Regionalizing Oman

United Nations University Series on Regionalism

Volume 6

Series Editors:

PHILIPPE DE LOMBAERDE AND LUK VAN LANGENHOVE

The United Nations University Series on Regionalism, launched by UNU-CRIS and Springer, offers a platform for innovative work on (supra-national) regionalism from a global and inter-disciplinary perspective. It includes the policy-oriented *World Reports on Regional Integration*, published in collaboration with other UN agencies, but it is also open for theoretical, methodological and empirical contributions from academics and policy-makers worldwide.

Book proposals will be reviewed by an International Editorial Board.

The series editors are particularly interested in book proposals dealing with:

- comparative regionalism;
- comparative work on regional organizations;
- inter-regionalism;
- the role of regions in a multi-level governance context;
- the interactions between the UN and the regions;
- the regional dimensions of the reform processes of multilateral institutions;
- the dynamics of cross-border micro-regions and their interactions with supra-national regions;
- methodological issues in regionalism studies.

Accepted book proposals can receive editorial support from UNU-CRIS for the preparation of manuscripts.

Please send book proposals to: pdelombaerde@cris.unu.edu and lvanlangenhove@cris.unu.edu.

For further volumes:
http://www.springer.com/series/7716

Steffen Wippel
Editor

Regionalizing Oman

Political, Economic and Social Dynamics

Springer

Editor
Steffen Wippel
Department for Economy and Social Geography of Arab World
University of Leipzig
Leipzig, Germany

Zentrum Moderner Orient (ZMO)
Berlin, Germany

ISBN 978-94-007-6820-8 ISBN 978-94-007-6821-5 (eBook)
DOI 10.1007/978-94-007-6821-5
Springer Dordrecht Heidelberg New York London

Library of Congress Control Number: 2013940775

Printed on acid-free paper

Springer is part of Springer Science+Business Media (www.springer.com)

Preface

"Regionalizing", the supralocal structuring process and the locally characteristic specificity of a region, is a comprehensive task in terms of content and a theoretically as well as conceptually demanding challenge. This appraisal applies to Oman in particular inasmuch as academic preoccupation *with* and *in* the country at the South Eastern corner of the Arabian Peninsula can look back only on a few decades.

Indeed Idrisi (12th c.),[1] Marco Polo (13th c.) and Ibn Battuta (14th c.) already reported on this part of the world at an early time, where, as we know today, the famous country (Magan) was located, from which Assyrian copper came. We owe our first detailed descriptions of local peculiarities and political conditions in the sixteenth century to Portuguese sources. Travellers like Kaempfer (17th c.), Francklin, Hamilton, Jenour and Niebuhr (18th c.) and Berghaus, Buckingham, Mansur, Ruschenberger and Wellstedt, to cite at least a few examples of the numerous reporters of the nineteenth century, already drew more precise contours of the South East Arabian country and people. Their reports definitely allow us to deduce first evidence of local and region specific characteristics. And, theirs would later be enriched by the numerous, mostly purpose-related reports and power-serving gazetteers of British colonial officers (19th/20th c.). Even if she cannot be scientifically pinned down, the Omani-Zanzibari Princess Salme bint Said bin Sultan Al Said should not and need not go unmentioned in this context. After her escape to Germany and her marriage to the Hamburg merchant Ruete, as Emilie Said-Ruete, with her books (around 1890), she anticipated in a way the intention of Regionalizing Oman trenchantly and from a very personal perspective.

But the "regionalization" ambitiously pursued in this volume and in its individual contributions is – as already remarked – noteworthy against the following background: in the late 1960s, Oman ranked among the most backward countries on earth, as a large number of publications have meanwhile depicted, sometimes quite dramatically. With the discovery of petroleum and on the basis of its commercial

[1]Details on the literature cited in the following can be found in Düster and Scholz (1980) and Scholz (1990, 2009).

exploitation (1969), as well as with the takeover of government by the young Sultan Qaboos bin Said (1970), a totally new phase in the social, political, infrastructural and economic development of Oman started. The accompanying opening of the country allowed, for the first time, among other things, international and in particular independent academic research in Oman, which was encouraged, welcomed and promoted notably by H.H. Sayyed Tariq bin Taimur Al-Said. This process, setting off hesitantly and actually systematically established only in the 1980s, has continued for barely four decades. Thus, the fact that this book fruitfully addresses such a challenging topic is notable in four ways:

First, the topic of the volume reflects the current interest of the international "community of sciences" in the country of Oman.

Second, the various contributions demonstrate the manifold local particularities of the Omani culture and society, as well as of their recent development.

Third, it must be emphasised that colleagues from Omani research institutions meanwhile also participate in the scientific debate and can apply for and receive financial support from the government.

Fourth, *Regionalizing Oman* finally articulates the position and recognition that the Sultanate has meanwhile obtained within the wider region, but also internationally in terms of politics, culture, and economics.

Therefore and in the view of someone like me, who has promoted and attentively accompanied the development of contemporary research in Oman from the beginning, *Regionalizing Oman* is a scientific milestone *in* and *for* the academic Oman. Certainly, this volume will receive adequate attention in the international "community of sciences". And it is to be hoped that it will also attract broad interest in Oman.

Berlin, Germany Fred Scholz

References

Düster, J., & Scholz, F. (1980). *Bibliographie über das Sultanat Oman*. Hamburg: Deutsches Orient-Institut.

Scholz, F. (Ed.). (2009). *Oman-German cultural and scientific relations*. Symposium during the "Oman Cultural Week", Free University of Berlin, June 2008. Berlin: Hans Schiler.

Scholz, F. (1990). *Muscat, Sultanat Oman: Geographische Skizze einer einmaligen arabischen Stadt*. Berlin: Das Arabische Buch.

Acknowledgements

A book of this kind cannot be published without the support and collaboration of many persons and institutions. First of all, it owes very much to all the contributors to this volume, as well as to the preceding conference "Regionalizing Oman – Political, Economic and Social Dynamics" that was held at the University of Leipzig, Germany in March 2010. I well remember especially the authors who submitted their papers in time and responded patiently to my manifold comments and requests. Very special thanks go to my student assistants from the Institute of Oriental Studies at Leipzig University: Julia Oheim was responsible for most of the organisational part of the conference, which made the meeting a success and the financial aspect viable; Michael Benz, who also already helped during the conference and subsequently developed his own academic interest in the issues dealt with, and who in particular had the biggest share in copy-editing the papers to this publication, which he did scrupulously and with much patience, when it came to the innumerable details. In addition, Svenja Becherer, responsible for publications at the *Zentrum Moderner Orient* (ZMO), Berlin, was willing to format and typeset the three latest articles in her very experienced manner. I also do not want to forget Mitch Cohen, who as a native speaker made the incredibly professional linguistic proofreading of all the texts and also was very tolerant when I wanted to re-discuss numerous author-specific reformulations. Yet, there still remains a certain inconsistency in spelling Arab terms. Finally, I would like to thank Esther Otten, Publishing Editor, and Miranda Dijksman and Hendrikje Tuerlings, Assistants, from Springer Business + Media, Dordrecht, The Netherlands, as well as Philippe de Lombaerde and Luk van Langenhove, editors of the United Nations University Series on Regionalism, launched by UNU-CRIS and Springer, for having quickly accepted the idea of the book and for having helpfully accompanied the publication and indulgently awaited the submission of the manuscript that saw several delays for various reasons. I also want to express my gratitude to the anonymous reviewers for their positive evaluation of the initial book proposal.

Yet, it was not only the personal input and laborious work of academic colleagues and professional partners that helped realize the publication and make it what it is, but also the necessary and generous financial support from several research institutions in Germany. For the most part, the Fritz Thyssen Foundation for Research Promotion had financed the aforementioned conference in Leipzig under the reference number 30.10.0.007. Additional funds came from the research project on Oman, briefly presented in the following introductory chapter, at the Institute for Oriental Studies at Leipzig University and funded by the *Deutsche Forschungsgemeinschaft* (DFG) under the reference numbers GE 749/8-1 (April 2008 to March 2010) and GE 749/8-2 (October 2010 to September 2011). A part of the project funds not only helped to organize the conference, but also to finance the copy-editing of this publication by Michael Benz and the proofreading of most papers by a native speaker. Additional conference costs were kindly covered by funds from the postgraduate programme "Critical Junctures of Globalization" at the Research Academy Leipzig, University of Leipzig, and from Sultan Qaboos University, Muscat. In the framework of the research project, my colleague and formal project leader Jörg Gertel, Professor for the Economy and Social Geography of the Arab World at Leipzig University, kindly left me a very free hand in pursuing the conference and the publications. Finally, the *Zentrum Moderner Orient* took over the proofreading and copy-editing of my own articles. My complementary and partly parallel research project "Tanger – Salalah: Globalising 'Regional Cities'" was also located here, funded by the Federal Ministry for Education and Research (BMBF) under the reference number 30/8845 (August 2008 to March 2010 and October 2011 to December 2013), which gave additional intellectual input.

I am very grateful to all the above individuals and institutions for their help and support in preparing and publishing this joint volume. However, the responsibility for the overall quality and content of this publication remains exclusively with me, the editor.

Leipzig/Berlin, Germany, June 2012 Steffen Wippel

Contents

Chapter 1
"Regionalizing Oman": A New Interest of Research on Oman and Its Spatial Dimensions

Steffen Wippel

1.1 Introduction

"Regionalizing Oman" aims to explore the diverse regional settings and contexts, of various sizes and scopes and on diverging geographical scales, to which people related to the area of present day's Sultanate, consciously or implicitly, contribute by their thoughts and acts and in which they live and operate. At the same time, this volume intends to show the amplitude of current research on Oman that enhances our understanding of the country and its people beyond some established perspectives and methodologies.[1] In the following, this introductory chapter presents the background of the book – especially the renewed interest of researchers from a wide range of social science disciplines in the Gulf area and, in the wake of it, in Oman – and the book's general outline before it sums up each chapter of the volume individually.

1.2 Research on Oman: A Renewed Interest and Current Developments

A first wave of studies on modern Oman came in the 1970s, when the country underwent a strong modernization push accompanying the windfall benefits of the oil boom of the time and after the current Sultan Qaboos had overthrown his father.

[1] For criticism of established methodologies in social research and new approaches that go beyond (exclusive) recourse to the territorial nation state and conventionally conceived world regions, see Wippel, Lorenz and Mattheis as well as Bromber, in the first, conceptual part of this volume.

S. Wippel (✉)
Zentrum Moderner Orient (ZMO), Kirchweg 33, 14129 Berlin, Germany
e-mail: steffen.wippel@t-online.de; steffen.wippel@zmo.de

S. Wippel (ed.), *Regionalizing Oman: Political, Economic and Social Dynamics*, United Nations University Series on Regionalism 6, DOI 10.1007/978-94-007-6821-5_1,

Several publications studied the political and, with it, the economic and social development of the Sultanate (for the first three decades, see e.g. Townsend 1977; Skeet 1974, 1992; Peterson 1978; Allen 1987).[2] These studies were often produced by former British and American officers, advisors and experts in the service of the Sultan and the regional oil industry. Rather than presenting critical analyses of on-going processes, they tended to reproduce the eulogising tenor of official statements and the new historiography of, in essence, a reborn Oman in the post-1970 "Renaissance", which was said to represent a total break with the past dark age.

In contrast, Fred Scholz, a social geographer and development specialist at the Free University of Berlin, was a protagonist of modern Oman studies in Germany who inspired a range of scholars to work on social developments in the country. Their research interest covered urban development (Scholz 1990, 2004a, b) as well as nomadism (Janzen 1980, translated in 1986; Zimmermann 1981; Scholz 1981; Bierschenk 1984), besides general geographical studies on Oman and the "smaller Gulf states" (Janzen and Scholz 1979; Scholz 1980, 1985, 1999). At the same time, anthropologists such as Wikan (1982) and Barth (1983), paid early attention to the post-coup Sultanate. Academic curiosity also focused early on Zanzibar, which in the nineteenth century temporarily even constituted the centre of the Omani empire (Bhacker 1992; Abdul Sheriff 1987; Bennett 1978), immigrants from India and Persia and their role in trade and administration (Allen 1981) and the interest of foreign powers in Oman (Al Wasmī 1986). Other studies explored the economic development of the young oil-producing country (e.g. Scholz 1977; Looney 1991). First anthologies assembling articles on different aspects of Oman have been Pridham (1987) and, in a larger context, Bonnenfant (1982).

With the apogee of interest in the 1970s and 1980s, the country was subsequently mostly ignored in the broader, but until the late 1990s still very limited, Gulf Studies. The Persian-Arab Gulf[3] has for some time been a domain for political, military and economic experts, whose research has mostly been limited to the geostrategic issues of an oil-rich and at the same time politically sensitive region. But in the course of the 2000s, it attracted attention from a wide range of social disciplines, with urban studies specialists and cultural geographers demonstrating a particularly high level of interest. Initially, Dubai's promotion on the global map was especially in the focus of initially more euphemistic, then increasingly critical and more theoretically based studies analysing the vulnerability of its post-oil and postmodern development strategies (e.g. Marchal 2001; Davis 2006, 2008; Davidson 2008; Scharfenort 2009; Hvidt 2009; Schmid 2009). But despite the sustained focus on the urban and economic development of the expanding agglomerations of the region, since the end of the decade perspectives have widened to include a broader range not only of cities and countries, but also of topics investigated and of academic

[2] The following references are selective. For a more exhaustive bibliography, see Düster and Scholz (1980).

[3] For the dispute about the "right" denomination of the Gulf, see Wippel (in this volume). The term "Arab Gulf", taken as a socio-economic project in its own right in contrast to the traditional use of the term "Persian Gulf", has meanwhile found wider recognition.

disciplines involved.[4] Current projects look, for instance, at the development of tourism (Henderson 2006; Steiner 2009, 2010), of sports (Bromber and Krawietz 2013) and of work migration (e.g. Cadène and Dumortier 2009; Piolet 2009) in the countries of the region, including the resulting political, economic and social challenges and (trans)regional references.

This also fuelled a new rise in Omani studies. A first testimonial to this renewed interest is the edited volume by Lavergne and Dumortier (2002), covering political, economic, social and cultural facets from different angles and disciplinary backgrounds. Similarly, the book edited by Kapiszewski, Al-Salimi and Pikulski (2006) treats the multiple aspects of the country in a kaleidoscopic manner. Additional books and articles published over the last decade give a broader overview of the development of contemporary Oman; these include Le Cour Grandmaison (2000), Allen and Rigsbee (2000), Owtram (2004), Peterson (2004a, b) and Ghubash (2006), mostly centring on the political system of the Sultanate (cf. also Kechichian 2005, 2008; Valeri 2007c, 2008). Especially Valeri 2007a (translated and updated in 2009), who also contributes to this anthology, gives a deep insight into the specific intertwining of political and socio-cultural dimensions. The author is also interested in processes of nation-building and the search for identity of specific groups such as the Zanzibar Omanis (Valeri 2005, 2007b). Chatty (1996) and Beaudevin (2007), both also authors in the present volume, investigate transnational connections from anthropological perspectives.

Several authors started to analyse Oman's macroeconomic profile and its attempts since the late 1990s at economic diversification in preparation for the post-oil era (Molavi 1998; Mansur and Treichel 1999; Scholz 2001; Valeri 2005; Looney 2009). In contrast, publications on tourism, for which Oman was late to open itself to, are still rare (such as Mershen 2007). Issues of international economic relations are more often approached in the framework of enquiries on Oman's foreign policy. Further, publications primarily take an overall perspective focused on regional economic and political institutions in which Oman is a member.[5] Last but not least, studies by Kechichian (1995), Manea (2001), Rabi (2005) and Al-Khalili (2009) investigate Oman's largely independent and balanced foreign policy since the 1970s, including some regional aspects. Relations with immediate neighbours have been especially studied (Halliday 1999; Pasha 1999; Al-Sayegh 2002). Historically oriented studies show again present-day Oman's close cultural, economic an political interconnection with, presence in and influence on areas across the Indian Ocean in South Asia and Eastern Africa from pre-Islamic times to the nineteenth century (e.g. Agius 2002; Nicolini 2004; Goswami 2011).[6] Due to these manifold historical

[4] Currently, another edited volume with multidisciplinary contributions on the semiotics of architecture and infrastructure in the Arab Gulf region is under preparation (Bromber et al. 2013).

[5] For references, see Zorob and Wippel (both in this volume). For earlier contributions on national perspectives on regional cooperation, see El-Rayyes (1987) and Anthony (1987).

[6] This research interest has also been demonstrated by another international conference, "The Ibadism of Oman – Its Overseas Development and its Perception Overseas", at the University of Tübingen, Germany, in May 2011, to be followed by another reader.

contacts with the world, contemporary Omani society shows strong ethnic, social and religious diversity and multiple transnational connections (Peterson 2004c, d; on the role of Zanzibar Omanis, Valeri 2003; Müller-Mahn 2005; Al-Rasheed 2005). A range of publications, mostly coming from geography, anthropology and archaeology, display further empirical and theoretical interests.

With all of this, the scope of issues and the range of authors have meanwhile widened considerably; contributions come from several social disciplines and the number of publications on Oman is increasing. Approaches are also broadening, from mostly territorially related developments to a wider range of issues on different spatial scales. But whereas supra- and transnational regional aspects are beginning to be apprehended more deeply, there are still few studies on the infranational scale. In part, research projects are still on-going inside Oman (especially at the national Sultan Qaboos University and the German University of Technology, both in Muscat) and outside, but their main results have not yet been published. This edited volume endeavours to include some of the most recent insights and to present a platform that brings together people from different academic fields.

1.3 Outline of the Volume: Its Conceptual Focus and Addressed Readership

This volume addresses the historical structures and current dynamics of Oman's regionalization processes and their political, economic and social dimensions. Oman, which is often automatically classified as part of the "Arab world" or the MENA (Middle East and North Africa) region, is conceptualized in this publication instead as being constructed via its articulations with several "regions" at the macro and micro levels.

Conceptually, studies often start from established metageographies, relating either to continentally or culturally defined world regions or to the territorial state as a basis of analysis. However, a conceptually contrasted discourse has developed on space and region as social constructs that are continuously constituted and reconstituted by public discourse and social action. Theoretical debates also focus on large-scale cultural, social and economic flows that concentrate and intersect in heavily globalised and globally radiating centres. The discourse also highlights the predominance of network societies and flow economies in a globalizing world. Hence, regional contexts are increasingly viewed as fluid and fragile, shifting and overlapping phenomena. A comprehensive understanding thus must include macro-, meso- and micro-perspectives on several intrinsically linked and interpenetrating spatial scales.

However, such more recent theoretical approaches are not irreconcilable with those long-established; rather, they open a wide spectrum of spatial perspectives on countries such as Oman. Although territories are still important as special formations of regions, they are subject to regular reconstruction, are objects of conflict and exist on diverse scales (such as national administrative subdivisions, institutionalised cross-border regions or international regional integration areas). Other regionalization processes have more to do with the perspective of flow, movement and communication. The emerging specific (trans)local, (trans)national and (trans)regional linkages and their spatial contexts can be reconstructed through the movement of people, goods or capital. Additionally, regionalization refers to mental and discursive constructions of regions.

Oman is integrated into multiple processes of regionalisation, which this volume wants to demonstrate. Already historically, the contemporary territory of the Sultanate was tightly embedded into regional flows and contacts. Up to today, it has a pivotal position between several conventional world regions – Asia, Europe and Africa. Relational forms of regionalization in Oman are, for example, established by nomads moving and circulating seasonally or over extended periods, by fluctuating flows of "foreign" migrants transforming transnational and urban landscapes or by their insertion into translocal and regional economic trade flows. At the same time, in territorial terms, as a young nation state, Oman has long been struggling to define its borders. On the sub-national level, reterritorialization occurred until recently, while internationally the Sultanate started to implement regional agreements, which also include forms of territorial regulation and control.

Concomitantly, space-related identities developed in relation to historical, reinvented or current regional articulations, and the country is marketed, in a regionally contextualized manner, as a trade hub, production site or tourist destination. Emerging macro-regional contexts include, e.g., the Gulf area in a narrower or broader understanding and large parts of the Indian Ocean rim, its adjacent seas and its wider hinterland. At local levels, societies are experiencing ambivalent processes of disembedding, i.e. the detachment of social relations from local contexts of interaction, and re-embedding, reflecting the on-going negotiation of social and territorial boundaries. Transnational and translocal links (e.g. with parts of neighbouring Yemen, the Emirates or Oman's former strongholds in East Africa, particularly Zanzibar) that do not necessarily include or refer to the national state level, bind all this together.

Against this conceptual background, the book pursues four major axes of research:

- Oman's integration into global and regional flows of goods, capital, people and ideas;
- the multi-scaled political negotiation of such integration (or disintegration) processes;
- the consequences of such processes and forms of regionalization for (trans)local actors;
- ideas and strategic communication of regional belonging and the constitution of regions.

Each chapter deals with one or more of these issues. Given the nature of the book – its conceptual input, the breadth of empirical, yet theoretically informed case studies and the range of authors and disciplines included – it is aimed at an international public of researchers and students. It addresses scholars in area studies such as Islamic, Middle East and Gulf Studies and to a certain extent in broader Asian, African and Indian Ocean Studies. Other readers might be found in disciplines such as International Politics and Economics, especially with a theoretical or empirical focus on regionalism and regionalization processes, development studies and the broader field of social and cultural studies, who are interested in issues of a current "spatial turn" in and across their disciplines.

The increasing interest in Oman as a research field in particular defines another audience. Furthermore, this volume complements existing works as an introduction to the main characteristics and recent developments of the Sultanate. It even goes further, being eager to pursue a conceptual focus and covering a multiplicity of aspects from a common theoretically informed perspective. It also updates earlier readers: over the last few years, the world has changed considerably, and new conceptual developments have occurred, while interest in Gulf and Indian Ocean Studies has increased and covers the broader range of social and cultural studies, and research on Oman in particular has also grown stronger.

1.4 The Background: The Editor's Projects and the Leipzig Conference in 2010

This volume is an outcome of an international conference also entitled "Regionalizing Oman – Political, Economic and Social Dynamics", which was organized at the Department for the Economy and Social Geography of the Arab World, Institute for Oriental Studies, at the University of Leipzig, Germany, on 25 and 26 March 2010.[7] It is based on an interdisciplinary and transregional dialogue between scholars from different fields such as political science, economics, social and cultural geography, history, Islamic studies, anthropology and linguistics as well as Middle Eastern and African area studies. In contrast to the traditional domination of Anglo-American scholars in Omani studies, authors contributing to this volume mainly come from European and Gulf universities and research institutions with different national backgrounds and have longstanding experience and reputations in their respective research specialities. Most contributors were selected from presenters at the Leipzig workshop in 2010, and some additional authors have been invited to join the volume.

The starting point for the workshop and the joint volume was the research project "Between the Arab World and the Indian Ocean: Oman's Regional Economic Orientations", which the editor carried out from 2008 to 2011 at the Institute for

[7] For the most part, the Fritz Thyssen Foundation for Research Promotion financed the conference under the reference number 30.10.0.007. Additional funds came from the DFG project on Oman presented in the next paragraph, the postgraduate programme "Critical Junctures of Globalization" at the Research Academy Leipzig and from Sultan Qaboos University, Muscat.

Oriental Studies at Leipzig University.[8] On the one hand, this project had to do with debates on the importance of "space" and "region" in geography and in the social sciences; on the other hand, it took up new conceptual approaches to political and economic "regionalism" and "regionalization". The project thereby adopted a macro-perspective on economic structures, connections, flows and imaginations resulting from a multitude of agreements, activities and ideas. This understanding was applied to a country at the interface of several important world regions. Besides the Arab world and the Gulf, the Indian Ocean region from Eastern Africa to South Eastern Asia has been of special interest. At the same time, the project intended to close empirical gaps in research on Oman's trade and integration policy.

In parallel, complementary aspects have been investigated in a second project "Tanger – Salalah: Globalising 'Regional Cities'" at the *Zentrum Moderner Orient* (ZMO), *Geisteswissenschaftliche Zentren Berlin*. First concentrating on the Oman case, it will later compare two port cities that are both being developed into the biggest container hubs in the Middle East and North Africa.[9] These localities are taken as gates between inside and outside and as nodal points in the worldwide network of human and material flows, which are continuously reconfigured by human action. A special focus is being placed on their regional orientations on several spatial scales. The project thereby meets the need to study economically important processes of regionalisation and globalisation not only on the national state level, but also in smaller regional or local contexts.[10]

1.5 Contributions: Multiple Perspectives on "Regionalizing Oman"

The book is divided into four major parts. The first one is conceptually oriented and deals with various concepts that seek to understand processes of "regionalisation" and "region-building". It is followed by three more sections, constituted by empirically oriented, yet also theoretically well-informed articles that consider the translocal, transnational and transregional movement of people, micro- and macro-regionalisations through economic practices, and state and society in regional and global perspectives respectively. Each chapter of this joint publication deals with one or more of the major axes of research presented above. While

[8] The project was funded by the German Research Council (DFG) under the reference numbers GE 749/8-1 (April 2008 to March 2010) and GE 749/8-2 (October 2010 to September 2011). A part of the project funds not only helped to organize the aforementioned conference, but also to finance a student assistant, Michael Benz, who was very helpful in the copy editing of this publication.

[9] The Federal Ministry for Education and Research (BMBF) funded this project under the reference number 30/8845 (August 2008 to March 2010 and October 2011 to December 2013).

[10] Further conceptual findings, in particular in the following chapter, result from previous work on territorialisation and regionalisation processes in the larger West Saharan region.

the conceptual focus of the book is on the various regional contexts of Oman, each author develops and adopts his or her own terminology according to his or her respective discipline, perspective and research environment. The volume is framed by an introductory and a conclusive part.

1.5.1 Introduction

First, Fred Scholz, Professor Emeritus at the Centre for Development Studies (ZELF), Institute of Geographical Sciences, Free University Berlin, who was one of the protagonists of social science research on Oman, in particular in German geography, since the early 1970s, was so kind as to introduce the volume with a short preface.

Then, in this chapter, *"Regionalizing Oman": A New Interest of Research on Oman and its Spatial Dimensions*, the editor of the volume presents the outline of the book, touching on the renewed interest of researchers from a wide range of social science disciplines in Oman. The presentation of the chapters shows the multiple possible perspectives on "Regionalizing Oman". *Steffen Wippel* is presently a Senior Researcher at the *Zentrum Moderner Orient* (ZMO), Berlin and at the same time a Lecturer (*Privatdozent*) at the Department for Research on the Contemporary Middle East, Friedrich Alexander University Erlangen-Nuremberg, Germany. At the time of the preparation of this volume, he also was a research fellow at the Department for the Economy and Social Geography of the Arab World at the Institute for Oriental Studies, University of Leipzig.

1.5.2 Part I: Concepts of Regionalisation and Region-Building

The mainly conceptually oriented Part I considers concepts of regionalisation and region-building and presents various approaches that accentuate certain dimensions of these processes and come from different disciplinary backgrounds. The conceptual explanations and the subsequent empirical case studies are thoroughly interlinked, allowing for multiple cross-references and theoretically informed results in the following parts of the book.

In the second chapter, *Steffen Wippel*, ZMO, gives some *Conceptual Considerations on "Space" and "Region": Political, Economic and Social Dynamics of Region-Building*. The author starts with a critique of the "methodological nationalism" and rigid regional "metageographies" that predominate in research as well as in the broader public. He then develops a broader understanding of regions as social constructs and of processes of region-building in line with the wide range of approaches that can be subsumed under the current transdisciplinary "spatial turn".

Chapter 3, called *Theorizing Regionalism(s): When "Regions" Emerge and Interact*, reviews theoretical perspectives dealing with the phenomenon of "regionalism". The authors *Ulrike Lorenz*, Assistant Professor at the Chair of International Politics, University of Potsdam, and *Frank Mattheis*, research fellow at the Global and European Studies Institute of the University of Leipzig, Germany, discuss approaches from the main disciplines, namely International Relations, New Regionalism and Critical Political Geography. They develop an extended notion of the region as a social space and arena for a multiplicity of actors in such a way as to include its specific occurrence in the South. The authors outline interregionalism as an emergence of regional interaction that brings out certain characteristics of regions in their institutionalised form. Empirical evidence from the South Atlantic illustrates the character of interregionalism outside of Europe.

Katrin Bromber, a senior researcher at the *Zentrum Moderner Orient* (ZMO) in Berlin and Lecturer (*Privatdozent*) at the University of Vienna, Austria, in her chapter *Working with "Translocality": Conceptual Implications and Analytical Consequences* introduces another conceptual perspective. The term "translocality" came up in the mid-1990s in discussions about the social production of place and space. It goes beyond geographical notions and questions cultures as closed entities bound to nation states. The inflationary and often unreflected use of diverse "trans"-terminologies exposed such notions to the danger of becoming empty catchall phrases. Chapter 4 therefore interrogates translocality with regard to its diverse conceptualizations, as a research perspective, a middle-range theory or a social fact, for its potential analytical value. Taking the example of the Indian Ocean – a *seascape* that is produced and transformed through movement – the chapter discusses one possible gateway to the study of a translocal phenomenon.

1.5.3 Part II: The Translocal, Transnational and Transregional Movement of People

Following the conceptual considerations, *Part II* focuses on the translocal, transnational and (trans)regional movement of people, their practices and imaginations, be they contemporary labour migrants, returnees from Eastern Africa or nomadic tribal members. Their border crossing activities are, if not contrary to, at least in a complex relationship with official attempts at territorial control, state-led development or nation-building.

In their chapter *"We are Part of Zanzibar" – Translocal Practices and Imaginative Geographies in Contemporary Oman-Zanzibar Relations* (Chap. 5), *Julia Verne*, Research Assistant in the Department of Human Geography at the Goethe University Frankfurt am Main, Germany, and *Detlef Müller-Mahn*, Professor of Population and Social Geography at the University of Bayreuth, illustrate how contemporary connections between the two places are lived and experienced by Zanzibar Omanis. Particularly since the Zanzibar Revolution in 1964, relations have been marked by contested political views and conflicting versions. While from the perspective of Oman these links meanwhile often seem to be of only minor significance, in Zanzibar they have been of high ideological value and a dominant argument in political controversies. However, instead of engaging in such macro-level debates, the authors focus on the everyday practices and imaginations of those actually constituting the translocal connections. Only this, they argue, can provide a deeper understanding of the ambiguity and complexity of these personal relations, thus adding an important dimension to Oman's current translocal links.

Health issues constitute another starting point to investigate the Sultanate's regional bonds. Chapter 6, *Of Red Cells, Translocality and Origins: Inherited Blood Disorders in Oman* by *Claire Beaudevin*, teaching anthropology at Paris Descartes University and a postdoctoral researcher at the *Centre de Recherche Médecine, Sciences, Santé, Santé Mentale, Société* (Cermes3) in Paris, reveals some of the Sultanate's past and present forms of translocality, too, and aims at describing the networks Oman belongs to. The ethnographic study focuses on a particular case of serious genetic diseases that are frequently stigmatized as consequences of a "traditional" behaviour that encourages local consanguineous marriages – symbolically linked to the interior of Oman – as opposed to "respectable" modernism that advocates avoidance of endogamy – supposedly characteristic of the urban coastal areas. Social representations of these diseases include transnational genealogical reconstructions and point to links with more distant areas. Furthermore, their diagnosis and treatment involve numerous local and regional interactions.

In his chapter *Oman-India Relations: Exploring the Long-Term Migration Dynamics* (Chap. 7), *Samir Pradhan*, a senior consultant in macroeconomic research at a leading consultancy in Qatar, shows that the historical legacy of the robust bilateral relationship enduring over many centuries goes back to the Byzantine trading and migration links. Whereas in the earlier era, Indian merchants virtually controlled the Omani economic domain and thereby revolutionized the commercial landscape, the oil and post-oil era witnessed an influx of skilled and semi-skilled Indian migrants becoming the foot soldiers in the economic ascension of the Sultanate. While the pattern and level of engagement between locals and Indians have transformed today, they speak volumes about the role of migration in the process of regionalization. Nevertheless, the role and status of Indian migrants have changed in conformity with the pace and scale of Oman's economic development, being contingent upon the prevailing political, social and cultural undercurrents.

Finally, Chap. 8, *Negotiating Authenticity and Translocality in Oman: the "Desertscapes" of the Harasiis Tribe*, examines the contestation around multiple belongings in the building of the Omani nation. Recent decades have seen the government of Oman increase its efforts to create a broadly homogenised "national identity". *Dawn Chatty*, University Reader in Anthropology and Forced Migration and Deputy Director of the Refugee Studies Centre, Department of International Development, University of Oxford, UK, explores the ways the Harasiis have negotiated their claims of authenticity. The largely mobile, camel- and goat-herding community has seen its belonging to translocal "desertscapes" contested as various government agencies make efforts to settle them, move them off this particular corner of South East Arabia and turn them into cheap day labourers. These translocal pastoral people, however, have used modern technology – particularly vehicles – to maintain their claims to the desert landscape not only of Oman but also across the modern borders to neighbouring countries.

1.5.4 Part III: Micro- and Macro-regionalisation Through Economic Practices

Contributions to the third part take a closer look particularly at economic issues and regionalisation processes that are mainly based on multiple trade links, regional development policies or politics of regionalism. They consider the ambivalence of deliberate construction as well as the emerging character of regions on micro- and macro-levels. This part starts with a historic perspective before turning to more institutionalised forms of regionalism and to emerging trans- and intra-state processes of regionalisation.

Chapter 9, *Re-reading the Role of Oman within its International Trade Relations. From the Sixteenth through to the Nineteenth Centuries*, considers the question whether Oman was part of a global unity that long preceded economic unification of the world over the last five centuries. For *Beatrice Nicolini*, who teaches African History and Institutions in the Faculties of Political Science and of Letters and Philosophy at the Catholic University of the Sacred Heart, Milan, Italy, the history of Omani international trade relations has been closely connected to its maritime routes. Within this framework, the gradual emergence of new Omani dynasties resulted from the polarizations that followed the struggles against the Portuguese presence in the Persian/Arab Gulf and in the Indian Ocean during the sixteenth and seventeenth centuries. This gave rise to gradual and discontinuous processes of unification among the Omani groups, traditionally divided and in conflict with each other, which came to the fore in the progressive affirmation of the regional power of the Omani Arabs.

Whereas contemporary Oman is regularly considered to be situated in MENA/the Arab world, Chap. 10, *Oman and the Indian Ocean Rim – Economic Integration Across Conventional Meta-Regions*, takes a different perspective and sees it also as part of the Indian Ocean area. Referring to recent concepts across the disciplines emphasising a more open approach to regionalisation processes and the definition of regions, *Steffen Wippel*, Senior Researcher at the ZMO, Berlin, focuses on three dimensions: on the institutional aspect, such as membership in regional organisations; on the development of material links, mainly regional trade; and on the self-positioning of Oman with respect to its regional orientation and belonging. The author shows that Oman has strong economic links with Indian Ocean rim countries and actively places itself in the area. The main motives behind this are to be found in endeavours to prepare the national economy for the post-oil era. Finally, the chapter shows that the Indian Ocean is not a homogenous entity, but has differing shapes, in accordance with different temporal, institutional, material and discursive perspectives.

In another institutional setting, the Gulf Cooperation Council (GCC) decided at the turn of the last decade to speed up the process of economic integration. Oman, however, started simultaneously to negotiate a free trade agreement (FTA) with the USA. In her chapter *Oman Caught Between the GCC Common Market and Bilateral Free Trade with the US: Is it Worth Breaking the Rules?* (Chap. 11), *Anja Zorob*, Senior Researcher and Assistant Dean, coordinating the PhD Program in Development Studies at the Institute of Development Research and

Development Policy (IEE), Ruhr University Bochum, Germany, states that, according to theory, signing an FTA with an external partner while at the same time belonging to a customs union means that the country in question is betraying the common external tariff. Yet, the question remains what kind of institutional settings must be in place to enable the small economy to economically benefit from such a far-ranging agreement. In addition, Omani companies, the public administration and the political leadership alike might face a difficult task in the future to be able to reconcile the implementation of the FTA with the GCC-internal process of integration.

Regional linkages also play an important role for the small Omani exclave of Musandam. They helped to establish a transnational trade network, which today connects various countries around the vital Strait of Hormuz. In Chap. 12, titled *Musandam and Its Trade with Iran. Regional Linkages across the Strait of Hormuz*, *Michael Benz*, who finished his MA in Arabic Studies with a focus on Economics and Social Geography at the University of Leipzig in 2011 and is currently preparing his PhD thesis, analyses this underinvestigated phenomenon. It is of great political and economic interest for the Omani government and intensely affects the social and economic situation on the peninsula, where the everyday lives of the inhabitants are undergoing a fundamental transformation. While from some perspectives Musandam seems to be a typical exclave, it is a highly uncommon exception for various historical, geographical and political reasons.

Turning from the transnational to the national, Chap. 13 asks: *Is Littoralization Reconfiguring the Omani Territory?* For *Belgacem Mokhtar*, Assistant Professor of Economic Geography and Planning at Sultan Qaboos University in Muscat, Oman, the concept of territory expresses the projection of specific human structures onto a specific area in terms of an unambiguous spatial representation. Littoralization designates the outcome of translocal movements of people and activities towards the coast with the accompanying infrastructures, urban spread and harmful environmental impacts. In Oman, with the conspicuous population increase of the last four decades, the demographic centre of gravity is shifting from the traditional inner regions towards the littoral fringes. This development has helped to overcome the traditional vulnerability of the inherited and dislocated territories. Regional groups and tribes do not have a territorial basis anymore, but actually move in a bigger space, live from new activities and belong to a larger territory than the tribal ones; henceforth, they identify themselves with the territorial nation-state.

In this subnational context, the chapter *The Impact of Shopping Malls on Traditional Retail Stores in Muscat. Case Study of al-Seeb Wilayat* (Chap. 14), written by *Montasser Abdelghani*, an Assistant Professor of Social and Urban Geography also at the Department of Geography, Sultan Qaboos University in Oman, analyses the relationship between transnational shopping centres, on the one hand, and retail trade in traditional markets, on the other. Many cities in Oman have witnessed a change in the function of retail trade and seen new components added to it, e.g. the emergence of giant hypermarkets. Since their appearance at the beginning of the third millennium, shopping centres are a symbol of globalization and modernization. They have dramatically changed not only the traditional Omani retailing structure, but also consumption behaviour.

1.5.5 Part IV: State and Society in Regional and Global Perspectives

Finally, the last part of the joint volume analyses political and socio-cultural issues from regional and global perspectives. This includes reconstruction of regional history and persisting sub-national identities and power structures, regional geopolitical matters and issues of education and language between the local and the global.

In Chap. 15, *Michaela Hoffmann-Ruf*, working in a DFG-funded project at the Rheinische Friedrich-Wilhelms-Universität Bonn and a docent in the Department of Art and History of the Islamic Orient at the Linden State Museum of Ethnology, Stuttgart, investigates *Private Documents as a Source for Regional History: The Archive of the 'Abrīyīn of al-Ḥamrā'*. The letters in this archive tell of the everyday life of a rural Omani community and reflect the interactions of its members on a local and regional level, thereby broadening the scope of existing macro-historical accounts. For the tribal leaders, the function of the letters is manifold, ranging from a substitute for personal meetings to the transmission of various kinds of information that help them to maintain and stabilize their political influence. One of the spatial aspects reflected in the letters is the actual geographic range of the contacts; another is that of the tribal territory. The correspondences show that the "landscape" of al-Ḥamrā' formed a historical and symbolic space that was created by the people involved, their perspectives and needs. Accordingly, these structures show variations dependent on time, place and actor.

Subsequently, Chap. 16, titled *Domesticating Local Elites. Sheikhs, Walis and State-Building under Sultan Qaboos*, focuses on the crucial role of local notables for understanding the political relationship between the centre and the periphery in today's Oman. The promotion of a new national identity centred on the person of Qaboos has decisively served the current ruler's strategy of legitimisation. At the same time, according to *Marc Valeri*, Lecturer in Political Economy and Director of the MA in Gulf Studies at the Institute of Arab and Islamic Studies, University of Exeter, UK, the regime has worked to neutralise the impact of local solidarities by "encapsulating" them within the central state. While the most important sheikhs have been offered economic opportunities and top positions in the state apparatus, minor notables have been "bureaucratized" as intermediaries between individuals and the administration. As a result, no social recognition remains beside that granted by the state, which has appropriated the symbolic spaces that local authorities controlled before 1970.

Gulshan Dietl, Professor at the School of International Studies, Jawaharlal Nehru University, New Delhi, India, turns again to Oman's northern exclave. Her chapter

Musandam: Creating a New Region Across the Water (Chap. 17) proposes to locate the country in both its neighbourhoods – the Arab Gulf States to its west and the Iranian landmass across the water to its east. The peninsula's special location has granted Oman the status of a Gulf state and secured it a berth on the Gulf Cooperation Council. It also gives Oman a joint control, with Iran, of the Strait of Hormuz. The "Musandam phenomenon", as a result, explains Omani foreign policy behaviour to a very large extent. More specifically, it makes Oman's "special relationship" with Iran well worth scrutinizing, turning to domestic economic considerations, internal dynamics within the GCC and the co-sharing of the Strait.

The chapter *The Political Economy of Internationalization and Privatization of Higher Education in the Sultanate of Oman* by *Torsten Brandenburg*, a researcher at the Center for Research on the Arab World (CERAW), Johannes Gutenberg University Mainz, Germany, outlines Oman's higher education policy. It aims at describing the origins of the government-funded higher education system since the late 1970s and assessing the rationales of its fundamental redesign since the early 1990s. Finally, Chap. 18 investigates the effects of the economic liberalization of higher education, by analysing the emerging models of cooperation providing cross-border educational services. Although Oman is adopting primarily Western educational concepts, its recent higher education policy also sets off in a new direction. It is a local exception within the postmodern higher education landscape of the Arabian Peninsula as it integrates international and local education paradigms and juggles market- and publicly-driven initiatives.

Rahma Al-Mahrooqi, Assistant Professor at the Department of English Language and Literature, and *Victoria Tuzlukova*, Head of the Professional Development & Research Unit, The Language Center, both at Sultan Qaboos University, Muscat, Oman, contribute Chap. 19 on *Bringing the Global and the Local Together through English in Oman*. Their chapter examines the ways English has assisted in modernizing Oman and its smooth entry into the global community. It discusses the role of English as a means of shaping social and cultural spaces in Oman, including Omani cultural manifestation and promotion around the world. The Omani culture is not only seen as valuable to Oman, but also as a part of the human heritage, reflecting the impact of different historical, economic and social events that have shaped and reshaped the world throughout history. Taking a look at how the two sides of the coin have been brought together will help find middle ground where Oman can foster its unique identity while adapting to the accelerating changes in the globalised world.

1.5.6 Conclusion

The joint volume rounds off with *Concluding Remarks* by *Steffen Wippel*, ZMO Berlin, on *Regionalizing Oman beyond Conventional Metageographies*. This final chapter resumes the preceding articles in view of Oman's diverse regionalisations in different social fields, on different scales, in different directions and from different actors' and authors' perspectives.

References

Agius, D. A. (2002). *In the wake of the dhow: The Arabian Gulf and Oman*. Reading: Ithaca Press.

Al Wasmī, K. (1986). *Oman entre l'indépendance et l'occupation coloniale: Recherches sur l'histoire moderne d'Oman dans ses relations régionales et internationales (1789–1904)*. Geneva/Paris: Labor et Fides.

Al-Khalili, M. (2009). *Oman's foreign policy: Foundation and practice*. Westport: Praeger Security International.

Allen, C. H., Jr. (1981). The Indian merchant community of Masqaṭ. *Bulletin of the School of Oriental and African Studies, 44*(1), 39–53.

Allen, C. H., Jr. (1987). *Oman: Modernization of the Sultanate*. Boulder/London: Westview Press/Croom Helm.

Allen, C. H., Jr., & Rigsbee, W. L., II. (2000). *Oman under Qaboos: From coup to constitution 1970–1996*. London/Portland: Frank Cass.

Al-Rasheed, M. (2005). Transnational connections and national identity: Zanzibari Omanis in Muscat. In P. Dresch & J. P. Piscatori (Eds.), *Monarchies and nations: Globalisation and identity in the Arab states of the Gulf* (pp. 96–113). London: Tauris.

Al-Sayegh, F. (2002). The UAE and Oman: Opportunities and challenges in the twenty-first century. *Middle East Policy, 9*(3), 124–137.

Anthony, J. D. (1987). Oman, the Gulf and the United States. In B.R. Pridham (Ed.), *Oman: Economic, social and strategic developments* (pp. 177–194). London/Wolfeboro: Croom Helm.

Barth, F. (1983). *Sohar: Culture and society in an Omani town*. Baltimore/London: Johns Hopkins University Press.

Beaudevin, C. (2007). Quid des hématies des descendants de Sindbad? Les tribulations d'une anthropologue de la santé au Sultanat d'Oman. In O. Leservoisier & L. Vidal (Eds.), *L'Anthropologie face à ses objets: Nouveaux contextes ethnographiques* (pp. 123–135). Paris: Éd. des archives contemporaines.

Bennett, N. R. (1978). *A history of the Arab state of Zanzibar*. London: Methuen.

Bhacker, R. M. (1992). *Trade and empire in Muscat and Zanzibar: Roots of British domination*. London/New York: Routledge.

Bierschenk, T. (1984). *Weltmarkt, Stammesgesellschaft und Staatsformation in Südostarabien (Sultanat Oman)*. Saarbrücken/Fort Lauderdale: Breitenbach.

Bonnenfant, P. (Ed.). (1982). *La péninsule arabique d'aujourd'hui, Tome II: Etudes par pays*. Paris: Ed. du CNRS.

Bromber, K., & Krawietz, B. (2013). The United Arab Emirates, Qatar and Bahrain as a modern sport hub. In K. Bromber, B. Krawietz, & J. Maguire (Eds.), *Sport across Asia: Politics, cultures, and identities* (pp. 189–211). New York: Routledge.

Bromber, K., Krawietz, B., et al. (Eds.) (2013). *Under construction. Logics of urbanism in the Gulf region*. In preparation.

Cadène, P., & Dumortier, B. (2009). Les Pays du Conseil de Coopération du Golfe: À Nouvelles Tendances Migratoires, Nouvelles Politiques? *Maghreb-Machrek, 199*, 101–119.

Chatty, D. (1996). *Mobile pastoralists: Development planning and social change in Oman*. New York: Columbia University Press.

Davidson, C. M. (2008). *Dubai: The vulnerability of success*. London: Hurst.

Davis, M. (2006). Fear and money in Dubai. *New Left review, 41*, 47–68.

Davis, M. (2008). *Le stade Dubaï du capitalisme*. Paris: Les Prairies ordinaires.

Düster, J., & Scholz, F. (1980). *Bibliographie über das Sultanat Oman*. Hamburg: Deutsches Orient-Institut.

El-Rayyes, R. N. (1987). Oman's role in the Gulf co-operation council and the region. In B. R. Pridham (Ed.), *Oman: Economic, social and strategic developments* (pp. 195–208). London: Croom Helm.

Ghubash, H. (2006). *Oman: The Islamic democratic tradition*. London/New York: Routledge.

Goswami, C. (2011). *The call of the sea: Kachchhi traders in Muscat and Zanzibar, c. 1800–1880*. New Delhi: Orient Black Swan.

Halliday, F. (1999, 28 October). *Oman and Yemen: an historic re-encounter*. Paper, Anglo-Omani/British-Yemeni Societies. http://www.al-bab.com/bys/articles/halliday00.htm. Accessed 5 May 2008.

Henderson, J. C. (2006). Tourism in Dubai: Overcoming barriers to destination development. *International Journal of Tourism Research, 8*(2), 87–99.

Hvidt, M. (2009). The Dubai model: An outline of key development-process elements in Dubai. *International Journal of Middle East Studies, 41*(3), 397–418.

Janzen, J. (1980). *Die Nomaden Dhofars/Sultanat Oman: Traditionelle Lebensformen im Wandel*. Bamberg: Fach Geographie an der Universität im Selbstverlag.

Janzen, J. (1986). *Nomads in the Sultanate of Oman: Tradition and development in Dhofar*. Boulder: Westview Press.

Janzen, J., & Scholz, F. (1979). Die Weihrauchwirtschaft Dhofārs (Sultanat Oman). In H. Peter, M. Peter, & P. Hugo (Eds.), *Fragen geographischer Forschung: Festschrift des Instituts für Geographie zum 60. Geburtstag von Alfred Leidlmair* (pp. 501–541). Innsbruck: Selbstverlag des Instituts für Geographie der Universität Innsbruck.

Kapiszewski, A., Al-Salimi, A., & Pikulski, A. (Eds.). (2006). *Modern Oman: Studies on politics, economy, environment and culture of the Sultanate*. Krakow: Księgarnia Akademicka.

Kechichian, J. A. (1995). *Oman and the world: The emergence of an independent foreign policy*. Santa Monica: Rand.

Kechichian, J. A. (2005). *Political participation and stability in the Sultanate of Oman*. Dubai: Research Papers/Gulf Research Center.

Kechichian, J. A. (2008). A vision of Oman: State of the Sultanate, speeches by Qaboos bin said, 1970–2006. *Middle East Policy, 15*(3), 112–133.

Lavergne, M., & Dumortier, B. (Eds.). (2002). *L'Oman contemporain: Etat, territoire, identité*. Paris: Karthala.

Le Cour Grandmaison, B. (2000). *Le Sultanat d'Oman*. Paris: Karthala.

Looney, R. E. (1991). An economic assessment of Oman's industrial diversification efforts. *Orient, 32*(2), 217–235.

Looney, R E. (2009, June). *The Omani and Bahraini paths to development: Rare and contrasting oil-based economic success stories*. Research Paper 2009/38. Helsinki: UNU World Institute for Development Economics Research (UNU-WIDER).

Manea, E. (2001). *Regional politics in the developing world: The case of the Arab Peninsula, Yemen, Saudi Arabia, Oman*. Ph.D. in Philosophy, Faculty of Arts, University of Zurich.

Mansur, A., & Treichel, V. (Eds.). (1999). *Oman beyond the oil horizon: Policies toward sustainable growth*. Occasional Paper 185. Washington, DC: International monetary fund.

Marchal, R. (Ed.). (2001). *Dubaï: Cité globale*. Paris: Ed. du CNRS.

Mershen, B. (2007). Development and community-based tourism in Oman: Challenges and opportunities. In R. F. Daher (Ed.), *Tourism in the middle east – Continuity, change and transformation* (pp. 188–214). Clevedon/Tonewade/North York, Ontario: Channel View.

Molavi, A. (1998). Oman's economy: Back on track. *Middle East Policy, 5*(4), 1–10.

Müller-Mahn, D. (2005). Sansibar und der Wandel arabischer Händler-Netzwerke in Ostafrika. *Geographische Rundschau, 57*(11), 32–40.

Nicolini, B. (2004). *Makran, Oman, and Zanzibar: Three-terminal cultural corridor in the Western Indian Ocean (1799–1856)*. Leiden/Boston: Brill.

Owtram, F. (2004). *A modern history of Oman: Formation of the state since 1920*. London/New York: I.B. Tauris.

Pasha, A. K. (Ed.). (1999). *India and Oman: History, state, economy and foreign policy*. Delhi: Gyan Sagar.

Peterson, J. E. (1978). *Oman in the twentieth century: Political foundations of an emerging state*. London/New York: Croom Helm/Barnes & Noble.

Peterson, J. E. (2004a). Oman: Three and a half decades of change and development. *Middle East Policy, 11*(2), 125–137.

Peterson, J E. (2004b). *The emergence of post-traditional Oman*. Durham middle east Papers 78, Sir William Luce Fellowship Paper 5. Durham: University of Durham.

Peterson, J. E. (2004c). Oman's diverse society: Northern Oman. *Middle East Journal, 58*(1), 32–51.

Peterson, J. E. (2004d). Oman's diverse society: Southern Oman. *Middle East Journal, 58*(2), 254–269.

Piolet, V. (2009). Les emirats et royaumes arabes: Les travailleurs migrants au pays des free zones. *Hérodote, 133*(2), 136–151.

Pridham, B. R. (Ed.). (1987). *Oman: Economic, social and strategic developments*. London/ Wolfeboro: Croom Helm.

Rabi, U. (2005). Oman's foreign policy: The art of keeping all channels of communication open. *Orient, 46*(4), 549–564.

Scharfenort, N. (2009). *Urbane Visionen am Arabischen Golf: Die "Post-Oil-Cities" Abu Dhabi, Dubai und Sharjah*. Frankfurt am Main/New York: Campus.

Schmid, H. (2009). *Economy of fascination: Dubai and Las Vegas as themed urban landscapes*. Berlin/Stuttgart: Borntraeger.

Scholz, F. (1977). Sultanat Oman: Ein Entwicklungsland im Südosten der Arabischen Halbinsel: Beschreibung der Entwicklung vor und nach 1970 und Versuch einer Analyse der Hintergründe und Perspektiven. *Die Erde, 108*, 2–74.

Scholz, F. (1980). *Sultanate of Oman, part 1: A geographical introduction to the country of Oman, its natural resources, its people, its settlements, its economy, and its modern development (reader)*. Stuttgart: Ernst Klett.

Scholz, F. (1981). *Beduinen im Zeichen des Erdöls: Studien zur Entwicklung im beduinischen Lebensraum Südost-Arabiens. Beihefte zum Tübinger atlas des Vorderen Orients: Reihe B, Geisteswissenschaften 45*. Wiesbaden: Reichert.

Scholz, F. (Ed.). (1985). *Die kleinen Golfstaaten: Reichtum und Unterentwicklung – ein Widerspruch?* Stuttgart: Klett.

Scholz, F. (1990). *Muscat, Sultanat Oman: Geographische Skizze einer einmaligen arabischen Stadt*. Berlin: Das Arabische Buch.

Scholz, F. (Ed.). (1999). *Die kleinen Golfstaaten* (2nd ed., completely revised ed.). Gotha/Stuttgart: Klett-Perthes.

Scholz, F. (2001). Oman und die arabischen Scheichtümer am Golf – Herausforderung an die zukünftige Landesentwicklung. *Petermanns Geographische Mitteilungen, 145*(2), 58–67.

Scholz, F. (2004a). Muscat. Hauptstadt des Sultanats Oman. In M. Günter (Ed.), *Die Arabische Welt im Spiegel der Kulturgeographie* (pp. 70–79). Mainz: ZEFAW.

Scholz, F. (2004b). Nizwa – das Zentrum Inner-Omans: Traditionelle und heutige Bedeutung. In G. Meyer (Ed.), *Die Arabische Welt im Spiegel der Kulturgeographie* (pp. 80–91). Mainz: ZEFAW.

Sheriff, A. (1987). *Slaves, spices & ivory in Zanzibar: Integration of an east African commercial empire into the world economy, 1770–1873*. London/Nairobi/Athens: James Currey/Heinemann Kenya/Tanzania Publishing House/Ohio University Press.

Skeet, I. (1974). *Muscat and Oman: The end of an era*. London: Faber & Faber.

Skeet, I. (1992). *Oman: Politics and development*. New York: St. Martin's Press.

Steiner, C. (2009). *Tourismuskrisen und organisationales Lernen: Akteursstrategien in der Hotelwirtschaft der Arabischen Welt, Eine Pragmatische Geographie*. Bielefeld: Transcript.

Steiner, C. (2010). From heritage to hyperreality? Prospects for tourism development in the Middle East between Petra and the Palm. *Journal of Tourism and Cultural Change, 8*(4), 243–256.

Townsend, J. (1977). *Oman: The making of a modern state*. London: Croom Helm.

Valeri, M. (2003). Réveil laborieux pour l'Etat-Qabous: Identité nationale et légitimité politique dans l'Oman d'aujourd'hui. *Maghreb-Machrek, 177*, 37–58.

Valeri, M. (2005). *Le sultanat d'Oman en quête d'un second souffle: Un régime aux prises avec la nécessaire diversification de son economie et l'émergence de revendications identitaires. Les Etudes du CERI 122*. Paris: CERI.

Valeri, M. (2007a). *Le sultanat d'Oman: Une révolution en trompe-l'œil*. Paris: Karthala.

Valeri, M. (2007b). Nation-building and communities in Oman since 1970: The Swahili-speaking Omani in search for identity. *African Affairs, 424*(106), 479–496.
Valeri, M. (2007c). State-building, liberalization from above and political legitimacy in the Sultanate of Oman. In O. Schlumberger (Ed.), *Debating Arab authoritarianism, dynamics and durability in nondemocratic regimes* (pp. 143–158). Stanford: Stanford University Press.
Valeri, M. (2008). Le Conseil d'Oman: Une instance bicamérale de consolidation de l'autoritarisme sultanien. *Revue Internationale de Politique Comparée, 15*(2), 189–204.
Valeri, M. (2009). *Oman, politics and society in the Qaboos-state*. London/New York: Hurst, Columbia University Press.
Wikan, U. (1982). *Behind the veil in Arabia: Women in Oman*. Baltimore/London: Johns Hopkins University Press.
Zimmermann, W. (1981). *Tradition und Integration mobiler Lebensformgruppen: Eine empirische Studie über Beduinen und Fischer in Musandam/Sultanat Oman*. Ph.D. thesis, Georg-August-Universität Göttingen, Göttingen.

Part I
Concepts of Regionalisation and Region-Building

Chapter 2
Conceptual Considerations of "Space" and "Region": Political, Economic and Social Dynamics of Region-Building

Steffen Wippel

2.1 Introduction: Recent Perspectives on Regionalisation

The present volume investigates the various and changing regionalisations of Oman. Yet, for a long time in social research a static and essentialist image of "space" and "region" prevailed, which took such configurations as given. According to this mostly implicit idea, social activities went on in predefined spatial contexts. Only with the more recent dissemination of approaches based in cultural studies and social constructivism did these rigid and container-like images start to dissolve. A broad "spatial turn" developed, which included many social science disciplines. Social space is now mostly interpreted as being socially constituted, i.e. continuously produced, reconfigured and transformed by human acts, ideas and communication. There is no uniform understanding, but a multitude of perspectives complement each other and offer different possibilities to conceptualize space, leading to discussion of diverse regional contexts. Recent approaches try to apprehend the multiplicity of spatial levels and the reaches of human activities and imaginations, from micro- to macro-scales (or from the "local" to the "global") and in diverse sub-, trans- and supranational contexts.

The diffuseness of the terms "region" and "regionalisation" results from the great diversity of definitions (shown by Miggelbrink 2002: 95), which however can also be understood as complementary rather than mutually exclusive. Different perspectives, classification procedures and fields of study condition the particular extent of regions and their limits. It will be shown that, rather than having clear-cut borders, such regional contexts intersect or gradually pass from one to the other at fluid interstices of reduced interaction. However, attempts are regularly made, especially in strategic communication, to rigidify the borders of regional entities and to match different

S. Wippel (✉)
Zentrum Moderner Orient (ZMO), Kirchweg 33, 14129 Berlin, Germany
e-mail: steffen.wippel@t-online.de; steffen.wippel@zmo.de

S. Wippel (ed.), *Regionalizing Oman: Political, Economic and Social Dynamics*, United Nations University Series on Regionalism 6, DOI 10.1007/978-94-007-6821-5_2,

functional areas. In the general debate on space, regions can therefore be understood in a larger sense as temporally variant, rapidly shifting spatial structures constituted by material and discursive social practices, which represent, even if not always unambiguously, political, economic and other social processes and transformations. At the same time, they constitute media, contexts and arenas of social agency and discourse (cf. also Miggelbrink 2002: 155). In this general understanding, "regionalisation" encompasses a broad variety of region-building processes and geographical structuring of the world.

In the following, this chapter will highlight presently circulating ideas and current debates that will be of relevance for the conceptual profile of the book and for a large number of contributions to it. But the chapter cannot be comprehensive and remains very much linked to the author's own institutional and disciplinary research career. Without repeatedly mentioning it, a lot of the following exposition is based on the work of Wippel (2008), which gives further details and sources.

The paper starts by examining two established spatial methodologies, "methodological nationalism" and conventional regional "metageographies", which rely on socio-spatial containers and thereby contribute to distorting our spatial understanding of the world. The article then briefly turns again to the new conceptualizations of space in the course of the expanding "spatial turn". It also includes constructivist considerations and helps to develop a broader understanding of regionalisation processes, which go beyond the building of territories. Subsequently, this conceptual overview will discuss the role of the state in the wave of intensified globalization and point to a more nuanced understanding of concomitant processes of de- and reterritorialisation. This in particular includes the formation of larger economic blocks. Thus, among the current trans- and post-disciplinary concepts, special reference will then be made to the "New Regionalism Approach" that goes far beyond conventional theories on regional integration to include a multiplicity of forms and actors. The "making of geography" based on processes "from below" is studied in another section. This includes remarks on the widely discussed emergence of "spaces of flows" as well as of "everyday regionalisations". In contrast, the (re-)emergence of "geopolitics" – and more recently "geoeconomics" – in the political field and new critical research perspectives on them are worth a further conceptual consideration. This is followed by new ideas on border-crossing "transstate", "transnational" and "translocal" networks, flows and spaces. Finally, this chapter considers the multiplicity and blurredness of spatial scales.

The two subsequent chapters will enlarge and deepen this conceptual introduction to the edited volume on "Regionalizing Oman" and discuss in more detail two specific concepts. Lorenz and Mattheis will centre on the "New Regionalism Approach" in combination with concepts from critical political geography, whereas Bromber presents the idea of "translocality" as it developed in the field of non-European, mostly historical studies. Some of the subsequent empirical chapters will also present in detail their individual approaches in the framework of the broader discussion on "region" and "regionalisation".

2.2 "Methodological Nationalism" and the Emergence of the Territorial Nation State

In terms of space, the study of human agency and social relations is still rather often limited to the dimension of the territorial nation state (TNS). This perspective is due to the fact that modern mainstream social sciences fundamentally understand the social world through the lens of "methodological nationalism" (Wimmer and Glick Schiller 2002) – or, in almost coinciding terms, of "state centrism" (Brenner 1999; Beck 2002) and "methodological territorialism" (Larner and Le Heron 2002: 754).[1] On the one hand, this basic research programme essentially equates or merges nation, state and territory into a single phenomenon. On the other hand, the TNS is conceived as preceding society and encompassing all areas of social life. States constitute discrete, contiguous geographical containers and define mutually exclusive fields of social, economic, political and cultural interaction, relations, flows and movements. Only a restricted number of passages allow – and help to regulate – interconnections between them; this includes a strict separation of "domestic" and "foreign" affairs, in which states are considered the only and homogenous actors. The state and its territory became the reference point for all other (sub-, trans- or supra-state) processes that are classified in relation to it. Even if the ideal of the TNS has rarely corresponded to actual control and regulation on the ground, it became so seemingly perennial and natural in the contemporary social imaginary that its rather unique and recent coming into existence was rarely made an own object of investigation.

In contrast, especially critical approaches in Political Geography and International Relations theory warn against the "territorial trap" (Agnew 1994; Agnew and Corbridge 1995). Their intention is to understand territories as historically and socially produced artefacts that are the result of discursive practises as well as of political, economic, cultural and social agency (cf. also Delaney 2005; Paasi 2003). Territorial arrangements are regarded as becoming effective only after their social formation. Social groups create and appropriate territories to exert power, to control the area in question and to enforce norms and rules on human beings. Closely linked with a state's territoriality is its exclusive sovereignty, which well-established ideas regard as constitutive for its capacity to act (Taylor 1995; Delaney 2005; Agnew 2005).

Several authors historicise the modern TNS and describe it as the long-term result of multiple structural changes from approximately the thirteenth through twentieth centuries (Schroer 2006; Agnew 1994, and authors cited in the following). It replaced previous political forms including empires that showed complex, often unstable and hierarchical spatial structures (e.g. Murphy 1996; Taylor 1995). Blurred, expansionist

[1] There were always heterodox strands that showed a preference for other spatial and social scales of analysis: the Marxian tradition in particular was preoccupied with "global" capitalism and "world" system theory; in contrast, "methodological individualism", in particular in (micro-) economics, represents the other end of the spectrum.

frontiers and fluid, permeable borderlands gradually developed into rigid and linear boundaries that defined the limits of society and community. Increasingly, the modern state started to bundle sovereignty over all aspects of social life on a territorial basis, thus developing from a power (and initially also a religious) container into a wealth and finally a cultural and social container (Taylor 1994, 1995). In the nineteenth century, "interstate" relations also became "international" as well as "interterritorial" after the division of land surface was completed.

The territorial characteristics of the post-war order impacted considerably on general perception and, in particular, on social research and made the state container the privileged unit for analysing social phenomena (Murphy 1996: 102 f.). This conceptual preference also reflects the close intertwining of the formation of modern social sciences with the culmination of TNS development in the Western world (Wimmer and Glick Schiller 2002; Brenner 1999). Last but not least, the pervasive representation of the state's territorial organisation in maps has shaped our understanding of the world from childhood on (Taylor 1995: 8 f.; see also Ben Arrous 2009); and most statistics, used as an essential basis of research, are produced by state institutions on a territorial basis.

Yet, with its focus on describing and analysing social processes within the TNS context, methodological nationalism impedes the understanding of important phenomena, especially in an era if accelerated globalisation. For a long-time, social sciences largely ignored and cut off trans-border connections, relations and processes unfolding between predefined territories. This also limited the ability of social scientists to adequately perceive on-going processes above or below the level of the TNS. Therefore, to overcome established methodologies, we need to come to a more appropriate image of a complex mosaic of overlapping and interpenetrating morphologies, scales and nodes that fill up the world.

In the following, several authors in this book will point out the fiction of a united TNS vs. the endeavours to create such a homogenous entity with a common history. Existing and shifting antagonisms and dichotomies within the contemporary Omani territory – such as coast vs. interior, North vs. South, rural vs. urban areas, Imamate vs. Sultanate and central government vs. local tribes – are especially emphasised (see Nicolini, Chatty, Valeri, Moktar and Beaudevin). In her study, Hoffmann-Ruf explicitly challenges established national macro-historiography. She also points to fluctuating tribal territories, whereas Nicolini highlights "premodern", less territorially bound forms of exercise of state power. Vice versa, Mokhtar as well as Al-Mahrooqi and Tuzlukova underline that some current processes contribute to reinforce national territoriality and identity at the same time.

2.3 Continental World Regions and Fixed "Metageographies"

What is true for the TNS applies similarly to the common thinking in a small number of – mostly (quasi-)continental – world regions as seemingly given and fixed spatial structures. Lewis and Wigen (1997) interpret such conventionally regarded, mutually exclusive regional containers as historically produced and mentally rigidified macro-regional "metageographies" that have been classified in accordance with seemingly objective criteria. They only allow one regional assignment that is continuously conveyed by media, politics and research as well as reproduced in the broader public. At the same time, their repeatedly communicated shapes can often be easily recognised and memorised.

Yet again, regions are not natural, aprioristic units, but changing, socially constituted geographical phenomena. Subject to political and social circumstances, ideas of regional spaces and their limits change repeatedly. Initially mostly delineated in accordance with physical features, the interference of the territorial principle made states the building blocks of world regions. However, what belongs to which specific region is heavily disputed, the more so as these attributions are normatively charged and used as worldviews, ideologies and programs to transport political ambitions (cf. also Fassmann and Wardenga 1999).[2] This is often part of larger subdivisions of the world into apparently clearly defined "cultural continents", present from older German cultural geography (e.g. Newig 1986) to the realist school of International Relations (Huntington 1993), easily leading to confrontational scenarios. Specific interest groups continuously and strategically promote and negotiate the creation of such "imagined geographies" (Said 1995: esp. 49 ff.). Their institutionalisation is reflected in symbols, signs and names, as well as in increasing regional consciousness (Jauhiainen 2004; Evers and Kaiser 2000). Often several conceptions of regions compete, and their boundaries are rather fuzzy.

In the academic realm, "area studies" in particular contributed to the creation of rigid "conceptual empires" (van Schendel 2005: 276; cf. also Kratoska et al. 2005). They concentrated on world regions conceived as static and contiguous containers that became more and more reified. The connections and relationships between them were thereby increasingly ignored. Correspondingly, Khalidi complained that

> [i]n the study of the 'Middle East', for example, complex processes which transcend regions, such as trade, capital and labor flows between countries all around the rim of the Indian Ocean, which in differing forms appear to have been quite significant for a very long time, have been given far less attention than they deserve (1998: 75).

In particular, the "Middle East" in its different shapes and designations constitutes such a metageographically fixed region. Authors like Krause (1993), Scheffler (2003) and Escher (2005) show its constructedness and multiple, changing definitions, mostly based on cultural essentialism or political interests.

Current nomenclature was imposed from outside the region, starting with older names pointing to the "East", reflecting Eurocentric perspectives. The inherent homogenisation and dichotomization of the "own" and the "other" has famously been denounced by Said (1995). Designations such as "Near" and "Middle East" were primarily coined in Western political chancelleries in the late nineteenth century to express political aspirations in the areas between the Mediterranean, Central Asia and India.[3]

[2]For constructions of "(Central) Europe", cf. for instance Schultz (1997, 1999).

[3]Paralleling this, in the West the French colonial administration separated a "white" North Africa from "black" Sub-Saharan Africa, which shows important effects until today (Wippel 2008).

Included areas differed noticeably in different languages and changed considerably over time. More neutral terms such as "Western Asia" are mainly employed by international organisations, whereas increasingly we find the identification as "Middle East and North Africa" (MENA), which however still is not used consistently. Similar problems of clear definition occur for the "Arab world" (cf. also Popp 2004) or subregional entities (for the Maghreb, Wippel 2005), depending on the use of ethno-linguistic, institutional or ideological criteria.

Attempts to define the region in cultural terms prevail until today. Others tried to define constitutive economic characteristics such as "rentierism" (Bobek 1979; Beblawi and Luciani 1987). Finally, the problems of clear definition lead to a sample of multiple phenomenological and descriptive criteria that include several natural, social, cultural and economic dimensions of the "Islamic-Oriental world" (Wirth 1980; Büttner and Scholz 1993). The ambiguity and change of regional terms, their vague and varying definition and geographical extension show that in fact no single, consistent conception of regions exists and that the conceptions vary in accordance with social contexts and issues. In contrast to (often strategically) communicated images, they rather constitute relatively recent, heterogeneous and disputed, continuously renegotiated constructs. Essentially, we are dealing with loosely-knit relational structures and multiple non-contiguous configurations that can only be described using open, temporary definitions and from different perspectives displaying manifold, overlapping and multiscalar belonging.

Correspondingly, subsequent chapters will rarely place Oman and its people and society within the Arab world or wider MENA region (alone), but (also) in other smaller and larger regional contexts, such as the Gulf (e.g. Zorob, Dietl, Benz) and the Indian Ocean (Nicolini, Wippel, etc.) – in quite different extensions and understandings – or show the close "bilateral", state and non-state links with Iran (Dietl), India (Pradhan), Zanzibar (Verne and Müller-Mahn) or the USA (Zorob).

2.4 "Spatial Turn": Deconstructing Spatial Rigidities in Social and Cultural Studies

Methodological nationalism and regional metageographies often constitute implicit and hidden presuppositions of social research rather than explicitly declared and consciously applied perspectives. The inherent spatial dimension of social phenomena has long been ignored to an even greater degree. Instead there has been a relative preference for time, especially in the modern Western worldview, in accordance with contemporaneous ideas of progress, dynamics and development.

But since approximately the 1980s, a new interest in social space started to develop across the disciplines, mostly kicked off by early debates in human geography about the appropriateness of existing concepts of space, but also in sociology, in particular based on Lefebvre's (1974) seminal work on "the production of space".[4] The expanding "spatial turn" was not only pushed by a general interest in the spatiality of human life, but also, and essentially, included new theoretical and conceptual approaches, mostly taking recourse to perspectives introduced by the larger "cultural turn" and social constructivism. This, however, is based on a wide range of disciplinary discourses and research backgrounds and represents diverging states of the art of meta-theoretical considerations. Some authors contribute action-oriented approaches, whereas other researchers advocate exclusive discourse-orientation. Many scholars plead for a microscopic approach, and especially flow-perspectives are *en vogue*. Still others, despite many controversies, recognize the complementarity of different approaches.

Yet, all of them contribute to overcoming the aforementioned methodologies and to breaking up static, closed and homogeneous images of territorial states and world regions. Finally, the spatial turn also drew interest in specific fields of history and political science, yet rarely in orthodox economics. In accordance with the multiple meanings of this turn, the following studies will all show an interest in the spatial qualities of social interaction and, more or less, apply specific space-centred concepts or interpret their results in the light of them.

2.5 Globalisation and the State: Concomitant Processes of Deterritorialisation and Reterritorialisation

Protagonists of globalisation theories often point to the fact that globalisation trends go hand in hand with the detachment of social agency from rigid territories (e.g. Bahrenberg and Kuhm 2000; Bahrenberg 2002; Werlen 2000, 2004). The territorial state is said to be increasingly losing its ability to regulate and control society vis-à-vis transnational and global actors. Globalisation is interpreted as a placeless, distanceless and borderless, territorially disembedded process. Fixed places and borders are accordingly replaced by global circulation, flows and geographical mobility and by transnational – quite often meaning "transstate" and "transterritorial" – interconnections and networks (e.g. Castells 1996). Consequently, Taylor (1994) asks whether, after having been "filled", the container is not increasingly "leaking". After the decline of its roles as an economic and a power container, it also seems to be losing its qualities as a social and cultural container with the globalisation of lifestyles, multiple citizenships and transnational flows of migrants.

Yet, many of the same authors who reflect about the "territorial trap" also warn against overgeneralising trends and effects. For them, the TNS continues to be

[4] For the German debate, see contributions, e.g., by Werlen (2004), Hard (2003), Bahrenberg 2002 in geography and Löw (2001), Schroer (2006) in sociology. They also give historical overviews of debates on space in both disciplines (see also Miggelbrink 2002). For the more recent "spatial turn", see Bachmann-Medick (2006: esp. 284 ff.).

powerful enough to shape social processes and to be an important framework for organising daily life (see, e.g., Paasi 2003; Agnew 2005; Schroer 2006; Taylor 1994, 1995). The realisation of the non-aprioristic character of container-like spaces does not contradict their empirically observable construction and attractiveness in daily practice. Contrary to the apologetic literature on its decline, the state still resists, proves to be highly efficient and seems to be still rather "filled" as a container.

Especially in political geography and IR theory, it is recognised that the TNS, despite all tendencies of dissolution, is still important for the national and international political system (cf. also Merle 1996; for the Arab world, Holm and Joenniemi 2001). As a cultural container, it still provides important bonds of identity. It is also difficult to observe a general retreat of the state from economic life. Economic geographers underline that enterprises are still embedded in and dependent on concrete social, cultural and institutional contexts, which are mostly defined on the TNS level (Bathelt and Glückler 2002; Glückler and Bathelt 2003; similarly Brenner 1999). Rules of origin that show national and regional territorial references are increasingly important for expanding trade and production chains. Other studies show that, even with their progressive opening, state borders still matter for trade and other flows (Helliwell 1998; Wolf 2000).

Between the reification of the TNS and territorially unbound globalisation, scholars with such critical stances (Agnew 1994; Delaney 2005; cf. also Paasi 2003; Brenner 1999; Miggelbrink 2002; from a historian's perspective, Osterhammel 2001) emphasise the transformation of statehood and territoriality. Their dynamic character reveals that the ideal of the sovereign TNS has never been an exact description of reality, and historically several forms of statehood, territoriality and society coexisted. At the same time, the state is currently recreated beyond the traditional container. Instead of decline, authors often acknowledge an "evasion" to other forms of statehood, with synchronous working of inter- and transstateness (Taylor 1995). Thus, deterritorialisation goes hand in hand with reterritorialisation and the creation of new political spaces (Schroer 2006; Brenner 1999). With the redistribution of regulation, control and power on spatial levels other than the TNS, a complex, multiscalar territorial system emerges (see also Paasi 2003; Merle 1996: 305 ff., Taylor 1994). At the same time, we need to consider the development and effects of discursive practices on state territorial sovereignty and linked strategies and rituals (Delaney 2005: 52 ff.).

In regard to globalisation trends, in the following, Abdelghani, for instance, will highlight the role of transnational companies and global consumption patterns in the intranational regionalisation of retail trade, whereas Brandenburg starts from the Westernization and privatisation of higher education to compare it in a regional Gulf perspective. Other authors come back to reterritorialisation processes on the supranational level (Zorob, Wippel), with Zorob in particular referring to the role of rules of origin. In contrast, Benz points to the specificities of a discontinuous state territory and mentions in fact shared, overlapping political and economic sovereignties. Valeri shows the redrawing of substate regions as well as the territorialisation in a modern sense of the tribal leaders' role when incorporated into the state apparatus. In fact, nobody negates the continuing, but changing role of the state.

2.6 The "New Regionalism Approach": From Conventional Integration Steps to a Multiplicity of Forms and Actors

The process described above includes the construction of new regional economic blocs. In the political and economic realm, region-building for a long time has been understood as "regionalism". This in particular refers to conscious and planned processes, initiated and politically controlled "from above", which lead to the *de jure* institutionalisation of inter- and suprastate cooperation and integration of several territorial nation states into a new and larger container (Oman 1994; Pomfret 1997 and many others). Bi- and multilateral agreements create common contractual spaces that might be strengthened by further joint institutions and can become more formal organisations. Political theory focused on issues like security and the balance of national interests (Pollack 2001; Schulz et al. 2001). In contrast, conventional international economics analysed a series of consecutive, increasingly deeper integration steps (see also Zorob, in this volume) – in a finally "given" regional setting. Especially after the Second World War, the number of regional cooperation schemes grew considerably. The European integration project was not the only one. Many more emerged among developing countries, normally designed in accordance with the phased model. Yet, these endeavours have not been too successful, partly because of structural impediments in the global economy, but also because local political elites were not disposed to abandon, even partly, newly acquired sovereignty.

However, since the turn to the 1990s, in practical political endeavours as well as in interdisciplinary theoretical considerations, a "new regionalism" is emerging. On the one hand, the number of registered regional agreements, in particular on trade, grew again markedly. Also countries in the Middle East and Southern Asia, which for a long time had shown the most important reluctance to integrate, have negotiated a growing number of such arrangements. On the other hand, the "New Regionalism Approach" (NRA) that finally encompasses a multiplicity of perspectives and methods is eager to break up state-centred and Eurocentric approaches and points to new – or rather formerly ignored – characteristics of regionalisation. Authors who can be subsumed under this label (e.g., Hettne and Söderbaum 2000; Bøås et al. 1999, 2005; Schulz et al. 2001; Lorenz and Mattheis, in this volume), in particular, turn to the diversity of forms "on the ground" and with that their spatial qualities. Forms and trajectories of regionalisation processes are more and more regarded as open, diverging and complex. Such newer approaches also highlight the overlapping of geographical spaces, institutions and tasks. They emphasise diverging levels of "regionness" and the smooth transition and complex interaction between formalised territorialisations “from above” and emerging regionalisations “from below”. It is not the state alone that produces regionalisation, but rather, even if it remains a central actor, a large number of other state and non-state, national and transnational actors with differing motives, interests, strategies and powers intervene.

We can thereby observe an increasing differentiation of regional cooperation, for instance in the EU, based on a vanguard core group, a graded surrounding or some kind of “variable geometry” of integration (Wessels 1994; Deubner 2003). In addition, “open regionalism” following the Asian-Pacific pattern aims at parallel, common vertical integration into the world economy. Horizontally, it allows for multidirectional orientations including simultaneous membership in and geographical overlapping of regional agreements (Leong 2000; Soesastro 1998, etc.). The multitude of interwoven, complementary as well as competing bi- and multilateral treaties concluded in recent years contributes to the emergence of regional networks of agreements, despite all problems such a “spaghetti-bowl regionalism” (Bhagwati and Panagariya 1999) brings with it.

Thus, economic and political cooperation agreements often form more or less coherent regions. New geographical spaces emerge, which transgress conventionally regarded continents and world regions. On the one hand, this is based on “interregional” accords, particularly across vast oceans, and bilateral agreements in particular sometimes cover great distances. On the other hand, it comprises interstices that hitherto have been regarded as empty spaces and natural barriers to relations and contacts, rather than as zones of exchange and transit. Such “transregional” areas – compared with the standard subdivision of the world – develop in particular in interjacent, literally “medi-terranean” spaces along sea coasts or across maritime basins, dispersed archipelagos or great deserts (Attinà 1996; cf. also Veltz 1997: 268, Lewis and Wigen 1997: 199). Simultaneously, formal cooperation not only develops among territorial nation states, but also between substate regions to form transnational “region states” (Ohmae 1993), “growth triangles” (Tang and Thant 1998) and “development corridors” (Söderbaum and Taylor 2007).[5] Altogether, differentiated, open and micro-regionalisms make it increasingly difficult to determine the definite limits of the influence of regional institutions and entail blurred and “fuzzy” boundaries of spaces of cooperation (for the EU, Christiansen et al. 2000; Melakopides 2000).

Finally, in the context of growing globalisation and medialisation, institutionalised regionalism increasingly needs explanation and legitimisation for the broader public. Strategic debates about integration policies and about regional and cultural belonging fix such regions in people’s minds. Long-term regional orientations can contribute considerably to the emergence of common regional identities. Arguments often refer to relations (and myths) of the past, which are revived and at the same time developed further and formalized.

[5]For the different levels of cooperation, see also the trilogy on macro-, meso- and micro-regionalism by Gamble and Payne (1996), Hook and Kearns (1999), Breslin and Hook (2002).

In this volume, Lorenz and Mattheis engage in depth with concepts such as the NRA and interregionalism. Empirical studies consider Oman's simultaneous economic agreements, either based on the conventional step-wise, European integration model or on the shallow type of open regionalism. Whereas Zorob focuses especially on variable geometries and emerging incompatibilities of multidirectional integration, Wippel, who also refers to the NRA, mainly reflects on the interweaving of formal, material and symbolic dimensions of economic regionalisation. Finally, Benz concentrates on a specific case of mostly informal micro-regionalism. Moreover, many contributions relate to physical features, such as oceans (e.g. Nicolini, Wippel), maritime straits (Dietl, Benz) or deserts (Chatty), that constitute conduits and areas of intense social and economic interaction.

2.7 The Daily "Making of Geography": The Emergence of Spaces of Flows, Movement and Entanglement

Spatial contexts emerge in the course of human agency. Current interaction-oriented perspectives centre on space-creating relations, movements and flows. When people interact, connections between them are built up, which may result in temporary or lasting networks, which concentrate and intersect in specific hubs and nodes.[6] In these relations, people themselves move and exchange goods, information and ideas that often converge into bigger flows. These, in turn, can bring about spatially concentrated interlacement, which temporarily consolidates and stabilises. Especially under contemporary conditions, "'flows' have become the generic (and hegemonic) metaphor of globalisation" (Larner and Le Heron 2002: 755). Together with a shift of interest from politics to economics, research started to focus on the increased mobility of goods, labour and capital; studies of the circulation of images, signs and information followed.

For Castells (1996, 1998), new, expanding technologies of communication are fuelling a shift from hierarchies to networks as the main organising principle of society. The "space of flows" supersedes the "space of places" based on physical space and closed spatial entities. For the constitution of the emerging global "network" and "information society", faster and faster circulating flows are of central importance. Local hubs that permit relations and exchange in these networks do not exist of themselves any more, but are determined in such a relational perspective by the processes in the networks. Subsequently, Appadurai (1996) in particular extended the debate to the cultural field, emphasizing several categories of flows undermining TNS-based institutions and creating new "media-", "ideo-", "ethno-", "finance-" and "technoscapes". The social sciences in general adopted the idea of flows as central characteristics of the contemporary global order.

[6] For network-oriented approaches in the study of the Islamic world, see Loimeier and Reichmuth (1996), Harders (2000).

In parallel, an action-centred human geography asks how human activities and behaviour create and define spatial patterns. According to Werlen (2000, 2004), "everyday regionalisations" are related to diverse kinds of social "geography-making" (cf. also Weichhart 2000), by which people, through their daily actions, relate the world to themselves and shape it materially and symbolically. With a specific focus on African contexts, Ben Arrous (2009, developing his text from 1996) highlights the importance of a relational "geography from below". He, too, refers to the spatial dimension of social dynamics and historical processes, which produce a multitude of varying and moving spatial arrangements, boundaries, hubs and networks.[7] Such subaltern spaces resist, contest and subvert the principle of territorial division, though not necessarily in binary opposition to territories, but rather in a dialectical, reciprocally constitutive relation.

As a result, authors like Werlen (2000, 2004; similarly Läpple 1991; Weichhart 2000; Jauhiainen 2004) distinguish several types of region-making. They acknowledge the structuring role of physical space as a substrate of social agency, as well as of politico-administrative territories as an outcome of norm-oriented agency. However, especially under late modern conditions of temporal and spatial "disanchoring" (*Entankerung*) of ways of life, two types of regionalisation are of special importance. Thus, "daily geographies of production and consumption" result from purpose-oriented, mainly economic agency and show the embeddedness of life in increasingly large and complex spatial contexts. In contrast, communication-oriented, primarily cultural agency leads to "informative-significative regionalisations" including the subjective, symbolic and emotional appropriation of space and its naturalisation and reification.

Networks and (spaces of) flows also constitute central fields of research in subsequent chapters, and many consider geographies from below and everyday regionalisations, based on material, social and emotional ties (e.g., Verne and Müller-Mahn, Beaudevin), including changing consumption geographies (Abdelghani).

2.8 From a Realist to a Critical Understanding of Making "Geopolitics"

With a widespread interest in spatial dimensions of human life, geopolitics – as an academic discipline and a field of political practice – also came back to the fore. In essence, geopolitics investigates connections between politics and space, in particular between state and territory (Mamadouh 1998; Helmig 2007; Agnew and Corbridge 1995). When it came up since the late nineteenth century, it essentially postulated the strategic political and economic importance of spatial contexts. International relations, expansion efforts and in general the mastering of space by territorial states have been a central focus. Biologism and natural determinism

[7] For a region constantly moving and changing, see also Marfaing and Wippel (2004).

resulted in arguing in favour of a fateful space-oriented *realpolitik*. Geopolitical maps exposing spatial perils, potential alliances and partitions of the world between the great powers have been effective representations of this way of thinking.

Its exaggerations and misuse by totalitarian regimes had largely discredited geopolitics after World War II, even if geopolitical strategies still have been practiced, especially during the Cold War. Its public renaissance was related to new global complexities and challenges from the breakdown of the Bretton Woods system through the collapse of the Soviet empire to the events of 9/11. On the one hand, re-emerging "realist" geopolitics, starting from given spatial constellations to develop space-related strategies of domination, presence and access, still has considerable influence on political practice. In this "neo-classical" conception (for the classification of concepts, see Mamadouh 1998), the state is still mostly conceived as a single, coherent actor with a clear set of national interests. Huntington (1993) in particular refilled overcome Cold War dichotomies from such a realist tradition with new cultural categories. A more "subversive" geopolitics, developed in the French research context (especially by Lacoste 2000), insistently contested these traditional conceptions, but at the same time "engaged" in practical politics, too. Central for it are "geopolitical situations", in which territorial claims, ideas and representations of diverse social groups engage in rivalry on different spatial scales and the role of media and public opinion in creating and developing them.

On the other hand, critical, purely academic approaches try to uncover essentialist spatial images and to deconstruct apparently given "spatial conditions" as socially constituted. Political geography turned again to geopolitical topics in the attempt to understand practical politics and international relations. Action-centred research analyses social and material conditions of political agency, emerging spatial power constellations and new territories, as well as forms of fragile statehood. In parallel, a post-structuralist "critical" approach regards geopolitics as a discursive practice that finally (re)produces the spatial order of international politics. It first of all endeavours to deconstruct powerful representations and imaginations of space in international relations, including constructions of the "other", territorial ideologies and practices of naming and their instrumentalisation for political purposes. Yet, other authors (e.g., Agnew 1994; Agnew and Corbridge 1995) plead for considering entangling discursive and material practices simultaneously.

Yet, with a globalising economy, attempts at economic cooperation and competition in global and regional contexts started to replace interest in purely military and political geostrategies. Therefore, more recently, we can observe a shift to more "geoeconomic" considerations. They developed mainly as a realist perspective in the 1990s and denied the dwindling importance or irrelevance of the state vis-à-vis global business networks (Spanger 1998). With the decreasing importance of military power and territorial dominance, the logic of international conflicts and "vital interests" has been transposed to the field of trade policy (especially by Luttwak 1990). As political power is said to depend on economic strength, states have to compete for national revenues, welfare and employment. Whereas the US-induced debate focuses on economic conflict strategies and regulations as a zero-sum game among industrialised countries, French scholars consider a broader range of economic actors and strategies again, which rather complement than supplement pure geopolitics (e.g. Lorot 1999). For them, countries outside the Western world, too, pursue international policies and offensive strategies to conquer markets and gain technological and economic supremacy. Simultaneously, the national territorial logic is seen as expanding to other scalar levels, in particular to the formation and institutionalisation of regional trade blocs.

In a broad understanding, many of the actors studied in the following undertake practical geopolitics, too. Yet, it is especially Dietl who deals with geopolitical matters in a more realist perspective, whereas others, more implicitly, investigate geoeconomic strategies (Zorob, Wippel).

2.9 The Rhetoric of "Transes": Transstate, Transnational and Translocal Networks, Flows and Spaces

Economic activities in particular have been increasingly conceived as transgressing natural and territorial boundaries. Correspondingly, there is a call to study human beings and objects in their "transareal" activities, movements and relations, which create links between existing places and regions as well as new complex, sometimes consolidated, sometimes ephemeral spatial configurations that go beyond the borders of the TNS container (and well-established world regions, too). With this, a multiple rhetoric of "trans"-approaches arose, which mostly focus on processes "from below".

Inconsistencies regularly exist between nationally or regionally institutionalised territories and spaces of interlacing and interweaving (e.g. Weichhart 2000: 551; Delaney 2005: 27 f., 63 ff; Ben Arrous 2009). This not only concerns relations and flows that have a formal character, but also informal movements, up to illegal practices, which are not controlled by state or regional authorities or which are even immediately directed against regulations from above. The focus of conceptual approaches dealing with these kinds of links is especially on the ambivalent meaning of borders between transgressed territories. On the one hand, they constitute barriers to trade and other movements and are often difficult to surmount and provide repeated sources of conflict. On the other hand, they are interfaces between different territories, tempting actors to overcome them, offer specific opportunities for social and economic interaction and signify geographical and social proximity (cf. also Meagher 1996; Nugent and Asiwaju 1996; Bantle and Egbert 1996).

For such contacts and flows transcending territorial delimitations, Bach (2003, 2004) coined the term "transstate regionalism". In particular he refers to Africa, where the phenomenon emerged in colonial times, when territorial borders multiplied. Today, reasons can be found in the financial, economic and political problems of concerned states that neglect their border areas and suffer from policies of economic adjustment or international sanctions. This also means that border areas are often socially and economically much closer linked to neighbouring countries than to their own "mother states". Some places and even whole countries developed into (trans)regional "hubs" in widely spanned trade and migration networks. Border-crossing relations become transstate activities in particular when they are able to penetrate entire territories as well as the institutions of affected states. Yet, states do not necessarily try to suppress such flows, which often exhibit a venting function. Even more, many state representatives may benefit from bribes or personally take part in these activities.

The concept of "transnationalisation", too, contradicts the idea that transgression of borders constitutes a rather exceptional, one-time "container hopping". It refers to social, cultural, economic and political structures and processes resulting from continued and repeated relations, interactions and practices of non-state actors across TNS borders. The term has become particularly prominent in migration sociology with reference to people, who not only emigrate – and perhaps remigrate – once between two states and societies, but in practice regularly move between, simultaneously reside in and continuously maintain ties with both of them (Pries 2002, 2004). These migrants are embedded in plurilocal cross-border networks; however, this approach does not ignore the enduring importance and influence of nation states. The term "transnational" also applies to non-governmental organisations, enterprises and financial capital, which have a consolidated presence in several countries. Even more, a transnational historiography claims a perspective that goes beyond national history rewritten onto legal or imagined territorial boundaries (Osterhammel 2001). It refers to groups, to their interconnections, networks and movements that transgress fixed national territories and continental regions as part of a world history that in particular includes the perspective from the "South".

Finally, the concept of "translocality" essentially investigates concrete movements of people, goods and ideas across multiform – political and geographical, but also social and cultural – borders and great distances and the emergence of geographical, cultural and social "interspaces", where new norms, identities and values are created (von Oppen 2004; Freitag and von Oppen 2010; Bromber, in this volume). It takes into consideration processes of the generation and institutionalisation of new spatial and socio-cultural structures that challenge established orders. The term "translocality" is preferred to the better-known "transnationalisation", because it also encompasses movements and processes prior to and beyond the TNS that in the non-European world were first established in the course of the twentieth century. It also covers links for which a physical change of place is not necessary, but which rely on communicative and imagined connections and spaces. This specifically allows taking into consideration rarely regarded contacts between the regions of the "South" and the resulting constitution of and change in spaces of mobility beyond conventional regional categories. Corresponding empirical research was done at the *Zentrum Moderner Orient* in Berlin on (trans-)Saharan spaces (Marfaing and Wippel 2004) and the Indian Ocean worlds. Here, "seascapes" and "sandscapes" (Deutsch and Reinwald 2002; Reinwald 2004) have been perspectives that developed further from considerations of several "(land)scapes" by Appadurai (1996), who had originally introduced the notion of "translocal communities".

As for networks and flows, most subsequent considerations also took an interest in the diverse kinds of "trans"-links and flows. First, Bromber presents practical research experiences with the translocality approach. Institutions such as clinics and shopping malls are described as having transnational or translocal character (Beaudevin, Abdelghani). Benz presents an illustrative case of transstate regionalism, whereas Chatty studies a transnational and translocal tribal community. In both cases, actors are not only disadvantaged by established territorial orders, but also profit from differentials across state borders. Verne and Müller-Mahn apply the translocality approach to their case study on the complex Oman-Zanzibar relationship. Transnational and translocal networks, flows and connections are also central to the geography of chronic diseases (Beaudevin) and to Indian migrant, merchant and businessmen communities in Oman (Pradhan). Mokhtar tries to link translocality and territory in the idea of "littoralisation", the current seaward-oriented trend inside Oman, from a macroscopic perspective. Different forms and shapes of sea- and desertscapes have an important role in the chapters that follow (e.g. by Nicolini, Verne and Müller-Mahn, Chatty, Wippel); other authors clearly refer to perspective-related landscapes of a local community (Hoffman-Ruf) or of higher education in the Gulf area (Brandenburg).

2.10 Blurred Spatial Scales Between the Local and the Global

Social processes unfold on different spatial levels. Such a "geography of scale" ranges – below, beyond and across nation states – from the smallest micro-regional contexts through meso- and macro-regions to quasi- and trans-continental world regions (Swyngedouw 1997; Läpple 1991). Whereas action- and subject-oriented approaches, e.g. in social geography, often favour the former scales, the latter ones are more generally regarded by economic and political studies in regionalism. In general, "region" is understood as a spatial category that ranges between "the local" and "the global" with the TNS as a particular case.

Several authors point out that spatial scales are not fixed and aprioristic containers, either, that only frame and organise social entities, but that they, too, are historical social constructs of material and discursive origin, which challenge established metageographies (see also Brenner 1999; Sassen 2003; Löw 2001). Often, in a conscious "politics of scale", certain spatial scales are created deliberately. Social conflicts contribute to the existence and the role of different spatial layers that in turn serve as important dimensions of regulation, control and power. At the same time, they run the risk of being mentally reified, including in the fields of research and politics, as the previous discussion of the TNS and world regions has already shown.

Different spatial scales are closely interlinked. Metaphors of "levels" of social life organized in an ascending spatial order don't seem to work well today when we have to deal with phenomena like global cities, diasporic communities and transnational protest movements. Systemic approaches, for instance, focus on interactions between social and spatial micro-, meso- and macro-structures (Ritter 1991 and his empirical study on Qatar 1985). There is a continuous rescaling of activities and organisational contexts; new scales are regularly created and others called into question – just as the state level is supplemented by sub- and supranational scales. Sometimes, in periods of exacerbated conflict and crisis, abrupt shifts of scales can occur. Even more, actions and their effects (or resulting flows and connections) regularly leap spatial scales and are rather difficult to be assigned to them without ambiguity (cf. also van Schendel 2005: 294, 296). In addition, perceptions and conceptions of space and space-related identities oscillate between scalar layers, depending on the contexts of action (Weichhart 1990: 75 ff.).

Continuous and accelerating rescaling results in an increasing "scale mismatch" between levels of action, organisation and appropriation. Instead of thinking in separated layers, we need to reconceive them as complementary and interpenetrating. Whereas, according to Sassen (2003), the concept of "glocalisation" (Robertson 1995) still starts from a clear and hierarchical distinction of spatial scales and the jumping between them, she prefers the term "multiscalar globalisation" emphasising their interlocking and close interconnectedness. In consequence, scales often mix and boundaries between them increasingly blur.

Finally, several authors in this volume demonstrate the different scales on which social agency and regionalisation take place and which often blend and are difficult to differentiate, for instance, different geographical ranges of contacts of a local rural community (Hoffmann-Ruf) as well as the interference among local, regional and global cultures (Al-Mahrooqi and Tuzlukova), the narrower and wider (trans) local and (trans)national regional scales of "therapeutic journeys" (Beaudevin) and the global, regional and local geographical contexts of the Musandam Peninsula (Dietl, Benz).

2.11 A Complex Understanding of "Regionalisation"

In studying Oman's diverse regionalisations, the present volume endeavours to go beyond the exclusive spatial categories of the territorial nation state and conventional world regions – without, conversely, ignoring them – and to develop a broader and more varied understanding of regional contexts. It thereby strives to show the multiple, often simultaneous, overlapping and perspective-related regional configurations and settings Oman, in the present and in the past, contributes to and is a part of. Thus, in the following, after exploring in more detail two of the aforementioned conceptual approaches – "new regionalism" and "translocality" – authors' empirical studies will cover a great variety of regionalisation processes, from the historical regional connections of al-Hamra (in contemporary Oman's al-Dakhiliya governorate) and the Sultanate's exclave Musandam's economic transnational links to the country's re-emerging relations with the Indian Ocean area and economic bonds with the United States. Yet, the limits of linguistic expression, powerful established methodologies of research, especially the necessary reliance on existing institutions, official documents and available data, and the continuing regulative, organisational and coercive power of the TNS make repeated reference to the territorial state as well as to the major world regions unavoidable – for instance, when exploring sub-, trans- and supra-"national" (or, actually, -territorial, -state) regional connections, flows and relations.

References

Agnew, J. (1994). The territorial trap: The geographical assumptions of international relations theory. *Review of International Political Economy, 1*(1), 53–80.

Agnew, J. (2005). Sovereignty regimes: Territoriality and state authority in contemporary world politics. *Annals of the Association of American Geographers, 95*(2), 437–461.

Agnew, J., & Corbridge, S. (1995). *Mastering space. Hegemony, territory and international political economy*. London/New York: Routledge.

Appadurai, A. (1996). *Modernity at large, cultural dimensions of globalization*. Minneapolis/London: University of Minnesota Press.

Attinà, F. (1996). *Regional cooperation in global perspective. The case of the "Mediterranean" regions*. Jean Monnet working papers in comparative and international politics 04.96. Catania: University of Catania, Department of Political Studies, Jean Monnet Chair of European Comparative Politics.

Bach, D. (2003). New regionalism as an alias: Regionalization through trans-state networks. In J. Andrew Grant & F. Söderbaum (Eds.), *The new regionalism in Africa* (pp. 21–30). Hants/Burlington: Ashgate.

Bach, D. (2004). Régionalisme et régionalisation à travers le prisme de l'aire saharo-sahélienne. In L. Marfaing & S. Wippel (Eds.), *Les relations transsahariennes à l'époque contemporaine. Un espace en constante mutation* (pp. 457–479). Paris/Berlin: Karthala/ZMO.

Bachmann-Medick, D. (2006). *Cultural Turns. Neuorientierungen in den Kulturwissenschaften*. Reinbek bei Hamburg: Rowohlt.

Bahrenberg, G. (2002). Globalisierung und Regionalisierung: die "Enträumlichung" der Region. *Geographische Zeitschrift, 90*(1), 52–63.

Bahrenberg, G., & Kuhm, K. (2000). Regionalität – ein Phänomen der Weltgesellschaft. *Informationen zur Raumentwicklung, 9*(10), 623–634.

Bantle, S., & Egbert, H. (1996). *Borders create opportunities. An economic analysis of cross-border small-scale trading. Diskussionspapiere 50*. Berlin: Das Arabische Buch.

Bathelt, H., & Glückler, J. (2002). *Wirtschaftsgeographie. Ökonomische Beziehungen in räumlicher Perspektive*. Stuttgart: Eugen Ulmer.

Beblawi, H., & Luciani, G. (Eds.). (1987). *The rentier state*. London/New York: Croom Helm.

Beck, U. (2002). *Macht und Gegenmacht im globalen Zeitalter. Neue weltpolitische Ökonomie*. Frankfurt am Main: Suhrkamp. (English: Beck, U. (2005). *Power in the global age: A new global political economy*. Malden: Polity).

Ben Arrous, M. (1996). *L'Etat, ses dissidences et leurs territoires. La géographie par le bas en Afrique* (Document de travail du CODESRIA 3). Dakar: CODESRIA.

Ben Arrous, M. (2009). La géographie par le bas: Introduction à une aventure collective. In M. Ben Arrous & L. Ki-Zerbo (Eds.), *Etudes africaines de géographie par le bas – African studies in Geography from below* (pp. 2–38). Dakar: CODESRIA.

Bhagwati, J., & Panagariya, A. (1999). Preferential trade areas and multilateralism – strangers, friends, or foes? In J. Bhagwati, P. Krishna, & A. Panagariya (Eds.), *Trading blocs. Alternative approaches to analyzing preferential trade agreements* (pp. 33–100). Cambridge/London: MIT Press.

Bøås, M., Marchand, M. H., & Shaw, T. M. (1999). The weave-world: Regionalisms in the south in the new millennium. *Third World Quarterly, 20*(5), 1061–1070.

Bøås, M., Marchand, M. H., & Shaw, T. M. (2005). The political economy of regions and regionalisms. An introduction to our critical, revisionist inquiries. In M. Bøås, M. H. Marchand, & T. M. Shaw (Eds.), *The political economy of regions and regionalisms* (pp. 1–12). Houndmills, Basingstoke/New York: Palgrave Macmillan.

Bobek, H. (1979). Rentenkapitalismus und Entwicklung im Iran. In G. Schweizer (Ed.), *Interdisziplinäre Iran-Forschung. Beiträge aus Kulturgeographie, Ethnologie, Soziologie und Neuerer Geschichte* (pp. 113–123). Wiesbaden: Dr. Ludwig Reichert.

Brenner, N. (1999). Beyond state-centrism? Space, territoriality, and geographical scale in globalization studies. *Theory and Society, 28*, 39–78.

Breslin, S., & Hook, G. D. (Eds.). (2002). *Microregionalism and world order*. Basingstoke/New York: Palgrave Macmillan.

Büttner, F., & Scholz, F. (1993). Islamisch-orientalische Welt: Kulturtradition und Unterentwicklung. In D. Nohlen & F. Nuscheler (Eds.), *Handbuch der Dritten Welt, Vol. 6: Nordafrika und Naher Osten* (3rd ed., pp. 16–66). Bonn: J.H.W. Dietz Nachf.

Castells, M. (1996). *The information age: Economy, society and culture. Vol. 1: The rise of the network society*. Cambridge/Oxford: Blackwell.

Castells, M. (1998). *The information age: Economy, society and culture. Vol. 3: End of millennium*. Cambridge/Oxford: Blackwell.

Christiansen, T., Petito, F., & Tonra, B. (2000). Fuzzy politics around fuzzy borders: The European Union's 'near Abroad'. *Cooperation and Conflict, 35*(4), 389–415.

Delaney, D. (2005). *Territory. A short introduction*. Malden/Oxford/Carlton: Blackwell.

Deubner, C. (2003). Differenzierte Integration: Übergangserscheinung oder Strukturmerkmal der künftigen Europäischen Union? *Aus Politik und Zeitgeschichte, 01–02*, 24–32.

Deutsch, J.-G., & Reinwald, B. (Eds.). (2002). *Space on the move. Transformations of the Indian Ocean's seascape in the nineteenth and twentieth century*. Berlin: Klaus Schwarz.

Escher, A. (2005). Arabische Welt, Islamische Welt oder Orient? Ein Plädoyer für "Arabische Welt" und "Islamische Welt" gegen "Orient". *Praxis Geographie, 35*(3), 4–11.

Evers, H-D., & Kaiser, M. (2000). *Two continents, one area: Eurasia*. Working paper 328. Bielefeld: Universität Bielefeld, Fakultät für Soziologie, Forschungsschwerpunkt Entwicklungssoziologie.

Fassmann, H., & Wardenga, U. (1999). Der Begriff Mitteleuropa in politisch-geographischer Sicht. *Geographische Rundschau, 51*(1), 26–31.

Freitag, U., & von Oppen, A. (2010). Introduction. 'Translocality': An approach to connection and transfer in area studies. In U. Freitag & A. von Oppen (Eds.), *Translocality: The study of globalising processes from a southern perspective* (pp. 1–21). Leiden: Brill.

Gamble, A., & Payne, A. J. (Eds.). (1996). *Regionalism and world order*. New York: St. Martin's Press.

Glückler, J., & Bathelt, H. (2003). Relationale Wirtschaftsgeographie: Grundperspektive und Schlüsselkonzepte. In H. Gebhardt, P. Reuber, & G. Wolkersdorfer (Eds.), *Kulturgeographie. Aktuelle Ansätze und Entwicklungen* (pp. 171–190). Heidelberg/Berlin: Spektrum Akademischer Verlag.

Hard, G. (2003). *Dimensionen des geographischen Denkens. Aufsätze zur Theorie der Geographie* (Vol. 2). Göttingen: Vandenhoeck & Ruprecht.

Harders, C. (2000). Dimensionen des Netzwerkansatzes. Einführende theoretische Überlegungen. In R. Loimeier (Ed.), *Die islamische Welt als Netzwerk. Möglichkeiten und Grenzen des Netzwerkansatzes im islamischen Kontext* (pp. 17–51). Würzburg: Ergon.

Helliwell, J. F. (1998). *How much do national borders matter?* Washington, DC: Brookings Institution Press.

Helmig, J. (2007). Geopolitik – Annäherung an ein schwieriges Konzept. *Aus Politik und Zeitgeschichte, 20–21*, 31–37.

Hettne, B., & Söderbaum, F. (2000). Theorising the rise of regionness. *New Political Economy, 5*(3), 457–473.

Holm, U., & Joenniemi, P. (2001). *North, south and the figure of Europe: Changing relationships* (Working paper 11). Copenhagen: Copenhagen Peace Research Institute.

Hook, G., & Kearns, I. (Eds.). (1999). *Subregionalism and world order*. Basingstoke: Macmillan.
Huntington, S. P. (1993). The clash of civilizations? *Foreign Politics, 72*(3), 22–49.
Jauhiainen, J. S. (2004). Baltic Sea region – Netzwerke und Innovationen. In W. Gamerith, P. Messerli, P. Meusberger, et al. (Eds.), *Alpenwelt – Gebirgswelten, Inseln, Brücken, Grenzen* (pp. 563–572). Heidelberg/Bern: Deutsche Gesellschaft für Geographie.
Khalidi, R. (1998). The "Middle East" as a framework of analysis: Re-mapping a region in the era of globalization. *Comparative Studies of South Asia, Africa and the Middle East, 18*(1), 74–80.
Kratoska, P. H., Raben, R., & Schulte Nordholt, H. (2005). Locating Southeast Asia. In P. H. Kratoska, R. Raben, & H. Schulte Nordholt (Eds.), *Locating south east Asia. Geographies of knowledge and politics of space* (pp. 1–19). Singapore/Athens: Singapore University Press/ Ohio University Press.
Krause, R. F. (1993). Orient, Naher und Mittlerer Osten. Die Begriffe im Wandel der Zeit. *Geographische Rundschau, 45*(1), 4–9.
Lacoste, Y. (2000). Rivalries for territory. *Geopolitics, 5*(2), 120–158.
Läpple, D. (1991). Essay über den Raum. Für ein gesellschaftswissenschaftliches Raumkonzept. In H. Häußermann, D. Ipsen, T. Krämer-Badoni, et al. (Eds.), *Stadt und Raum, Soziologische Analysen* (pp. 157–207). Pfaffenweiler: Centaurus.
Larner, W., & Le Heron, R. (2002). The spaces and subjects of a globalising economy: A situated exploration of method. *Environment and Planning D: Society and Space, 20*(6), 753–774.
Lefebvre, H. (1974). *La production de l'espace*. Paris: Anthropos.
Leong, S. (2000). The East Asian economic caucus (EAEC): 'Formalized' regionalism being denied. In B. Hettne, A. Inotai, & O. Sunkel (Eds.), *National perspectives on the new regionalism in the South* (Vol. 3, pp. 57–107). Houndmills, Basingstoke/London/New York: Macmillan Press/St. Martin's Press.
Lewis, M. W., & Wigen, K. E. (1997). *The myth of continents. A critique of metageography*. Berkeley/Los Angeles/London: University of California Press.
Loimeier, R., & Reichmuth, S. (1996). Zur Dynamik religiös-politischer Netzwerke in muslimischen Gesellschaften. *Die Welt des Islams, 36*(2), 145–185.
Lorot, P. (1999). La nouvelle grammaire des rivalités internationales. In P. Lorot (Ed.), *Introduction à la géoéconomie* (pp. 11–20). Paris: Economica.
Löw, M. (2001). *Raumsoziologie*. Frankfurt am Main: Suhrkamp.
Luttwak, E. N. (1990). From geopolitics to geo-economics. Logic of conflict, grammar of commerce. *The National Interest, 20*, 17–23.
Mamadouh, V. (1998). Geopolitics in the nineties: One flag, many meanings. *GeoJournal, 464*, 237–253.
Marfaing, L., & Wippel, S. (Eds.). (2004). *Les relations transsahariennes à l'époque contemporaine. Un espace en constante mutation*. Paris/Berlin: Karthala/ZMO.
Meagher, K. (1996). Le commerce parallèle en Afrique de l'Ouest. Intégration informelle ou subversion économique? In R. Lavergne (Ed.), *Intégration et coopération régionales en Afrique de l'Ouest* (pp. 197–222). Paris/Ottawa: Karthala/CRDI.
Melakopides, C. (2000). On the Mediterranean "fuzzy edge" of the EU: The candidacies of Malta, Cyprus and Turkey. *European Integration, 22*(3), 299–334.
Merle, M. (1996). Un système international sans territoire? In B. Badie & M.-C. Smouts (Eds.), *L'international sans territoire* (pp. 289–309). Paris: L'Harmattan.
Miggelbrink, J. (2002). *Der gezähmte Blick. Zum Wandel des Diskurses über "Raum" und "Region" in humangeographischen Forschungsansätzen des ausgehenden 20. Jahrhunderts*. Leipzig: Institut für Länderkunde.
Murphy, A. B. (1996). The sovereign state system as political-territorial ideal: Historical and contemporary considerations. In T. J. Biersteker & C. Weber (Eds.), *State sovereignty as social construct* (pp. 81–120). Cambridge/Melbourne: Cambridge University Press.
Newig, J. (1986). Drei Welten oder eine Welt: Die Kulturerdteile. *Geographische Rundschau, 38*(5), 262–266.
Nugent, P., & Asiwaju, A. I. (1996). Introduction. The paradox of African boundaries. In P. Nugent & A. I. Asiwaju (Eds.), *African boundaries, barriers, conduits and opportunities* (pp. 1–17). London/New York: Pinter.

Ohmae, K. (1993). The rise of the region state. *Foreign Affairs, 72*(2), 78–87.
Oman, C. (1994). *Globalisation and regionalisation. The challenge for developing countries.* Paris: OECD.
Osterhammel, J. (2001). Transnationale Gesellschaftsgeschichte: Erweiterung oder Alternative? *Geschichte und Gesellschaft, 27*(3), 464–479.
Paasi, A. (2003). Territory. In J. Agnew, K. Mitchell, & G. Toal (Gearóid Ó Tuathail) (Eds.), *A companion to political geography* (pp. 109–122). Malden et al.: Blackwell.
Pollack, M. A. (2001). International relations theory and European integration. *Journal of Common Market Studies, 39*(2), 221–244.
Pomfret, R. (1997). *The economics of regional trading arrangements*. Oxford: Clarendon.
Popp, H. (2004). Die Arabische Welt – was ist das eigentlich? In G. Meyer (Ed.), *Die Arabische Welt im Spiegel der Kulturgeographie* (pp. 8–29). Mainz: Universität Mainz, Geographisches Institut.
Pries, L. (2002). Transnationalisierung der sozialen Welt? *Berliner Journal für Soziologie, 2*, 263–272.
Pries, L. (2004). Transnationalism and migration: New challenges for the social sciences and education. In S. Luchtenberg (Ed.), *Migration, education and change* (pp. 15–39). London/New York: Routledge.
Reinwald, B. (2004). Espace(s) en mouvement? Quelques réflexions comparatives sur des processus translocaux. In L. Marfaing & S. Wippel (Eds.), *Les relations transsahariennes à l'époque contemporaine. Un espace en constante mutation* (pp. 443–455). Paris/Berlin: Karthala/ZMO.
Ritter, W. (1985). *Qatar: Ein arabisches Erdölemirat.* Nuremberg: Wirtschafts- und Sozialgeographisches Institut der Friedrich-Alexander-Universität.
Ritter, W. (1991). *Allgemeine Wirtschaftsgeographie, Eine systemtheoretisch orientierte Einführung*. Munich/Vienna: R. Oldenbourg.
Robertson, R. (1995). Time-space and homogeneity-heterogeneity. In M. Featherstone, S. Lash, & R. Robertson (Eds.), *Global modernities* (pp. 25–44). London/Thousand Oaks/New Delhi: Sage.
Said, E. W. (1995). *Orientalism: Western conceptions of the orient.* London/New York: Penguin. First ed. 1978. London: Routledge & Kegan Paul Ltd.
Sassen, S. (2003). Globalization or denationalization? *Review of International Political Economy, 10*(1), 1–22.
Scheffler, T. (2003). 'Fertile Crescent', 'Orient', 'Middle East': The changing maps of Southwest Asia. *European Review of History/Revue européenne d'Histoire, 10*(2), 253–272.
Schroer, M. (2006). *Räume, Orte, Grenzen. Auf dem Weg zu einer Soziologie des Raums*. Frankfurt am Main: Suhrkamp.
Schultz, H.-D. (1997). Räume sind nicht, Räume werden gemacht. Zur Genese "Mitteleuropas" in der Deutschen Geographie. *Europa Regional, 5*(1), 2–14.
Schultz, H.-D. (1999). *Europa als geographisches Konstrukt.* Jena: Friedrich-Schiller-Universität Jena, Institut für Geographie.
Schulz, M., Söderbaum, F., & Öjendal, J. (2001). Introduction. A framework for understanding regionalization. In M. Schulz, F. Söderbaum, & J. Öjendal (Eds.), *Regionalization in a globalising world. A comparative perspective on forms, actors and processes* (pp. 1–21). London/New York: Zed Books.
Söderbaum, F., & Taylor, I. (2007). *Micro-regionalism in Africa: Competing region-building in the Maputo Development Corridor* (UNU-CRIS Working Papers W-6). http://www.cris.unu.edu/fileadmin/workingpapers/20070504105447.W-2007-6.pdf. Accessed 30 Mar 2013.
Soesastro, H. (1998). "Offener Regionalismus" im asiatisch-pazifischen Raum. In H. W. Maull (Ed.), *Regionalismus in Asien-Pazifik* (Arbeitspapiere zur Internationalen Politik 98, pp. 7–58). Bonn: DGAP.
Spanger, H.-J. (1998). *Globalisierung, Geoökonomie und der Euro*. Frankfurt: Hessische Stiftung Friedens- und Konfliktforschung.
Swyngedouw, E. (1997). Excluding the other: The production of scale and scaled politics. In R. Lee & J. Wills (Eds.), *Geographies of economies* (pp. 167–176). London/New York: Arnold.

Tang, M., & Thant, M. (1998). Growth triangles: Conceptual and operational considerations. In M. Tang, M. Thant, & H. Kakazu (Eds.), *Growth triangles in Asia. A new approach to regional economic cooperation* (2nd ed., pp. 23–48). Hong Kong: Oxford University Press.
Taylor, P. J. (1994). The state as container: Territoriality in the modern world-system. *Progress in Human Geography, 18*(2), 151–162.
Taylor, P. J. (1995). Beyond containers: Internationality, interstateness, interterritoriality. *Progress in Human Geography, 19*(1), 1–15.
van Schendel, W. (2005). Geographies of knowing, geographies of ignorance: Jumping scale in Southeast Asia. In P. H. Kratoska, R. Raben, & H. S. Nordholt (Eds.), *Locating South East Asia, Geographies of knowledge and politics of space* (pp. 275–307). Singapore/Athens: Singapore University Press/Ohio University Press.
Veltz, P. (1997). Une organisation géoéconomique à niveaux multiples. *Politique Etrangère, 62*(2), 265–276.
von Oppen, A. (2004). L'évolution d'un programme de recherche: la "translocalité" au Centre de Recherche sur l'Orient Moderne (ZMO), Berlin. In L. Marfaing & S. Wippel (Eds.), *Les relations transsahariennes à l'époque contemporaine. Un espace en constante mutation* (pp. 401–414). Paris/Berlin: Karthala/ZMO.
Weichhart, P. (1990). *Raumbezogene Identität. Bausteine zu einer Theorie räumlich-sozialer Kognition und Identifikation.* Stuttgart: Steiner.
Weichhart, P. (2000). Designerregionen – Antworten auf die Herausforderungen des globalen Standortwettbewerbs? *Informationen zur Raumentwicklung, 9–10*, 549–566.
Werlen, B. (2000). Alltägliche Regionalisierungen unter räumlich-zeitlich entankerten Lebensbedingungen. *Informationen zur Raumentwicklung, 9–10*, 611–621.
Werlen, B. (2004). *Sozialgeographie. Eine Einführung.* Bern/Stuttgart/Vienna: UTB, Haupt.
Wessels, W. (1994). Integrationspolitische Konzepte im Realitätstest. *Wirtschaftsdienst, 74*(10), 499–503.
Wimmer, A., & Glick Schiller, N. (2002). Methodological nationalism and beyond: Nation-state building, migration and the social sciences. *Global Network, 2*(4), 301–334.
Wippel, S. (2005). Regionale Integration im Maghreb: Wirtschaftliche, kognitive und räumliche Aspekte. In S. Wippel (Ed.), *Wirtschaft im Vorderen Orient. Interdisziplinäre Perspektiven* (pp. 112–141). Berlin: Klaus Schwarz.
Wippel, S. (2008). *Territorialisierungen und Regionalisierungen im nordwestlichen Afrika – Wirtschaft, Politik und Raum in den marokkanisch-mauretanischen Beziehungen.* Habilitation thesis. Philosophische Fakultät und Fachbereich Theologie, Friedrich-Alexander-Universität Erlangen-Nürnberg. (Published 2012 as: *Wirtschaft, Politik und Raum. Territoriale und regionale Prozesse in der westlichen Sahara.* Berlin: Hans Schiler).
Wirth, E. (1980). Einleitung: Der Orient – Versuch einer Definition und Abgrenzung. In H. Mensching, & E. Wirth (Eds.), *Nordafrika und Vorderasien. Der Orient* (pp. 11–19, Revised and updated ed.). Frankfurt am Main: Fischer.
Wolf, H. C. (2000). Intranational home bias in trade. *The Review of Economics and Statistics, 82*(4), 555–563.

Chapter 3
Theorizing Regionalism(s): When "Regions" Emerge and Interact

Ulrike Lorenz-Carl and Frank Mattheis

3.1 Introduction

At the latest with the proliferation of regional trade agreements (RTAs) in the last two decades, the concept of "the region" has come to the forefront of social science research – not only in International Relations (IR), but also in neighbouring social science disciplines like geography, anthropology and economics. Some scholars see an emerging "world of regions" (Katzenstein 2005), while others associate the term with concepts of empires (Hardt and Negri 2000) or describe it as a "project" within the wider phenomenon of globalisation (Hveem 2003) as "almost every country in the world has chosen to meet the challenge of globalisation in part through a regional response" (Bulmer-Thomas 2001: 363). However, despite an ever-growing number of publications, knowledge about actors and processes shaping and producing our world seems still insufficient, and "philosophical confusion reigns supreme in much writing about place, space and region" (Agnew 1999: 93–95, cf. Lorenz-Carl and Rempe 2013). Related academic disciplines are struggling with theorizing the concept and little consensus exists between, but also within the disciplines and their respective conceptualisations, terminologies and ideologies. Particularly between political and economic readings of regionalism, there is a vastly diverging understanding, whereby the latter is sympathetic towards a purely economic regionalism while the former primarily understands political regionalism as a viable solution for the allegedly diminishing competences of the state in a

U. Lorenz-Carl (✉)
Faculty of Economics and Social Sciences, University of Potsdam,
August-Bebel-Straße 89, 14482 Potsdam, Germany
e-mail: ulrike.lorenz-carl@uni-potsdam.de

F. Mattheis
Centre for Area Studies, University of Leipzig, Thomaskirchhof 20,
04109 Leipzig, Germany
e-mail: mattheis@uni-leipzig.de

S. Wippel (ed.), *Regionalizing Oman: Political, Economic and Social Dynamics*, United Nations University Series on Regionalism 6, DOI 10.1007/978-94-007-6821-5_3,

globalising world. In both fields, literature focuses on explaining why regionalism, meaning the idea of ordering economic and consequently political relations on a regional basis, has again emerged after the integration sclerosis of the 1970s, as well as on which effects are to be expected from these current developments.

At the same time, the spatiality of the phenomenon and its ontological configurations have been widely ignored by both camps, whereas Critical Political Geography has advanced towards a sophisticated discussion on the matter. Surprisingly, exchange between the disciplines is only in its infancy (Fawn 2009; Paasi 2009; Lorenz 2010; Lorenz and Cornelissen 2011). A theoretical approach called New Regionalism, for example, has been eager to overcome the disciplinary boundaries between IR, Comparative Politics and Area Studies. But, as this chapter argues, it still carries a tendency to enforce disciplinary divides instead of engaging with a conceptual rethinking of "region" per se.[1]

This chapter thus sets out to move towards an inclusive approach to grasp the multiplicity the concept of region holds. The chapter will, in a first step, revisit existing theories of economic and political regionalism and discuss how different forms and different functions of region are addressed and reflected. It will, secondly, introduce the recent conceptualisation of region in Critical Political Geography, followed by a discussion of an adaptive concept of regional integration and Interregionalism as a most recent theoretical approach. The chapter will conclude by linking the respective discussions with an "Omani point of view" on the study of regionalism(s).

3.2 Multiple Epistemologies: New Regionalism(s) and the "IR Trap"

As aptly assessed by Warleigh-Lack (2008: 43), "theorising regionalism has never been straightforward". For the majority of academic researchers, the focus of research lies not on ontological facets, but on the phenomenon of regionalism and the institutionalisation of regional organisations, where "region" becomes "an epistemology, a way of knowing the world" (Paasi 2004: 539). Since regionalism is a widely used term that has carried differing meanings in different periods of social science research, a source of confusion has been the use of the term "regionalism" for both the politico-economic phenomenon as well as for the theoretical approaches analysing the ideas, objectives and ideologies related to a delimited geographical area or institution (Marchand et al. 1999: 900; Söderbaum 2004: 5). Broadly speaking, literature on regionalism suffers from an epistemological and conceptual

[1]Analogously to the differentiation in ir/IR of using small letters when referring to the political project or "ideology" and using upper case when referring to the theoretical concept, this chapter will refer to regional integration and (new) regionalism as political projects, and to New Regionalism as the theoretical concept and debate (cf. Higgott 2005: 576).

"spaghetti bowl" – "a tangle of conflicting, overlapping and competing terminologies" (Baldwin 2008: 5) that can broadly be differentiated by chronological order and thematic orientation. With regards to the former, regionalism and its corresponding theories are divided into an early phase of regional integration in the 1950s and 1960s and into attempts towards regionalism in relation to globalisation starting again in the 1980s. Especially on the latter, Hettne and Söderbaum (2008: 62) suggest "that it is time to bury the distinction" not only between an Old and a New Regionalism, but also to bridge the gap between Area and European Studies. Regarding a thematic orientation, regionalism is furthermore either concerned with an *economic dimension* and here mainly with preferential trade relations and agreements, with theories focusing for example on the implications of such agreements or the various steps towards establishing a monetary union as part of economic integration (Pomfret 1997; Viner 1950: chapter 8); or it is driven as part of a *political dimension* by the key idea of creating a security community with theoretical approaches focusing on the development of politically integrated communities (Deutsch 1968).

3.2.1 Economic Regionalism

The basic idea of economic regionalism relates to one of the most fundamental actions between two or more parties:[2] it aims at preferential trade relations between two or more trading partners. Most famously introduced by Adam Smith in the *Wealth of Nations* back in 1776, the question again became central to the "small-think regionalism" (Baldwin 2008: 3) of the post-Second World War architecture in the 1950s, which however not only asked about potential gains for states when joining a preferential trade agreement, but also about trade agreements as promoters of creating and maintaining peace between states.[3] Assessing developments in Europe and also in Latin America and other parts of the world where FTAs were established, theories discussed respective "measures that entail the suppression of some forms of discrimination" (Balassa 1961: 2) and consequently focussed on economic integration, especially on customs unions (Viner 1950) and the processes leading to their establishment that were most famously outlined by Balassa's postulation of a linear model of sequential integration.[4] This "closed regionalism" constituted the basis for many of the trade blocs formed in

[2]The terms "economic regionalism" and "economic regional integration" are thereby often used interchangeably.

[3]Although Adam Smith is mostly referred to as an economist, (Cafruny and Ryner (2009): 221) raise a valid point in arguing that *The Wealth of Nations* "represented a unified conception of social science" well before the fragmentations of social sciences into individual disciplines.

[4]Balassa's model foresees the process starting with a free trade area, which transforms into a customs union and a common market before reaching the stage of an economic union and "complete economic integration".

the 1960s and 1970s between developing countries and was very protectionist, comprising high external trade barriers. These preferential trading conditions, however, did not lead to economic gains for all the member states of the respective trade blocs.[5] Particularly for developing countries, potential economic gains from regionalism were, and still are, highly debatable (Faini and Grilli 1997: 224; Majluf 2004: 6).

Institutional dynamics did not figure prominently in this first wave of economic integration theories; however, with the crisis of the Bretton Woods system, the limitations of "economics of integration", which had developed into a specialised domain for, mainly, neoclassical economics, were exposed and drew attention to the political dimensions of international economic affairs and led to a revival of international political economy (Cafruny and Ryner 2009: 237). The exponential growth of regional trade blocks in the late 1980s and the slowing of the GATT talks after 1990 led to the development of "big-think regionalism", which instead asks about the gains of states focused on systemic implications and led to the two most-cited lines of inquiry: would regionalism serve as a stepping stone (Krugman 1991, 1993) or stumbling block (Bhagwati 1991) to world welfare and multilateralism? This new regionalism was outward-oriented towards trade within a multilateral environment conditioned by the pressures of globalisation to seek efficiency through larger markets, as well as to attract foreign investment and access foreign technologies.[6] And while the first wave of economic integration theory focused almost entirely on states as sole actors within trade blocs, economic regionalism also considered "major political actors in society, [for example] business, labour, and environmentalists" (Lawrence 1999: 26), as well as customers as relevant actors, since "foreign trade and foreign investment […had] become increasingly complementary" (ibid.: 26). Regarding the "scope of region" and the role of states in economic regionalism, Schiff and Winters (2003: 201) interestingly point towards a critical aspect of regionalism when stating that "joining an RIA [Regional Integration Agreement] necessarily requires surrendering some immediate control over policymaking and losing some political autonomy". This surrendering, for example by creating institutions to facilitate joint decision-making, is however not seen as problematic and not as necessarily leading to the suppression of the state and to limiting its sovereignty, but rather as enhancing the position of members of an RIA in international negotiations. The "region" serves as a territorially defined arena for positioning effective economic governance. Different levels of sovereignty can thus exist in parallel as long as they lead to economic growth.

[5]For the time between the 1960s and the late 1980s, Baldwin (2008: 13) assesses that "regionalism was a simple matter", consisting of, on the one hand, the "the EEC which encompassed a third of world trade in a highly effective customs union" and, on the other hand, "a slew of RTAs among developing nations that covered a trivial fraction of world trade and in any case never operated effectively".

[6]The extensive debate in economics on the new regionalism cannot be deepened here, but has been sophisticatedly scrutinised by Schiff and Winters (2003) and Baldwin (2008), among others.

3.2.2 Political Regionalism

The first wave of theories of regionalism from a political science point of view was dominated by the competing strands of either neofunctionalism or intergovernmentalism. Whereas neofunctionalism argues that specific government functions can be exercised more efficiently by means of regional cooperation than by the individual states (Haas 1958;), intergovernmentalism draws heavily on realist assumptions about the role of states and views the continuing centrality of the national governments as sovereign actors as the explanatory factor for European integration where "sovereign nation-states 'decide' on regional cooperation when their 'national interests' prove to be compatible" (Schirm 2002: 6; also Hoffmann 1964, 1966).[7] Both approaches share an inward-orientated focus in which the region – meaning the European Economic Community – is understood as a territorial entity characterised by the proximity of its Member States while essentially ignoring influences from potential external actors. Works from "old" or rather from the "first wave" (Hettne 2005: 548) of regionalism theory focused on the then emerging European Economic Community, whose aim was to foster regional integration among the Western European post-World War II states.

In contrast, the second wave of Regionalism Studies moved away from the earlier inward-orientated regional integration theories and opened up towards critical International Political Economy (IPE) (Bach 1999; Bøås et al. 2005; Hettne and Söderbaum 2000; Hurrell 2007; Hveem 1999; Lee 2003; Söderbaum and Shaw 2003; Söderbaum 2004), making the impact of rising levels of regional social and economic exchange and the links between politico-economic integration, institutions and identity the core of this "New" Regionalism (Hurrell 2007: 132; also Söderbaum 2004). Distinguishing between *regionalism* as a "body of ideas, values and concrete objectives" and *regionalisation* as a "process of change from relative heterogeneity and lack of cooperation towards increased cooperation, integration, coherence and identity in a variety of fields" (Söderbaum 2004: 4), New Regionalism sees its innovation compared with the early regionalism theories in transcending the dichotomy between state and non-state actors, as well as by opening up to a reflectivist approach (Söderbaum 2004: 55). It departs from a rejection of the notion of space(= state)-as-container in favour of a multilevel framework, which defines regions as dynamic processes for social interaction that come into being and are shaped discursively and materially and (although some models neglect this aspect) trail long histories of economics, politics, or ethnicity that make regions highly complex and multi-spatial entities whose existence is anything but granted. Critics

[7] The debate developed further with Moravcsik's (1993) suggestion of a more rigorous version of intergovernmentalism – liberal intergovernmentalism – and Sandholtz and Stone Sweet's (1998) positing of the concept of supranational governance, which assumes different levels of supranationalism existing within different policy sectors. This debate has however been forcefully led elsewhere and will not be deepened in this chapter.

of New Regionalism have however argued that New Regionalism does not offer a theoretical alternative or even a theoretical model for the study of regionalism. Similarly, in the light of a socially constructed nature of regions, (Neumann 2003; also Browning 2003) criticises New Regionalism for not sufficiently addressing the question of how regions come into being. Albeit regions are understood as "entities whose contents and borders are in a process of change, the existence of a region is taken as a given [...and] treated as *a priori*" (Neumann 2003: 165–166).

The differing notions between the first and second wave of regionalism theories about the scope of region mark a key difference for this chapter. Early works understood regions either as "international subsystems" (Haas 1970; Nye 1968), as levels of integration and interdependence within (Russett 1967) or as "larger units" (Bull 2002: 255) constituting an "alternative level" to the nation-state (Adler 1997). First-wave scholars thereby focused almost entirely on the EEC, while New Regionalism scholars share the tendency to reject the EU and its model of regional integration as a role model for regionalism (Bøås et al. 2005; Warleigh and Rosamond 2006; Warleigh-Lack 2008). This stance has however led New Regionalism to turn a blind eye on more recent developments in European Studies that could in fact offer a toolbox for scrutinising variations of EU/EC models. More crucially, however, despite their understanding of regions as socially constructed processes, large parts of New Regionalism research still assesses that, "like a nation, [... the region] is an 'imagined community', and like a nation it has a territorial base" (Hettne 2003: 7). Such theoretical conceptualisation has not yet fully transcended IR thinking and theorising and thus remains in the "IR trap": reading regions ultimately as alternative units to the state falls short not only in capturing the changing role of the state within a globalising world, but also on a broader scale regarding a conceptualisation of multilevel relations in a globalising world. In such IR-trapped theorising, regions constitute yet another container for social action, and the advancement of a constructivist approach will inevitably hit the theoretical glass ceiling of a continued division of today's world into, quite literally, manageable parts.

3.3 The Concept of "Region" in Critical Political Geography

IR and Critical Political Geography have not been regular dinner partners, but since in recent years both are increasingly confronted with their disciplinary boundaries and rising calls for interdisciplinary approaches, awareness of and interest in each other's work has increased, but little has been taken place beyond this. European Studies scholars like Alex Warleigh-Lack have realised that

> [t]here is ... an emergent view that attempting a narrow definition of the term 'region' is not likely to be productive, and that instead theorists should concentrate on understanding the various processes of regionalisation that are unfurling across the globe (2008: 51).

Yet again, different notions of region conform to different schools of thought and, perhaps even more important, to different disciplines that so far have rather talked past each other than with each other.

To theorise "region" beyond an understanding of an accumulation of states, it seems natural to turn to geography, where regions – literally – have been given more space. Admittedly, geography scholars have also struggled to define the concept. While earlier works focused on physical characteristics such as geology, climate or vegetation "smaller" than the states of which they were a part, more recent works either conceptualise regions as "urban-metropolitan agglomerations … focusing on commonalities of production patterns, labour markets and market linkages" as part of economic new regionalism or as "representing regions as territorial and political sub-national administrative units" from a political New Regionalism point of view (Fawn 2009: 5; Harrison 2006: 26). Lovering's (1999: 384) critique disapproves of these differing theoretical approaches as a "set of stories about how parts of a regional economy might work, placed next to a set of policy ideas which might just be useful in some cases" (emphasis in the original) which distract those whom he calls "regional geographers" from engaging with their "supposedly foundational concept".

The re-introduction of space as an analytical concept as an outcome of the so-called "spatial turn" is one of the major advancements in understanding the present transformations of a globalising world and can be attributed to Lefebvre's seminal work on the *Production of Space* (1991 [1974]). However, his "three moments of social space" found little scholarly resonance in the 1980s, competing against Althusser's structural Marxism and the influential research on urbanisation of his former student Manuel Castells that was published a year before the *Production of Space* (Merrifield 2002: 168).[8] The importance of Lefebvre's work lies in his understanding of space as active, rather than as a passive surface for the reproduction of activity (ibid.: 172). In identifying the "spatial triad" of "representations of space" as conceptualised space, "representational spaces" as "directly lived through its associated images and symbols" and "spatial practice", abstract space is related to its real social existence (Lefebvre 1991: 33–39). His triad internalises lived, perceived and conceived notions of space that make up everyday life and inspired a new generation of scholars to "think space" and to turn from reading globalisation as a phenomenon of modernity in which space was considered a less relevant category towards inscribing it into a postmodern understanding.[9] The claim that space is obsolete was altered towards considering its multilevel-character and the plurality of spatial relations (Schroer 2008: 131). So despite the prognoses of the development of both temporal and spatial compression (Harvey 1990; also Cairncross 1997), in which space would become obsolete, space has, on the contrary, become even *more* relevant for two reasons: on the one hand, it is needed to challenge the characteristics of existing notion of "social containers", while at the same time it has drawn attention to space as an alternative analytical arena to overcome the state/international dichotomy (Schroer 2008: 131).

[8]It was David Harvey who introduced Lefebvre's work to the Anglophone audience.

[9]His work also influenced Edward Soja's work on Postmodern Geographies in 1989, but while social sciences intoned the call for a spatial turn, geosciences claimed the need for a "geographical turn" of science (cf. Lévy 1999).

As one of the first to address this matter in the 1990s, Agnew (1994: 53) directed attention to what he called the "territorial trap": even though political practices require territorial anchorage, the processes set in motion by such practices are not territorially fixed and no longer fall along a binary divide of domestic/foreign, East/West or real/imagined based on states as "containers of society".[10] Therefore, the reading of "region" as an alternative unit of analysis or as a "mesoscale" unit between the local and national scales is to be refuted (Agnew 2000: 106) in favour of a conceptualisation of "region" that departs from drawing geographical lines.[11] Allen analyses differences in geographical distributions, the corresponding fuzziness of an overlapping of respective borders and intra-regional differentiation. He concludes "that difference is … constituted more through interconnection than through opposition". In his line of argument, a region is

> "not bounded off from but linked to, and in part constituted in its character through its linkage to, other regions. We are so used to the idea of geographical definition that not drawing boundaries seems to go beyond our thinking of 'region'" (ibid.: 55).

With this reading, "region" becomes a self-contained object (cf. Weichhart 1995: 36), which is spoken about as a representational entity and not as a spatial projection and abstraction of social and economic realities, which are primarily relations and interactions between individuals.[12] This is where Critical Political Geography joins New Regionalism in arguing against viewing states or world regions as territorial containers and units of analysis, but proposes instead a relational reading of regions since "one cannot understand a particular scale without analysing its relationship to other scales, since the meaning and importance of each scale is unavoidably embedded in its interscalar relationships" (Purcell 2003: 318). The blind spot of this approach to think region relationally is however twofold: the first blind spot lies in limiting an analysis to the question of how such relationships were produced and are reproduced and how they contribute to the production of a regional order. But it points to a necessary actor-centred conceptualisation and the relevance of power relations and their representations for escaping a "spatial voluntarism" (Jones 2009: 493). The engagement with the concept of power, in particular, is a weakness of region studies and New Regionalism so far. If regions are neither to be understood as given and passive units, regardless of the perspectives of questions addressed to the relevant spaces, nor as exclusive, autonomous entities operating "above human beings" (Paasi 2001: 16), the challenge is to develop a notion transcending both the "container thinking" and a purely relational model of regional space, a notion

[10] As mentioned above, this approach was indeed taken up by International Relations and New Regionalism scholars like Bøås, Marchand and Shaw (2005) in recognizing the relevance of space and spatiality for the study of regions and that utilizing insights gathered in parallel disciplines like critical geography or cultural studies would contribute to their own understanding of regionalism. These findings were however not further developed.

[11] In fact, Allen refrains from drawing any geographical lines in his study.

[12] In his 1995 article, Weichhart claims that there is no accepted theory of space ("Raumtheorie").

conceptualising regions as ordering schemes and concepts that are constantly renegotiated (see, in part, Pradhan's chapter on Oman-India ties).

The second blind spot lies in the treatment of the state. The argument that addressing states as unitary actors obfuscates the complexity of processes that "make a state" and at the same time "make regions" points correctly to a problematic ontology. As already stated, understanding a region *a priori* as a group of states can be appropriate in some cases and for some research problems, but does not cover those processes that reach beyond this kind of geographical delimitation. There is no need on either account to banish the state from analysis; rather, analytical understanding of the state's exclusivity and unity is required. Obviously, despite the many scenarios that proclaimed the dissolving of the state, states are adapting to on-going transformations. Their *de jure* existence is questioned in few cases, but what seems to be decreasing is the exclusive legitimacy of national governments in directing the courses of issue areas. They are not only challenged by the increasing influence of non-state actors, but also by an increasing number of actors within "the state" who participate in policy making processes that parallel national governments. City networks or permanent representations of federal states with the EU are successful examples of such parallel participation. The question should therefore be more *how* states adapt and where which new characteristic comes to the fore, rather than simply concluding that "the state" does not fit (Taylor 2010). It is in regard to this struggle of bringing "the state" and also "the region" together with an emerging global order that Critical Political Geography might have the most to offer to.

3.4 Towards an Adaptive Concept of Regional Integration

When dealing with the phenomenon of regional integration in the world, interstate institutions are at the centre of attention. Transborder regions are generally excluded, as their informality leads to different structures and perceptions. However, in many non-European regions – including the Arab world – formal contracts tend to be shadowed by other structures of power. Applying a broader notion of regionalism to the regional level offers the opportunity to include a wider range of actors and processes. This perspective still puts a multi-state region in the centre of attention, but contextualises institutions in the setting of the Third World. As opposed to a rigid focus on organigrams and signed agreements, it can emphasize the redefinition of the region exercised by state and/or non-state actors either in formal or informal ways.[13] The general bias of regional integration studies towards state-led formal institutions can thereby be compensated by extending the range of actors, even though state agents usually retain most of the power. Furthermore, one needs to emphasize the

[13] Müller-Mahn and Verne (in this volume), for example, relate their case study of the movement of Omani Zanzibaris and Zanzibari Omanis to "soft" concepts of translocal practices and imaginative geographies.

temporary, flexible and dynamic aspect of regional endeavours. It is rarely a linear or singular process and cannot be solely associated with one specific organisation. In fact, regional integration can be limited to certain areas or actors during specific periods, but can also be extended to a comprehensive approach in other cases. Each mode of regional integration serves certain purposes and interests. Therefore, the actors involved have to be examined in order to properly understand how the pursued mode is embedded into their broader strategies and interests. Similarly, a change or crisis in one mode of regionalism does not necessarily imply disintegration but rather refers to a modification concerning the areas to be governed, the actors involved or the goals to be achieved.

What sets regional integration apart from other levels of governance such as the nation-state is first and foremost the scale. We must be able to identify a geographical supranational space (a region) that is interdependent in at least one area (finance, trade, labour, infrastructure, production networks etc.) or is being reshaped so as to become interdependent. A region usually cannot rely on the same ideational foundations and political structures as the nation-state (see Dietl's chapter, in this volume, on the creation of the wider "Musandam" area as a "new region"). Traditional vehicles of power such as political parties, bureaucracies, armies and so forth are deeply incorporated into the nation. At the same time, the prevalence of regionalised interdependences (or at least an agenda to install such interdependence) sets the region apart as a distinguishable space within a more broadly defined context such as global governance. It is often not easy to identify the range of actors that is involved, affected or benefiting in regionally defined areas, since they are usually embedded within a national environment and their regional interests might merely be a projection of interests originating at the national level.

Since the study of regional integration originated around the creation of the European Communities and since the European Union remains the most investigated case, the application of the related insights and concepts to other parts of the world has been a prominent way to examine regional schemes outside of Europe. To date, nothing resembling a theory of Arab integration has been articulated. However, a narrow approach might draw our attention away from the particularities and varieties of modes of governance in other regions. For the concept of regional governance to be universally useful, it needs to avoid Eurocentric tendencies. These assumptions may lead us to further considerations. If we conceive the European experience as a phenomenon that, albeit singular, has to be located within a broader concept of regionalism, the latter would need to be detached and broad enough to accommodate other existing forms. Conversely, if the European experience represents a unique phenomenon, the concept of regional integration has to account for these idiosyncrasies by offering an approach that is applicable to regions outside of Europe.

In either case, the notion of different modes of regional governance implies that we need to be able to identify significant differences with respect to their rules, their purpose and their functioning. Moreover, we must account for the possibility of new modes of regional integration that emerge and eventually replace existing ones (Auerbach 2007). A prevalent mode can be put under pressure if the area it is supposed to govern (usually trade or security) experiences a crisis. Such crises have been a recurring phenomenon in the Arab world and have negatively affected the regional governance to be provided by the GCC (on the GCC and the role of Oman, see Zorob's chapter in this volume; Wippel's chapter engages with economic integration across metaregions with a case study of Oman and the Indian Ocean Rim). As a consequence, alternative modes receive the support of the established actors who fear a loss of influence or benefits. Simultaneously, a crisis can reshape the economic area by bringing in new actors or strengthening others. Emerging actors could also push alternative types of regionalism that reflect their specific interests. These alternatives can be novel modes that are designed to fit the specific challenges of the crisis. In addition they can also be modes that already existed in the preceding period but were hitherto not supported enough to become the dominant mode.

A comprehensive concept of regional governance must also consider that it is not positive per se, even though there might be several potential positively defined effects. For one, a mode of governance might cause detrimental unintended effects as it unfolds unforeseen dynamics. For another, we cannot restrict our analysis to modes of governance that are designed to promote common regional welfare. Governance structures dominated by kleptocratic state elites or certain private sectors serve a purpose that may not coincide with a genuinely regional interest, even if they claim to (Söderbaum and Taylor 2003). It is an important task to uncover the involvement of various interest groups in order to understand why regional governance does not necessarily imply the provision of regional public goods. A basic but necessary question concerns the shape and aims of regional integration. Regional organisations are set up to provide governance in a variety of areas, and the same applies to informal networks of governance. Uncovering the areas and actors of regional governance is more than a mere descriptive task. It helps to identify the varieties of regionalism that a comprehensive concept must be able to include. Furthermore, a comparative approach can point out similarities and therefore hint at potential encompassing characteristics of regionalism. Comparing the GCC to other struggling regional organisations in the global South, for instance, could help to uncover mechanisms at play that might not become obvious when doing a benchmark-oriented comparison with the EU.

3.5 Interregionalism

Just as nation-states require and seek the acceptance of their sovereignty by other nations, self-defined regions require and seek to be accepted by other actors in the global political system. One important approach is to establish relations with other regional entities, i.e. interregionalism. This strategy has been pursued most prominently by the European Union but has also been employed by regionalisms of the South. Unlike regionalism, the term interregionalism primarily refers to relations that occur between formalised, non-overlapping regional organisations.

States forming a region install certain powers in a common institution or at least use the latter as a vehicle to implement national foreign relations.

The EU has made interregionalism an important strategy in its external affairs.[14] It aspires to be the hub in a supposedly emerging multilateral world and thus conducts relations with or within most major intergovernmental organisations in the world. Inside the EU, the sense of singularity and the conviction that its mode of governance contains several benefits has become a raison d'être (Barroso 2010). On the basis of this notion, the EU proposes to conduct formalised relations with other regional blocks in the world. Whether as a trading partner[15] or an aid donor,[16] the EU has been committed to an interregional approach.

The importance attached to fostering interregional relations is connected to two institutional logics from the hub's perspective. Firstly, an emulation of the EU model around the world would provide a crucial indicator for success. If other emerging regional organisations are modelled after the EU, the latter will be able to defend its position as archetype. Secondly, the legitimisation of the EU would be further enhanced if it were able to take over a sizeable part of the traditional national monopoly of foreign affairs, namely relations with regional entities. In order to achieve a proliferation of regionalisms and assure their connection with the EU, the latter can rely on two capacities: being a model and making funds available. The function of the EU as a model for other regional organisations is twofold. It can be passively perceived and imitated by foreign elites or it can actively pursue the propagation of beneficial aspects. The EU has not been a solely passive actor in this process. Many of the research and study programs on EU-related themes receive financial and logistic support.[17] These are designed to attract and/or shape potential policy makers.

Outside the academic realm, the EU also dedicates considerable effort to marketing itself. The delegations of the European Commission around the globe play a crucial role in diffusing the image of a benevolent EU that is thus a model worth emulating (Dykmann 2006). The EU also devotes a considerable budget to directly supporting regionalisation efforts worldwide. It is the only regional organisation worldwide to do so at a noteworthy scale.[18] The link between its mode of regional integration and achieving prosperity and peace is a focal point of the EU's own

[14] Cf. http://www.eeas.europa.eu/regions/index_en.htm. Accessed 23 August 2010.

[15] Cf. http://ec.europa.eu/trade/creating-opportunities/bilateral-relations/regions/. Accessed 22 January 2011.

[16] Cf. http://ec.europa.eu/aidco/where/neighbourhood/regional_cooperation/irc/index_en.xml. Accessed 22 January 2011.

[17] Prominent examples of such support are the Jean Monnet Programme (cf. http://www.eu-un.europa.eu/articles/en/article_8339_en.htm), a range of projects under the Seventh Framework Programme (cf. http://cordis.europa.eu/fp7/home_en.html), as well as higher education programs and scholarships for potential future foreign elites such as Erasmus Mundus (http://eacea.ec.europa.eu/erasmus_mundus/programme/about_erasmus_mundus_en.php) and Alβan (cf. http://www.programalban.org/; all accessed 30 December 2010).

[18] Bear in mind that even a small fraction of the EU's external funding can correspond to a significant budget share in a receiving regional organisation.

identity and therefore of its support to other organisations. In order to spur similar effects in developing countries, the EU has been dedicating important shares of its development budget to region-building (European Commission 1995). This also underlines its ambitions to strengthen its position as a hub among regionalisms worldwide and is an important instrument to facilitate and control the diffusion of its mode of governance. In principle, many of the mechanisms of interregionalism outlined above also apply to regional organisations of the South, even though the latter usually do not intend to promote their own model. Therefore, recognition from other regional organisations plays a more important role than active support. However, there are two major structural differences. First of all, developing countries simply cannot rely on similar resources. Staff, budget and capacity are far smaller. While the EU is envisioning a budget of almost nine billion Euro in 2011 for its section "EU as a global player"[19] alone, the total budget of regional organisations like Mercosur[20] and SADC[21] is less than 1 percent of that sum. This obviously means that these organisations cannot afford costly permanent delegations to other regions or even a dedicated department of extra-regional affairs. Secondly, the institutions are usually themselves not designed to conduct external relations on their own. Despite the emulation of many other organs, this seems to be one of the EU structures left aside. Mercosur, for instance, merely relies on a working group composed of officers from national ministries. SADC offers the possibility to accredit ambassadors, but has not established an explicit counterpart in its own institution, let alone set up representations abroad.

In both cases, the most consolidated external relations are in place with their umbrella organisations. Mercosur and SADC are in fact sub-organisations of the ALADI (Latin American Integration Association) and African Union respectively, which claim continental dimensions. The legal structures of the regional organisations are partly dependent on these more encompassing bodies. This entails an important degree of intertwining, even though both organisations operate largely autonomously with regard to concrete issues in many fields. In the South American case, where Uruguay is the seat of both organisations, each member state even sends one ambassador as a permanent representative to both Mercosur and ALADI (but not to Uruguay). Additionally, there is an overlap with other sub-continental organisations in both cases, be it on economic[22] or political[23] issues. Member states often choose to engage in parallel negotiations within different regional organisations or even with external actors to increase their negotiating power and their strategic options.

---

[19]Cf. http://ec.europa.eu/budget/figures/2011/2011_en.cfm (accessed 30 June 2011).

[20]The Common Market of the South (Mercado Común del Sur) currently consists of Argentina, Brazil, Paraguay and Uruguay.

[21]The Southern African Development Community consists of all 15 countries located at or below latitude 5° S.

[22]Cf. the overlapping membership in SADC and COMESA (Common Market for Eastern and Southern Africa), which both aspire to become free trade agreements and customs unions.

[23]Cf. the creation of Community of South American Nations in 2004 (later renamed UNASUR) that competes with Mercosur as a main interlocutor for external interregional relations.

The extra-regional outreach is first and foremost with the EU or with hegemonic non-members. In contrast, South-South interregionalism is generally characterised by ad hoc and cyclical endeavours. This eclecticism, however, is not comprehensive enough to entail diversity in its external approach. It follows impulses that are derived from national interests and priorities. The case of South Atlantic interregionalism between Mercosur and SADC exemplifies the mechanisms at work. Up to the 1990s, regional organisations in both regions were mainly inward-looking and thus not focused on extra-regional relations. Most South-South relations came about via binational ties or multilateral arenas such as UNCTAD or the Non-Aligned Movement. The more outward-looking type of regionalism that emerged with the rise of the neoliberal paradigm in the early 1990s was more prone to insertion into the global economic system, and the regions were thus more likely to develop extra-continental relations. Hence, there were various attempts in the 1990s to exchange ideas about regional integration (South African Institute of International Affairs 1999). Initially, this was characterized by the African interest in learning from Mercosur, as it seemed a cost-effective way to move towards a common market while maintaining national sovereignty. However, this seemed to be a somewhat misinformed view of the initial progress Mercosur had made. The struggles to move beyond an imperfect free trade area as well as the financial crises in the late 1990s and early 2000s led to a fading interest, both from the African political elites and the multinational enterprises initially financing the bulk of the meetings. While there have been only vague declarations towards cooperation between SADC and Mercosur, relations between the Southern African Customs Union and Mercosur have assumed a formalised stage through the negotiations of a preferential trade agreement. Its signing mainly corresponds to the strategy of the dominant powers Brazil and South Africa to play an increasing role in the global political economy via South-South linkages.

Interregionalism in the case of the South Atlantic is thus mainly to be seen as a channel for regional powers to achieve certain foreign policy goals. These powers are thus following a strategy that differs from that of the major powers such as the U.S., which does not frame its relations to other regional organisations within NAFTA, as Zorob's chapter in the volume shows. However, the region-to-region approach that has emerged in the South Atlantic remains at that stage, and the South Atlantic can hardly be described as a region of its own. For now, only state actors are pursuing this approach, while there are almost no interregional dynamics on the part of private or civil society actors. As long as these dynamics remain an outcome of isolated and sporadic occurrences, they will remain a strategy of political elites. In this respect, the case of the South Atlantic contrasts with other emerging unconventional regions such as the Indian Ocean, which displays such dynamics and partially appears as a region in its own right, transcending predefined continental regions.[24]

[24] Cf. Wippel's chapter in this volume with a focus on the Indian Ocean Rim Association for Regional Integration.

South American relations with North Africa and the Middle East seem even more restricted than with Southern Africa. Mercosur has an interest in concluding free trade agreements with certain countries, such as Morocco, Israel and Egypt, as well as the GCC. This is based on economic complementarities. The Mercosur is a highly competitive agro-exporter while many countries of the region are net food importers. On the political level, first consultations have been held during the Summit of South America-Arab Countries (ASPA) in 2005 in Brasilia. These encounters help countries to identify interests similar to those of peers in more distant and unknown regions but substantial common positioning and coalition building in multilateral arenas has yet to emerge.

3.6 Conclusion

This chapter set out to move towards an inclusive approach so as to grasp the multiplicity the concept of region holds. For this exercise, the focus has been on macro- or suprastate regions.[25] Clearly, the term "region" can be a very relevant and useful one in this context when addressing the changes and reconfigurations of a variety of key issues such as sovereignty, nation-state, world order and hegemony. To this end we need to take into account the term's various notions and their application. We can refer to a region in the sense of an organisational body or of a spatial multilevel project, depending on the issues at stake. In the first case, we need to account for a region being more than just the sum of its member states. The case of interregionalism exemplifies this with respect to institutional settings, as conducting interregional relations is a key issue for regional organisations to increase the leverage of both the single member states and the grouping. The hitherto marginal interregionalism between groupings in the global South is gaining importance in this context as well but is equally limited to states or actors embedded into the state. The region is both a setting and an instrument for emerging powers that seek more influence in the international political economy.

Drawing from critical political geography (see Agnew 2008; Brenner 1999; Ó Tuathail and Luke 1994), we open our theoretical scope towards understanding "region" as a relational arena produced through interactions between various actors beyond fixed geographical, political, economic or any other boundaries. We argue that conceptualising them as territorially delimited and fixed entities neatly existing side by side will not allow us to capture the on-going global transformations in which interactions on non-global levels play a decisive, yet theoretically neglected role. This also supports our initial argument for opening up theoretical work on regionalism towards a more spatial understanding of such processes. To re-conceptualise "the region", and coming back to our initial argument, "difference is …

[25] Cf. the chapters by Bromber, and Verne and Müller-Mahn (in this volume) for a micro-perspective on translocal connections.

constituted more through interconnection than through opposition" and "not bounded off from but linked to, and in part constituted in its character through its linkage to, other regions". On this matter, theoretical works on regions and regionalism could benefit from drawing on recent theory development on the denationalisation and relocalisation of global processes (see Sassen 2007; Fawn 2009; Paasi 2009; Lorenz 2011).

And while the EU certainly remains the most influential regional scheme in the world, it is necessary to equally include other regionalisms and to avoid viewing them through an EU lens. In this regard, trying to understand processes of regionalism from an "Omani point of view" sets up a worthwhile experiment in looking beyond structural conditions towards interrelated regional networks that transcend national and institutional boundaries in a multiplicity of ways, as presented in this volume.

References

Adler, E. (1997). Imagined security communities. Cognitive regions in international relations. *Journal of International Studies, 26*(2), 249–277.

Agnew, J. (1994). The territorial trap. The geographical assumptions of international relations theory. *Review of International Political Economy, 1*(1), 53–80.

Agnew, J. (1999). Region on the mind does not equal region of the mind. *Progress in Human Geography, 23*(1), 91–96.

Agnew, J. (2000). From the political economy of regions to regional political economy. *Progress in Human Geography, 24*(1), 101–110.

Agnew, J. (2008). Borders on the mind. Re-framing border thinking. *Ethics & Global Politics, 1*(4), 1–17.

Auerbach, N. (2007). The meanings of neoliberalism. In R. K. Roy, A. Denzau, & T. Willett (Eds.), *Neoliberalism: Global experiments with a shared mental model* (pp. 26–50). London: Routledge.

Bach, D. (Ed.). (1999). *Regionalisation in Africa. Integration and disintegration.* Oxford: James Currey.

Balassa, B. (1961). *The theory of economic integration.* London: Allen & Unwin.

Baldwin, R. (2008). *Big-think regionalism. A critical survey* (NBER Working Paper 14056). Cambridge: National Bureau of Economic Research.

Barroso, J. M. (2010). *Keynote Speech at the GARNET 2010 Conference.* Brussels.

Bhagwati, J. N. (1991). *The world trading system at risk.* Harvester Wheatsheaf: Hemel Hempstead.

Bøås, M., Marchand, M., & Shaw, T. (2005). The political economy of regions and regionalisms. An introduction to our critical, revisionist inquiries. In M. Bøås, M. Marchand, & T. Shaw (Eds.), *The political economy of regions and regionalism* (pp. 1–12). Basingstoke/New York: Palgrave MacMillan.

Brenner, N. (1999). Beyond state-centrism? Space, territoriality, and geographical scale in globalization studies. *Theory and Society, 28*, 39–78.

Browning, C. (2003). The region-building approach revisited. The continued othering of Russia in discourse or region-building in the European north. *Geopolitics, 8*(1), 45–71.

Bull, H. (2002). *The anarchical society. A study of order in world politics.* Basingstoke/New York: Palgrave.

Bulmer-Thomas, V. (2001). Regional integration in Latin America and the Caribbean. *Bulletin of Latin American Research, 20*(3), 961–995.

Cafruny, A., & Ryner, M. (2009). Critical political economy. In A. Wiener & T. Diez (Eds.), *European integration theory* (pp. 221–240). Oxford/New York: Oxford University Press.

Cairncross, F. (1997). *The death of distance. How the communications revolution will change our lives*. Boston: Harvard Business School Press.

Deutsch, K. (1968). *Political community and the north Atlantic area: International organization in the light of historical experience*. Princeton: Princeton University Press.

Dykmann, K. (2006). Perceptions and politics: The foreign relations of the European union with Latin America. In *Schriftenreihe des Instituts für Iberoamerika-Kunde, 63*. Frankfurt am Main: Vervuert.

European Commission. (1995). *European community support for regional economic integration efforts among developing countries*. COM(95)219. Brussels: European Commission.

Faini, R., & Grilli, E. (Eds.). (1997). *Multilateralism and regionalism after the Uruguay round*. Basingstoke/New York: Macmillan Press.

Fawn, R. (2009). 'Regions' and their study. Wherefrom, what for and whereto? *Review of International Studies, 35*(1), 5–34.

Haas, M. (1958). *The uniting of Europe. Political, social and economic forces 1950–1957*. Stanford: Stanford University Press.

Haas, M. (1970). International subsystems. Stability and polarity. *The American Political Science Review, 64*(1), 98–123.

Hardt, M., & Negri, A. (2000). *Empire*. Cambridge/London: Harvard University Press.

Harrison, J. (2006). Re-reading the new regionalism. A sympathetic critique. *Space and Polity, 10*(1), 21–46.

Harvey, D. (1990). *The condition of postmodernity. An enquiry into the origins of cultural change*. Cambridge: Blackwell.

Hettne, B. (2003). The new regionalism revisited. In F. Söderbaum & T. Shaw (Eds.), *Theories of new regionalism* (pp. 22–42). Basingstoke/New York: Palgrave Macmillan.

Hettne, B. (2005). Beyond the "New" regionalism. *New Political Economy, 10*(4), 543–571.

Hettne, B., & Söderbaum, F. (2000). Theorising the rise of regionness. *New Political Economy, 5*(3), 457–473.

Hettne, B., & Söderbaum, F. (2008). The future of regionalism. Old divides, new frontiers. In A. Cooper, C. Hughes, & P. De Lombaerde (Eds.), *Regionalisation and global governance. The taming of globalisation?* (pp. 61–95). Abingdon/New York: Routledge.

Higgott, R. (2005). The theory and practice of global and regional governance. Accommodating American exceptionalism and European pluralism. *European Foreign Affairs Review, 10*(4), 575–594.

Hoffmann, S. (1964). The European process at Atlantic crosspurposes. *Journal of Common Market Studies, 31*(1), 85–101.

Hoffmann, S. (1966). Obstinate or obsolete? the fate of the nation state and the case of western Europe. *Daedalus, 95*(3), 862–915.

Hurrell, A. (2007). One world? many worlds? the place of regions in the study of international society. *International Affairs, 83*(1), 127–146.

Hveem, H. (1999). Political regionalism. Master or servant of economic internationalization? In H. Hettne, A. Inotai, & O. Sunkel (Eds.), *Globalism and the new regionalism* (pp. 85–115). Basingstoke/London: Macmillan Press.

Hveem, H. (2003). The regional project in global governance. In F. Söderbaum & T. Shaw (Eds.), *Theories of new regionalism* (pp. 81–98). Basingstoke/New York: Palgrave Macmillan.

Jones, E. (2009). The economic mythology of European integration. *Journal of Common Market Studies, 48*(1), 89–109.

Katzenstein, P. (2005). *A world of regions. Asia and Europe in the American imperium*. New York: Ithaca.

Krugman, P. (1991). Is bilateralism bad? In E. Helpman & A. Razin (Eds.), *International trade and trade policy*. Cambridge: MIT Press.

Krugman, P. (1993). Regionalism vs. Multilateralism. Analytic notes. In J. De Melo & A. Panagariya (Eds.), *New dimensions in regional integration* (pp. 84–89). Cambridge: Cambridge University Press.

Lawrence, R. (1999). Regionalism, multilateralism, and deeper integration. Changing paradigms for developing countries. In R. Mendoza, P. Low, & B. Kotschwar (Eds.), *Trade rules in the making. Challenges in regional and multilateral negotiations* (pp. 23–46). Washington: Brookings Institution.

Lee, M. (2003). *The political economy of regionalism in southern Africa*. Cape Town: University of Cape Town Press.

Lefebvre, H. (1991). *The production of space*. Oxford/Cambridge: Blackwell.

Lévy, J. (1999). *Le tournant géographique. Penser l'espace pour lire le monde*. Paris: Berlin.

Lorenz-Carl, U. & Rempe, M. (Eds.) (2013). *Mapping Agency. Comparing Regionalisms in Africa*. Aldershot: Ashgate.

Lorenz, U. (2010). Negotiating regions, reordering international relations? the economic partnership agreements as signifier for a new global order. *Journal of International Relations and Development, 14*(1), 50–60.

Lorenz, U. (2011). *Negotiating trade agreements, transforming regional order. The economic partnership agreement negotiations between the EU and Southern Africa*. Unpublished Ph.D. thesis, University of Leipzig, Leipzig.

Lorenz, U., & Cornelissen, S. (2011). Regional organisation, regional Arena. The SADC in southern Africa. In T. Shaw, J. A. Grant, & S. Cornelissen (Eds.), *Research companion to regionalisms* (pp. 240–255). Aldershot: Ashgate.

Lovering, J. (1999). Theory led by policy. The inadequacies of the "new regionalism". *International Journal of Urban and Regional Research, 23*(2), 379–395.

Majluf, L. A. (2004). *Swimming in the spaghetti bowl. Challenges for developing countries under the "new regionalism"*. New York/Geneva: UNCTAD. Policy Issues in International Trade and Commodities Study Series, No. 27.

Marchand, M., Bøås, M., & Shaw, T. (1999). The political economy of new regionalisms. *Third World Quarterly, 20*(5), 897–910.

Merrifield, A. (2002). Henri Lefebvre. A socialist in space. In M. Crang & N. Thrift (Eds.), *Thinking space* (pp. 167–182). London/New York: Routledge.

Moravcsik, A. (1993). Preferences and power in the European community. A liberal intergovernmentalist approach. *Journal of Common Market Studies, 31*(4), 473–524.

Neumann, I. (2003). A region-building approach. In F. Söderbaum & T. Shaw (Eds.), *Theories of new regionalism* (pp. 160–178). Basingstoke/New York: Palgrave Macmillan.

Nye, J. (1968). Patterns and catalysts in regional integration. In J. Nye (Ed.), *International regionalism*. Cambridge: Harvard University Press.

Paasi, A. (2001). Europe as social process and discourse. Considerations of place, boundaries and identity. *European Journal of Urban and Regional Studies, 8*(1), 7–28.

Paasi, A. (2004). Place and region. Looking through the prism of scale. *Progress in Human Geography, 28*(4), 536–546.

Paasi, A. (2009). The resurgence of the "region" and "regional identity". theoretical perspectives and empirical observations on regional dynamics in Europe. *Review of International Studies, 35*(1), 121–146.

Pomfret, R. (1997). *Development economics*. Prentice Hall: London/New York.

Purcell, M. (2003). Islands of practice and the Marston/Brenner debate. Towards a more synthetic critical human geography. *Progress in Human Geography, 27*(3), 317–332.

Russett, B. (1967). *International regions and the international system. A study in political ecology*. Chicago: Rand McNally & Company.

Sandholtz, W., & Stone Sweet, A. (1998). *European integration and supranational governance*. Oxford: Oxford University Press.

Sassen, S. (Ed.). (2007). *Deciphering the global. Its scales, spaces and subjects*. Abingdon: Routledge.

Schiff, M., & Winters, L. A. (2003). *Regional integration and development*. Washington, DC/ Oxford: World Bank, Oxford University Press.

Schirm, S. (2002). *Globalization and the new regionalism. Global markets, domestic politics and regional cooperation*. Cambridge: Polity.

Schroer, M. (2008). "Bringing the space back in" – Zur Relevanz des Raumes als soziologische Kategorie. In J. Döring & T. Thielmann (Eds.), *Spatial turn. Das Raumparadigma in den Kultur- und Sozialwissenschaften* (pp. 125–148). Bielefeld: transcript Verlag.

Söderbaum, F. (2004). *The political economy of regionalism. The case of southern Africa*. Basingstoke/New York: Palgrave Macmillan.

Söderbaum, F., & Shaw, T. (Eds.). (2003). *Theories of new regionalism*. Basingstoke/New York: Palgrave Macmillan.

Söderbaum, F., & Taylor, I. (Eds.). (2003). *Regionalism and uneven development in southern Africa. The case of the Maputo development corridor*. Aldershot: Ashgate.

South African Institute of International Affairs. (1999). *Exploring south-south dialogue: Mercosur in Latin America and SADC in southern Africa*. Johannesburg: SAIIA.

Taylor, I. (2010). *The international relations of Sub-Saharan Africa*. New York/London: Continuum.

Tuathail, G. Ó., & Luke, T. (1994). Present at the (Dis)integration. Deterritorialization and reterritorialization in the new wor(l)d order. *Annals of the Association of American Geographers, 84*(3), 381–398.

Viner, J. (1950). *The customs union issue*. New York: Carnegie Endowment for International Peace.

Warleigh, A., & Rosamond. B. (2006, April 25–30). *Theorising regional integration comparatively. An Introduction*. Paper to the ECPR Joint Sessions of Workshops, Nicosia, Cyprus.

Warleigh-Lack, A. (2008). Studying regionalisation comparatively. A conceptual framework. In A. Cooper, C. Hughes, & P. De Lombaerde (Eds.), *Regionalisation and global governance. The taming of globalisation?* (pp. 43–60). Abingdon/New York: Routledge.

Weichhart, P. (1995). Die region. Chimäre, artefakt Oder strukturprinzip sozialer systeme? In G. Brunn (Ed.), *Region und Regionsbildung in Europa* (pp. 25–43). Baden-Baden: Nomos.

Chapter 4
Working with "Translocality": Conceptual Implications and Analytical Consequences

Katrin Bromber

4.1 Introduction

How can we approach "acting at a distance"? This question has occupied the social sciences since the early 1990s. The expansion of interest in "a variety of economic, social and political linkages that cross borders and span the world" has generated a vast body of literature (Vertovec 2001: 1). Whereas the "crossing" is labelled with the prefix "trans-", the "What is actually crossed?" varies in accordance with the specific conceptual viewpoint. Since Arjun Appadurai introduced the paradigm, "translocality" is used to describe social and cultural representations of a globalizing world that is characterized by the movement of people, goods and ideas across borders (Appadurai 1995: 204–225). It shares the semantic field with other trans-terminology such as "transnationalism" or "transculturation", but also with studies of "border culture", "culture of mobility" and "cosmopolitanism". These interrelated concepts can be seen as true attempts to overcome methodological nationalism (Chernillo 2006: 5–22) as well as a contribution to systematically questioning the notion of culture as a closed entity.[1] From their specific disciplinary background, researchers study interconnectedness/entanglement (*Verflechtung*) and overlaps as well as fragmentation and disparity.

"Translocality", on the one hand, means spatial mobility as such and, on the other hand, physical, political, social and cultural spaces and localities that are shaped by it. According to Ferdinand de Jong, research on the transformative and reproductive potential of flows is one way to conceptualize a translocal community in a globalizing world. He showed how the transformation of ritual practice

[1]The discussion in the 1980s and 1990s, especially within the field of cultural anthropology, demanded the abandonment of "culture" as an analytical tool.

K. Bromber (✉)
Zentrum Moderner Orient (ZMO), Kirchweg 33, 14129 Berlin, Germany
e-mail: katrin.bromber@zmo.de

S. Wippel (ed.), *Regionalizing Oman: Political, Economic and Social Dynamics*, United Nations University Series on Regionalism 6, DOI 10.1007/978-94-007-6821-5_4,

increased the self-reproductive capability of a community whose members have migrated to places as far as Paris or Amsterdam. He argued against Arjun Appadurai's observation that globalizing processes lead to a "growing disjuncture between territory, subjectivity and collective social action" and, as a consequence, the "deterritorialization of social life" (de Jong 1999: 316).

What this example hints at is that "translocality" has been conceptualized from the mid-1990s onwards as going beyond geographical notions. It is deeply rooted in discussions about the social production of place and space. However, Ferdinand de Jong, like other authors, neither revealed what he actually means by translocality nor did he share his ideas about the added value of using such a term or even of revealing its *Begriffsgeschichte* (conceptual history). It is a further example of how the inflationary and often unreflected use of "trans-terminology" exposes it to the danger of becoming empty signifiers – i.e. catch-all phrases completely lacking any theoretical or analytical depth.

This essay makes an attempt to conceptualize "translocality" from a very distinct perspective – the Indian Ocean. This focus, firstly, derives from and makes use of a specific research context. Between 2000 and 2007, two successive multidisciplinary group projects based at the Centre for Modern Oriental Studies (ZMO) in Berlin studied the Western Indian Ocean as space produced and transformed by movement.[2] Secondly, it links with a number of contributions to this volume. They not only show Oman's connectedness to various nodal points within the Indian Ocean, but also discuss both Oman's perspective on and direct responsibility to the region.

Taking translocality as an entry point, this chapter starts with a more general question: What does a focus on South-South relations, meaning relations between and within Africa, Asia and the Middle East, produce? Does it create a broad conceptual option or a very distinct notion of the term, which may result in operational limits on it?[3] Taking the latter half of the question seriously, the second part of this chapter introduces the concept of the "seascape". In its very specific meaning, "seascape" denotes the maritime social and cultural landscape of the Indian Ocean. As a conceptual term, it attempts to operationalize the theoretical implications of translocality.

4.2 Translocality: A Perspective, a Middle-Range Theory or a Social Fact?

In their introduction to *Translocality. An approach to connection and transfer in area studies*, Achim von Oppen and Ulrike Freitag defined translocality both as "a descriptive tool" for the specific empirical realities in Africa, Asia and the Middle

---

[2]On the conceptual level, this research project successfully cooperated with the group projects on translocal relations in the Sahara-Sahel zone. For further information see www.zmo.de/forschung/projekte_2004_2005.html.

[3]Comparison with North–South relations or with relations within the North would certainly be a very interesting yet demanding endeavour.

East and as "a perspective" for conceptualizing research on these realities (Freitag and von Oppen 2010: 3). The critique of globalization studies, as voiced by Frederick Cooper, pointed out that it often ignored the historical depth of connection and entanglement and obscured that a variety of processes that create flows and linkages across territories are very uneven (Cooper 2001: 189–213). Translocality, instead, aims at a better accounting for the diversity of Asian and African experiences and agency in transformational processes. It can be seen as a conscious attempt to transcend the elitist focus of much of global history, to contribute to a social history "from below" and to overcome Eurocentrism. Disproportionate attention is often given to translocal traffic from the "periphery" to the "centre", the "rest" to the "West". It is as if there were no significant flows of people moving around within the "rest". Unsurprisingly, it is often these latter people whose experiences of migrancy are the most traumatic.[4] Recent years, however, have seen a number of good studies that attempt to fill this gap by looking not only at cyberspace and global cities, but also at refugee camps in the East and South, immigrant sweatshops in the West or global prostitution networks.

Hence in the descriptive sense, translocality can be understood as

> the sum of phenomena which result from a multitude of circulations and transfers. It designates the outcome of concrete movements of people, goods, ideas and symbols which span spatial distances and cross boundaries, be they geographical, cultural or political (Freitag and von Oppen 2010: 5).

It considers not only movement, whether concrete or potential, but also its opposite – the constraints and failure of movements that often result in immobility. It thus evades the teleological trap of being used as a normative category. Especially in social settings in which translocality was or is constant, there must be institutions to control it. The introduction of the British passport and immigration regulations in the Western Indian Ocean in the 1930s, for example, increasingly restricted the Hadhrami and Omani labour migration to and the settlement patterns of diasporic families on the East African coast. These regulatory measures not only ran counter to long-established links, they also fed directly into the redefinitions of status and identity. So-called Arabs gradually became "aliens" in the localities they had made their home.[5] For the thousands of Zanzibaris, often of Omani descent, who were expelled from the island in 1964, Zanzibar signified a "place of longing" rather than a "place of be-longing". With the political changes of the 1990s, when Tanzania opened up, seemingly old links between the East African coast and the Arab Peninsula revived. In fact, as Verne's and Müller-Mahn's paper shows, they were invested with new meaning. Zanzibar has gradually regained its "metonymy of possibilities", both in its affirmative and in its critical forms. Hence, translocality has to conceptualize connectedness through movement as well as through imagination or hope. The dialectics between movement, real or imagined, and constraints re-produce a locality as trans-locality. Translocalities are, thus, not only nodal points as such, but "nodes of reference".

---

[4] For a fundamental critique, see Hamzah 2005: 117–119.

[5] For a detailed analysis, see Hartwig 2002: 21.

What follows is that translocality as a research perspective has to account for the fact that the interactions and connections have far more diverse and often even contradictory effects. It therefore "proposes a more open and less linear view on the manifold ways in which the global world is constituted" (Freitag and von Oppen 2010: 6). The very different scales and types of *trans*-gression and (re-)creation of "local" distinctions have to be observed. Hence, studying the Indian Ocean in the dimension of connection through Islamic education and scholarship, for example, results in a quite different picture than looking at it with the intention to investigate colonial strategies of territorialisation, i.e. converting the Western Indian Ocean into a "British Lake".

Without going further into the details that can be found in the volume with the title *Translocality. The study of globalising processes from a Southern perspective*, (Freitag and von Oppen 2010: 3) defining translocality as a perspective also has its pitfalls. Namely, this technical term of philosophy designates the fact that all knowledge is perspective, i.e. that it relates to *needs* (and in particular, *vital* needs of the cognizant being). Nietzsche grounded perspectivism in the nature of conscience, which requires a general and conceptual representation of the world *opposed* to the individual reality of beings (Nietzsche 1973: §§110, 111, 354). Defining translocality as a perspective, then, comes down to grounding it in an anti-rationalist theory of knowledge, which means that while its experiential quality can be celebrated, it cannot be charted – hence, a concept or theory cannot be derived from it.

Perspectivism can also flirt with metaphorism gone wild, if not outright hallucination. The otherwise serious Peter Mandaville suddenly sees "fluid creatures leak openly from their dilapidated habitats, mixing and matching as they encounter each other in travel" (Mandaville 2001: 97).

However, the problem people encounter when actually working with translocality – irrespective of whether its quality is conceptualized as a perspective, as an analytical tool or as a social fact – was how to turn it into an operational concept that "holds together" a huge diversity of objects, contexts and disciplinary methodologies. Hence, it has to be broken down into its disparate extensions, i.e. to develop middle-range concepts that link the specificities of the empirical with the general assumptions of the theoretical.

4.3 The Operational Concept of the *Seascape*[6]

The attempt of the *Indian Ocean Research Initiative* (INORI) to unravel the complex heterogeneity of the societies on the Indian Ocean rim that have been profoundly affected by the long-term exchange resulted in such a middle-range concept: the

[6]For a detailed description of the seascape paradigm, see Reinwald 2002: 9–20.

"seascape".[7] Working in a multidisciplinary research context focussing on different actors, the key idea was to give meaning to the specific material modes of cohesion that made the Indian Ocean region a historical and symbolic space that was structured by movement. With a clear focus on agency in everyday life as well as on its perceived potentiality, the "landscape" paradigm provided a conceptual gateway for collaborative work. In the 1980s and 1990s, a substantial body of literature was produced, especially within African Studies, that had thought about the material and imaginative practices by which "natural" and "cultural" environments are appropriated. Ute Luig and Achim von Oppen have convincingly argued that "landscapes" are "made" and contested through physical, social and political practice. Instead of considering this process to be "a sedimentation" of history, they conceptualize it as a continuous reworking of past experience and future potentialities (Luig and von Oppen 1997: 7). Such an approach allows a general comparative analysis of different – conflicting and converging – "ways of seeing" the Indian Ocean, which have to be considered when conducting research on different actors. What is more, this approach includes from the outset what Eric Hirsch has described as the "productive tension" between everyday practice and the potential social "beyond" (Hirsch 1995: 1–30). It furthermore counters the argument that the *Begriff* (concept) "Indian Ocean" is only a "useful heuristic device", rather than an object of study in the narrow sense of the word (Parkin and Headley 2000: 2).

Without recalling the notion of the "liquid continent",[8] the "landscape" under study has a maritime connotation. Thus, the variant form "seascape", meaning a maritime social and cultural landscape, seemed appropriate. However, the maritime connotation had to be critically assessed, also in relation to such notions as "maritime culture". Adriaan Prins' study *Sailing from Lamu*, in which he developed the notion of maritime culture, provides the reader with a positive and a negative lesson. The positive one is that transoceanic, littoral and interior flows overlap in the mediation of culture and that people blend elements through appropriation. Prins' conclusion, however, is that "maritime events produce a certain style [...] which permeates the whole culture" (Prins 1965: 264). The assumption that social groups actually agree on the values expressed or mirrored in all of their cultural activities runs the risk of overstretching the argument. The developments in Zanzibar in the 1950s and 1960s, to stay with this example, indicate that Prins' model neither accounts for those who turn their back on the

[7] INORI was founded by the members of the group project "Indian Ocean – Space on the Move", which was based at the Centre for Modern Oriental Studies in Berlin. The following researchers were involved: Ravi Ahuja examined working patterns of maritime labour in colonial India. Jan-Georg Deutsch studied social biographies in Zanzibar, Friedhelm Hartwig worked on Hadhrami diasporic family histories. Brigitte Reinwald investigated the processing and representation of intercultural relations in film, and I studied the perception and construction of ethnic and cultural difference in Swahili newspapers of the 1950s and 1960s.

[8] A term coined in discussions to situate the study of the Mediterranean, the Atlantic and the Indian Ocean within and in opposition to area studies.

sea but are nevertheless part of the polity, nor for the impact of internal social division that generate conflict. The newspaper discourse about citizenship on Zanzibar during this period is very revealing in this respect (Glassman 2011: 147–176). Whereas *Mwongozi* (The Leader), the mouthpiece of the allegedly Arab-dominated Zanzibar Nationalist Party, conceptualized the island as part of the Indian Ocean seascape, *Afrika Kwetu* (Africa – Our Home), the newspaper that was closely linked to the Afro-Shirazi Party, considered Zanzibar part of an African landscape that includes the island. These absolutely contradictory notions fed into the political controversies that resulted in bloodshed and the dislocation of thousands of people in 1964 and beyond (Bromber 2002: 89).

Apart from Prins' wider "Lamu world" of the 1960s with its seemingly unchanging "anthropological present",[9] a critical review of more recent literature revealed and confirmed the need for a more rigorous periodization and historisation of the "flows" and "sediments" of trans-oceanic cultural encounters. One of the key questions is the extent to which the Indian Ocean seascape was reorganized and redefined in the context of the further integration of the region into the capitalist world economy, of colonial expansion and of the emergence of post-colonial nation states as well as integration into the post-World War II political world system. On the one hand, this involves measuring the impact of technological and infrastructural transformations, accelerated urbanization and new means of mass communication. On the other hand, it had to account for political and juridical interventions aimed at controlling and regulating the movement of people, goods and ideas.

Taking the actors' perspective seriously makes it obvious that established periodizations do not work. The works of the German historian Reinhard Koselleck inspire us to even complicate the picture by identifying different "layers of time" that intersect (Koselleck 2002, 2003). Furthermore, the Indian Ocean as a spatial category is a point to discuss. The study of related spatial and temporal dimensions of "movement" and "sedimentation" from the actors' perspective helps to understand the "Transformation of the Seascape – Indian Ocean".[10] Based on ideas about the social production of space, in particular the classical study by the French philosopher Henri Lefebvre, the Indian Ocean is conceptualised as multifaceted, produced and maintained by relations that govern the interaction within society. As a relational configuration of constantly moving objects and subjects, it is linked to aspects of time and agency. Thinking further in this direction, one can say that individual actors and groups produce their unique spaces that overlay one another. This does not mean that there are as many spaces as there are individuals, which would lead to a subjectivist approach and, consequently, to the impossibility of conceptualising spatial relations. It rather opens up a dialectical understanding of

[9] Although from a completely different perspective, this approach was reproduced in Kitiri N. Chaudhuri's works, in which he assumes unchanging Indian Ocean civilizations that have reproduced themselves over a thousand years' time span. By so doing, he replaces Braudel's concept of longe durée by stationary time and the principle of invariance.

[10] This was the title of a follow-up group project on the Indian Ocean at the ZMO between 2003–2007.

spatial processes as two layers of space "interpenetrating" each other or as one "superimposed" on the other (Lefebvre 1991: 86).

Instead of looking at the production of localities, or trans-localities as Verne and Müller-Mahn call them, through movement, the ZMO approach studies the transformative qualities of the movement itself. During World War II, hundreds of thousands of East and Central African soldiers were drafted into the British Empire Forces. Nearly 160,000 of them saw out-of-area deployment in South Asia or Madagascar. The majority originated from the vast inland territories. Their journey across the ocean did not start at Kilindini Harbour, the strategically most important East African port, which was located in Kenya. No, it started much earlier in the military camps that lay deep in the interior. Hence, when speaking about the Indian Ocean as a socially produced space during the war, we have to admit that it reached far into the mainland. Temporally, for the majority of East African soldiers, the war began no earlier than 1941, but did not end until 1946 or even later after their return from South Asia and their subsequent discharge. For those of them who remained within the forces, fighting did not stop at all, since they became a rapid intervention force in the Indian Ocean, for example to fight the communists in Malaya in the 1950s. The temporal points of reference for most of them might not be the great battles of the Second World War, and definitely not 8 May 1945, since they were part of the South East Asia Command. Arguably, experiences such as their transfer to a new camp, entailing the separation from comrades or a beloved girl, shaped their individual or shared periodization of the war in a fundamental way (Bromber 2009: 24–28). Argued with Fernand Braudel's "hundred horizons" (Braudel 1949), the Indian Ocean has to be conceptualized as a pulsating and constantly transforming object of study.

Do such radical interventions in time and space fundamentally put even the idea of territoriality into question? Yes, if we assume the possibility of distinguishable political, cultural or economic regions that are congruent with clearly identifiable societies, civilizations or nation states. No, on the one hand, if we acknowledge that "external" forces and internal dynamics had lasting influence on the development of the "internal" history of the Indian Ocean and, on the other hand, if we accept the fluidity and permeability of temporal, spatial and epistemological borders.

4.4 By Way of Conclusion

Translocality, if it is carefully reworked, has the potential of becoming more than a perspective, but a medium-range theory about social change through movement. It is more encompassing than transnationalism, because it transcends the nation state as analytical framework and thus accounts for an historical depth. It evades the trap of assuming or still working with cultures and civilizations, as transculturalism still does to a great extend. Since it also includes unsuccessful movement and institutionalization, it evades the teleological trap of linearity. Since it takes the South-South linkages seriously, it could even have the potential of being a true response to Orientalism. However, it has to be made functional by operational concepts, working paradigms such as "locality", "landscape or seascape" or "networks", which substantiate the theoretical claims and sharpen the theory. Otherwise, and here I quote Ben Arrous, translocality runs the risk of remaining an "omnibus concept", one into which everyone puts whatever he or she wants or sees fit (Ben Arrous 2004: 415–442).

In studying Oman, a middle-range theoretical approach such as translocality, mediated by a concept such as the INORI's seascape, is useful in at least two ways. Firstly, because of its geographical position, Oman has been included in larger debates on the Indian Ocean and the relevant academic literature right from the start. Secondly, Oman faces the sea. This very fact opens up the possibility of questioning its usual location within the Arab world and of offering alternative ways of conceptualisation. Instead of a static, often essentialised inclusion in an "Arab" context, the translocal approach focuses on the dynamics of entanglement and the social transformations resulting from them. In other words: it is historical from the outset.

Beaudevin's ethnographic study on blood diseases, for example, deals with different communities and social fields, revealing some of the Sultanate's past and present inscriptions of social dynamics. She demonstrates how the treatment of the diseases links Oman to trans- or multinational networks. Using the example of South Asian migrants to Oman, Pradhan's contribution shows how related patterns of movement and settlement changed in accordance with socio-economic circumstances, while the importance of these migrants, especially for Oman's economy, might be read as a continuity. Whereas his study focuses on links across the Indian Ocean, Chatty's chapter looks at "translocality" in the South Arabian "sandscape". She discusses how pastoral communities make use of cross-border movements to escape and undermine attempts by the Omani state to include them in a unified national body, i.e. with a common language, a fixed territory and one identity, while clearly ignoring important social (tribal) structures and an allegedly prosperous past. However, a glorious past is also a central part of a constructed Omani identity. As Nicolini explains, this is to a great deal linked to former maritime trade relations, which shaped the seascape of the Western Indian Ocean in a specific way. Wippel's contribution supports the argument of Oman's economic orientation toward the sea. On the one hand, he emphasizes the dialectic of flows and institutionalization. On the other hand, he shows that branding strategies clearly situate Oman as part of the Indian Ocean. The Indian Ocean is conceptualized in different ways depending on the focus, i.e. branding, flows or institutions. The orientation of infrastructures and industrial activities and the related movements of people and goods to the coast result not only in new spatial configurations as such. As Belgacem argues, they lead to negative effects, too, since translocal, sea-oriented processes have led to an unprecedented regional polarization within Oman. The ambivalence of translocal sea-oriented economic relations is also dealt with in Dietl's chapter, which demonstrates that different, i.e. Omani and Iranian, government institutions can regard one and the same kind of trade as legal or illegal, respectively.

Although the aforementioned contributions do not all deal explicitly with translocality, be it as a concept, an analytical tool or a perspective, they can contribute to the larger debate in a fruitful way. On the basis of their specific empirical research, they generate new gateways to the study of the Indian Ocean as a socially produced space, as a maritime social and cultural landscape.

References

Appadurai, A. (1995). The production of locality. In R. Fardon (Ed.), *Counterworks. Managing the diversity of knowledge* (pp. 204–225). New York: Routledge.

Ben Arrous, M. (2004). La translocalité, pour quoi faire? In S. Wippel & L. Marfaing (Eds.), *Les relations transsahariennes à l'époque contemporaine. Un espace en constante mutation* (pp. 415–442). Paris/Berlin: Karthala – ZMO.

Braudel, F. (1949). *La Méditerranée et le Monde Méditerranéen a l'époque de Philippe II* (Vol. 3). Paris: Armand Colin.

Bromber, K. (2002). Who are the Zanzibari? newspaper debates on difference, 1948–1964. In J.-G. Deutsch & B. Reinwald (Eds.), *Space on the move. Transformations of the Indian Ocean seascape in the nineteenth and twentieth centuries* (pp. 75–89). Berlin: Klaus Schwarz Verlag.

Bromber, K. (2009). *Imperiale Propaganda. Die ostafrikanische Militärpresse im Zweiten Weltkrieg. ZMO-Studien 28*. Berlin: Klaus Schwarz Verlag.

Chernillo, D. (2006). Social theory's methodological nationalism. Myth and reality. *European Journal of Social Theory, 9*(1), 5–22.

Cooper, F. (2001). What is the concept of globalization good for? An African historian's perspective. *African Affairs, 100*, 189–213.

de Jong, F. (1999). The production of translocality. Initiation in the sacred grove in southern Senegal. In R. Fardon, W. van Binsbergen, & R. van Dijk (Eds.), *Modernity on a shoestring. Dimensions of globalization, consumption and development in Africa and beyond.* EIDOS: Leiden and London.

Freitag, U., & von Oppen, A. (2010). Introduction. 'Translocality': An approach to connection and transfer in area studies. In U. Freitag & A. von Oppen (Eds.), *Translocality. The study of globalising processes from a southern perspective*. Leiden: Brill.

Glassman, J. (2011). *War of stones. Racial thought and violence in colonial Zanzibar*. Bloomington: Indiana University Press.

Hamzah, D. (2005). Peter Mandaville, transnational Muslim politics: Reimagining the Umma, London: Routledge, 2001, 235 S. *The Middle East Studies Association Bulletin, 39*(1), 117–119.

Hartwig, F. (2002). The segmentation of the Indian Ocean region. Arabs and the implementation of immigration regulations in Zanzibar and British east Africa. In B. Reinwald & J.-G. Deutsch (Eds.), *Space on the move. Transformations of the Indian Ocean seascape in the nineteenth and twentieth century* (pp. 21–38). Berlin: Klaus Schwarz.

Hirsch, E. (1995). Landscape: Between place and space. In E. Hirsch & M. Hanlon (Eds.), *The anthropology of landscape. Perspectives on place and space* (pp. 1–30). Oxford: Oxford University Press.

Koselleck, R. (2002). *The practice of conceptual history. Timing history: Spacing concepts.* Stanford: Stanford University Press.

Koselleck, R. (2003). *Zeitschichten*. Suhrkamp: Frankfurt am Main.

Lefebvre, H. (1991). *The production of space* (Donald Nicholsen-Smith, Trans). Oxford: Blackwell.

Luig, U., & von Oppen, A. (1997). Landscape in Africa: Process and vision. An introductory essay. In U. Luig & A. von Oppen (Eds.), *The making of African landscapes*. Steiner: Wiesbaden.

Mandaville, P. G. (2001). *Transnational Muslim politics, reimagining the umma*. London: Routledge.

Nietzsche, F. (1973). Die fröhliche Wissenschaft. In G. Colli & M. Montinari (Eds.), *Kritische Gesamtausgabe: Idyllen aus Messina. Die Fröhliche Wissenschaft. Nachgelassene Fragmente. Frühjahr 1881 bis Sommer 1882*. Berlin: Walter de Gruyter.

Parkin, D., & Headley, S. C. (2000). *Islamic prayer across the Indian Ocean. Inside and outside the mosque*. London: Routledge.

Prins, A. H. J. (1965). *Sailing from lamu. A study of Islamic culture in Islamic east Africa*. Assen: van Gorcum.

Reinwald, B. (2002). Space on the move. Perspectives on the making of the Indian Ocean seascape. In B. Reinwald & J.-G. Deutsch (Eds.), *Space on the move. Transformations of the Indian Ocean seascape in the nineteenth and twentieth century*. Berlin: Klaus Schwarz.

Vertovec, S. (2001). *Migration and other modes of transnationalism: Towards conceptual cross-fertilization. 1*. http://rimd.reduaz.mx/documentos_miembros/1840116.pdf Accessed 16 Mar 2011.

Part II
The Translocal, Transnational and Transregional Movement of People

Chapter 5
"We Are Part of Zanzibar" – Translocal Practices and Imaginative Geographies in Contemporary Oman-Zanzibar Relations

Julia Verne and Detlef Müller-Mahn

5.1 Introduction: Zanzibar as a Translocality

> Our beautiful island of Zanzibar aptly termed the 'Island Metropolis of East Africa',
> the land of cloves and carved doors, has had a very changeful and romantic history.
> From time immemorial, ever since the discovery of the monsoons,
> adventurous voyagers from various parts of the world have visited these verdant shores
> and have contributed their share towards the fullness of the pageant
> that characterise the history of these isles of the sun (Young Arab Union 1936: 1).

In terms of size and population, Zanzibar can probably be considered no more than a small dot in the Indian Ocean. Nevertheless, due to its commercial and political history, it has become famous as a unique example of early transnationalism and globalisation resulting in a hybrid, cosmopolitan society. It has also become more popularly known as an attractive tourist site with paradise beaches, and the sound of the name Zanzibar itself is often held responsible for giving it the romantic and mythical touch so often attributed to it when talking about the island linking Africa to Arabia. Although dates and details concerning its early history are still contested, in general the history of Zanzibar is rather homogeneously presented as a history of interaction between islanders and various visitors, foregrounding processes of adaptation and incorporation (cf. Sheriff 2006; Saleh 2004). After the Portuguese domination in the sixteenth and early seventeenth centuries, with the growing influence

J. Verne (✉)
Department of Human Geography, Grüneburgplatz 1,
PEG-Gebauede, 60323 Frankfurt am Main, Germany
e-mail: verne@geo.uni-frankfurt.de

D. Müller-Mahn
Department of Geography, Meckenheimer Allee 166, 53115 Bonn, Germany
e-mail: mueller-mahn@geographie.uni-bonn.de

S. Wippel (ed.), *Regionalizing Oman: Political, Economic and Social Dynamics*, United Nations University Series on Regionalism 6, DOI 10.1007/978-94-007-6821-5_5,

of the Omani, Zanzibar turned into the commercial capital of East Africa, celebrating its peak of economic success in the mid-nineteenth century. Overall, Zanzibar has been observably shaped by the forces of merchant capitalism and the colonial expansion, first of the Omani, then of the British. As Bissell points out, "trade and travel, movement and migration were central to its growth as an entrepot in the nineteenth century, as the island became a dynamic cultural and commercial nexus linking Africa to Asia, the Arab world, Europe, and America" (Bissell 2007: 183). As a result, as Pouwels formulates it so well in his review of the book "Les Swahili entre Afrique et Arabie" (Le Guennec-Coppens and Caplan 1991), the Swahili coast including Zanzibar is conceptualised as an "intersection of multiple influences and networks from which individuals derive their identities, and through which they establish and maintain relations with others in their complex social universe through various forms of exchange" (Pouwels 1991: 411).

During the second half of the twentieth century, these networks have been expanded by sizeable Zanzibari communities in Europe, the USA and Canada, as well as on the Arabian Peninsula (esp. in Oman and the United Arab Emirates) (Mazrui and Sharif 1994: 132; Topan 2006). If the initial wave of Zanzibari migrants was triggered more directly by political persecution resulting from conflicts over Zanzibari identity, which led to what has been called the Zanzibar Revolution in 1964, subsequent waves were more a product of economic problems and a sense of being extremely underprivileged (Glassmann 2011; Mazrui and Sharif 1994; Maliyamkono 2000). Since 1964, Zanzibar has become an integral part of the United Republic of Tanzania, but retaining its own presidency, government ministries and a house of representatives, while still sending a delegation to the Tanzanian parliament. In contrast to its former commercial power, for the last two decades it has rather been characterised by economic decline, a contentious relationship to the mainland and recurrent political unrest.[1]

Nevertheless, the relevance of Zanzibar as a node of multiple relations has not been diminished, for to this day the imaginative as well as material ties between Zanzibar and its diaspora contribute essentially to its character. It is these contemporary relations, the ways they affect Zanzibar materially as well as discursively and influence current processes of place-making that form the centre of our research interest.

As a perspective that brings these connections to the fore, we therefore suggest the concept of "translocality" as a valuable lens through which to look at contemporary Zanzibar. "Translocality" is a term increasingly appearing in articles, but seldom defined. It seems almost taken for granted that the reader knows what is meant by it, although the use of the term as well as its context varies enormously (Bromber, in this volume). Whereas it is sometimes linked to a particular notion of the relationship

[1]The most recent elections in October 2010 resulted in a considerable change in government personnel and the inclusion of the opposition party (Civic United Front [CUF]) in the government (22 out of 50 seats in the House of Representatives are now held by members of the CUF). The effects this political change – considered a major step towards real democracy – may have on the economic situation of the islands cannot be assessed yet, however.

between "the local" and "the global", it is also used to refer to relationships between cities or simply to indicate that actions and practices that are taking place somewhere are somehow connected to actions and practices elsewhere. As a kind of counter-movement to the idea of seemingly free-floating transnational practices, an increasing number of scholars now try "to ground the discourse of the transnational in the place-making practices of the translocal" (Smith 2005: 243, cf. also Zhou and Tseng 2001). Also, when first used by Appadurai in 1996, the term "translocality" addressed the ways "in which ties of marriage, work, business and leisure weave together various circulating populations with kinds of 'locals'" (Appadurai 1996: 216). Popularised by Castells' image of "spaces of flows" instead of "spaces of places" (Castells 1996), this idea has been transferred to the understanding of place by putting a strong emphasis on places as unbounded and cross-cut by flows of people, things and information (cf. Amin and Thrift 2002: 3; Allen et al. 1999; Urry 2007). Most prominently in geography, Doreen Massey and her colleagues argue that it is the connections and relations between extensive flows of people, capital and power that constitute places, and instead of understanding them as internally bound and separated from the outside, they advocate regarding places as consisting of both relations "within" the place and the manifold connections reaching far beyond it (Massey 2004: 6). This means to "think of places in less territorial terms, as nodes, sites of exposure, connectivity, juxtaposition, interaction and trajectory" (Rogers 2005: 406) and to go beyond the notion of places "as spatially fixed geographical containers for social processes" (Sheller and Urry 2006: 209). In this respect, M. P. Smith has developed a concept of "translocalities" emphasising that what is considered local is not detached from other places but "a fluid cross-border space in which social actors interact with local and extra-local institutions and social processes in the formation of power, meaning, and identities" (Smith 2001: 174).

To view Zanzibar as a "translocality" therefore means to understand its continuous (re)construction through the movements of people, material objects and ideas through it (cf. Appadurai 1996; Hannerz 2003; Smith 2001). As Massey points out, "this is a notion of place where specificity (local uniqueness, a sense of place) derives not from some mythical internal roots nor from a history of relative isolation – now to be disrupted by globalisation – but precisely from the absolute particularity of the mixture of influences found together there" (Massey 1999: 41). Seeing Zanzibar through the lens of "translocality" leads to a conceptualisation that no longer simply emphasises the links between the islands and other places but positions it as a product of diverse forms of connection and relations, aiming to explore its links as its constitutive elements. Consequently, when attempting to get to grips with Zanzibar and its role and position in the wider Swahili network today, the complex relationships and connections themselves need to be examined. In a recently accomplished research project, we therefore explore the multiple relations between Zanzibar and its diaspora on the Tanzanian mainland, on the Arabian Peninsula and in the United Kingdom by especially focusing on contemporary trading connections.[2]

[2]The authors wish to express their gratitude to the Deutsche Forschungsgemeinschaft (DFG) for funding this project.

In this article we now want to focus on a particular connection that, apart from its economic relevance, has also been of high ideological and imaginative value and is advanced as a dominant argument in political controversies in Zanzibar. The relationship between Oman and Zanzibar is marked by very contested views and conflicting versions and has often been exploited for different political interests. Instead of engaging in these wider and more macro-level political and economic debates on the relationship between Oman and Zanzibar, we want to ground these in the everyday practices and imaginative geographies of individual people as lived and perceived today. Focusing on individual economic connections and private investments, we will explore how these actions are informed by and linked to changing imaginative geographies over time and over different generations. We will do so by looking at the relations from the perspective of "Zanzibaris" who are current residents of Oman, bringing together multi-sited research that has been done in Oman, Dubai and Zanzibar.

This paper thereby not only adds to the literature on contemporary Zanzibar, but also deals with Oman's recent engagement with its regional connections, which form the centre of this book. The aim of this paper, however, is not to give a complete overview or any representative account of current Oman-Zanzibar relations, but to present a qualitative insight that foregrounds their complexity and ambiguity and, thus, to broaden the perspective on these particular connections by adding and discussing what is actually happening in the everyday lives of the people who constitute this translocal relationship.

5.2 Turning the Focus Towards "Zanzibari" in Oman

Conceptualising Zanzibar as a "translocality" pushes us to focus on its diverse links and relations as its constitutive elements and therefore enables us to better account for the ways in which particular connections contribute to practices of place-making. In general, the term place-making is used to describe the process of filling a certain space with meaning, materially as well as discursively (cf. Cresswell 2006). Thus, material aspects such as building activities and investments characterise the outer appearance of a place as well as emotions related to it; these aspects are crucial in order for understanding the meaning of Zanzibar today. These place-making practices are not only organised and fostered by people living in Zanzibar, to a great extent they are also triggered and maintained by Zanzibari residing elsewhere. Their points of view, their practices and imaginations also have to be taken into account when trying to get to grips with Zanzibar as a translocal place. As stated above, we here want to concentrate on the contemporary connections between Zanzibar and Oman, grounding the often more macro-level discussions in the everyday lives of individuals, exploring how current relations are motivated, how they are lived and experienced, what they consist of and in what ways they contribute to practices of place-making in Zanzibar.

An important moment for the movement of Zanzibari to the Arabian Peninsula was the so called Zanzibar Revolution in 1964. What started as a unidirectional movement between Zanzibar and several Arabian countries willing to take in political refugees has been followed by a more general mobility of people of Omani ancestry who had resided along the East African coast, as well as in places in Europe and the United States. Meanwhile, family reunions and movements to as well as out of the country have led to a fluctuating Zanzibari population in Oman that overall still seems to be constantly increasing. Yet, it is hard to tell how many Zanzibari are currently residing in Oman, since they are not listed as a separate category and the great majority of them have been fully included as Omani nationals in the official population statistics and censuses. The apparent lack of distinction in the official records indicates the government's interest in stressing the idea of national unity and integrity. Since the 1970s Omani nationality law considers children of Omani nationals born abroad to be full citizens. Townsend (1977), for example, estimated that by the end of 1975 between 8,000 and 10,000 Zanzibari had settled in Oman; the number is thought to have increased to 100,000 today (Valeri 2007: 486). According to Al Rasheed (2005: 100), Zanzibari themselves claim to be even more, suggesting numbers of 300,000 at the end of the nineties. Regardless of the exact number, they have come to form a considerable community in Oman and they played and are still playing a crucial role in the process of nation building and the creation and negotiation of an Omani identity.

Generally, Zanzibari in Oman can be differentiated into two or even three different categories, which mainly depend on the time of their or their ancestors' migration to East Africa. There are still a number of different, contesting views about the time of the first contact between the Arabian Peninsula and the East African coast. Some are convinced that constant and close ethnic, cultural, economic and political links were forged between the South Arabian kingdoms and the East African coast already during the early part of the first millennium BC. Others rely on the first definite mention of Oman-Africa connections in 700–705 AD, when rulers of the interior of Oman travelled to Africa to escape the Umayyad attacks (Bhacker 2001). What is certain is that by 1,700 the Omani had managed to establish a loose hegemony over the Swahili coast (Gilbert 2007: 165); and, having successfully defeated the Portuguese, in 1832 Zanzibar became the seat of an Omani Empire with Sultan Said bin Sultan (1804–1856) moving his court to the island (Sheriff 1987: 26).

From the beginning, these links brought with them flows of migration. As Sheriff points out, "the initial attraction of the East African region for Omani rulers had been the caravan trade, with rapidly increasing demand for ivory and enslaved persons throughout the eighteenth and nineteenth century due to the appetites of global capitalist markets" (Sheriff 1987: 175). As trade boomed, some of the wealth began to be invested in the establishment of plantations, clustered in certain areas of the coast, most prominently in Pemba (Cooper 1977; Glassmann 2011), which further stimulated elite Arabs to migrate from Oman to Zanzibar (Cooper 1977: 54). The Al Busaidi rulers and sections of Omani tribal nobility and religious scholars came to control the political, religious and economic affairs of the island, and, assisted by Hindu and Muslim Indian merchants, Omani therefore became the commercial and political elite in Zanzibar (cf. Myers 2000: 432). While some carefully preserved their "pure Oman blood", others took African wives, but generally they all retained their tribal ancestry as well as their Ibadi and Sunni faith (Peterson 2004: 46). Over the years, most of them became more and more "swahilisised", and over the generations many even lost their knowledge of Arabic (Al Rasheed 2005: 98). The descendants of these early Omani migrants in East Africa form the first category of Zanzibari in Oman today. The second category of Zanzibari in Oman is the offspring of those who moved to Zanzibar mainly during the first half of the twentieth century. These mostly fled economic hardship, tribal rivalries and the political oppression of the autocratic rule of Sultan Said bin Taymur (1932–1970). Unlike the earlier waves of migrants who soon enjoyed economic and political power and formed an urban aristocracy whose position was based on clove growing, commerce, and government employment, they never enjoyed the same possibilities to upgrade their social and economic status and generally engaged in shopkeeping, peddling and various rather small-scale trades (Middleton 1992; Prins 1961). Many also entered the clove plantation economy in Zanzibar or moved deeper and deeper into the mainland to look for attractive revenues in the trading business on the periphery. A third category is sometimes posited to address those Omani originating especially from Sur and al-Sharqqiya who regularly moved between Oman and East Africa already as early as in the tenth century, resulting in translocal families split between these places (Le Cour Grandmaison 1989: 176). This would include, for example, the al-Harthi and al-Barwani, who maintained close connections between Oman and the East African coast since their involvement in the early slave trade. Nevertheless, despite these differences in the time of emigration from Oman, what these groups have in common is that they all (re)migrated to Oman after the Zanzibar Revolution on 12 January 1964.

In the aftermath of the political upheaval, residents who were considered Arabs were deported; the last Sultan, Sayyid Jamshid bin Abdallah bin Khalifa bin Harib, fled to Portsmouth in the United Kingdom; and many were killed. Whereas an estimated 6,000–10,000 died (cf. Cameron 2004: 105; Clayton 1981; Gilbert 2007: 170), it is assumed that about 30,000 out of approximately 50,000 people of Arab origin were forcibly expelled or fled at their own initiative, many of them heading towards Arabia (cf. Bakari 2001: 193; Loimeier 2009: 52). Though Zanzibar had long been part of the Sultanate of Oman and many of the refugees could clearly trace their relatives to Oman, the Omani government under the rule of Sultan Said bin Taymur (1932–1970) refused to organise a collective repatriation process and, through the end of 1964, agreed only to accommodate 3,700 Zanzibari (Peterson 2004: 46). Only when Sultan Qaboos overthrew his father in July 1970 were some of the Zanzibari who had first settled in other Arabian countries, such as the United Arab Emirates (then still the Trucial Sheikhdoms), Kuwait, Egypt and Saudi Arabia, or in Europe, able to move to Oman when they were invited to join forces and contribute to the "awakening of the country" (Valeri 2007: 485). In this context, Zanzibari have come to form a considerable community in Oman; it has played and is still playing a crucial role in the process of nation building and the creation and negotiation of an Omani identity.

Only over the last couple of years have academics started to engage with the situation of Zanzibari in Oman. Al Rasheed (2005), for example, traces the life histories and experiences of those Zanzibari who returned to Oman in the 1970s, putting special emphasis on the transnational context of what has become a Muscat elite. On the other hand, Peterson (2004) and Valeri (2007) focus instead on the role of Zanzibari for the Oman nation-state, examining their group feeling (*asabiyya*) and identity as a valuable contribution to the study of modern state-led processes of Oman nation building. Despite the different contexts (transnational vs. national), what is commonly agreed on is that the Zanzibari refugees were welcome participants, especially in the early phases of Oman's development after 1970, not only because they were educated and possessed skills that were in high demand, such as knowledge of English, but also because they were considered Omani insiders on grounds of their ancestry, while at the same time being outsiders to the rivalrous tribal alliances due to their long absence (Al Rasheed 2005: 102; Valeri 2007: 485; Peterson 2004: 46). Nevertheless, whereas the Zanzibari in Oman were on the one hand appreciated for their education and their proficiency in English, on the other hand, they had to face negative attitudes and refusal due to their "Africanness", most clearly recognisable in their Swahili language and their weakness in Arabic, which some retain to this day, as well as their more liberal and "cosmopolitan" traits (Al Rasheed 2005: 103; Valeri 2007: 489). Regarding integration in the job market, Zanzibari were initially strongly represented in the national oil company (Petroleum Development Oman), as well as in the Ministry of Defence, the Omani intelligence agency and the police (Al Rasheed 2005: 102–103; Valeri 2007: 494; Peterson 2004: 47–51). It was in these strategically important government bodies that qualified staff of Omani origin were most urgently needed in the early years of the young Sultan's government. To this day, the Omani-Zanzibari also seem to have developed a strong position in the tourism sector.

While these recent publications so far mainly examine how the Zanzibari fit into Oman society and their connections within it, we now want to broaden this perspective by focusing on the connections going abroad, back to Zanzibar. The topicality of these relations is vividly expressed by the recent book by Al Riyami (2009), a Zanzibari Omani himself, in which he presents his view on the history of Zanzibar and Oman. The book was a bestseller in Oman – selling 5,000 copies in the first couple of weeks – and was sold out shortly after its publication.[3] The situation of Zanzibari in Oman and the historical relationship between the two places have clearly remained an intensely discussed topic of national concern, fuelled by books like Riyami's and the recent publication of another Zanzibari Omani entitled *Kwaheri ukoloni, kwaheri uhuru* (Ghassany 2010, in English: Goodbye Colonialism, Goodbye Freedom), in which the author sheds new light on the happenings of 1964, as well as by group discussions in online networks such as Facebook, in which historical photographs are shared. What has been dealt with far less is the current interaction between Oman and Zanzibar based on individual relationships. Against the background of the situation of Zanzibari in Oman as presented, we will therefore engage with the ways Zanzibari Omani relate and contribute to the place-making of Zanzibar today. As we will point out, this long-standing relationship between the Arabian Peninsula and Zanzibar not

[3] A translation into English is in progress.

only has been, but still is of enormous importance for many of their everyday practices and imaginative geographies. Only including these contemporary relations and revealing what Zanzibar means to Zanzibari Omani makes it possible to account for the translocal geographies of Oman today.

5.3 Imaginative and Material Relations to Zanzibar: Keeping Connected and/or Being Tied Together

After the Zanzibari Revolution in 1964, the political isolationist course prohibited foreigners, with the exception of technical experts from the Eastern bloc, from entering Zanzibar. Arab visitors were explicitly forbidden and the connections between Zanzibar and Oman were generally limited and under the strict observation of the state. The Revolutionary Government was determined to undermine or even completely cut relations with Oman and its neighbours as a means of safeguarding the "African" Revolution by minimising Arab influence and completely isolating the exiled people who had taken refuge there (Bakari 2001: 193). Mainly as an effect of the financial crisis and the urgent need for foreign investments, Zanzibar began economically and politically opening up again in the late 1980s, also resuming and reawakening relations to the Arab world (Gilbert 2007: 172–173). Under the rule of Zanzibar's President Ali Hassan Mwinyi, who travelled to Oman in 1985, relations between Oman and Zanzibar were gradually restored to the extent that Oman established a Consulate in Zanzibar. Especially since the 1990s, a tentative reengagement with the island by Zanzibari living in Oman could be observed, leading to an increased mobility between the two places, family reunions and for some even a return movement.

Based on our qualitative research, consisting of narrative interviews and participant observation in Oman and Zanzibar between 2006 and 2011, we will in the following present the everyday practices and imaginative geographies of individual people living and experiencing the relations between Oman and Zanzibar. We thereby try to provide deeper insight into what these contemporary relations consist of and how they are motivated and maintained.

5.3.1 Emotional Ties Between Oman and Zanzibar

A first theme that emerges in conversations with Zanzibari Omani in Oman[4] often is the emotional dimension of their relationship to Zanzibar. Most of the people we talked to were born and grew up in Zanzibar and had to experience the Zanzibar

[4]In Oman, our research was mainly conducted in Muscat. In addition, several trips were undertaken to Ibra – a place in the interior from which many families migrated to East Africa – accompanying Zanzibari Omani on their weekend trips to visit their remaining relatives.

Revolution either as a child or as a young adult. Many of them have very clear and intense memories of their childhood in Zanzibar, a place they had to leave abruptly when their families decided to abandon the islands and seek refuge on the Arabian Peninsula. Some of them even had to escape on their own, hiding on one of the boats travelling north along the East African coast, not knowing if they would ever see their relatives again.

Thus, what most of the Zanzibari Omani we talked to share are memories of a childhood in Zanzibar, which ended in a horrifying experience of the violent political change in 1964. While some had to go through a risky flight and spent a couple of years as refugees before being allowed to enter Oman, others simply moved to Muscat, where the great majority of them soon succeeded in (re)establishing their careers and – if they had not already done so – starting a family. Many of them easily found a job and, after a while, came to occupy important positions in the petroleum industry, the military, the police, the government or private companies (some also founded their own business). However, despite the similarity of their life paths and the generally very positive memories of Zanzibar before the Revolution, the emotional ties to Zanzibar expressed in our conversations vary enormously and can roughly be separated into three groups.

First, it is noticeable that some still seem to feel more closely attached to Zanzibar than to Oman. Statements such as "We are part of Zanzibar, I have my origins there, that is our country" show that these people consider Zanzibar their proper place of belonging. Despite having spent most of their life in Oman, it is Zanzibar that "has left a very special mark in our psyche". And, although being physically present in Oman for many years, they say that "our hearts are still in Zanzibar". To the degree that Zanzibar is closely related to their past, it is assigned a high relevance today, being crucial to their identities. The conversations with this group of people often centre on very positive images of Zanzibar as green and lush islands, full of delicious fruits and beautiful landscapes. Contrary to the view of a hierarchical social structure prior to the Zanzibar Revolution, certainly prominent among the more "African" Zanzibari, they recollect harmony and communality, bringing examples of friendly relationships beyond ethnic and social differences that in their opinion dominated life in Zanzibar at that time. In these memories, Zanzibar is generally described as a paradisical place, a place of dreams and longing, forcibly destroyed by the political events in 1964 and the economic decline in their aftermath. And even though such sad developments forced these Zanzibari Omani to leave the islands, they report that their emotional bonds remain very positive and close. Their historical image of Zanzibar, as preserved and created in their memories, generally forms the centre of these positive emotions.

For others, however, the memories of early experiences in Zanzibar appear far more detached from today's emotional bonds to the islands. Even though Zanzibar is the place where they were born and which is thus full of childhood memories, they do not consider it particularly meaningful to them in their current situation. Zanzibar is rather viewed as a place of the past that has emotionally been left behind. In their views, the relations to Zanzibar that have remained consist only of family relations, as many of them still have a lot of relatives there. And as they state, "That will be the only tie, that will be the only feeling." So, while acknowledging the meaningfulness and importance of Zanzibar for their childhood, these Zanzibari Omani speak of the islands today simply as a place where some of their relatives live, denying any other emotional attachment. And, although a little less frequently, we even encountered some Zanzibari Omani who strongly denied having any emotional attachment to the islands at all. As one of our interviewees put it: "I don't regard it as my home at all, if it's on fire, if it drowns, it doesn't bother me." Together with a similar statement, another informant expressed his gratefulness to the Sultan who had offered him and the other refugees from East Africa a new home in Oman: "When Sultan Qaboos opened the door for us, it was the best place to come."

As this brief overview of the various positions we confronted in our first interviews shows, independent of their contents, the statements concerning their emotional relations to Zanzibar generally sound very clear and straightforward – either regarding their personal ties as very positive and deeply emotional or expressing a more pragmatic approach, with Zanzibar sometimes even being described as completely devoid of any significance. But in the course of the conversations, especially when together with a group of Zanzibari Omani, it soon became clear that it is often not as simple and clear-cut as the discourses above might suggest. Even among those who initially denied any emotional ties to the islands, conversation sooner or later turned to Zanzibar. They too delve into the news received from relatives or engage in heated discussions about the political and economic situation in Zanzibar. In the following, we thus want to turn our attention to the actual practices linking Zanzibar and Oman today, allowing us to provide a more complex picture of current relations between these two places.

5.3.2 Material Ties Between Oman and Zanzibar

It is hard to meet any Zanzibari Omani in Muscat who does not follow the news in Zanzibar or at least listen attentively when friends or relatives exchange stories about the islands, either received online or told in one of the numerous phone calls connecting Oman to East Africa.[5] Independent of emotional relationships with Zanzibar – not only as they were presented to us in our interviews, but also as we were able to observe in discourses among themselves in more informal settings in people's homes, at family gatherings, on day trips etc. – they all seem to be involved in one way or another.

Apart from this more general concern for happenings on the islands and the exchange of news, many of the practices are related to material ties. Sending clothes,

[5] While some exchange messages with friends and relatives in Zanzibar almost daily, calls are generally made to notify each other of important happenings such as weddings, hospitalisation or death, often combined with the exchange of the latest gossip. Because of its own instant messaging system that involves no additional costs, the Blackberry phone has achieved great popularity in recent years, making this kind of exchange even more casual and turning communication with friends and relatives abroad into an everyday activity.

new or second-hand, paying school fees and sending money for medical treatment or just to contribute to their relatives' monthly income by sending USD 100 or more are the most common ways to support relatives in Zanzibar. And while some still emphasise that these material ties are an effect of their emotional bonds to Zanzibar, others make clear that they simply feel obliged to provide economic support. Even if they don't feel close to Zanzibar, even if they would like to turn their back on the islands, it seems impossible to them not to meet their relatives' demands.

Many Zanzibari Omani families regularly receive visitors from Zanzibar, often female relatives who are eager to spend up to 3 months in *Arabuni* (Arabia). And even though most of them see this as a meaningful expression of the harmonious relationship between families in both places, others blatantly admit that "they like the sort of life here because we are supporting them!", pointing more critically to the often one-sided direction of material exchange. But this does not mean that they don't want to help their relatives – most of them do or at least say they do – but that, even if they didn't want to, they feel that they do not really have a choice. Material flows thus do not necessarily correspond to emotional ties.

The same can be observed, but considerably less so, in the context of Zanzibar Omani travelling to Zanzibar. Apart from visiting sick relatives and attending weddings or funerals, most other practices, such as regaining formerly confiscated property, buying land or building a house, generally seem to be driven by some kind of emotional attachment to the island. At least some are convinced that this can only be done for emotional reasons since, in their opinion, it lacks any rational thinking: "Their parents have invested there, they lived there, they built, they had everything, and then all of it was confiscated. Now, to find a son of that same father going back there, putting thousands of Omani Rial to rebuild that house, that is stupid!" Particularly when walking along the beach of Bwejuu, a small village of the east coast of Zanzibar, where the majority of the luxurious houses on the shoreline are owned by Zanzibari Omanis, one cannot help having the impression that this is a way to create the "paradise" that features so prominently in their memories. At any rate, in recent decades Zanzibar has become a favourite place for Zanzibari Omani to spend their summer holiday and "escape the heat" of Muscat. And, while meeting old friends on one of the *barazas* (a bench or veranda in front of the house, often integrated into the wall of the building, which serves as a common meeting place; cf. Kresse 2007: 73) in Stone Town or having dinner at the recently renovated Forodhani Gardens, many of them seem to dream about "going home" or spending at least a considerable part of the year in Zanzibar, as some retirees do.

But, even though many of the activities might indeed be triggered by positive emotions towards Zanzibar, it would be wrong to deny that there also is an awareness that not attending a wedding, not taking part in the mourning of a relative, not visiting their parents in hospital, or not taking every opportunity to request former property could mean severely damaging family relations between the two places. How complicated the relationship between "having to be there", "wanting to be there" and "not wanting to be there" can be, becomes especially clear when observing personal business relations between Oman and Zanzibar.

5.3.3 *Personal Business Ties Between Oman and Zanzibar*

A common way of trying to make the material ties between the two places beneficial for both sides is to establish personal business ties. The wish to help their relatives in Zanzibar earn their living leads to a business idea – most often related to trade. Sending money[6] to open a shop or sending goods for them to sell, they hope to trigger a successful business endeavour from which they too will profit or at least in which they won't lose.

> *Many people tried, I was sending things to the people so that they can do something and help themselves. I just want to get out what I pay. But it didn't work well, because they couldn't pay me back* (Interview 3, 2006).

Often enough, enthusiasm and hope soon give way to resignation and the realisation that the outcome is generally not in their hands. Even though some of the projects succeed and many Zanzibari traders maintain very helpful connections to relatives in Oman and Zanzibar to facilitate their business, others flourish only for a short time before demanding more money, and yet others do not even get off the ground because the money sent from Oman has to be used for more urgent purposes instead. But even if these endeavours do not work out, and many Zanzibari Omani express their criticism and frustration about these kinds of business ties, in the majority of the cases they still continue – maybe with a different kind of trade, or with another relative. And if they do not continue their engagement, they don't want their reluctance to be noticed: "I don't want to recommend that he open a shop in Dar because then I would have to support him financially".

5.4 "We Are Part of Zanzibar": Caught Between Desire and Obligation, Romanticism and Pragmatism

By conceptualising Zanzibar as a ‚translocality', in this article, we tried to turn the attention to the ways in which the place is shaped materially and imaginatively by its translocal connections. Even though its cosmopolitan character is often proclaimed and almost taken for granted, more thorough engagement in translocal relations remains rare today. Particularly the connections between Oman and Zanzibar seem to rest comfortably in historical imagination, while current ways of interaction, the various movements and struggles that go into sustaining these longstanding relations are almost left untouched. Looking at today's emotional as well as material ties between Oman and Zanzibar from the perspective of Zanzibari Omani, however, provides interesting insights not only into the complexity and manifold character of these relations, but also and especially into the ambivalence involved.

[6]Sums may vary from a couple of hundred dollars to several thousand, depending on the personal situation of the sender.

Conversations with Zanzibari Omani about their emotional ties to Zanzibar often centre on the history between the two places, the history of Zanzibar and the role Omanis played in it. "It's our history, I love the history, maybe because I love the place," one of our interviewees said, and, indeed, deep emotions towards the islands are often narrated in conjunction with imaginations of the past. However, what this translocal perspective on contemporary Oman-Zanzibar connections has shown is that trying to get to grips with the meaning of Zanzibar for Zanzibari Omani today requires going beyond discourses and actually engaging with their everyday practices and material relationships. The stories told about the maritime history of Oman and Zanzibar, the successful times of the Indian Ocean dhow trade, the images of lush islands and fine Zanzibari culture do not always match the practices linking the two places. Nor do the protestations of indifference towards Zanzibar always find their equivalence in actions. Positive emotional ties do not necessarily result in extensive material relations and frequent visits, disinterest does not necessarily result in cutting off material connections and visits and, despite "low profitability" and "frequent failure", business relations still go on. Overall, translocal connections between Oman and Zanzibar are thus characterised by an extreme ambivalence; they consist of contradictions and tensions between expressed emotions and actual practices, negotiating between romanticism and pragmatism, desire and obligation.

Being an Omani citizen with a deep connection to Zanzibar is not always easy, because people's lives have been affected by disrupted histories and experiences of migration and cultural distinction. On the one hand, Zanzibari Omani do share some characteristics such as the ability to communicate in a language other than Arabic or their love for Swahili cuisine, which distinguish them from other Omani nationals. Decorating their homes in Oman with furniture brought from Zanzibar, displaying pictures of the islands and particularly of the historic sites of Stone Town or the famous Indian Ocean dhows, or putting up enlarged reproductions of faded photographs of ancestors in their ceremonial dress in Zanzibar all serve as indicators of their Swahili background. On the other hand, Zanzibari Omani have always been very keen to prove that they are loyal members of the Omani society. As one of our interviewees poignantly expressed: "You identify with both [Oman and Zanzibar]. One should not be told to choose between your father and your mother, they are both your parents." But the relationship to one's parents is just not always as harmonious as one would wish it to be.

References

Al Rasheed, M. (2005). Transnational connections and a national identity – Zanzibari Omanis in Muscat. In P. Dresch & J. Piscatori (Eds.), *Monarchies and nations – Globalisation and identity in the Arab states of the Gulf* (pp. 96–113). London: I.B. Tauris.

Al Riyami, N. (2009). *ZanÊibār: šahÒīyāt wa-aÎdā*t *1828–1972* [Zanzibar: People and events 1828–1972]. London: Dār al-Íikma.

Allen, J., Massey, D., & Pryke, M. (1999). *Unsettling cities: Movement/settlement*. London: Routledge.

Amin, A., & Thrift, N. (2002). *Cities: Reimagining the urban*. Cambridge: Polity Press.
Appadurai, A. (1996). *Modernity at large: Cultural dimensions of globalisation*. Minneapolis: University of Minnesota Press.
Bakari, M. A. (2001). *The democratisation process in Zanzibar. A retarded transition*. Hamburg: GIGA-Hamburg.
Bhacker, M. R. (2001). *Trade and empire in Muscat and Zanzibar*. London: Routledge.
Bissell, W. C. (2007). Casting a long shadow: Colonial categories, cultural identities, and cosmopolitan spaces in globalizing Africa. *African Identities, 5*(2), 181–197.
Cameron, G. (2004). Political violence, ethnicity and the agrarian question in Zanzibar. In P. Caplan & F. Topan (Eds.), *Swahili modernities: Culture, politics and identity on the east coast of Africa* (pp. 103–119). Trenton: Africa World Press.
Castells, M. (1996). *The rise of the network society*. Oxford: Blackwell.
Clayton, A. (1981). *The Zanzibar revolution and its aftermath*. London: C. Hurst & Co.
Cooper, F. (1977). *Plantation slavery on the east coast of Africa*. New Halen: Yale University Press.
Cresswell, T. (2006). *On the move*. London: Routledge.
Ghassany, H. (2010). *Kwaheri ukoloni, kwaheri uhuru. Zanzibar na mapinduzi ya Afrabia*. Raleigh: Lulu.
Gilbert, E. (2007). Oman and Zanzibar: The historical roots of a global community. In H. Prabha Ray & E. A. Alpers (Eds.), *Cross currents and community networks. The history of the Indian Ocean* (pp. 163–178). Oxford: Oxford University Press.
Glassmann, J. (2011). *War or words, war of stones*. Bloomington: Indiana University Press.
Hannerz, U. (2003). Being there…and there…and there! Reflections on multi-site ethnography. *Ethnography, 4*, 201–216.
Kresse, K. (2007). *Philosophising in Mombasa: Knowledge, Islam and intellectual practice on the Swahili coast*. Edinburgh: Edinburgh University Press.
Le Cour Grandmaison, C. (1989). Rich cousins, poor cousins: Hidden stratification among the Omani Arabs in East Africa. *Africa, 59*(2), 176–184.
Le Guennec-Coppens, F., & Caplan, P. (1991). *Les Swahili entre Afrique et Arabie*. Paris: Karthala.
Loimeier, R. (2009). *Between social skills and marketable skills: The politics of Islamic education in 20th century Zanzibar*. Leiden: Brill.
Maliyamkono, T. L. (2000). *The political plight of Zanzibar*. Dar es Salaam: Tema Publishers.
Massey, D. (1999). *Power-geometries and the politics of space and time* (Hettner Lecture 1998). Heidelberg: Department of Geography, University of Heidelberg.
Massey, D. (2004). *Space, place and gender*. Minneapolis: University of Minnesota Press.
Mazrui, A., & Sharif, I. N. (1994). *The Swahili: Idiom and identity of an African people*. Trenton: Africa World Press.
Middleton, J. (1992). *The world of the Swahili – An African mercantile civilisation*. London: Yale University Press.
Myers, G. (2000). Narrative representations of revolutionary Zanzibar. *Journal of Historical Geography, 26*(3), 429–448.
Peterson, J. E. (2004). Oman's diverse society: Northern Oman. *Middle East Journal, 58*(1), 31–51.
Pouwels, R. (1991). Swahili networks. *Cahiers d'Etudes africaines, 123*, 411–415.
Prins, A. H. J. (1961). *The Swahili-speaking peoples of Zanzibar and the east African coast*. London: International African Institute.
Rogers, A. (2005). Observations on transnational urbanism: Broadening and narrowing the field. *Journal of Ethnic and Migration Studies, 31*, 403–407.
Saleh, M. (2004). Going with the times: Swahili norms and values today. In P. Caplan & F. Topan (Eds.), *Swahili modernities: Culture, politics and identity on the east coast of Africa* (pp. 145–155). Trenton: Africa World Press.
Sheller, M., & Urry, J. (2006). The new mobilities paradigm. *Environment and Planning A, 38*.
Sheriff, A. (1987). *Slaves, spices and ivory in Zanzibar*. London: James Curry.

Sheriff, A. (2006). Between the worlds: The littoral peoples of the Indian Ocean. In R. Loimeier & R. Seesemann (Eds.), *The global worlds of the Swahili* (pp. 15–30). Münster: LIT.
Smith, M. P. (2001). *Transnational urbanism*. Oxford: Blackwell.
Smith, M. P. (2005). Transnational urbanism revisited. *Journal of Ethnic and Migration Studies, 31*, 235–244.
Topan, F. (2006). From coastal to global: The erosion of the Swahili "paradox". In R. Loimeier & R. Seesemann (Eds.), *The global worlds of the Swahili* (pp. 55–66). Muenster: LIT.
Townsend, J. (1977). *Oman: The making of a modern state*. London: Helm.
Urry, J. (2007). *Mobilities*. Cambridge: Polity Press.
Valeri, M. (2007). Nation building and communities in Oman since 1970: The Swahili-speaking Omani in search for identity. *African Affairs, 106*, 497–506.
Young Arab Union. (1936). *The Silver jubilee book of his highness the Sultan of Zanzibar* (pp. 1911–1936). Zanzibar: Young Arab League.
Zhou, Y., & Tseng, Y. F. (2001). Regrounding the 'ungrounded empires': Localisation as the geographical catalyst for transnationalism. *Global Networks, 1*, 131–154.

Chapter 6
Of Red Cells, Translocality and Origins: Inherited Blood Disorders in Oman

Claire Beaudevin

Drawing on the example of inherited blood disorders (IBD), this chapter aims at showing how health issues can shape both people's understanding of a territory and the territory itself. While a sick individual is often pictured as lying motionlessly in a bed – an island of stillness surrounded by moving social groups and networks – this chapter emphasizes that the patients' chronic affection involves most of them in local and transnational networks, flows and symbolic geographies. More precisely, I aim to explore the different forms of IBD-related translocality in Oman; as Katrin Bromber underscores,

> 'Translocality', on the one hand, means spatial mobility as such and, on the other hand, physical, political, social and cultural spaces and localities that are shaped by it. [...] It considers not only movement, whether concrete or potential, but also its opposite – the constraints and failure of movements that often result in immobility (Bromber, in this volume).

This chapter discusses how, from this point of view, there is a common translocal dimension in flows of patients within Oman, "therapeutic journeys" abroad, the social stakes of genetics research, genealogical reconstructions of Oman's past and the everyday shackles of chronicity.

C. Beaudevin (✉)
Cermes3 (Centre de recherche Médecine, sciences, santé, santé mentale et société), Paris/Villejuif, France
e-mail: claire@beaudevin.net

S. Wippel (ed.), *Regionalizing Oman: Political, Economic and Social Dynamics*, United Nations University Series on Regionalism 6, DOI 10.1007/978-94-007-6821-5_6,

6.1 Background: The Anthropology of Health and Inherited Blood Disorders

This chapter draws on an anthropological research[1] and deals with genetic health in the Sultanate. More specifically, the research was conducted on sickle-cell anaemia and thalassaemia and their social representations, through an ethnographic approach.[2] Medical anthropology's definition of health is much broader than the medicine-related issues or solely the biological state of well-being. It encompasses the entire healthcare system (the official sector as well as complementary and alternative medicines), patients and family networks, health professionals, medical research etc.

My research focused on the particular case of two inherited blood disorders: sickle-cell anaemia and thalassaemia. A short medical description of these two hereditary diseases is necessary to grasp the complexity of their social management and representations. Inherited blood disorders are serious genetic chronic conditions, affecting red blood cells and inducing acute unpredictable pain crises, bone malformations, multiple organ failure etc. They are generally diagnosed in very young children because of the first clinical symptoms' outbreak. Without treatment, these diseases are usually lethal during early childhood. Their genetic transmission pattern is recessive, which means an affected individual is always born from the fecundation of gametes both carrying the affected genes. Thus, he or she systematically owns two copies of these genes, causing the disease. If the parents transmit only one affected gene, the child will only be a carrier of the disease and will not suffer any symptom. However, he or she will be able to transmit these affected genes to his or her own offspring. It is important to stress that when two carriers have children together, the risk of an affected newborn is 25 % in every pregnancy.

6.2 Health and Translocality Within Oman

6.2.1 *3-Digit Numbers, the WHO and a Pyramid: Administrative Constructions of "Health Spaces"*

The Ministry of Health (MoH) in Oman was created on 22 August 1970, a month after the current Sultan's accession to power; its first modest annual budget was set at three million pounds sterling (Ministry of Health 1972). The MoH published its first report in 1972, which described a Dantesque field situation:

[1]Cf. Beaudevin 2010. The research was partly hosted by Sultan Qaboos University and granted ethical approval by the relevant committee of the Omani Ministry of Health. Fieldwork has been conducted between 2005 and 2009.

[2]Ethnography is a comprehensive combination of participant observation, informal conversations and semi-structured interviews, as well as review of the local press and relevant archives. It usually involves a long presence in the field; for this study, the fieldwork lasted about 18 months.

Fig. 6.1 Regional health services (Ten regions as administered by the MoH) (Source: Ministry of Health 2008)

there were fewer than 100 staff members in the whole country (including drivers and the Minister himself) and

> […] the staff was poorly paid and had few facilities in the form of supplies, equipment, transport and accommodation to be able to provide a satisfactory service. In all respects the ministry had to start from scratch, to build up a health service where almost none existed (Ministry of Health 1972: 2).

Logistic situation was Spartan at this time:

> *There was no transportation and phone numbers had 3 digits. […] We created sort of an instant Ministry of Health* (interview, Dr 'Asîm al-Jamâli, former Ministry of Health 2008).[3]

In 1971, immediately following the creation of the MoH, Oman became a member of the World Health Organization (WHO) (Turing 1980). Because of the double necessity for the new government to bring the health situation under control and to build its legitimacy, from then on the Omani health care system was designed in close cooperation with the WHO. Its contemporary organization hence follows the main WHO guidelines for a pyramidal health care services organization and referral. The health institutions network is organized in ten health regions (Fig. 6.1) and composed of

[3]Quotes from interviews are given in italics.

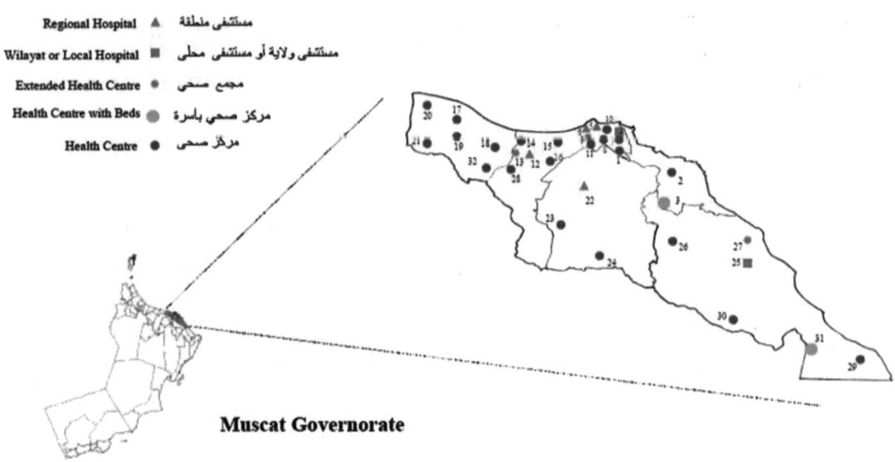

Fig. 6.2 Public health care institutions of the Muscat governorate (Source: Ministry of Health 2008)

local health centres providing primary health care[4]; regional hospitals for secondary (i.e. more specific) care; and tertiary hospitals for advanced care (in Muscat).[5]

The core rule in such a system is that patients must first search for treatment in the local facilities. If necessary, doctors then make referral decisions. As a result, patients affected by chronic and serious diseases such as inherited blood disorders have to follow the rules of this referral system. It is noteworthy that the specialized care they need – regular transfusions, multiple joint prosthesis, etc. – is not available outside of public institutions. This public health policy is applied all over the Sultanate, hence regular flows of patients are noticeable. Patients affected by IBD, once diagnosed, are referred to Muscat's tertiary care institutions, regardless of where they are from. Their two main destinations are Sultan Qaboos University Hospital (the country's only research and teaching hospital) and the Royal Hospital (Fig. 6.2).

6.2.2 *A Burden That Leads to a Routine Mobility: Patients Travelling Up and Down Oman*

Ethnographic data show that their illness is the only reason for many patients – especially women – to travel, within the Sultanate or abroad. In small rural communities, this mobility represents a particularly visible sign of their condition and is

[4]Defined as "the first level of contact of individuals, the family and community with the national health system bringing health care as close as possible to where people live and work, [that] constitutes the first element of a continuing health care process" (World Health Organization 1978: article VI).

[5]See Fig. 6.2 showing the different levels of health care institutions in the Muscat region.

part of their social identity of sick persons. Given that blood transfusion, treatment reassessment, check-ups and specific blood tests are often necessary on a monthly basis for inherited blood disorders patients, being able to travel to Muscat's tertiary care hospitals is the core step of survival management. For people regularly travelling from afar to the capital area, the meaning of "local" is shifted and broadened and tends to include Muscat, too, regardless of how distant it is.

The administrative pyramidal organization described above and the trips it requires lead patients to regard the capital area as a survival zone. In contrast, more remote places are often pictured as chancy and hazardous: as a matter of fact, distance makes every acute pain crisis or every infection more worrying – because of the impossibility to get properly treated in the nearest emergency room by one's "usual" physician from the referral hospital.

Most of the patients I met share their time between home, school and hospital, the three steps of their commuting routine. However, the very pace of this routine is important medical information, since it is a clue to their state of health: for sickle-cell anaemia patients, the frequency of admission is a criterion to assess the severity of their affection; for thalassaemia patients, the equivalent is the frequency of necessary transfusions.

Once they have admitted the necessity of this routine mobility, patients and families often implement pragmatic strategies. Yahya,[6] for instance, explains why he was treated in several hospitals before choosing Sultan Qaboos University Hospital (SQUH):

> *From Nahda Hospital, I moved to the Royal because my doctor was moving there. [...] I followed him. Then he retired. And I had very bad experiences with the ER [emergency room; C.B.] in the Royal. I escaped and found another hospital. I ended in the Armed Forces Hospital and there I had another bad experience. Fortunately, I ended up in SQUH and there... I was relieved to be treated in SQUH* (interview, Nov. 2008).

IBD patients' specific translocality is thus composite, comprising fruitless attempts to find the proper physician; incessant home-hospital commuting; the obstacles that limit the latter; and the improvements of their medical condition that sometimes make travelling to the hospital less necessary.

6.2.3 "My Family from the Interior Doesn't Know Anything but Religious Books": Omani Social Genography

Several contributions in this volume show how historical events related to religion, politics or migrations participate in symbolically organizing the Omani territory and its social representations (e.g. Hoffmann-Ruf or Verne and Müller-Mahn, in this volume). Health phenomena themselves – and particularly inherited blood disorders – can also contribute to this shaping process. Actually, IBD in Oman are frequently

[6] All names are pseudonyms, as agreed with the interviewees. Only the identities of the officials interviewed in their professional context remain unchanged.

stigmatized as a consequence of consanguineous marriages and of general "lack of awareness", which is seen as a "traditional" behaviour. Many people are firmly opposed to marrying kin: they tend to adhere to the disapproving medical discourse about consanguinity or wish to move away from the burden of cousin marriage. In this manner, Abdulrahman laments his parents' decision to get married despite the fact they are relatives: they are first cousins; he is affected by sickle-cell anaemia. To him, the causality is obvious, and the legitimacy of medical discourse irrefutable:

> *The Ministry of Health does not do anything to decrease the number of births of affected children. It's not complicated: they should only say: if you marry a relative, it's dangerous for the children* (interview, May 2005).

Marrying relatives is indeed pictured as a dangerous, but also a retrograde decision, as in Hamad's discourse, who identifies such marriages with Saudi Arabia, for many young Omanis the archetype of backward-looking society:

> *In Saudi Arabia, they marry relatives. This is why there are so many affected people there. They don't want to get married outside of the family* (Hamad, husband of a sickle-cell anaemia patient, interview, May 2008).

Many patients and health practitioners I met symbolically relate this stigmatization to a spatial opposition different from the Saudi/Omani one: the common dichotomy between the interior of Oman and the coastal areas.[7] The interior is indeed often depicted as a socially backward area, opposed to "respectable" coastal urbanized areas, where modernism is said to advocate avoidance of intermarriage. Ahmad, one of the patients I interviewed, gives a clear example of these representations:

> *My family from the interior doesn't know anything but religious books to heal. No medicine, no genetics* (interview, Nov. 2006).

Besides these representations that draw a geography of intermarriage, one can also notice another geographic dimension. Despite a growing mobility of populations inside the Sultanate, strong social, political and economical links exist between tribes and their place of origin. These links are often perceived as absolute and unchanging. As a result, numerous patients and some health practitioners, confusing tribal name with supposed tribal place of origin, spread rumours of variations of prevalence[8] of IBD from one region to another. For example, the Batinah is said to be affected by thalassaemia, whereas the Sharqiya region is known as a "sickle-cell area". Therefore, numerous people, affected or not, build a mental map of the Sultanate based on the supposed number of affected inhabitants.[9]

This idiosyncratic mapping combines prevalence figures with perceptions of consanguinity frequency. Thus, one can say that social representations of inherited blood disorders and their causes are embodied in the country's territory itself.

---

[7] For a discussion of this opposition, see Valeri (2009), Mokhtar (in this volume).

[8] A public health term that designates the number of cases of a precise disorder that are known in a population at a precise moment, compared with the total size of this population.

[9] This aspect is related to lay representations of communities and ancestry in Oman that will be addressed below.

6.3 Transnational Networks and Flows Related to Inherited Blood Disorders

The issue of health induces transnational flows of technologies, money, knowledge or individuals and hence constitutes a relevant starting point to investigate the Sultanate's regional integration. In the particular case of inherited blood disorders, their diagnostic process, their different treatments and even the patients' survival involve numerous local and/or regional interactions that can be observed at the macro- as well as the micro-social scale. This section will deal with some of them: expatriate health practitioners and Omanis trained abroad; international scientific networks; health care policies; and pursuit of treatment abroad.

6.3.1 Transcultural Therapeutic Relationships, Travelling DNA and "Genetic El Dorado": Medical Expertise and Scientific Knowledge Flows

It is public knowledge that migrant workers are numerous in Oman, including in the medical and paramedical professions. The College of Medicine was created in 1986 in Sultan Qaboos University and does not train enough doctors to fill the vacancies of the public hospitals. There are about 12,000 nurses in Oman (Ministry of Health 2010: 4.3), many of them women from India.[10] 42 % of the health care sector employees are non-Omanis; in institutions run by MoH, 70 % of the medical doctors and 36 % of the nurses are non-Omanis (Ministry of Health 2010: 4.8).[11] As a result, clinical situations themselves are frequently translocal: the language used can be English, if the practitioner does not speak Arabic, and the power relationship is shaped in accordance with the pattern learned by the doctor during his or her studies. However, such paradigm conflicts – because of past relative mobility of the protagonists – can also occur when Omanis "back-from-Africa" (Valeri 2007: 486) or Omanis who studied abroad for a long time experience the asymmetrical and paternalistic therapeutic relationship that is common in Oman.

Oman is not only a destination for health professionals: regarding genetics, specifically, there are quite dense connections between the Sultanate and several European countries, where Omanis are trained as doctors or lab technicians. These are mainly the UK and France at the moment, with a recent opening towards the Netherlands for training technicians for the Ministry of Health. These bonds with Europe have other dimensions since, given the lack of genetic analysis facilities

[10]Especially from Kerala. For an anthropological study of this specific migration route and its contemporary consequences, see Percot (2006).

[11]In the private health care sector, Omanization has reached about 7 % (Ministry of Health 2010: 4.7).

in Oman,[12] these expertise flows from Europe towards Oman are accompanied by reverse DNA samples flows: samples are analyzed in European labs using specific advanced tests unavailable in the Gulf, and results are usually shared, frequently being published in medical journals by multinational author teams (for two examples, see Rajab et al. 1999; El-Gayar et al. 2009). These international studies are more and more frequent.[13] Oman indeed represents a kind of "genetic El Dorado" for geneticists from Europe and America: the common family pattern supposes numerous children, and more than 56 % of Omani couples are relatives (24.1 % are first cousins) (Rajab and Patton 2000).[14] This guarantees investigators relative ease in genetic studies and increases the chances of discovering new syndromes and mutations (Mégarbané 2003). "No branch of medicine affords more opportunity for the diagnosis of rare disorders than clinical genetics", state Reardon and Donnai (2007: 225); this is all the more true in a country where advanced prenatal diagnosis is not common and many newborns are affected by genetic dismorphologies. Besides, the local gene pool is very specific, due to the country's history (slave trade, migrations, settlements). The historical particularities of Oman are thus interesting to biomedical researchers, but are sometimes mingled with biological specificities. Attempting to answer the key public health question "whom should we screen first for inherited blood disorders?", scientists in Oman have designed a tribal database of people affected by inherited blood disorders (Rajab and Patton 1999). This approach takes for granted that tribes can be considered biologically cohesive units and it obliterates their history of splitting, merging, political alliances, etc.

In these matters, because of its relatively small size and its numerous specificities, the Omani gene pool and the way it appeals to scientific covetousness can be compared to the gene pool of Iceland, where deCODE Genetics, a private company, planned to access and use the DNA information of the entire Icelandic population – for research and business purposes (for a detailed study of these events, see Fortun 2008).

6.3.2 A Regional Burden: Genetic Health Issues Shared with Neighbouring Countries

Inherited blood disorders are a burden shared by the Gulf countries and, more broadly, by most Middle East and Mediterranean countries. Within the GCC, this led to an official network of concern involving regional Ministries of Health: international conferences gather representatives of governments in search of public health solutions. The Omani government's interest in screening and preventing IBD is part of this

[12] This situation will probably change in the near future, since a specialized genetics centre was inaugurated in 2012 in the capital, next to the Royal Hospital.

[13] See for instance the "Oman Family Study" carried out by the Texas Biomedical Research Institute (http://txbiomed.org/departments/genetics_detail.aspx?p=48; accessed 7 August 2011).

[14] These figures are similar in neighbouring countries: in Saudi Arabia for example, these values are 56 % and 22.4 % respectively (El-Mouzan et al. 2007).

regional trend – especially noticeable in the UAE, Bahrain and Saudi Arabia. Generally speaking, genetics is a public health interest since the early 2000s; the media have long focused clearly on the issue, as shown in the article published in an Emirati newspaper: "Arabs have highest rate of genetic disorders" (Muslim 2006).

There was no regional coordination of genetics policies and research until the Centre for Arab Genomic Studies (CAGS, funded by a local royal family member[15]) was inaugurated in Dubai in 2003. CAGS is a nexus of genomics activities in the Gulf and hosts a biobank used to build the "Catalogue for Transmission Genetics in Arabs".[16] Its Council brings together numerous Arab geneticists and aims at defining public health orientations toward inherited disorders. IBD are one of the CAGS targets and one of the official health priorities set up among GCC countries. Their management and treatment leads to massive expenses for the health care systems, and public health policies are thus designed to include mandatory premarital genetic testing – new genetic screening and counselling services are being progressively implemented by the governments: in 2004 in Saudi Arabia, 2006 in Dubai and currently designed in Oman.

As stated above, the regional context is characterized by a significant rate of consanguineous marriages. These alliances are valued by families, but condemned by numerous health professionals and not recommended by the authorities. However, recent public health policies in Oman and the UAE tend to discourage citizens from marrying relatives. This huge range of representations (and the practices they involve) between "consanguinity as economic choice" and "consanguinity as genetic burden" (Bonte 1994, 2007; Khlat 1989) still has to be investigated in the region.

6.3.3 Elsewhere Is a Panacea: Therapeutic Journeys[17]

Medical anthropology studies individuals' help-seeking patterns: family members' advice, a visit to a traditional healer, religious support, medical investigations (in one's own society or abroad), etc. These different choices constitute individual therapeutic itineraries.

This can start at a patient's doorstep, since patients may move from their home to one of the numerous Ayurveda or Chinese medical Centres blossoming all over Oman – thus creating a bridge with Indian or Chinese medical traditions. But the trip can be longer than a local step of the therapeutic itinerary, and this is what I call therapeutic journeys. I deliberately avoid the phrase "medical tourism", since tourism connotes private funding and a voluntary decision, whereas travelling to get treatment can be government-funded and is not necessarily the patient's decision.[18]

[15]Sheikh Hamdan Bin Rashid Al Maktoum's foundation, which awards funds to medical sciences projects (http://www.hmaward.org.ae, accessed 7 August 2011).

[16]See http://www.cags.org.ae/ctga_search.html. Accessed 7 August 2011.

[17]For manifold ethnographic examples and anthropological analysis of therapeutic journeys, see three special issues: Roberts and Scheper-Hughes (2011b), Naraindas and Bastos (2011), and Smith-Morris and Manderson 2010.

[18]This contribution is not the proper place for a longer semantic discussion, but Roberts and Scheper-Hughes (2011a) interestingly speak about "medical migrations".

However, despite the different connotation, the denotation of "therapeutic journey" is close to the one of "medical tourism": "super-speciality hospitals and clinics that repair and replace organs and body parts, or assist infertile people in their quest for conception" (Naraindas and Bastos 2011: 1).

Travelling to seek medical treatment is a growing phenomenon: since 2005, India is the second-most frequent destination for therapeutic journeys worldwide (after Thailand); more than a million visitors come into the country every year (Pordié 2013). Nonetheless, seeking treatment abroad is not a new phenomenon in Oman; thinking about treatment possibilities outside of one's own country was not rare before 1970, especially for people living next to the Emirates. Yahya's therapeutic itinerary is a good example:

> *I was born in Zanzibar; five years later, we left for Dubai. I had typhoid and was very weak. Before then, I never had any pain. In Dubai, they didn't know these diseases and they thought I had to take iron. So, for a period of three months they injected me with iron and gave me camel liver to eat. My father heard that in Bahrain they knew how to treat this, so we went to Bahrain. Once there, after only one week, they made the diagnosis of sickle-cell* (interview, Nov. 2008).

After 1970, this continued, since many treatments were not available in the country yet. Nowadays, the government acknowledges this help-seeking pattern, and two special offices (in the MoH and the Dîwân) are in charge of treatments abroad.[19] Both of these offices, after review of a patient's medical files, may provide funding and practical support for therapeutic journeys, theoretically as long as the needed treatment is not available in Oman. Destinations depend on the expertise that can be found in the chosen country, but strong networks do exist. For example: Pakistan is a common destination for kidney transplants and India for joint replacement surgery. To overcome the difficulties in getting visas to the Schengen space, most of the patients travelling to Europe for treatment are sent by the MoH, or use strong personal connections. A 25-year-old sickle-cell patient I met in the University Hospital explains the process:

> *The Dîwân paid for all the treatments I had in the USA and in the UK. I remember, once, in the States, the treatment cost OMR 18,000. For every trip, we have to see a doctor who gives the medical file, the strongest possible [i.e., advocating in the most efficient way for treatment abroad; C.B.], then my father gives it to someone he knows in the Dîwân, someone who has helped us a lot. Then, the Minister of Dîwân has to sign... Well, first we have to prove that the treatment does not exist here, or that it's better abroad. The Minister decides afterwards* (interview, Nov. 2008).

There are no available figures on the total number of travelling Omani patients, since many of them do not declare their aim to be treated when leaving Oman. Between 1990 and 2007, 54 IBD patients were sent abroad by the MoH (Ministry of Health 2008: 9.61), but unofficial figures state 30 patients very year.

---

[19]Literally: "office", "administration". I borrow Valeri's definition in the Omani context (2009: 180): "This administration has the role of filtering files coming to the ruler, while managing national and private affairs which do not concern any other department but do not require the Sultan's personal intervention."

It is important to note that the majority of Omanis think of medical care as a transnational system, even if they cannot afford the journey. Going abroad – and especially sending a close family member abroad – is considered a social duty, a proof that the family has helped the patient as much as possible. Fatma, a mother of two thalassaemia patients, describes the familial pressure regarding her children:

> *The entire family wants me to send them abroad for treatment. They [i.e., family members] are very well educated, you know* (interview, May 2008).

Thus, choosing to travel for treatment is not always linked to a medical decision: it can also be a way to follow fashion – getting one's orthopaedic surgery in Chennai even if it is available in Oman – or to satisfy social expectations. Besides, therapeutic journeys are undoubtedly a way to escape the highly interconnected Omani society, in order to benefit from relative anonymity.

These patient flows have practical consequences; one of them is the production of transnational spaces through therapeutic journeys. Oman exists outside of its borders, through the ethnoscape (Appadurai 2005 [1996]) built by the patient flow, i.e., the space/landscape created by movements of these individuals belonging to the same society. In this meta-national, partly virtual[20] and deterritorialized space, patients and families can reproduce everyday practices from Oman – this is facilitated, for example, by the presence of Arabic translators in Indian or Thai private hospitals. These facilitative measures are also visible in Oman: privately funded biomedical journeys are facilitated by private companies that run hospitals in Asia and have offices in Oman. Companies use these offices and their good reputation in Asia to attract foreign customers to their hospitals.[21]

Health care practices thus create connections between Oman and East Africa, India, China, South-East Asia and Europe. The study of these bonds leads to the same conclusion found in several of this volume's papers (see Wippel, Verne and Müller-Mahn, and Pradhan): MENA is not the only or most relevant analytic regional inscription for the Sultanate.

6.4 A "Biological Remnant of History"[22]: Perceptions of IBD's Distant Origins

Inherited disorders have long been described as group-specific diseases: sickle-cell anaemia was discovered in 1910 in a Black American patient (Herrick 1910) and thus considered to be confined to Black populations; thalassaemia was characterized

[20] For example, through the search for medical information on the Internet or the necessary e-mail exchanges with the medical team, prior to the journey.

[21] See for example the webpage of the Indian company Apollo, dedicated to "International patients", http://www.apollohospitals.com/international_patient_services.php (Accessed 7 August 2011). For an anthropological analysis of the hospitals' websites in the context of therapeutic journeys, see Sobo et al. (2011).

[22] I borrow this phrase from Jean Benoist (2004).

among Mediterranean populations (Whipple and Bradford 1932). Later, population genomics studies tackled these diseases. This field aims to trace human migrations since prehistoric times. Its main interest is not individuals themselves, but their gene pool and particularly the mutation processes occurring over centuries and the relationships between elements of this pool (Susanne et al. 2003: 365). From this angle, genes can be considered historical documents, since their analysis provides information about the individual's ancestors' migrations.

For this reason, the representations of inherited blood disorders have – worldwide – been deeply constructed in terms of ancestry and affected by a significant racialization process. This has led to lay perceptions of these diseases as "diseases of origins". About sickle-cell disease, for instance:

> [this disease], which – because of its hereditary character – was already the core of an "origins issue", gradually appeared as a "disease of origins". This happened not only on the conceptual level (notions of original root, geographical isolate, homogenous biological unit, population, origin group, etc.) but was also how patients viewed their own identity (Bonnet 2009: 13; my translation).

In the United States, for instance, sickle-cell anaemia has for long been considered a marker of African ancestry (see for instance Tapper 1999): until the 1970s, the disease was frequently called a "Black-related disease", "Negro blood" or "disease of Black people" in medical journals. In Europe, thalassaemia is mainly known as an Italian and Greek disease. This stigmatizing racialization process is partly based on a misunderstanding of the findings of population genomics: the appearance of the sickle-cell anaemia mutation in West Africa 3,000 years ago has certainly been documented for a long time, but this does not allow us to categorize the disease as African or any affected individual as African. Gene pool dispersion and human migrations patterns have contributed to draw a much more complex picture.

Nonetheless, in Oman as elsewhere, inherited blood disorders are often considered ancestry markers, a biological remnant of the country's history. Partial scientific information interacts with social representations of different ethnolinguistic groups present in Oman. Representations of these groups' roles are strongly shaped by representations of past Omani possessions in Africa, of slave trade, and of migrations from Asia to Oman. As a result, some people link the diseases with a supposed ethnic origin. For example:

> *My cousin is from Zanzibar, that's why she is sick [with sickle-cell anaemia]: abnormal blood comes from Africa* (Abdulrahman, sickle-cell anaemia patient, interview, May 2005).
>
> *For a long time, Omanis from Africa could not come back. Then they arrived and they brought sickle-cell genes* (an Omani doctor, interview, Nov. 2008).

These representations do not heed the scattering of the diseases in most of the groups of Omani society and all over the Sultanate's territory, or the fact that genes spreading within a population is a very slow process and can be observed only over several generations.

Mentioning these perceptions may appear trivial but is not, insofar as they take place within the Omani diversity system (Barth 1983: 83) that weaves the society in an entanglement of hierarchical categories (of self- and exogenous assignments). An individual's social status is a precise point that can be located within a multidimensional system, as the result of a subtle balancing process heeding several social categories (gender, tribe, intra-tribal status – that is noble, slave descent, etc. –, supposed "degree of Arabness", skin colour, place of birth, native language, financial status etc.). An eloquent example is the role of spatial mobility in this system, the symbolic advantage lying in an Omani place of birth for "back-from-Africa" Omanis (Valeri 2007: 486): many who lived in Zanzibar (the core of the former Omani maritime empire) consider themselves as "more" Omani than those who were born and raised on the Tanzanian coast.

Thus, the simplification process that links a disease with an origin – with the pattern: "sickle-cell anaemia=Africa" and "thalassaemia=Asia" – is theoretically incompatible with this multidimensional categorization. These diseases are scattered throughout all of Omani society. In everyday interactions, this distribution challenges the social classificatory competency of Omani people: it is difficult to think about the heredity lottery within the existing social categories of the classificatory web described above. Often, people cannot make head or tail of their observations: several patients, considering sickle-cell anaemia synonymous with African ancestry, could not explain the presence of the disease in their family and, at the same time, preserve the genealogic representations of the lineage. Because of the ancestry representations they carry, inherited blood disorders are a constant reminder of the Omani population's diverse origins, whereas the national identity crafted by the regime since 1970 does not include them. IBD cast a harsh light on the various groups formed by translocality in Oman's recent past: those "who stayed", those "who went away and married there", those "who returned", those "who could not come back" …

6.5 Conclusion

This paper emphasizes that health, and here specifically genetic health, not only consists of objective physical manifestations but is also shaped by (and shapes) social issues and events. More precisely, whether one considers patients' routine mobility; transcultural therapeutic relationships; health journeys (and a multitude of failed attempts), or other things, health helps shape relationships of individuals to their own country's territory as well as their representations and uses of distant territories. Health – and especially chronic disorders – is as such a translocal issue, contributing to create social and political spaces.

The anthropological study of inherited blood disorders in Oman intertwines key aspects of the Sultanate's society. Some have been dealt with in this paper: state policies and their impact on everyday life (health care infrastructure's spatial organization); ancient political and religious dissensions between the coast and the interior (that lead to a social "genography"); importance of foreign workers in vital sectors (place of non-Omani healthcare practitioners); regional synergism with other

GCC members (common concern about IBD and screening policies); ancient trade connections with Asia (that also take shape in the flows of patients seeking treatment in India); the deep inscription of the country's past migration and colonial history in contemporary social life (remnants of this history in the perceptions of IBD).

Acknowledgments I want to express my gratitude to patients, families and health practitioners, who trusted me and let me settle in their everyday life, in hospitals or at home, in Muscat and elsewhere.

References

Appadurai, A. (2005 [1996]). *Après le colonialisme* (Petite Bibliothèque). Paris: Payot & Rivages.

Barth, F. (1983). *Sohar: Culture and society in an Omani town*. Baltimore/London: John Hopkins University Press.

Beaudevin, C. (2010). *Faqr al-dam, "l'indigence du sang", comme héritage. Représentations et enjeux sociaux des hémoglobinopathies héréditaires au sultanat d'Oman* [Faqr al-dam (indigence of the blood) as inheritance. Representations and social stakes of hereditary haemoglobinopathies in the Sultanate of Oman]. Ph.D. thesis in Social Anthropology, Université Paul Cézanne – Aix-Marseille III, Aix-en-Provence (France).

Benoist, J. (2004). A propos de: Agnès Lainé (Ed.), La drépanocytose. Regards croisés sur une maladie orpheline. *Bulletin Amades*, 58. http://amades.revues.org/index584.html. Accessed 8 Aug 2011.

Bonnet, D. (2009). *Repenser l'hérédité*. Paris: Editions des archives contemporaines.

Bonte, P. (Ed.). (1994). *Epouser au plus proche. Inceste, prohibitions et stratégies matrimoniales autour de la Méditerranée*. Paris: Editions de l'EHESS.

Bonte, P. (2007). Le choix du conjoint dans les sociétés musulmanes maghrébines contemporaines. Evolutions sociales et réformes juridiques. *Anthropology of the Middle East, 2*(1), 1–19.

El-Gayar, S., Ganesh, A., et al. (2009). Molecular analysis of CYP1B1 in Omani patients with primary congenital glaucoma: A pilot study. *Molecular Vision, 8*(15), 1325–1331.

El-Mouzan, M. I., Al-Salloum, A. A., et al. (2007). Regional variations in the prevalence of consanguinity in Saudi Arabia. *Saudi Medical Journal, 28*(12), 1881–1884.

Fortun, M. (2008). *Promising genomics. Iceland and deCODE genetics in a world of speculation*. Berkeley: University of California Press.

Herrick, J. B. (1910). Peculiar elongated and sickle-shaped red blood corpuscles in a case of severe anemia. *Archives of Internal Medicine, 6*, 517–521.

Khlat, M. (1989). *Les Mariages consanguins à Beyrouth. Traditions matrimoniales et santé publiques*. Paris: PUF/Institut National d'Etudes Démographiques.

Mégarbané, A. (2003). *Projets Nord-Sud en génétique: coopération ou colonialisme scientifique?* L'Observatoire de la Génétique, 9(janvier-février). http://www.omics-ethics.org/observatoire/cadrages/cadr2003/c_no9_03/c_no9_03_1.html. Accessed 8 Aug 2011.

Ministry of Health. (1972). *A report of the Ministry of Health –August 1970 to November 1972*. Muscat: Ministry of Health.

Ministry of Health. (2008). *Annual health report 2007*. Muscat: Department of Health Information and Statistics, Directorate General of Planning.

Ministry of Health. (2010). *Annual health report 2009*. Muscat: Department of Health Information and Statistics, Directorate General of Planning.

Muslim, N. (2006, February 21). Arabs have highest rate of genetic disorders. *Gulf News*. http://gulfnews.com/news/gulf/uae/health/arabs-have-highest-rate-of-genetic-disorders-1.226021. Accessed 8 May 2013.

Naraindas, H., & Bastos, C. (2011). Healing holidays? Itinerant patients, therapeutic locales and the quest for health. *Anthropology & Medicine, 18*(1).

Percot, M. (2006). Indian nurses in the Gulf: Two generations of female migration. *South Asia Research, 26*(1), 41–62.

Pordié, L. (2013). Spaces of connectivity, shifting temporality. Enquiries in transnational health. *European Journal of Transnational Studies 5*(1).

Rajab, A., & Patton, M. A. (1999). Development and use of a national haemoglobinopathy register in Oman. *Community Genetics, 2*(1), 47–48.

Rajab, A., & Patton, M. A. (2000). A study of consanguinity in the Sultanate of Oman. *Annals of Human Biology, 27*(3), 321–326.

Rajab, A., Patton, M. A., & Modell, B. (1999). Analysis of the population structure in Oman. *Community Genetics, 2*(1), 23–25.

Reardon, W., & Donnai, D. (2007). Dysmorphology demystified. *Archives of Disease in Childhood. Fetal and Neonatal Edition, 92*, 225–229.

Roberts, E. F. S., & Scheper-Hughes, N. (2011a). Introduction: Medical migrations. *Body & Society, 17*(2 & 3), 1–30.

Roberts, E. F. S., & Scheper-Hughes, N. (Eds.). (2011b). Medical Migrations. *Body & Society, 17*(2–3).

Smith-Morris, C., & Manderson, L. (2010). Medical travel. *Medical Anthropology, 29*(4).

Sobo, E. J., Herlihy, E., & Bicker, M. (2011). Selling medical travel to US patient-consumers: The cultural appeal of website marketing messages. *Anthropology & Medicine, 18*(1), 119–136.

Susanne, C., Rebato, E., & Chiarelli, B. (Eds.). (2003). *Anthropologie biologique. Evolution et biologie humaine*. Brussels: De Boeck.

Tapper, M. (1999). *In the blood. Sickle cell anemia and the politics of race (critical histories)*. Philadelphia: University of Pennsylvania Press.

Turing, P. (1980, May 9). Striking success in control of disease. *The Times*, p. v.

Valeri, M. (2007). Nation-building and communities in Oman since 1970: The Swahili-speaking Omani in search of identity. *African Affairs, 106*(424), 479–496.

Valeri, M. (2009). *Oman. Politics and society in the Qaboos state*. London/New York: Hurst/Columbia University Press.

Whipple, G. H., & Bradford, W. L. (1932). Racial or familial anemia of children: Associated with fundamental disturbances of bone and pigment metabolism. *The American Journal of the Medical Sciences, 44*, 336–365.

World Health Organization. (1978). *Declaration of Alma-Ata*. Adopted at the International Conference on Primary Health Care, Alma-Ata, USSR, 6–12 Sept 1978.

Chapter 7
Oman-India Relations: Exploring the Long-Term Migration Dynamics

Samir Pradhan

7.1 Introduction

For centuries, the Gulf region[1] was a major point on the sea routes between the Fertile Crescent[2] and India, a centre for the international pearl trade and at various times an entrepot for regional trade between the Crescent and the old Silk Road. Indian presence in the Gulf region predates that period as far as the third millennium BC, when trade and travel flourished between the erstwhile Indian kingdoms and the Arab world. Archaeological evidence from the great Indus Valley civilization period confirms the movement of peoples between the regions. The historical legacies of international trade between the two regions points to barter exchanges of textiles and spices for dates, pearls and semiprecious stones. Importantly, during this period, the Indian business community, especially wealthy individual merchants, set up their base in the region. The major thrust came after the discovery of oil in the region and the consequent economic development of the desert economies, propelling imports of goods, services and manpower from the neighbouring Asian region. As huge chunks of people from India migrated to the Gulf in their quest for

[1]For analytical convenience, "Gulf region" refers to the geopolitical entity comprising member states of the Gulf Cooperation Council, namely Bahrain, Kuwait, Oman, Qatar, Saudi Arabia and the United Arab Emirates (UAE). Reference to other neighbouring countries, namely Iraq, Iran and Yemen, has also been made when required.

[2]James Henry Breasted, a University of Chicago archaeologist, coined the term "Fertile Crescent" around 1900, referring to a crescent-shaped region in the Middle East, originally incorporating the Levant and Ancient Mesopotamia and extending to ancient Egypt. The region is referred to as the "Cradle of Civilization" due to its rich soil and is also believed to be the original location of the Garden of Eden in the Bible because of its fertility. For details, see Columbia University Press (2008).

S. Pradhan, Ph.D. (✉)
UAE based Economic Researcher, Macroeconomics Research,
Tanween, PO Box 33175, Doha, Qatar
e-mail: pradhan.samir75@gmail.com; sampradel06@gmail.com

S. Wippel (ed.), *Regionalizing Oman: Political, Economic and Social Dynamics*, United Nations University Series on Regionalism 6, DOI 10.1007/978-94-007-6821-5_7,

wealth and prosperity, so did the business communities in their effort to serve these expatriate consumers as well as the wealthy import-dependent Arabs. The succeeding periods witnessed phenomenal labour migration from the heavily populated subcontinent as the oil-fuelled development process in the Gulf gathered momentum. Simultaneously, individual business houses from the subcontinent started to expand their base by entering into partnerships with Gulf business communities. And the legacy continued, although the pattern of economic engagement has transformed considerably over the years. In essence, the Indian community has played a pivotal role in the transformation of the Gulf economic scenario from primeval commercial exchanges to high-tech-based corporate practices and innovative consumer services.

Against such a backdrop, the major objective of this chapter is to explore Oman-India migration dynamics and to map the socio-cultural and economic interaction between the Omani and Indian migrants from the pre-oil era to recent times. This chapter thereby touches upon the factors by which migration influences the process of regionalisation. The remaining part of the chapter consists of four sections: Sect. 7.2 gives a brief historical account of the evolution of Indian migration to Oman primarily facilitated through commercial exchanges and Indian business communities' settlement. Section 7.3 deals with the current trends and patterns of Indian migration to Oman, starting from the oil era and moving to the post-oil era. Section 7.4 describes the level and pattern of engagement between Omani and Indian migrants and their perceptions of each other and the prevailing policy paradigm. The last section summarizes and concludes the chapter.[3]

7.2 Evolution and History: Indian Merchants in Oman

Oman's tryst with India probably began very early in the commercial history of the Indian Ocean when maritime trade was conducted between Sumer and the Harappan civilization of the Indus valley (Allen and Calvin 1981; Thapar 1975). Some archaeologists believe that Magan, the source of copper for this ancient trade, was located somewhere in Oman, and this argument is supported by the numerous ancient copper-mining sites that have been discovered in the Hajar Mountains behind Sohar. While it is probably safe to assume that Indian merchants called on the coastal ports of Oman, it is impossible to determine when the first Indian merchant decided to establish a semi-permanent presence in Muscat or anywhere else on the Batina coast. However, evidence points to Indian settlement occurring no later than the fifteenth century. S. B. Miles reported the ruins of a Hindu temple at Qalhat (Miles 1966, as cited by Allen and Calvin 1981), the principal Omani port of the

[3]This revised version of the chapter was originally presented at the International Workshop on "Regionalizing Oman – Political, Economic and Social Dynamics", Institute of Oriental Studies, Leipzig University, Germany, 25–26 March 2010. The author would like to thank Steffen Wippel for his insightful comments and suggestions. The usual disclaimer applies.

fifteenth century. The argument for fifteenth-century settlement is supported further by de Albuquerque's report that Hindu merchants from Gujarat escaped from Khor Fakkan, a secondary port on the Shimiliya coast of northern Oman, before he sacked that town in 1507 (Walter de Gray Birch 1875, as cited by Allen and Calvin 1981).

Moreover, the period of Portuguese domination of the Indian Ocean reveals extensive information on Indian commercial activities in Oman and Muscat. It is reported that the Portuguese relied heavily on Indian Hindus in their attempts to secure a monopoly of the Indian Ocean/Arabian Gulf trade (Pearson 1973). In the seventeenth century, when the Portuguese lost Hormuz, Muscat became the headquarters of their Arabian Gulf operation and played an important role in their commercial policy.

During this period, Oman's most important trading destination was the Indian city of Thattha, located on the Indus River in Sindh province of present Pakistan. Thattha was an important trade centre between the Indian Ocean and Central Asia before the Portuguese sack of the city in the sixteenth century. During the period of Portuguese control of its trade, Thattha continued to be an active commercial centre, boasting 40,000 weavers of calico and loongees and artisans of every other class and 20,000 bankers, money changers, shopkeepers and sellers of grain (Allen and Calvin 1981). Thattha's main export items were cloth, including elegantly embroidered cashmere shawls, silk and cotton yarn, as well as opium, ghee, indigo and sugar. Thattha's commerce in these goods with Africa and the Gulf was so voluminous that the British believed that the Portuguese position in Muscat was entirely dependent on the customs duties they collected as a result of their policy of forcing all Africa- and Gulf-bound shipping to call at Muscat for licensing (Allen and Calvin 1981).

Hindu merchants were the primary facilitators of the robust trade between Muscat and Thattha by means of Portuguese ships and established warehouses and trading establishments at Muscat. As Allen and Calvin (1981: 36) has described, "Oral traditions of the Indian merchant community in Muscat allege that these Sindhis were the first 'Baniyas' to settle in Muscat and they were Bhattias (Bhattiya)."[4] Under the patronage of the Portuguese rulers of Muscat, the Sindhi Bhattiyas not only expanded their business pursuits, but also increasingly became active politically. As reported by Omani chroniclers Ibn Ruzayq and Al-Salimi, "a Baniya worshipper of the cow, named Narottam, acted as supply agent for the Portuguese garrison at Muscat, and the Portuguese commander seems to have accepted advice freely from his agent. However, the Baniya eventually became dissatisfied with the Portuguese, especially as the commander wished to marry his daughter, and helped the Ya'ariba rulers of Oman expel the Europeans from Muscat in 1650…." (Peterson 2004: 69).

[4]Bania is an occupational caste of bankers, moneylenders, dealers in grains and spices and in modern times, people involved in numerous commercial enterprises. Baniya is a distinct caste mostly coming from Western India and Central India but spread now all over India. Bhatia is a group of people and a caste originating from Sindh Province and Rajasthan, who are also merchants and traders.

Nevertheless, the strategic alliance with the Ya'ariba rulers fetched rich dividends to the Baniyas, as the community was exempted from paying the poll tax (jizya) and permission was granted for the construction of Hindu temple. It is noteworthy that the Sindhi Bhattiyas founded their temple in Muscat with the idol of the deity Govindraj transported from Basra, where Hindus were having problems. Moreover, as a mark of their obeisance to the Omani rulers and to demonstrate their strong ties to their adopted homeland, the Bhattias put an Omani dagger in their vestments.

Importantly, the civil war in the 1740s, which saw the establishment of the Al Bu Sa'id dynasty, did not affect the Hindu business community adversely and in fact the community continued to prosper and pursue their religious activities prominently under the patronage of the ruler Ahmad Bu Sa'id (1743–1782). This period also witnessed the establishment of three more Hindu temples. This is substantiated by the description of the Baniya community by Danish explorer Carsten Niebuhr during his fortnight visit to Muscat in January 1765. He remarked,

> In no other Mahomedan city are the Banians so numerous as in Maskat; their number in this city amounts to no fewer than twelve hundred. They are permitted to live agreeably to their own laws, to bring their wives hither, to set up idols in their chambers, and to burn their dead (Allen and Calvin 1981: 42).

The Dutch merchant Engelbert Kaempfer, visiting Muscat in 1688, also acknowledged the presence of Hindu Baniyas, as did the Italian physician Vincenzo Maurizi in the early nineteenth century, who put the number of Indian merchants at 4,000. The Indian Navy officer J.R. Wellsted, visiting Muscat in the 1830s, estimated the number of Baniyas in Muscat to be 1,500; he said they nearly monopolized the pearl trade in the Arabian Gulf and were prominent in the supply of grain from India and Indian cloth and piece-goods (Wellsted 1837). Thus by all accounts, it is certain that the Hindu community of Muscat and Oman, which consisted largely of principal merchants, dominated commercial life and had replaced the Al Bu Sa'id rulers of the town as the paramount economic power in Oman (Allen and Calvin 1981; Wellsted 1837).

Despite the initial success of the Sindhi Bhattias, the community faced severe adversities and ultimate demise during the period 1785 and 1820. This resulted in a massive exodus of Sindhis from Muscat. As outlined by Allen, three interrelated factors were the primary cause for this, namely; the economic collapse of Thattah, the shift in the commercial practices and policies of the rulers of Muscat, and the arrival of Kutchi Bhattias[5] in Muscat, which is relevant to the analytical scope of this chapter.

The growth of Kutchi Bhattiya's settlements and rapid domination of Muscat's commercial landscape is owed to the peculiar geographical location of Kutch and to the Kutchi ruler Godji II (1760–78), who was extremely active in the development

[5] They are named after their place of origin, Kutch, which lies to the east of the mouth of the Indus River, an area that is in many ways very similar to Oman in that it is an arid, rugged country that is virtually cut off from the rest of India by the sometimes impassable Rann of Kutch.

of Mandvi's[6] shipbuilding industry and also who is credited for Kutch's commercial expansion in the Arabian Gulf in the late eighteenth century. The Kutchis had every advantage over the Sindhis; as noted by Allen and Calvin (1981: 46),

> they were not in competition with the sayyids of Muscat as the Kutchis served largely as shippers rather than middle-men. Kutchi merchants transported the few products of Kutch, predominantly cotton yarn and piece goods, as well as goods from Bombay and the Gujarati ports, to Muscat where they could be sold to the sayyid or his agents. By contrast, the Sindhis had their business establishments in Muscat, and while they could have sold to the sayyid, Sindhi overheads and, consequently, prices were higher. A second Kutchi advantage was that they had a market for a wide range of the products that Muscat had to offer due to their secure trading network in India.

Soon, Kutchi Bhattiyas replaced Sindhi Bhattiyas and increased their commercial profile in Muscat to the point that they overwhelmingly dominated the commercial and economic affairs of the port after the ruler Sayyid Sa'id transferred his residence to Zanzibar after 1830. Even during Said's residence in Muscat, though the Kutchis did not establish an extended presence in the port, they established temporary commercial establishments in Muscat and few Kutchi Bhattiyas rose to prominence in the services of the entrepreneurial ruler. In this regard, the cases of two prominent Indian migrant Kutchi Bhattiyas are worth mentioning. One of them is the family business of Virji Purshottam Toprani, who still owns business establishments in Oman and whose contact with Oman is seven generations old and goes back to the days of his family patriarch Aranji Toprani, who sailed to Muscat from Mandvi in the late eighteenth century. The other illustrious example is that of the Gopal Mawji Bhimani family, whose grandfather was the first family member to trade in Muscat in the late eighteenth century. It has also been contended that Gopal Bhimani, apart from extending his business ventures, was also active in Muscat's politics: "Gopal was among the Baniyas who encouraged Sa'id ibn Sultan to conquer Zanzibar, and his business manager was active in the suppression of piracy" (Allen and Calvin 1981: 43). By 1840, the Kutchi Bhattiyas filled the commercial vacuum in Muscat, and the community population rose to 20,045 and became the principal economic power in Muscat. Even the death of Sa'id ibn Sultan in 1856 and the consequent rule of his son Thuwayni ibn Sa'id (1856–68) was never detrimental to the business interests of the Kutchis. As Thuwayni carried out his father's policy of abandoning lucrative trade in favour of gaining greater political influence and control in Oman, the Kutchis had to face no state competition. As a result, their business empire flourished while that of the rulers floundered in the succeeding period.

However, the major blow came to the otherwise bright economic future of the Kutchis with the internal political rumblings in Oman that saw the revivalist Ibadi

[6] Mandvi is also known as Musca-Mandvi after the neighbouring village of Musca. This name is very intriguing, since the Arabic chronicles often refer to Muscat as Muska. Allen Jr. visited Musca in May 1977 in search of information on the origin of the name of the town but met with little success. He further speculated that this village is probably named after Muscat, just as Mandvi's newest suburb, Swalli, is named after the Swahili coast.

movement spearheaded by Imam ‘Azzan ibn Qays changing the overall power equation. The new conservative government led by Imam ‘Azzan not only removed the Bhattias from their important financial posts, but also sought to extend Ibadi social regulations, including a ban on the use of tobacco and the playing of musical instruments and the imposition of dress requirements, to all the inhabitants of Muscat. Despite Imam Azzan's assurances of religious tolerance, there were numerous attacks on Baniyas due to their religious practices and ceremonies using bells, gongs and drums, which were perceived as being antithetical to the culture of the rulers. Consequently, the Indians began an exodus from Muscat, and the community dwindled to a mere 750 by 1870 (Allen and Calvin 1981).

Despite the exodus of families from Muscat and Oman, a number of prominent business family still survived there and also grew in importance during the moderate regime of Turki ibn Sa‘id (1871–88), which saw the emergence of a whole new group of young Kutchi Bhattias as the commercial leaders of Muscat. Prominent among them was Sheth Ratansi Purshottam Purecha, who came to dominate the trade and finances of the port after 1871. Ratansi played an important role in this expanded trade, as a leading arms merchant dealing with the London firm Schwarte and Hammer and the Hamburg arms dealer Moritz Magnus and active in exporting dates to the United States through the New York firm of William Hills. Upon this base, a number of other Banians established prosperous businesses that have continued to flourish in Muscat. These include Khimji Ramdas, Dayal Purshottam, Danji Murarji, Vallabdas Umarsi and Gopalji Walji.

There were also two other small communities of Indian origin, traditionally living together in the Kumbhar quarter of Matrah, just outside the town's walls. The name of the quarter apparently derived from the Indian caste of Kumbhars, traditionally potters in India, although the Kumbhar quarter in Matrah was well known for bread-baking. The quarter was also inhabited by Sonabara, apparently originating from the Indian caste of Sonis who were gold- and silversmiths. The Sonabara continue to specialize as goldsmiths, and in recent times many have taken the name al-Sayigh (Arabic for jeweller) as their family name. Although both communities appear to be Hindu in origin, they are Muslim today (Peterson 2004).

Another important group of Indians lived within the domains of the sultan, the Khwajas (Khojas). Very little is known about the Khwaja community of Oman, which goes by the name Lutti, and virtually nothing has been written about it. The Luwatiyya claim origins in Hyderabad, Sindh and are therefore occasionally given the nickname Hyderabadi.[7] The pattern of Lutti settlement in Oman was very similar to that of the Kutchi Bhattias. The earliest Luttis came in the wake of the establishment of the Al Bu Sa‘id state in Muscat in 1785. The disruptions of ‘Azzan ibn Qays' reign may have had the same impact on the Lutti commercial community as it had on the Bhattias. Following the re-establishment of moderate Al Bu Sa‘id rule in 1871, a new group of Luwatiyya came to Oman and came to dominate the community. The Luwatiyya operated within the same kind of mercantile system that the

[7] They were predominantly Sunni Muslims.

Baniyas utilized, and there were Khwajas in most of the Gulf ports, Bombay, Karachi, Zanzibar and Mombasa. Besides dealing in the standard products, like textiles, grain and dates, the Khwajas also had a virtual monopoly of the trade in dried fish from Muscat, as this was a product in which the Hindu merchants, for religious reasons, would not deal. Khwajas were also involved in various skilled crafts, like carpentry and boat building. Unlike the Baniyas, the Luwatiyya chose to make Matrah their home, and the community was concentrated in a cluster known as Sur Luwatiyya, adjoining the market. The Sur was off limits to non-Luwatiyya and was strictly residential. Despite their permanent settlement in Matrah, the Luwatiyya remained segregated from their Arab neighbours. Although Lutti men would occasionally take Omani women for brides, Lutti women always married within the community. Khwajki, a mixture of Sindhi and Kutchi, was the principal language spoken within the household, but Arabic was fairly widely used. The community had an elected Shaykh and council of elders that governed communal affairs. Worship took place in a Jama'at khana located within the walls of the Sur.

It is important to note that despite economic competition, the Baniyas of Muscat retained a fairly high degree of community solidarity. The community was represented in political matters by the nagar seth or mukhia, the most respected man in the community. During the later nineteenth century, a Bhimani held this office.[8] The Hindus celebrated their religious festivals, such as New Year (Diwali), with social gatherings and dinner parties. Usually a dish of the best food would be taken to the Sultan. Baniyas were also invited to the palace on special occasions, although they would not eat the food prepared by the ruler's non-Hindu cooks. For the most part, dietary laws were kept, and the community maintained a herd of cows to ensure a steady supply of dairy products. Kutchi or Gujarati remained the principal language spoken within the community, although most did learn Arabic for business purposes, and accounts were kept in Gujarati. Indian dress styles were maintained.

In general, the Muscat Hindus made no attempt to assimilate, whereas the Khojas and Baluchis were made Omani citizens – diluted Omanis, as they came to be called in later years. Moreover, in modern times, the Khojas or Lawatiyya have played only a limited role in politics, largely because of their concentration on commerce and because many other Omanis sometimes regard them as "foreigners". As outlined,

> by virtue of education, worldview, and experience, Lawatiyya undoubtedly should have been well represented in Oman's early cabinets of the 1970s and 1980s. But, although Lawatis are widespread throughout the government at most levels, Lawatis became ministers only in the 1990s, when a son of Hajji 'Ali Sultan, Maqbul, was appointed Minister of Commerce and Industry in 1993 and Muhammad Musa al-Yusuf received the new portfolio of Minister of State for Development Affairs in 1994 (although he had enjoyed ministerial rank as Secretary-General since 1989). Reflective of the community's relatively liberal outlook, Oman's first female under-secretary, Rajihah 'Abd al-Amir, and first female ambassador, Khadijah Hasan al-Lawati, were Lawati women. Still, perceptions of the Lawatiyah by other Omanis may be negatively impacted by the wealth of successful Lawati merchant families, the corruption of a few prominent Lawatis, and sectarian differences (Peterson 2004: 28).

[8] Bhimanis were Hindu trading families.

Thus, over the course of the nineteenth century, Indian merchants came to dominate the economic life of Muscat, replacing the Al Bu Sa'id rulers as the principal merchants of the city and acquiring fortunes that had once gone to the royal family. An important contribution of the Indian merchant group of the late nineteenth century was its "internationalization" of the trade of Muscat. That is to say that trade expanded beyond the confines of the Indian Ocean basin. The Indian merchants showed great adaptability in this area. European steamers were rapidly replacing Arab and Indian sailing ships, and the Indian merchants were able to import new products from Europe and America for their traditional markets and to export traditional goods to new markets overseas.

7.3 Indian Migration During the Oil and Post-oil Era

Before 1970, Oman was an isolated country despite its vibrant trading links and the presence of British and Indians in the supply chain. The Sultan prohibited Omanis from leaving the country without his permission and forbade them to wear Western clothes, though many defied and slipped out to live in exile. Movement within the country and in the capital itself was strictly restricted. The gates to the walled town of Muscat were closed 3 h before sunset. Apprehensive of a possible coup by other Arabs, the Sultan encouraged Indian merchants to build their homes and business establishments in the vicinity of the palace. The Sultan also recruited soldiers from Baluchistan for his armed forces and continuously sought advice from the Government of India. It was reported that a number of Indian officials were deputed to the police and the public works departments in Oman (Weiner 1982).

However, oil development in 1967 and the change of government in 1970[9] witnessed radical changes in the modernization of Oman with the process of economic development gaining momentum. Oil revenues were invested in the development of physical infrastructure including roads, ports, highways and office buildings and also in the development of industries such as fishing, refrigeration and processing, cement, petrochemicals, oil refining, a glass factory, steel rolling mills, copper plants etc. Since educated Omanis had already left the country and settled in neighbouring Gulf countries where they had good, well-paying jobs and since the educational system was underdeveloped, the demand for foreign labour increased with the pace and scale of economic development. In the early 1970s, an influx of migrant workers began, mainly from India and Pakistan. According to the Oman Labour department, by 1975, there were 70,000 foreign workers in Oman as against 99,000 nationals in the labour force. It is also reported that nearly 38,000 Omanis were employed overseas at that time (Weiner 1982). Since many of the Omanis are

[9] In 1970, the Sultan, Sa'id ibn Taymur, was overthrown by his son, Sultan Qabus ibn Sa'id Al Bu Sa'id with the help of the British.

traditionally engaged in agriculture and fishing, it is quite obvious that the urban labour force consisted overwhelmingly of foreigners. As a result, Omani society became the most culturally heterogeneous in the Gulf region, with a diverse mix of its local Ibadi Muslim population, a Baluchi community, an African population made up of descendants of former slaves, Shi‘is from Iran, two Sunni Arab tribal groups in the province of Dhofar, Arabs who returned from Zanzibar where they formed the ruling class, Hyderabadi and Kutchi merchants from Pakistan and India and skilled and semi-skilled workers from India and Pakistan.

In 1979, the Indian Embassy estimated that there were about 60,000 Indians in Oman. The majority were from Kerala and the remainder from Goa, Gujarat and the Punjab. At that time one Indian was technical adviser to the Sultan with managerial responsibilities for his private properties. The Sultan's palace itself was built by an Indian construction company that had its office in Oman till the 1990s. Indians were also employed in the government sector, especially in police service. During this period, the Indian business community was also active in Oman. The Sultan made a few exceptions in favour of a handful of Indian businessmen, who enjoyed the privilege of permission to own their own business without any local partner, which was rare at that time in the region.

It is a fact that the Indian merchants and migrants were structurally entrenched within the local economy and there were a strong nexus and mutually vested interests that facilitated the continuous flow of Indian migrants to Oman. In this regard, it is apt to highlight a case of a labour dispute involving Indian construction workers and a Cypriot-owned construction company in Oman (Weiner 1982). Under Omani law, an employer had to provide a minimum wage of 3.6 riyals daily, plus accommodation and food to the workers. However, this large construction company paid the Indians only 2 riyals, provided them with tents rather than wooden barracks for accommodation, had inadequate medical facilities, paid steamship rather than air transport to India and also concluded annual contracts instead of the mandatory 3-year contract. As a result, there was large-scale discontent among the workers. Despite warnings from government authorities, the company managed to call in the police and deported some of the workers to India. Other workers protested with the Indian mission, which informed the Omani government. The workers finally retreated when Omani police arrested 2,000 workers and deported 200 workers with Indian government intervention. There was a backlash in India and the Government of India (GoI) halted the emigration of all workers to Oman in February 1978. The Omani government, under pressure from business houses, requested that India lift the ban. In the state of Kerala, there was also a clamour to end it. Finally, in July 1978, the GoI lifted the ban, but refused to allow the workers to emigrate for employment with the offending company. Nevertheless, Oman remained an attractive destination for Indian workers (especially unskilled workers) in comparison with other Gulf countries, even though the workers get lower salaries in Oman than their counterparts in other Gulf states. In recent years, the number of unskilled workers migrating from India to Oman has increased, despite the current undergoing Omanisation policies in the labour market (see Table 7.1).

Table 7.1 Unskilled Indian emigrants to the Gulf and world

Country	2003	2004	2005	2006	2007
United Arab Emirates	143,804	175,262	194,412	254,774	312,695
Saudi Arabia	121,431	123,522	99,879	134,059	195,437
Qatar	14,251	16,325	50,222	76,324	88,483
Oman	36,816	33,275	40,931	67,992	95,462
Kuwait	54,434	52,064	39,124	47,449	48,467
Bahrain	24,778	22,980	30,060	37,688	29,966
GCC	395,514	423,428	454,628	618,286	770,510
Rest of the world	466,456	474,960	548,853	676,912	809,453

Source: Rajamony (2008)

Note: Figures include only Indians who have not completed school education and who obtained clearance from the Protector of Emigrants in India. Educated persons, those who travel on visit visas to seek employment etc. are not included in these figures

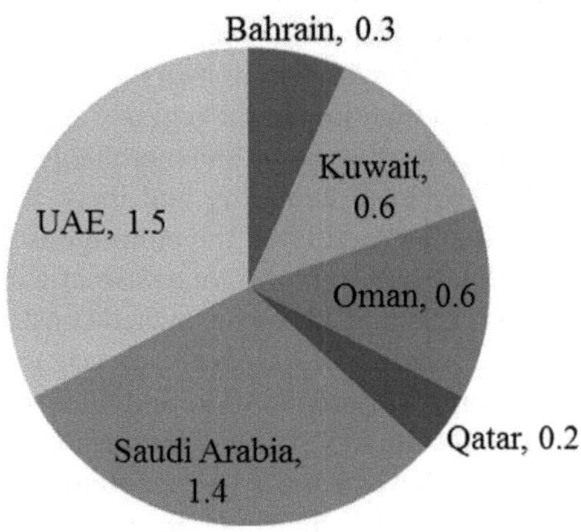

Fig. 7.1 Indian migrants in the GCC (Source: Indian Embassies in the GCC 2009)

Currently, nearly 4.6 million Indians live in the GCC countries, making them the largest expatriate community (Fig. 7.1).[10] The majority of the Indian population in the GCC is from the southern Indian States, including Andhra Pradesh, Tamil Nadu and Kerala. The rest come from Gujarat, Maharashtra, Goa, Punjab, Uttar Pradesh, Bihar and Rajasthan. The Indian expatriate community can be categorized into four broad groups, viz., (a) unskilled workers, employed in construction companies, municipalities, agricultural farms and as domestic workers; (b) skilled and semi-skilled workers; (c) professionals, such as doctors, engineers, accountants, employed in government and the private sector; and (d) businessmen.

There are around 0.6 million Indians[11] in Oman, constituting the largest expatriate community in the country. In 2008, Indians constituted 59 % of total expatriate

[10] In the absence of concrete data, figures pertaining to the number of Indians living in the GCC are estimates. However, Oman is an exception – data on Indians and other expatriates are available from the Ministry of Economy Annual Statistical Yearbook.

[11] However, no data is available on Indians who lack valid work permits.

Table 7.2 Expatriates in the Omani private sector by nationality

Year	2006		2007		2008	
Nationality	Number	Share (%)	Number	Share (%)	Number	Share (%)
Indians	307,877	60	395,657	62	466,188	59
Bangladeshis	64,726	13	77,936	12	125,325	16
Pakistanis	53,108	10	80,867	13	106,038	13
Sri Lankans	10,884	2	7,826	1	9,281	1
Filipinos	16,842	3	12,735	2	15,734	2
Egyptians	6,971	1	9,153	1	10,843	1
Other nationalities	50,305	10	54,273	9	61,526	8
Total	510,713	100	638,447	100	794,935	100

Source: Sultanate of Oman (2009)

Table 7.3 Expatriate civil service employees in Oman Ministries and Government Organizations by nationality

Year	2006		2007		2008	
Nationality	Number	Share (%)	Number	Share (%)	Number	Share (%)
Indians	5,884	38	5,659	38	5,532	39
Pakistanis	303	2	338	2	399	3
Other GCC	37	0	40	0	40	0
Egyptians	5,784	37	5,752	39	5,336	38
Jordanians	647	4	463	3	396	3
Sudanese	1,040	7	815	6	672	5
Other Arab	1,196	8	1,076	7	1,135	8
Other nationalities	597	4	585	4	553	4
Total	15,488	100	14,728	100	14,063	100

Source: Sultanate of Oman (2009)

workers in the Omani private sector and 39 % of all expatriate workers in the Omani government sector (see Tables 7.2 and 7.3). Coming from all parts of India, they include skilled workers and technicians, as well as professionals such as doctors, engineers, bankers, finance experts, managers etc., many holding middle and senior management positions in the corporate sector. Several Indians also hold responsible positions in Omani government departments and public undertakings: there are around 2,000 Indian doctors working in the country. The contribution of Indians to the development of Oman, particularly in the fields of commerce, healthcare, education, horticulture, finance, construction and communication is widely acknowledged. A number of Persons of Indian Origin (PIOs) have been granted Omani nationality, some of them receiving high awards of the Omani government. Mr. Kanaksi Khimji and Mr. P Mohammed Ali, both prominent members of the Indian community in Oman, received the Pravasi Bharatiya Samman Puraskar, the highest award conferred on overseas Indians, in January 2003 and January 2004 respectively. There are 15 Indian schools in the Sultanate. All schools follow the CBSE (Central Board of Secondary Education) pattern.

7.4 Omani Nationals and Indian Expatriates: The Level and Pattern of Engagement

As already described comprehensively above, in the pre-oil era, relations between the locals and Indian expatriates were purely economic, although sometimes political and largely mutually beneficial, and were very close due to the prevailing conditions in the Sultanate. The situation changed in the early part of the oil era with the new government and the large-scale migration of Indian skilled and semi-skilled workers. In the absence of any concrete evidence, it can be contended that the semi-skilled and skilled Indians always maintained good relations with the local Omanis in the economic domain and maintained their exclusivity. In 1974, the Sultan gave land to the Indian community to enable it to build a social centre. There were also number of Indian schools, Christian churches, several Hindu temples and gurudwara for the Sikh community. As rightly observed,

> Social life in Oman remains highly segmented. The Indian middle class has some social contract with English speaking other expatriates, but almost no social contract with the native Omanis (Weiner 1982: 72).

However, with changes in the economic dynamics and labour sector in Oman, the interaction between the locals and Indian expatriates has transformed considerably in the last decade. Before analysing the current phase of engagement, it is apt to delineate a contextual background of and a theoretical perspective for the issue.

7.4.1 Reliance on Foreign Labour: A Growing Concern and Dilemma

Over the last two decades, the growth in the number of foreign workers consistently outpaced the growth of the national workforce in Oman and other GCC countries. Unlike the oil era, when potential job creation through the expansion of public sector employment temporarily enhanced welfare by acting as a semi-automatic stabilizer, it soon became apparent that such a policy could not be sustained forever. For one thing, such a policy resulted in a misallocation of resources by diverting potential investment funds into public consumption (UNESCWA 2004). Second, with falling oil prices and consequently subdued growth accompanied by mounting fiscal pressures in the 1990s, the public sector was no longer in a position to create adequate jobs to absorb the new entrants into the labour market. Ultimately, this led to a rise in national unemployment rates. Though concrete data on employment is still difficult to source and collate, a few observations can be made from currently available information (Winckler 2002). The unemployment rate among nationals was 11.9 % in Oman (as per the December 1993 population census), 15 % in the UAE (1995), 15 % in Bahrain (1997), 20 % in Kuwait (1997) and 12 % in Saudi Arabia (1997).

Table 7.4 Growth of real GDP, Population and Labour Force in Oman and the GCC (1996–2007)

	1996–1999	2000–2004	2005	2006	2007
Real GDP growth (annual percentage change)					
Bahrain	4.0	5.6	7.9	6.5	6.6
Kuwait	1.2	6.8	11.5	6.4	4.6
Oman	2.9	4.6	5.6	7.0	6.9
Qatar	12.0	9.1	9.2	10.3	14.2
Saudi Arabia	2.1	3.7	6.1	4.3	4.1
United Arab Emirates	5.2	7.6	8.2	9.4	7.7
Population growth (per cent)					
Bahrain	3.0	3.0	2.0	2.0	2.0
Kuwait	4.0	3.1	2.9	2.3	2.2
Oman	2.5	1.1	1.3	1.8	2.1
Qatar	4.3	5.2	5.3	4.6	4.5
Saudi Arabia	2.5	2.4	2.6	2.5	2.4
United Arab Emirates	5.9	7.2	5.8	7.2	7.2
Labour force growth (annual percentage)					
Bahrain	4.0	2.7	2.7	2.7	2.7
Kuwait	6.4	5.3	5.0	5.0	5.0
Oman	3.5	1.0	1.4	0.8	0.8
Qatar	2.5	2.2	1.9	–0.5	1.4
Saudi Arabia	3.3	3.6	3.9	3.7	3.7
United Arab Emirates	6.0	7.2	5.8	7.2	7.2

Sources: IMF (2008: 140, 142), United Nations (2009) and national authorities

This current phase can be characterized as the "open unemployment of nationals" (Girgis 2000). The main factor behind this phenomenon is the preference of nationals to work in the public sector, mainly due to the substantial wage differentials with the private sector. This implies that the private sector in Oman, as in other GCC countries, relied fully on the cheap expatriate labour and the government could not impose the employment of nationals on the private sector for fear of harming their ability to retain competitive prices for their products (Table 7.4). As rightly observed,

> In the Gulf countries, segmented labour markets with differential wages for nationals and non-nationals contributed to the high unemployment rate. In the private sector, employers preferred to hire expatriate labour (mostly male), since nationals were generally unwilling to work at the same wage levels as non-nationals. On the other hand, the public sector has been responsible for the absorption of nationals, particularly in the employment of women. The sluggish economic growth of 1.2 percent and the rapid population growth of 3.4 percent during the period 1980–2000 reduced the governmental capacity to expand public-sector job opportunities, which led to the rising problem of unemployment of nationals in a number of countries (UNESCWA 1995: 8).

The paradox is that while nationals put heavy pressure on the labour market, especially in the public sector, the steady expansion of the private sector induced increases in low-cost expatriate labour.

The current unemployment situation in Oman and the Gulf region has serious implications. Although this phenomenon has been in existence for more than a decade, and despite high economic growth rates due to historically high oil prices and an increasing diversified economic structure especially in the first decade since the year 2000, anecdotal evidence continues to show glaring unemployment trends among nationals – with a high in the 15–30 % range in Saudi Arabia,[12] 10–15 % range in Oman, 14 % in UAE,[13] 7 % in Qatar, 4.5 % in Kuwait and 4 % in Bahrain. The nature of unemployment among Gulf nationals is a cause of serious concern that foretells the daunting challenge ahead in the quest for economic diversification. Unemployment in the GCC is both structural – since the demand for and the supply of labour do not match in the face of changes in the structure of the economy (Girgis 2000)[14] – and cyclical – owing to fluctuating oil prices and corresponding government spending. More importantly, the recent unemployment rates of the more educated are high, partly because of significant increases in the level of schooling and partly because the quality and type of education do not match labour market needs.[15] It has been argued that "to some degree unemployment among the educated can be attributed to 'queuing', that is graduates waiting for prospective employment in the government sector – this is more prevalent in the Gulf Cooperation Council economies" (UNESCWA 2004: 9).

While Oman, like its GCC neighbours, has modernized rapidly and the material aspects of its way of life have been transformed beyond recognition, the traditional and conservative socio-cultural and political aspects have been only marginally touched upon by the forces of the oil-fuelled modernization process. The character of the rapidly changing Omani society continues to be enmeshed in the transitional phase between modernity and post-modernity. While Oman has integrated considerably with the global economy, there are also more frequent and recent debates about the "limits to growth" and "growth at what cost", or "bridging the divide between quantitative growth and qualitative progress" – reflecting Omanis' increasing concern to retain their peculiar social and cultural traits that are tied to tradition and religion. In this particular paradigm, the presence of a huge foreign labour force of diverse national ethnic composition adds to the emerging fluidity.

The overall framework to analyse the economic and socio-cultural anxieties of nationals about the presence of large numbers of expatriates in Oman can thus be designated a problem of a "dilemma between retrospective culture and futuristic

[12] The National Bank of Kuwait reported independent estimates in its publication, the Kuwait Economic and Financial Review (April 2007: 2–10). However, as per the preliminary estimates released by Saudi Arabia's Ministry of Economy and Planning, the unemployment rate for Saudi nationals was 11.5 % in 2005 and 12 % in the year 2006.

[13] This is also confirmed in the earlier 2004 official study by Tanmia, the Human Resource Agency of the UAE government.

[14] This is evident, as national workers cannot find jobs that match their skills at the reservation wage rate, which is determined largely by the opportunity wage rate in the government sector – the traditional job haven for national workers.

[15] For the expansion of higher education in Oman, see Brandenburg's contribution (in this volume).

economy". In Oman, like other Gulf regions, there is clear distinction between the socio-cultural space and the economic space. Since the culture of a community is determined over a period of time and the contemporary culture is embedded in the social pattern, it is a retrospectively determined phenomenon. In contrast, the economic requirements of the development process determine the trends and patterns of labour migration to Oman and the Gulf region, rendering them futuristic. Thus from a broader perspective, contemporary Gulf society is in a state of "identity crisis" in which nationals are increasingly feeling isolated and are therefore apprehensive about everything considered foreign, including foreign labour. The ruling elites, meanwhile, strive to protect their peculiar culture and religious tradition without countering their global economic competitiveness. In this way, the Gulf presents a best case of global–local debate impinging upon various facets of national identities in the throes of globalization, which has crucial bearing on the future socio-cultural space of an increasingly economically interdependent society.

The above shows a number of different phenomena that have over time crystallized and become issues of debate within GCC political and intellectual circles. The following discusses key concerns raised by the Gulf national population about labour migration and Oman's continued reliance on large-scale imports of workers.

7.4.2 Anxieties About Economic Opportunity

For the moment, national unemployment is basically voluntary in Oman, as in the other GCC states. Given the vastness of economic opportunities and the continued ability of the state to provide public sector employment, the situation of significant unemployment has not yet translated into immediate and visible social consequences. Yet, as the Omani economy has begun to diversify and as the state's dependence on low hydrocarbon revenues lead to financial stringency, meaning both that employment in the public sector is increasingly unavailable and also that other sectors of society, such as women, are becoming an increasing force on the employment market, these social consequences can no longer be denied. What exists is a situation in which the educated youth's private sector employment opportunities are both limited and not very encouraging. It also needs to be mentioned that expatriates do not eat away into public sector opportunities for nationals in general. Nevertheless, the continued reliance on foreign workers has resulted in fewer incentives for nationals to pursue education and training, as there is a large degree of complacency that these foreign workers will be available to fill needed positions. This is a key dilemma for the government to consider, as it has concentrated on pouring large sums of money into the education and training of nationals. While this is a good step, the jury remains out on its overall effectiveness and one should be very cautious about thinking that it is only a matter of time until a skilled national labour force appears that is ready to turn the demographic imbalance around.

Another economic consequence is that there are also fiscal and income redistribution effects in the host country to contend with. This is a primary cause of anxieties

Table 7.5 Remittances outflows[a] from the Gulf region and world, 2008 (USD million)

Year	Bahrain	Kuwait	Oman	Saudi Arabia	GCC[b]	World
1975	263	276	208	554	1,301	11,912
1980	330	692	397	4,094	5,513	30,676
1985	778	1,044	950	5,199	7,971	33,189
1990	332	770	856	11,221	13,179	66,295
1995	500	1,354	1,537	16,594	19,985	98,648
2000	1,013	1,734	1,451	15,390	19,588	110,108
2001	1,287	1,784	1,532	15,120	19,723	118,785
2002	872	1,925	1,602	15,854	20,253	131,304
2003	1,082	2,144	1,672	14,783	19,681	146,551
2004	1,120	2,403	1,826	13,555	18,904	166,670
2005	1,223	2,648	2,257	13,996	20,124	184,040
2006	1,531	3,021	2,788	15,611	22,951	238,203
Remittances as a share of GDP 2006 (%)	9.5	3.7	9.0	4.5	–	0.5

Source: World Bank (2008)
[a]Workers' remittances, compensation of employees and migrants' transfers (debit); data for Qatar and the UAE is not available
[b]GCC total excluding Qatar and the UAE

among Omanis and other Gulf nationals, because foreigners – who feel uncertain because their status in the host countries is purely temporary – remit huge sums of money to their home countries. Table 7.5 describes the trends of remittance outflows from Oman and the Gulf region.

7.4.3 Socio-Cultural Anxieties

Currently, the Omani society is going through a phase of tremendous socio-cultural transformation precipitated by large-scale urbanization and increasing concern about national identity. Adding to the perplexity is the presence of a large-scale foreign labour force and its impact on the socio-cultural space. The issue of immigration and identity now appear at the top of the national security agenda. By determining or changing the basic demographic structure, questions of nationality go to the heart of Oman's basic character or identity. Simultaneously, it is obvious that the large influx or stock of migrants continues to maintain its cultural, linguistic and religious traditions. It is also unrealistic to think that nationals will exhibit a cavalier disregard for the preservation of the culture they share; they can be expected to desire immigration policies that nurture and protect their culture. Thus, immigration triggers these deep responses because it forces a people to address the question: who are we and who do we want to be (Meilaender 2001)?

This fear of being swamped by a large presence of foreigners from diverse cultural backgrounds is also rooted in the process of nation building with its emphasis on cultural homogeneity. Moreover, this perception has been heightened in recent years by the regional integration process' implications for the national identity and sovereignty of the member states of the GCC.

Importantly, among the various expatriate communities, Indians maintain strong bonds with the religion and culture of their countries of origin and do not wish to abandon their linguistic, religious and cultural practices.[16] In this respect, it is widely perceived that migration threatens communal identity and culture by directly altering the ethnic, cultural, religious and linguistic composition of the population, as political institutions cannot adequately accommodate even relatively small numbers without significant changes that raise sensitive issues of national identity. The local national population increasingly demands action from the government to address the demographic imbalances and to protect the spaces that allow nationals to feel protected and able to promote their own cultural values. A certain fortress mentality has been erected in which nationals feel besieged and powerless to stop the continued inflow of foreigners. In this context, not only a process of demographic imbalance needs to be addressed, but also the more likely process of a demographic blending in which the lines of identity between nationals and expatriates are becoming increasingly blurred. One example here is the well-known phenomenon of bilingualism and cultural mix resulting when Gulf children are reared by foreign nannies (mostly Asians). One UAE official has stated that, due to its dependence on foreign workers,

> This society is recreating generations of dependent personalities who request that domestics do everything for them. Our full reliance on domestics in the household is encouraging the growth of an unproductive family (Sabban 2002: 27).

Therefore, the ethnically homogenous society of the Gulf places higher value on preserving its ethnic character and regards the foreign population as a threat to stability and security.

Thus, it can be argued that the negative images of the expatriates have been reinforced by certain economic, social, political and ideological factors. Firstly, traditionally, the prevailing collective image of Gulf societies is that of an ethnically homogenous, closed society that proscribes any kind of uncertainty. This image combined with the lack of any kind of discussion about multiculturalism rendered it difficult to entertain any notion of acceptance of the other. Secondly, practices of differential treatment for similar migrants from different countries can lead to discontent and protests. For example, the criteria of higher pay for Westerners in comparison with other nationals reinforces the segmentation and can create frustration. Thirdly, geographical proximity to India has instilled in immigrants a sense of being temporary residents having short-lasting proximity with the Omani society; this weakens any bid for social integration by the immigrants themselves. Lastly, even with a law facilitating selective naturalization, the authorities feel that those ethnic or religious communities that have a higher fertility than the native communities may challenge the long-established model of national identity.

[16] See the conceptual article by Bromber on translocal connections (in this volume).

The bottom line of the above argumentation is that the large-size foreign labour force and the private sector's continued reliance on it are increasingly seen as pressing security issues that must be comprehensively dealt with. Kapiszewski (2001) was one of the first to point to the emerging security concerns as a result of the preponderance of foreigners. In this regard, it is worthwhile to highlight that thc recent spate of labour strikes and violence in labour camps in Bahrain, Kuwait and the UAE also adds to the Omani authorities' apprehension of social instability.

7.4.4 Policy Response and Outcome

Currently, the issue of foreign labour is more than an economic issue in Oman and other Gulf countries, with authorities viewing the issue as a national security threat with socio-political implications. This is being compounded by the international call for equal rights for the foreign labourers, and the authorities have adopted a "zero-tolerance" approach aimed at resorting to expatriates in the absence of any local or regional alternatives (Janardhan 2007). To illustrate how the issue of foreign labour has increasingly become a public issue of concern, it is useful to summarize the migration policy views of the GCC member countries as in Table 7.6.

What is clearly apparent is that while authorities tended to be comfortable with the immigration policies in place in the mid-1970s, this is no longer the case, as the issue of foreign labour reliance emerged at the top of the policy debate. In response to this changed perception, Oman and GCC authorities are putting in place several measures to redefine the labour market rules, including nationalization of the workforce and heavily regulating expatriates flows by means of stringent administrative rules and regulations. As the value of Omani oil revenues decreases, unemployment increases and nationals become more willing to accept occupations dominated until now by expatriates, jobs in many sectors are no longer open to expatriates in Oman.

Setting employment quotas has been the main direct policy plank of the GCC countries. The rationale behind the quota system is to place the burden of identifying, training and maintaining local personnel on the employers, who are often foreign companies. However, these policies have not been successful yet, due to the rigid labour market and the growing economic pressure that constantly demands foreign labour in the face of local skill shortage. In principle, Oman, like other Gulf countries, is concerned with its reliance on foreign labour and the looming threat of increased local unemployment. In practice, most of these countries are more concerned with maintaining the momentum of economic growth and are reluctant to risk their competitiveness by raising the cost of foreign labour. As rightly remarked by Shaham (2008: 9),

> this policy is really an extension of the old labor regime, trying to assure the rotation of the foreign labor force. It is unlikely to increase the employment of locals, it does not apply to the increasing number of skilled workers, and by mandating rotation it will further reduce the price of labor. Why pursue a policy so adverse to the proclaimed goal of increasing local employment? The rhetoric behind this proposal suggests that its primary goal is to abate social and political concerns.

Table 7.6 Immigration policy views of the Gulf countries

	1976		2007	
Country	Views on immigration	Public policy	Views on immigration	Public policy
Bahrain	Satisfactory	Maintain current levels of migration	Satisfactory	Maintain current levels of migration
Kuwait	Satisfactory	Maintain current levels of migration	High	Lower levels of migration
Oman	Satisfactory	Maintain current levels of migration	Too high	Lower levels of migration
Qatar	Satisfactory	Maintain current levels of migration	Too high	Lower levels of migration
Saudi Arabia	Too low	Raise levels	Too high	Lower levels of migration
United Arab Emirates	Satisfactory	Maintain current levels of migration	Too high	Lower levels of migration

Source: UNESCWA (2009)

7.5 Summary and Conclusions

Since the pre-oil era, as traders, entrepreneurs, moneylenders, bankers, customs farmers, financiers of the pearl trade etc., Indian migrants have developed into a critical mass in Omani economy and society. With their astute skills and close commercial relations with the rulers, they have tremendously contributed to Oman's economic modernization. Over the course of the nineteenth century, Indian merchants came to dominate the economic life of Muscat, replacing the Al Bu Sa'id rulers as the principal merchants of the city and acquiring fortunes that had once gone to the royal family. Indian merchants not only took control of trade and fiscal administration, but also expanded Muscat's commercial prominence by broadening the mercantile base of the port through trade with Europe and America. The integration of migrant Indians in Omani society further strengthened with the discovery of oil and the mass immigration of skilled as well as unskilled Indian labourers. It is difficult to imagine the contemporary Oman economic scene without taking into account the role played by Indian manpower. For Indian migrants, the security and working environment have been assured by the close association between the Indian community and the ruling regime in Oman, although there is stark asymmetry between the migrants and the native population.

Things may change with increasing apprehension about foreign labour because of glaring unemployment among Omani nationals and the increase in the number of nationals willing to work in sectors in which they previously refused to work. There can be no doubt that the flows of people and commodities have converged to contribute to the development of a multicultural society in conformity with many local sources of authority and social legitimization. Yet, the presence of a huge foreign labour force is a pervasive issue with considerable implications for Oman's economic and socio-cultural fabric and its political and international relations. The labour polemics and polarized viewpoints about the foreign labour issue point towards a situation of uncertainty that is contrary to the character of traditional society. While economic pressures have resulted in the growth of the foreign labour force and a quota on migration, perceived socio-cultural anxieties create a policy dilemma on how to manage governance. Oman, like other Gulf countries, is thus in a catch-22 situation. Simultaneously, relations between the expatriates and the nationals continue to be mutually suspicious, which is not conducive to a stable social structure in the future. It can be contended that how the Omani government and politically articulate groups within Omani society feel about Indian expatriates will largely decide the fate of this diaspora in the future.

Seen from a broader perspective, Indian migration to Oman at various times points to a confluence of various economic, political, social and cultural interactions, resulting in a process of "virtual" interregionalisation. This is a peculiar form of regionalisation where – in the absence of any formal institutional mechanisms – economic imperatives and mutual benefits have been the primary driver igniting and sustaining the process of interregionalisation based on labour migration in the case of India-Oman integration. The most important feature of this form of regionalisation is the diversity of interests (political, social and cultural) among actors (migrant Indians and local Omanis) that hinders full-scale integration and the convergence of purely economic benefits that glue them together. Moreover, in terms of regionalisation process, Indian migration to Oman has evolved a "critical mass" or "comfort zone" that has the potential to enable interregionalism. The "critical mass" or "comfort zone" refers to certain push and pull factors that drive and sustain migration from India to Oman. From the perspective of interregionalism, the critical mass is not confined to India and Oman only, but spreads across the Indian subcontinent and the Gulf region.

References

Allen, J., & Calvin, H. (1981). The Indian merchant community of MasqaỘ. *Bulletin of the School of Oriental and African Studies, 44*(1), 39–53.

Columbia University Press (Ed.). (2008). *Columbia encyclopedia*. Farmington Hills: Gale Group.

Girgis, M. (2000). *Nationals versus migrants: Coping with the change*. Paper submitted to the Mediterranean Development Forum Labour Workshop, Cairo, 5–8 Mar 2000.

IMF. (2008). *MENA economic developments and prospects: Regional integration for global competitiveness*. Washington, DC: International Monetary Fund.

Janardhan, N. (2007). Redefining Gulf labour market rules. In *Gulf yearbook* (pp. 36–49). Dubai: Gulf Research Center.

Kapiszewski, A. (2001). *Nationals and expatriates. Population and labour dilemmas of the GCC states*. Reading: Ithaca Press.

Meilaender, P. C. (2001). *Towards a theory of immigration*. New York: Palgrave.
Miles, S. B. (1966). *The countries and tribes of the Persian Gulf* (2nd ed.). London: Frank Cass.
National Bank of Kuwait. (2007, April). *Kuwait economic and financial review*. National Bank of Kuwait, Kuwait.
Pearson, M. N. (1973). Indigenous dominance in a colonial economy: The Goa rendas, 1600–1670. In J. Aubin (Ed.), *Mare luso-indicum: Etudes et documents sur l''histoire de l'océan Indien et des pays riverains à l'époque de la domination portugaise* (Vol. II, pp. 61–73). Geneva: Librairie Droz.
Peterson, J. E. (2004). Oman's diverse society: Northern Oman. *Middle East Journal, 58*(1), 254–270.
Rajamony, V. (2008, June). *India-UAE labor relations*. Dubai: Consulate General of India.
Sabban, R. (2002). *United Arab Emirates: Migrant women in the United Arab Emirates: The case of female domestic workers* (GENPROM Working Paper No. 10). http://www.ilo.org/wcmsp5/groups/public/---ed_emp/documents/publication/wcms_117955.pdf
Shaham, D. (2008). Foreign labor in the Arab Gulf: Challenges to nationalization, Al Nakhlah, *The Fletcher School Online Journal for Southwest Asia and Islamic Civilization*, pp. 1–14.
Sultanate of Oman. Ministry of National Economy. (2009). *Statistical year book*. Muscat: MoNE.
Tanmia. (2004). *Labour Survey in the UAE*. Dubai: Tanmia.
Thapar, R. (1975). A possible identification of Meluḷḷa, Dilmun and Makan. *Journal of the Economic and Social History of the Orient, 18*(1), 1–42.
UNESCWA. (2009, 2004, 1995). *Survey of economic and social developments*. Beirut: United Nations Economic and Social Commission for Western Asia.
United Nations (UN). (2009). *World population prospects: The 2008 review*. http://www.un.org/esa/population/publications/wpp2008/wpp2008_text_tables.pdf
Walter de Gray Birch, W. (Ed.). (1875). *Afonso de Albuquerque, The commentaries of the great Afonso Dalaboquerque, second Viceroy of India* (Vol. 1, pp. 99–100). London.
Weiner, M. (1982). International migration and development: Indians in the Persian Gulf. *Population and Development Review, 8*(1), 1–36.
Wellsted, L. (1837). Narrative of a journey into the interior of Oman, in 1835. *Journal of the Royal Geographical Society of London, 7*, 102–113.
Winckler, O. (2002). The demographic dilemma of the Arab world: The employment aspect. *Journal of Contemporary History, 37*(4), 617–636.
World Bank. (2008). *Migration and remittances factbook 2008*. Washington, DC: World Bank.

Chapter 8
Negotiating Authenticity and Translocality in Oman: The "Desertscapes" of the Harasiis Tribe

Dawn Chatty

8.1 Introduction

The Harasiis nomadic pastoral tribe have been for centuries the sole human inhabitants of the central desert of Oman, which the reigning sovereign in the 1930s named the Jiddat il-Harasiis. This remote tribe, organized around a subsistence economy based on raising camels and goats, has a wide presence not only in Oman but also in the present-day United Arab Emirates (UAE). Mobility over a vast and largely inhospitable rock and gravel plain – the Jiddat il-Harasiis – has been the principle feature of their resilient livelihood focussed on camel transport and more recently on trucks. The authenticity of their attachment to this translocal region is intimately tied to the traditional distinction in Islamic historiography between *bedu* in the deserts and *hadar* in the towns and cities. Recent decades in the Sultanate of Oman, however, have seen increasing pressure by government, international conservation agencies and multinational extractive industries to contest these peoples' claims of "translocal" desert belonging. This paper examines these processes, both national and regional, and explores the ways the Harasiis make their claims of authenticity and translocal belonging transparent.

8.2 Mobility, Translocality and Dislocation

History is written from the perspective of the settled. Those who move are generally regarded as threatening or at least unsettling to the sedentist order of affairs. Pastoral nomadic groups have, for centuries, been regarded as a threat to the

D. Chatty (✉)
Refugee Studies Centre, Oxford Department of International Development,
Queen Elizabeth House, University of Oxford, 3 Mansfield Road, Oxford, OX1 3TB, UK
St Cross College, St. Giles, Oxford, OX1 3LZ, UK
e-mail: dawn.chatty@stx.ox.ac.uk; dawn.chatty@qeh.ox.ac.uk

S. Wippel (ed.), *Regionalizing Oman: Political, Economic and Social Dynamics*, United Nations University Series on Regionalism 6, DOI 10.1007/978-94-007-6821-5_8,

margins of settled agriculture, or so Oriental and Occidental historiography tells us. However, the facts on the ground suggest a symbiotic system largely independent of settled society, but contributing to its effective workings by guaranteeing safe passage across deserts for wide-ranging East to West trade networks and religious pilgrimage. The pastoral nomadic tribes of the Arabian peninsula – in many regards marginal to settled life – have largely escaped the strictures of central authority and have established systems of mobility for livelihood risk reduction and resilience (cf. Gellner 1983; Scott 2009). These pastoral systems required extensive areas of low-resource desert and semi-desert land to survive. Negotiated movement of people and herds of livestock from deficit to surplus areas across these expanses was the foundational principle of life. The movement was not "nomadic", it was informed and deliberated among similar units from the same tribe; occasionally prolonged deficit in one area and surplus in another area outside of a particular tribe's traditional territory (*dar*) would be negotiated inter-tribally. Wide expanses of desert might go for years without people or herds, and other areas might experience constant use over many years, depending on unpredictable and unreliable rainfall or other forms of precipitation.

With the establishment of the modern nation-state in the twentieth century, many nomadic pastoral groups found their traditional territory suddenly "located" in several nation states. This translocality was more than mere physical emplacement; it was also a reality shaped by the movement of cultural, social and political ideas across spaces and localities (Appadurai 1996; also Bromber, in this volume; Jong 1999). The practice of movement of people and herds as risk management was unchanged. Yet over recent decades government officials and international civil servants came to see these movements across localities as threatening to the concept of the nation-state (Wilkinson 1983). Border crossings came to be partially patrolled and regularized, leaving many desert dwellers in difficulties. Their movements and thus their translocality came under threat.

At the same time, encroachment of these deserts by multinational oil companies and biodiversity conservation NGOs meant that some spaces and locations were removed from the orbit of movements of these desert dwellers. Instead of being dispossessed entirely from their traditional lands, they were slowly being "dislocated" from important sites, generally the richest spaces with tree cover (e.g. Yalooni in the Jiddat il-Harasiis) or depressions where oil and, in association with it, water were found. These dislocations on a small scale could be absorbed into the highly resilient pastoral land management system. But on a larger scale, the dislocation undermined the ability of the desert tribes to recover, renegotiate and identify sufficient localities for survival. In this paper, I understand translocality as

> the sum of phenomena which results from a multitude of circulations and transfers. It designates the outcome of concrete moments of people, goods, ideas and symbols which span spatial distances and cross boundaries, be they geographical, cultural or political (Freitag and von Oppen 2010: 5).

When these circulations are circumscribed, the people and cultures that conducted them are impoverished and their cultural survival is threatened.

8.3 Authenticity, Landscape and Identity

The desert-dwelling inhabitants of Oman, organized in kin-based "segmentary" groups of tribes are recognized as *bedu*, while tribes and extended families in the mountain and coastal settlements of the country are regarded as *hadar*.[1] This *bedu/hadar* distinction has deep roots in Muslim history and historiography (cf. Ibn Khaldûn 1958). From the perspective of the settled urban historian, the pinnacle of civilization was the city with its government, places of worship, schools and markets. The city and town dweller was *hadari*. The other extreme, the *badia* (desert), was defined by its lack of *hadar* or civilization and was represented by the social category of *badawi* or *bedu*. The latter were mainly the desert dwellers, with nomadic pastoral camel and sheep herding but also other livelihoods, such as beekeeping. The different landscapes of the *bedu* and *hadar* had important cultural and social dimensions in the understanding of human activity.[2] Furthermore, though the term *hadar/hadari* is hardly used any longer, the term *bedu* remains in contemporary use. For the *bedu*, such self-identification is a statement of tribal or ethnic identity and solidarity as well as attachment to the desert landscape, which is a physical background and social and cultural foreground constantly shaped and reshaped by social processes and interactions with the physical environment (Hirsch and O'Hanlon 1995). However, when non-*bedu* use the term, particularly contemporary government officials, it is often a statement of contempt, highlighting the presumed backwardness and primitiveness of this social category with no reference to the desert landscape.

Nationalism and identity are two concepts at the heart of the processes described above. The Sultanate of Oman had its modern "birth" in 1970 after a near-bloodless palace coup brought the Sultan Qaboos to the throne. From that moment the Sultan and his advisors have struggled to create an imagined political community of a unified nation (see Anderson 1983). The first few decades after the birth of this new nation saw campaigns to attract educated and professional Omanis in exile to return to create the modern state (Peterson 1978). This paper posits that once these outsiders and expatriates had integrated and transformed themselves into "insiders", they set about creating an "imagined" nation that was homogenous and modern. The authentic inhabitants in background and translocal landscapes such as the deserts (Hirsch and O'Hanlon 1995) thus became the "outsiders". The tension between the

[1]The French term "*bedouin*" derives from the Arabic *badia*, meaning the semi-arid steppe or desert. Those who live in the *badia* are described as *bedu*.

[2]Landscapes are complex phenomena. In addition to the physical features that geographers have focussed on until the last 30 years or so, is a widely accepted contemporary understanding that landscapes reflect human activity and are imbued with cultural values. Landscapes combine notions of time and space as well as political and social constructs. They evolve over time, are changed through human activity, and acquire many layers of sometimes contested meanings and versions of reality. Connections with landscapes form part of cultural and political identity; people feel they belong to certain places or regions (Aplin 2007; Jackson 1984).

outsider "traditions" and new insider "modernities" appears to be resolved in a representation that encapsulates the political and cultural fiction of a unified nation at the expense of the *bedu* tribes of the interior deserts; *bedu* claims to authenticity in the desertscapes are thus increasingly rejected.

8.4 Historical Background

Like so many states of the Middle East, Oman has been inhabited by successive waves of peoples. Settlement in Oman from the desert fringe came from two directions: one along the southern coast of Arabia from Yemen and the other through the northern gateway of al-Buraymi. The pastoral tribes in the middle of the country are the most remote and marginal peoples in Oman physically; culturally they form distinct, heterogeneous groups seemingly at odds with contemporary government efforts to create a unified state. Other migrations into Oman include the Baluch and Persian from Southwest Asia, African and Zanzibari from the east coast of Africa, and Hyderabadis from the Indian subcontinent. The latter have settled in the coastal regions and the mountain valleys mainly of the north of the country (for greater detail on ethnic composition, see Peterson 2004a, b) (Fig. 8.1).

Until 1970, the Sultanate of Oman could justifiable be described as the "Tibet of Arabia" (Eickelman 1989), so complete was its isolation from the rest of the world. This remoteness and sense of separateness of the state was largely created during the long reign of Sultan Said Al Said (1932–1970). It was a time when many urban Omanis fled the country seeking education and livelihood opportunities. During this period the tribes of the desert interior maintained their largely subsistence livelihoods, including local trade and barter with coastal settlements. What little transformation was taking place along the coastal and mountain settlements in the north of the country had little, if any impact, on the desert tribes.

Oil exploration commenced in Oman during the 1930s and a number of oil companies began making small payments to the Sultan to maintain their rights to exploration. In the central desert of Oman, both the Harasiis and the Jeneba nomadic pastoral tribes were affected by these activities. The Jeneba tribe, closely watching oil exploration in the area, laid claim to the Jiddat il-Harasiis, maintaining it was their land that they merely permitted the Harasiis to occupy. Sultan Said dismissed the Jeneba claim. Wilkinson, moreover, suggests that the Sultan's true motive in coming down on the side of the Harasiis was his confidence that the Harasiis had no relationship with his rival, the Ibadi Imam, and were thus potentially allies in his claim to future oil rights in the central desert interior (Wilkinson 1987).

Oil activity in Oman stopped during World War II and resumed in the early 1950s. Pastoral tribes in the north of the country bordering on areas under the control of the Ibadi Imam were increasingly drawn into the political fray, and armed conflict between the Sultan on the coast and the Ibadi Imam in the interior grew more frequent. For example, at Ibri, the pastoral Duru tribe, concerned to protect their "capital" and date gardens to the south of the town at Tan'am, entered into

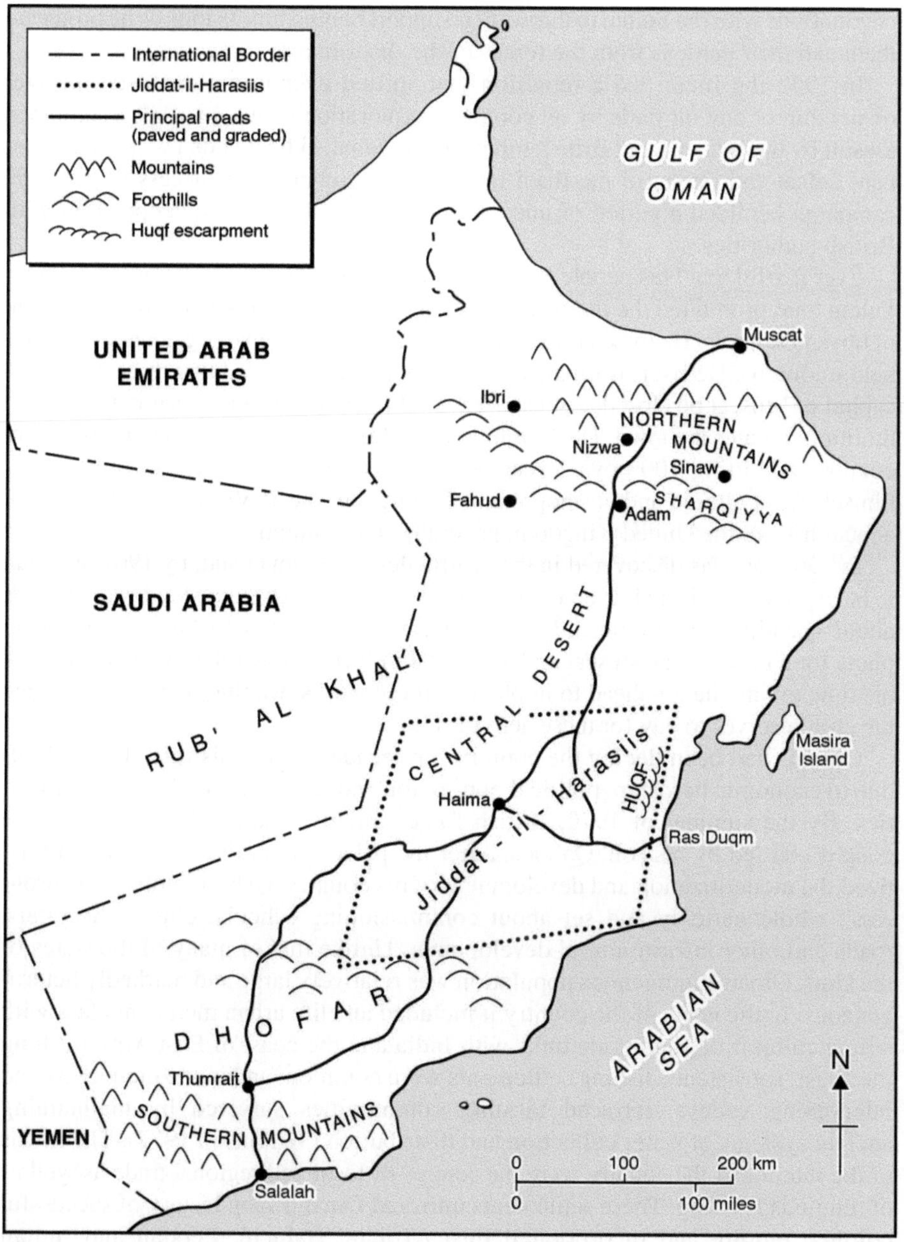

Fig. 8.1 Map Sultanate of Oman

negotiations with the Sultan to throw their support behind him as long as he protected them and their gardens from the forces of the Ibadi Imam.[3]

In 1952 the Imam led a rebellion that spilled over into a contestation over ownership of any oil finds by oil company exploration teams. In 1959 a combined assault by the Sultan's and British forces on the Jabal Akhdar ended with the permanent defeat and retreat of the Ibadi Imam and his rebels. The success of the 1959 campaign heralded a period of uncontested and genuinely close cooperation with British authorities.

Ever fearful that "his people" were not ready to move into the twentieth century, Sultan Said prohibited the importation of cars and severely restricted the enrolment of boys in schools. He took a direct interest in all matters regarding changes to long-held traditions. He banned sunglasses and torches and insisted that the gates of the capital of Muscat be closed at sunset. Those stuck outside had to wait until the next morning to enter the town. He permitted only three schools to operate in the entire country, admitting 100 boys a year whom he personally chose. Yet Sultan Said himself was cultured and cosmopolitan. Throughout the 1950s and 1960s he made annual trips to the United Kingdom, generally in the summer.

In 1964, oil was discovered in the central desert of Oman and, by 1967, it began to be exported. Projected revenues jumped dramatically, but Sultan Said was cautious about spending money he did not yet have. Thus, although he commissioned plans for a new port at Muscat and a hospital in Ibri, among other projects, he took his time giving the go-ahead to implement these works, waiting first to accumulate the cash reserves to pay for these activities.

Omanis had been fleeing the country for decades during his rule (1932–1970) due to economic hardship, political oppression and lack of educational opportunities. By the summer of 1970, British forces quietly instigated and supported a coup d'etat led by his son, Qaboos. After the palace coup, the new Sultan prioritized the modernization and development of his country. Qaboos embraced "progress" wholeheartedly and set about commissioning schools, clinics, hospitals, roads and other infrastructural development. Unlike that of many of the states of the Gulf, Oman's indigenous population was relatively large and markedly heterogeneous. In the north of the country it included an elite urban merchant class with strong cultural ties and trade links with India and the coast of East Africa. Along the coast, subsistence fishing settlements were common, and in the mountains and intervening valleys, terraced farming communities survived by maintaining ancient systems of water collection and distribution (Wilkinson 1977). The towns of the interior of the country were the centres of local and regional trade as well as of religious learning. These settlements mirrored Oman's long history of successful colonial empire and incorporated East African, Baluchi, Persian and Indian elements into the dominant culture.

---

[3]The long political and military struggle between Sultan Said and the Ibadi Imam over control of the interior of the country in the 1950s is studied in great detail by both Wilkinson (1987) and Peterson (2007).

Once he had established his reign, Sultan Qaboos reached out to all Omanis living abroad and encouraged them to return to the country as quickly as possible. This they did in large numbers from Bombay, Mombasa, Liverpool and other Western centres. Along with this returning "citizenry" came skilled European, particularly British, and South Asian expatriate workers to help build a government infrastructure nearly from scratch. The armed forces, the police force, the internal security service, the civil service and government ministries of health, education, social affairs and labour, agriculture and fisheries, water and electricity, communications and roads and other agencies were rapidly set up. The trappings of a modern state were put into place almost overnight. Thousands of miles of roads were tarmacked, and for the first time a modern road network connected Muscat to Salalah. The social and economic transformation of the coastal areas and the mountains behind in both the north and the south of the country, funded mainly by petroleum wealth, was enormous. The same was not true of the interior desert areas of the country or its nomadic pastoral peoples.

8.5 The Harasiis Tribe in Contemporary Oman

The Harasiis along with the Wahiba, the Duru and the Jeneba are the four main nomadic pastoral tribes in the central desert of Oman. The Wahiba tribe of about 7,000 people occupy the southern coast of Oman and the desert interior known as the Wahiba Sands. To the West of the Wahiba Sands is the Duru camel-raising tribe, numbering about 9,000. Spread out along much of Oman's southern coast and adjacent interior are the Jeneba, a large and widely dispersed tribe; their numbers are easily in excess of 12,000. To the south of the Duru and Wahiba are the Harasiis tribe. Moving over what was until the 1950s a vast, waterless plain of more than 42,000 km^2, the Harasiis are a "refugee" tribe. They are people largely of Dhofari origin who have been pushed into this most inhospitable core area of the central desert of Oman. They are the most remote and isolated of already marginal peoples. The region they inhabit separates north Oman from Dhofar and is the backwater of both regions. As such, the region has attracted individuals and groups expelled from their own tribes as punishment for major infractions of traditional codes of conduct and honour. The Harasiis tribe speaks a southern Arabian language related to Mahri, an indicator of its lack of contact and relative isolation certainly in the past few centuries (Johnstone 1977). The tribe's usufruct or rights to access graze and browse found in the Jiddat il-Harasiis were established in the 1930s when the Sultan and his political advisor, Bertram Thomas, decided to confer the name Jiddat il-Harasiis[4]

[4]The Jeneba tribe, it seems, protested that this territory was its own and the Harasiis were simply being accommodated there because they had no land of their own. However the Sultan decided that if the Jeneba wanted to go and live in the region it could be renamed "Jiddat il-Jeneba", but as long as the Harasiis were the sole occupiers of the Jiddat, it would bear their name (Thomas 1938).

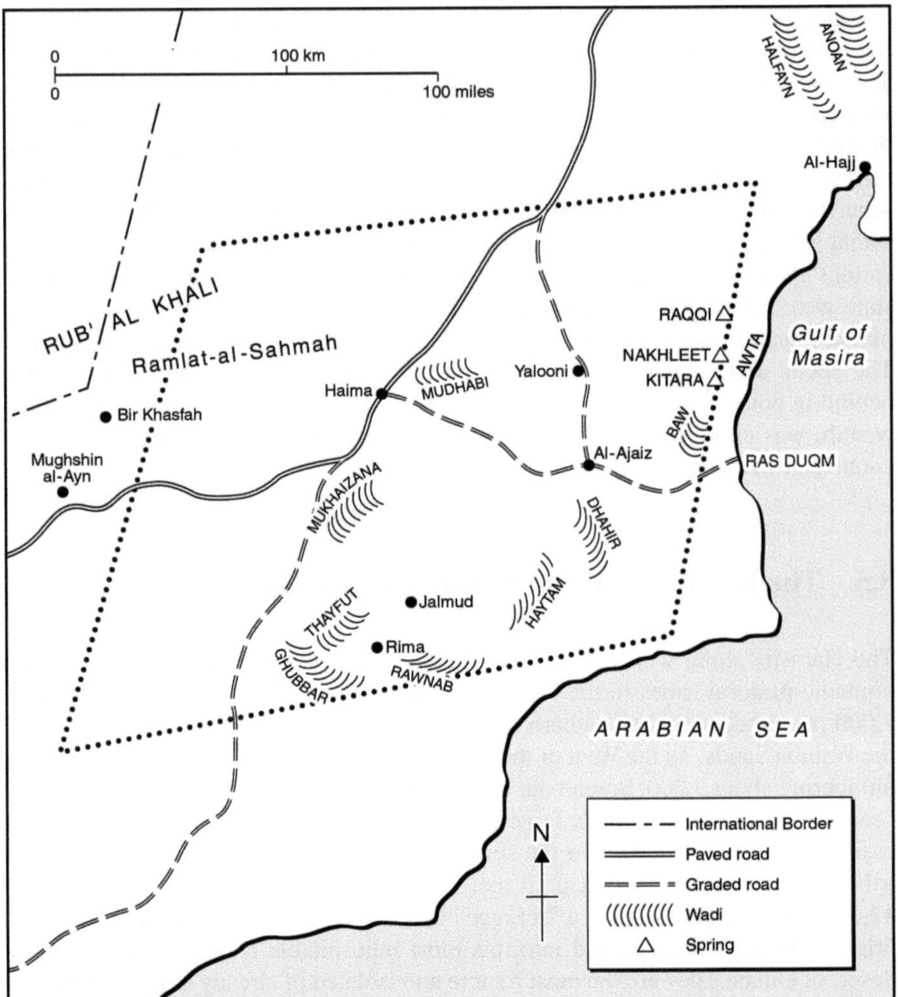

Fig. 8.2 Map of Jiddat il-Harasiis, Oman

upon the territory, which had fallen to them as much by occupancy as by the lack of desire of any other tribe to be there (Thomas 1938) (Fig. 8.2).

The tribe is small, numbering about 5,000 people. Although their claim to the Jiddat has been, on occasion, contested by other groups, no other tribe has actually attempted to move into this most desolate of landscapes, which has little if any seasonal grasses, no natural water sources and is unfit for human habitation during the scorching summer months. It was only with the oil activity of the 1950s that the fortunes of the Harasiis and their grazing lands on the Jiddat were transformed. In 1958 an exploratory party came to a point called Haima in the middle of the

Jiddat il-Harasiis and sank a water well there to support its oil activity. Another well was sunk at a point 70 km towards the coast, called al-Ajaiz. These two wells were the first water sources on the Jiddat il-Harasiis, an area approximately the size of Scotland. Al-Ajaiz became something of a magnet attracting pastoral families to its well and its seasonal browse. The Haima well was also used, but not to the same extent as that at Al Ajaiz, as the area surrounding Haima was a salt flat with very little grazing for the herds of camels and goats.

The traditional economy of the Harasiis was based on raising camels and goats by natural grazing for the production of milk, rather than meat. At the core of their way of life was migration determined by a combination of seasonal and ecological variables in the location of pasture and water. Survival of both herds and herders vitally demanded movement from deficit to surplus areas. Households were and are still generally extended family units, the average family being composed of nine members.

At the core of the household is the nuclear family of husband, wife and children. Generally two or three adults, of one degree of kinship or another, make up the rest of the household. On average a household keeps 100 goats, which are owned by and the responsibility of women and older girls. The average household also has 25 camels, of which 5 or 6 are generally kept near the homestead – these are the heavily pregnant or lactating ones. The remainder of the camels are left free to graze in the open desert. The whereabouts of these animals are very carefully monitored and an elaborate camel information exchange system operates among all the tribesmen. When they meet, tribesmen first exchange news about the conditions of pastures, then the whereabouts of various loose camels, and finally news items of various family members. Homesteads are generally moved a significant distance three or four times a year.[5]

Basic to the organization of all pastoral people is the existence of sedentary communities in adjacent areas and access to their agricultural products. The trading towns important to the Harasiis tribe have been along the northern desert foothills of the Sharqiyya, particularly Adam and Sinaw. The cash economy of the village was reinforced by the continual influx of "capital on the hoof". Transactions were completed and money exchanged hands. Significantly though, when the final purchases were made, the bulk of the money had simply moved from one end of the market to another – from the animal buyer's pocket to the merchants till. For the Harasiis, the relationship with the villages reinforced not a cash, but a subsistence economy. Until the late 1970s, this economic interaction was unchanged among the Harasiis and extended no further than these border desert villages and towns.

[5]In 1980 the Omani government cooperated with the United Nations to implement a 2-year anthropological study and needs assessment of the Harasiis tribe. I led this project and as a result was able to promote the opening of a boarding school in 1982 for boys and later a special day school for girls. Increasingly over the past two decades, Harasiis families have either camped near Haima or have taken up residence in "low-cost" housing units on the edge of the centre while the schools are in session.

8.6 Transforming and Contesting Authenticity

In the early months of 1980, shortly after my arrival in the Sultanate of Oman, I was offered an opportunity to join a small convoy of vehicles across the desert of Oman. The trip was to take a week and would start in Salalah, the capital of Dhofar, the southern region of Oman, to cross the deserts of Oman and end up in Muscat. It was not quite the retracing of the steps of the English explorers Bertram Thomas in the 1930s and Wilfred Thesiger in the 1940s, but it felt like it. The purpose of the journey was partially to permit a medical team to trace several lapsed tuberculosis patients from tribes in the Dhofari interior and, at the same time, to provide immunization vaccines to the children of these communities. Halfway through our journey we came across a small group of nomadic pastoral Harasiis families preparing for a wedding. We took the opportunity to stop and to seek their permission to begin the course of immunization against some of the six WHO-targeted childhood diseases (poliomyelitis, diphtheria, tetanus, measles and rubella). "Why," we were asked, "do you want to do this?" Our answer was, "The Sultan of Oman wishes to see all Omanis immunized against these diseases." "Why," they continued, "should he want to do this for us?" We were initially lost for an answer, having assumed that the notion of Omani citizenship and the sense of belonging to one nation had reached these parts. They had not yet.

In 1981, I began a 14-year close association with this small nomadic pastoral tribe. My role was to assist the government in extending social services to this remote community. A Royal Decree had been issued that government services were to be extended into the interior desert in a way that would not force its inhabitants to give up their traditional migratory way of life. A policy had been formulated that needed to move through a bureaucratic hierarchy and emerge as a set of discretionary decisions made locally and on the ground.[6] Sultan Qaboos had encouraged the government ministries to push "development" forward into the remote interior of the country to offer its people the same services that the government had extended to the settled folk in the rest of the country during the first 10 years of his reign. His perception of the desert landscape as a "created" physical, social and cultural environment inhabited by nomadic pastoral, was undoubtedly informed by his own mother's origins as a Qara tribeswoman in Dhofar.

Over a 2-year period, as a "Technical Assistance Expert" with the United Nations Development Programme (UNDP), and with the help of two Peace Corps volunteers, I was allowed by the Minister of Health and the Minister of Education to set up both mobile and sedentary health services as well as a weekly boarding school for boys with day enrolment for girls (Dyer 2006). Other government services relevant to these mobile pastoralists were more difficult to organize. Here the policy landscape saw the "hilltop" policy formulations of the Sultan, re-interpreted by the bureaucratic hierarchy

[6]Allen Rew has described the constraints on policy and practice in development as a pyramid landscape. There is the hilltop where policy is formulated; then the plateau where bureaucratic hierarchy prevails and at the base a broad expanse of discretionary practice and local coping strategies (Rew et al. 2000).

to create a landscape in the desert that attempted to reproduce the settled, "civilized" landscapes they were familiar with in the coastal and mountain valley settlement. For example, opening government offices in the remote tribal centre of Haima generally meant borrowing all the rules and regulations of a civil service developed around *hadari* – settled – needs. Thus government welfare benefits became possible for unmarried, widowed and divorced women, the handicapped and disabled. But elderly widowers or bachelors with no family to support them were excluded from government support. Harasiis concepts of welfare and aid extended to elderly men and women alike. There was recognition that in the extreme environment of the Jiddat il-Harasiis, generation was as important as gender in determining need.

Housing and shelter were particularly problematic, as government officials and ministers could not conceive of the desert being occupied in any other way than in permanent village settlements. The urban concepts of settled space reigned supreme. Thus the outsider's view of the desert landscape became more powerful than that of the insider inhabitant. The reality of the widespread dispersal of small household camps over the 40,000 km^2 of the Jiddat was inconceivable to government bureaucrats, whatever the Royal Decrees might have suggested. Hence our highly successful 1982 UNDP programme of canvas tent distribution among the Harasiis households met with obstruction and eventually failure when we tried to set it up as a recurrent government programme. In an interview with the Minster of Housing in Muscat in 1984 to plead for a continuation of the tent distribution programme, I was told that the Ministry had to be seen to be doing something useful in the interior and tents were not progressive. He needed permanent "mortar and cement", and thus government modern cement housing would have to be built – units of 20–30 British-designed two-story town houses; no matter that this mode of architectural space was more suitable to an English suburb than an Arabian desert.[7] The units were built in 1985 and stood empty for more than a decade, except when they were used to shelter Harasiis goat herds, or hired out to expatriate labourers imported by local traders and oil company subcontractors.

The distribution of potable water was another area of critical concern to the Harasiis tribe, but not fully understood by government, whose rules of auctioning time for agricultural irrigation were well established (see Wilkinson 1977). The tribal elders petitioned the government to finance a carefully constructed decentralized plan to distribute water to households spread out over the Jiddat il-Harasiis based on a horizontal organization in which all seven of the tribe's lineages were involved. The mid-level government bureaucrats, however, found it easier and more in line with the way Oman's towns and villages were organized to hand over the keys to the water bowser trucks to the tribal leaders recognized by the government and the oil company. For many years thereafter, water distribution rested in the hands of a few powerful individuals rather than with a syndicate as the tribal elders had hoped for.

Even the request for agricultural extension – a national programme widespread along the coast and in the interior towns of the country and well funded by various international agencies such as USAID and the oil company – failed to be granted to

[7] Interview with Minister of Housing, Ahmed Al Ghazali (1984).

the desert interior. Despite numerous requests for assistance from Harasiis tribal elders to improve breeding stock and to experiment in growing salt-resistant fodder, government ignorance of and disinterest in tribal subsistence and its potential for marketing meant that all livestock extension programmes were restricted to the coast and interior towns.[8]

For decades the oil company was perceived locally as the government in the desert. Its exploration activities had resulted in three water wells being left open and maintained for the use of the local Harasiis, a service that was widely appreciated. As the major employer in the region – albeit generally for unskilled and short-term work contracts – it had a grasp of the social makeup and organization of these nomadic pastoralists. Thus, when the international demand for greater social corporate responsibility resulted in the requirement that environmental and social impact assessments be conducted prior to any further oil extraction in the Central Desert of Oman, much was expected. However, many local and expatriate petroleum engineers' view was that the desert was a landscape full of promising mineral resources (i.e. gas and oil) and devoid of people; people, the company engineers maintained, only emerged from other regions opportunistically when the oil company set up camp.[9] This particular representation of the desert was mirrored in the expert social impact assessments commissioned by the oil companies. As late as 2006, Occidental carried out a preliminary environment impact assessment of one of the most important Harasiis grazing areas, Wadi Mukhaizana (Fucik 2006). The "findings" of this report were that the area was devoid of people – at the time of the 2-week study – and thus no social impact assessment would be necessary. It was empty of people at the time of the brief visit of the European consultant. But the absence of people and herds at that moment was related more to the lack of rain in that season than to an absence of tribal use rights to the wadi. Only 5 years earlier, the largest oil company in Oman had commissioned a social impact assessment of the same wadi and found significant numbers of authentic local Harasiis there (Rae and Chatty 2001). Notwithstanding this earlier impact assessment, Occidental has since developed a spaghetti junction of oil and gas infrastructure in the wadi, devastating the grazing area for a large number of Harasiis families. Harasiis rights to this land have been denied and no adequate compensation or restitution has been considered. Overall, the major oil companies in the central desert of Oman take the view that

[8]The Sultan asked the oil company to set up an experimental farm using artesian water in the desert to show how the "desert could bloom". Rahab Farm was successfully set up near Marmul in the southern province of Oman and proceeded to sell its alfalfa and other grasses locally. But its goat-breeding programme, which fascinated the local tribes, was closed down without any effort made to introduce these animals to local herds.

[9]These views are common globally in the dispute over petroleum exploration in areas of human habitation. In the Amazonian belt where tribes have sought to remain in isolation, efforts to stop petroleum exploration have resulted in the denial of their existence. Recently the president of Peru, Alan Garcia, was quoted as saying "the figure of the jungle native" is a ruse to prevent oil exploration. Daniel Saba, the former head of the state oil company in Peru, added more scornfully, "It is absurd to say there are uncontacted people when no one has seen them. So, who are these uncontacted tribes people are talking about?" (Carroll 2009: 27).

these concession areas are *terra nullius* or empty land (Gilbert 2007). They lay their pipelines across important tribal migration routes causing disruption if not obstruction for Harasiis herders trying to transport or move their herd from one grazing area to another.[10] A slow and gradual process of dislocation followed by displacement is occurring (Chatty 1994).

Furthermore, conservationists – both national and international – have regarded the central desert of Oman as their own backyard, ignoring the presence and authenticity of its local human inhabitants. Conservationists viewed the desert as a landscape as well, but one shaped by plants and animals, not people. Their concern was to restore a balance to this landscape by returning to it animals that had been hunted to extinction in the 1970s. Planned in the late 1970s, the international flagship conservation effort, the Arabian Oryx Re-introduction Project, was set up and put into effect in the Jiddat il-Harasiis. Between 1980 and 1996, 450 Arabian oryx were returned to "the wild" in the Jiddat il-Harasiis and Harsusi males were hired to track these animals. In 1994 Oman succeeded in getting this conservation project recognized formally as the UNESCO World Heritage Arabian Oryx Sanctuary. But ongoing and constant friction between the Western managers of the conservation project and the local Harasiis tribesmen regarding their "rights" to graze their domestic herds in large parts of their territory – now officially a UNESCO nature reserve – eventually led the Harasiis to distance themselves from the project and resulted in a lack or diminution of any sense of ownership or use rights.

Two representations of the desert landscape came to a head: a Western conservation protectionist vision of a pristine landscape of plants and animals and the local tribal vision of a landscape with sets of cultural and historical concepts relating people and domestic animals to desert spaces and places. When between 1996 and 1998 poaching and illegal capture of the oryx by rival tribes resulted in the loss of more than 350 animals, the Harasiis could do little to stop this downward spiral. Other tribes were actively acting out their disaffection. The Harasiis youth had become alienated, and the elders were no longer interested in the transformed landscape in the part of their traditional territory from which they had been dislocated. In 2007, The Arabian Oryx Sanctuary became the first World Heritage site to ever be deleted from the UNESCO list of World Heritage Sites. The justification for this unprecedented step was the rapid decline in oryx numbers (from 450 to 65) and the supposed degradation of its grazing area.

8.7 Responding to Increasing Dislocation

The Harasiis tribe has for centuries occupied the central desert of Oman as well as other remote and generally inaccessible regions when lack of precipitation or other weather or political extremes so demanded. Mobility among Harasiis households

[10]For a brief period of time in the early 1990s, one oil company did agree to bury any new pipelines at 5 km intervals across the desert to facilitate the requirement of the Harasiis and other nomadic pastoral tribes to move themselves and their animals around the desert floor.

has seen them split their family groups into satellite camps as they search out the best grazing land for their camels and their goats. Certainly, in the earlier parts of the twentieth century their presence across the wide desert region of southeast Arabia up to the borders to the Trucial Coast (currently the UAE) were well documented. The lack of definitive elaboration of borders between the Sultanate, the United Arab Emirates and Saudi Arabia has meant that these tribesmen have moved across "borders" since their "creation" in the twentieth century. Goods, people and ideas flowed across these regions and the Harasiis and other pastoral communities took advantage of differentials across these newly established modern states. One example highlighting the early openness of movement that has since been shut down is that of Hamad, a Harasiis camel herder and expert tracker and guide to hunting parties. Hamad worked for the government of Oman for over 25 years and recently retired with a state pension. For most of his life he has moved freely across the desertscapes of Oman, Saudi Arabia and the UAE. With family and herds spread out between the United Arab Emirates (UAE) and Oman, he has long maintained camps and – more recently – residences in the central desert of Oman and along the UAE-Saudi borderland. His vehicles have both UAE and Oman registration plates, and his family avails itself of health and education services in both locations. Several decades ago he applied for and received two passports, one Omani and the other from the UAE, to facilitate his movements across this translocality. In 2002, motivated by petty local jealousy among non-local oil company staff, he was reported to the local governor and told to turn in one of his two passports; dual nationality was supposedly no longer permitted to Oman citizens. Unwilling to challenge this demand, he has returned his Omani passport, but continues his cross-regional or translocal movements for the health of his family and his herds. His family spends much of the year in the UAE, several of his sons work for the UAE police force and his camels remain in Oman and are herded by Baluchi and Sindhi hired herds. He collects his pension from the local governor's office in the Omani central desert. His identity is as a Harasiis tribesman. Which passport he holds means little to him, as crossing the borders between Oman and the UAE is relatively easy, with little or no restriction.

The question "Why should he [the Sultan] want to do this for us?" that I was asked in 1981 when attempting to immunize Harasiis children, comes to mind here. The notion of Omani citizenship and sense of belonging to one nation cannot be comfortably squared with the translocality of Harasiis identity and belonging to the desertscapes of southeast Arabia.

8.8 Conclusion

The authenticity of the Harasiis and other nomadic pastoral tribes has been challenged by national governmental and multi-national bodies that have their own views on the landscapes of Oman and the wider region. Recognizing the tensions that exist between the traditional and modern and between the *bedu* and the *hadar* has meant that representations of landscapes are subject to hegemonic power. Space and place are not resolved in a singular representation that encapsulates the political fiction of a united state. There is no one absolute landscape, but rather a series of related and also contradictory perspectives. Omani policy formulations recognize elements of the authenticity of the Harasiis' vision of their desert landscapes. But bureaucratic hierarchy prioritizes and puts into practice landscape perspectives quite contrary: *hadar* landscapes imposed upon *bedu* territories; multinational extractive industry's perspectives of landscapes of no human imprint, but replete with natural resources under the surface; and conservation landscapes of pristine import momentarily unbalanced by humans' disregard for the equilibrium of flora and fauna. And in addition, settled perspectives make the translocal irregular or illegal. These visions explain the lack of interest in the authenticity of Harasiis culture, in the lack of government interest in developing or promoting Harasiis livestock raising economy and the oil companies lack of interest in Harasiis claims to spaces and places they have inhabited at one time or another for centuries. At the same time, Harasiis claims of mobile and translocal identities are denied.

The Harasiis are increasingly becoming dislocated by the current prospecting and extractive activity of the oil and gas industry. Their restricted access to areas adjacent to the former Arabian Oryx Sanctuary has also impacted heavily on their sense of mobility and grazing rights. Contemporary government unwillingness to recognize the importance of mobility in their way of life is threatening their freedom of movement, as families are increasingly finding themselves tied to government centres to access education, health and welfare for the vulnerable weak, the young and the old.

For the first four decades of Oman's modern nation-building history (from 1970 to the present), a truly integrationist approach seemed to hold in which all Omanis from whatever background were called upon to work together to build a new "modern" nation. Now, however, with much of the building in place, an assimilationist outlook and approach seems to have taken hold that is curiously out of step with global trends. Oman, in its recent failures to recognize the authenticity and translocality of its minority tribes, seems to have replaced an open-minded, ahead-of-its time, integrationist vision of the development of the modern state with a backward-looking assimilationist perspective at the expense of the country's unique *bedu* heritage.

These challenges to the authenticity of Harasiis tribe and their desert landscapes are being addressed in different ways. Attachment to place and space is difficult to transform. Disassociation is even harder. Some families are settling part of the extended group in government housing and hiring shepherds from Baluchistan and the Indian subcontinent to look after their mobile herds of goat and camel. Others are picking themselves up and moving their families to the United Arab Emirates, where the national perception of the desert landscape and the place of the *bedu* in it reflect their own vision. The Emirate government has built two *bedu* settlements made up of low-lying and spread-out bungalows near the Abu Dhabi/Saudi border that effectively address local perceptions of *bedu* culture, ideas of appropriate shelter and desert landscapes. Some Harasiis as well as other pastoral tribal elements from Oman, Saudi Arabia and Qatar have moved their families to these settlements.

The move is not permanent; nor is the settlement static. The Harasiis continue to move back and forth across borders. However the sense of "being *bedu*" is reinforced by the other tribal elements also moving into these created desert landscapes in Abu Dhabi. Mass education and mass communications (Eickelman 1992) also reinforces their sense of authenticity.[11] The United Arab Emirates national identity is closely tied with both the *bedu* in the interior and the *hadar* merchants in the coastal towns. Here several representations of landscapes encapsulate the imagined state, including that of the *hadar* and that of the *bedu*. As in the Kingdom of Jordan (see Layne 1994; Shryock 1995), *bedu* culture and its role in the development of the notion of national identity is important in the UAE. Unfortunately this is not the case of Oman. There seems to be in Oman no recognition yet that assimilating traditional or minority people who resist such policy is not the way to build a strong country (Blackburn 2007). Recognition of the tribes and their authenticity in the desertscapes of southeast Arabia would not radically pluralize Oman nor negatively impact on state-building processes.

References

Al Ghazali, A. (1984). *Interview*. Muscat: Ministry of Housing.

Anderson, B. (1983). *Imagined communities: Reflections on the origin and spread of nationalism*. London: Verso.

Aplin, G. (2007). World heritage cultural landscapes. *International Journal of Heritage Studies, 13*(6), 427–446.

Appadurai, A. (1996). *Modernity at large: Cultural dimensions of globalization*. Minneapolis: University of Minnesota Press.

Blackburn, C. (2007). Producing legitimacy: Reconciliation and the negotiation of aboriginal rights in Canada. *The Journal of the Royal Anthropological Institute, 13*, 621–638.

Carroll, R. (2009, July 4). Rumble in the Jungle. *The Guardian Weekend*, pp. 23–27.

Chatty, D. (1994). Petroleum exploitation and the displacement of pastoral nomadic households in Oman. In S. Shami (Ed.), *Population displacement and resettlement: Development and conflict in the Middle East* (pp. 89–106). New York: Center for Migration Studies.

de Jong, F. (1999). The production of translocality. Initiation in the sacred grove in Southern Senegal. In R. Richard, W. van Binsbergen, & R. van Dijk (Eds.), *Modernity on a shoestring. Dimensions of globalization, consumption and development in Africa and beyond* (pp. 315–340). Leiden/London: EIDOS.

Dyer, C. (Ed.). (2006). *The education of nomadic peoples: Current issues, future prospects*. Oxford: Berghahn Books.

Eickelman, D. (1989). *The Middle East: An anthropological approach*. Englewood Cliffs: Prentice Hall.

[11] Although the lack of continuous sources of electricity limits the use of the Internet and computers, the early and widespread use of mobile phones and satellite phones suggests that the Harasiis and other desert dwellers continue to maintain a greater affinity with the spoken than with the written word.

Eickelman, D. (1992). Mass higher education and the religious imagination in contemporary Arab societies. *American Ethnologist, 19*, 643–655.
Freitag, U., & von Oppen, A. (2010). Introduction: Translocality: An approach to connection and transfer in area studies. In U. Freitag & A. von Oppen (Eds.), *Translocality: The study of globalising processes from a Southern perspective* (pp. 1–24). Leiden: Brill.
Fucik, K. (2006). *Environmental impact assessment in Wadi Mukhaizana*. Muscat: Occidental Oil.
Gellner, E. (1983). *Nations and nationalism*. Oxford: Basil Blackwell.
Gilbert, J. (2007). Nomadic territories: A human rights approach to nomadic peoples' land rights. *Human Rights Law Review, 7*(4), 681–716.
Hirsch, E., & O'Hanlon, M. (Eds.). (1995). *The anthropology of landscape: Perspectives on place and space*. Oxford: Clarendon.
Jackson, J. (1984). *Discovering the vernacular landscape*. New Haven: Yale University Press.
Johnstone, T. M. (1977). *Harsusi lexicon*. Oxford: Oxford University Press.
Khaldûn, I. (1958). *The Muqaddimah: An introduction to history* (F. Rosenthal, Trans.). Princeton: Princeton University Press.
Layne, L. (1994). *Home and homeland: The dialogics of tribal and national identities in Jordan*. Princeton: Princeton University Press.
Peterson, J. (1978). *Oman in the twentieth century*. New York/London: Croom Helm.
Peterson, J. (2004a). Oman's diverse society: Northern Oman. *Middle East Journal, 58*(1), 32–51.
Peterson, J. (2004b). Oman's diverse society: Southern Oman. *Middle East Journal, 58*(2), 255–269.
Peterson, J. (2007). *Oman's insurgencies: The sultanate's struggle for supremacy*. London: Saqi.
Rae, J., & Chatty, D. (2001). *Participatory project appraisal for the Mukhaizana field development: A social impact study*. Muscat: Petroleum Development Oman LLC.
Rew, A., Fischer, E., & Pandey, B. (2000). *Addressing policy constraints and improving outcomes in development-induced displacement and resettlement projects*. Oxford: Refugee Studies Centre, University of Oxford.
Scott, J. (2009). *The art of not being governed: An anarchist history of Southeast Asia*. New Haven: Yale University Press.
Shryock, A. (1995). Popular genealogical nationalism: History writing and identity among the Balqa Tribes of Jordan. *Comparative Studies in Society and History, 37*(2), 325–357.
Thomas, B. (1938). *Arabia Felix: Across the empty quarter*. London: Reader's Union.
Wilkinson, J. (1977). *Water and tribal settlement in South-East Arabia: A study of the Aflaj of Oman*. Oxford: Oxford Clarendon Press.
Wilkinson, J. (1983). Traditional concepts of territory in South East Arabia. *The Geographical Journal, 149*(3), 201–315.
Wilkinson, J. (1987). *The Imamate tradition of Oman*. Cambridge: Cambridge University Press.

Part III
Micro and Macro Regionalisation Through Economic Practices

Chapter 9
Re-reading the Role of Oman Within Its International Trade Relations: From the Sixteenth Through to the Nineteenth Centuries

Beatrice Nicolini

9.1 A Working Hypothesis

This paper attempts to answer the following question: are we so sure that Oman[1] was part of a global unity that long preceded the economic unification of the world that began in the sixteenth century, and the more recent processes of globalisation?

To approach this idea, we should consider more than one methodological perspective, such as the cultural and political "films" represented by the land and sea aspects. What we call "water drunkenness" shaped many readings of Oman and the Indian Ocean. And one of the results was an Indian Ocean history focused – and still focusing – mainly on the sea. The consequences of these interpretations can be misleading; watching and studying Oman from the sea, on the sea and to the sea leaves crucial issues such as land and land dynamics sometimes too far out of sight.

The gradual emergence of new Omani dynasties resulted from the polarizations that followed the struggles against the Portuguese presence in the Persian/Arab Gulf[2] and in the Indian Ocean during the sixteenth and seventeenth centuries. This gave rise to gradual and discontinuous processes of unification among the Omani groups,[3] traditionally divided and in conflict with each other, which came to the fore in the progressive affirmation of what we could define as the international power of the Omani Arabs in the Gulf and in the Indian Ocean.

---

[1] The word Oman was used by Europeans to describe all of South-Eastern Arabia to the east of the sands of the Rub' al Khali.

[2] From here on referred to as the Gulf.

[3] Aware of the lively debate on this issue, with the term "groups" we obviously include the tribes.

B. Nicolini, Ph.D. (✉)
Faculty of Political and Social Sciences, Università Cattolica del Sacro Cuore,
Largo Gemelli, 1, 20123 Milan, Italy
e-mail: beatrice.nicolini@unicatt.it

S. Wippel (ed.), *Regionalizing Oman: Political, Economic and Social Dynamics*, United Nations University Series on Regionalism 6, DOI 10.1007/978-94-007-6821-5_9,

The history of Omani international trade relations is closely connected to the maritime routes across the Indian Ocean: sailing the Gulf and the Indian Ocean had always been dependent on the fact that the winds occur in an annual sequence with great regularity (Tibbetts 1981: 360; Sheriff 2009: 173–188). The balance created by the monsoons[4] was achieved over the space of a year with the following rhythm: from December to March the monsoon blows from Arabia and the western coasts of India in the northeast, pushing as far as Mogadishu. The winds are light and constant, the climate hot and dry. In April the monsoon starts to blow from the southwest, from East Africa towards the coasts of the Gulf, the climate cooler but much more humid. The rains are mainly in April and May, while the driest months are November and December. Moreover, along the East African coasts and in the islands of the Indian Ocean, the tropical climate is always tempered by sea breezes.[5] Sailing from the Arabian Peninsula in November in a south-south-westerly direction took 30–40 days in ideal weather conditions while, in December, thanks to the stabilization of the monsoon, the voyages took only 20–25 days. Consequently, thanks to the monsoons, Oman's international trade relations were historically maritime; although, as stated above, we must remember that Omani trade was intense by land as well. Maritime coastal and long-distance trade manifested an economy that was already highly sophisticated, developed and organized; therefore, the necessity of control of these sea trade routes was a crucial political issue.

During the sixteenth century, the Portuguese presence in the Gulf did not really affect Omani trade; nevertheless, after the loss of Hormuz in 1622, the Portuguese increased their influence at Muscat while the Ya'ariba, an Omani dynasty that ruled in Oman and along the East African coasts during the seventeenth century, threatened the Portuguese forts along the coast of Oman, as well as the pearl trade from Julfar – today Ras al-Khaimah, UAE – and the trade in horses from Muscat (Floor 2006: 324–328).

9.2 Oman Dynasties

During the seventeenth century, the Ya'ariba dynasty fostered Oman's foreign trade with an active naval policy against the Portuguese, combined with an expansion of its mercantile influence in sub-Saharan East Africa. During the eighteenth century the Ya'ariba stood at the head of a flourishing mercantile realm that was closely linked to the coastal cities and the principal islands of East Africa. The Ya'ariba Omani domination of East African littorals, which included Mombasa and the island of Pemba, was characteristic of quite normal changes in dominion over the seas,

[4]The term derives from the Arabic mawsin (pl. mawasin), season, and from the Portuguese monçao.

[5]The monsoon winds were also economically important before the introduction of steam navigation around the second half of the nineteenth century in the Indian Ocean.

without resulting in substantial alterations in traditional commercial organizations. The presence of Arab deputies was always mainly to control trade and impose taxes; this institution had its roots in the traditional Omani systems of exercising power through local representatives, as well as in political agreements with local rulers. In this regard, the Ya'ariba, often assisted by merchants and bankers from the coasts of western India and defended by Asian – i.e. Baluch – troops, sailed to the coasts of sub-Saharan East Africa and progressively spread into the interior of Central East Africa (Pallaver 2008: 44–50; Rockel 2006). After centuries of relative prosperity, since the second half of the eighteenth century the traditional thalassocratic system that had developed along the shores of the Indian Ocean was progressively shattered by the Europeans, who started to pursue their mercantile and territorial ambitions with determination from the seas to the land (*terra firma*).

The Ya'ariba society was a society of rich and powerful merchants and landlords, and numerous forts were built in Oman during the Ya'ariba period. The round fort of Nizwa was started by Sultan bin Saif I (r. 1649–1680), while his son Bal'arab (r. 1688–1692) built the magnificent fort of Jabrin. Saif bin Sultan I (r. 1692–1711) was the greatest of the Ya'ariba princes and was succeeded by his eldest son Sultan bin Saif II, who in turn was succeeded as Imam, in 1719, by his son Saif bin Sultan II, a boy of 12. Unable to find any further support for his cause in Oman, Saif bin Sultan II turned to Persia for help, and a large Persian force soon invaded his country. The Omanis suffered many defeats but were finally helped by Ahmad bin Sa'id (r. 1792–1804), a member of the small Al Bu Sa'id group who at that time was Governor of Sohar. He succeeded in driving out the Persians and, after having overcome the Ya'ariba family and its supporters from the Ghafari tribe, was elected Imam and founded the present Al Bu Sa'id dynasty (Smith 1999: 292).

The title of Imam gave Ahmad bin Sa'id Al Bu Sa'id a certain control over Oman, and under him and his successors the country expanded for more than a century. The Omanis extended their influence into the interior and into part of what is now the United Arab Emirates (UAE), consisting of the future states of Abu Dhabi, Ajman, al-Fujairah, Dubai, Ras al-Khaimah, Sharjah and Umm al-Qaywayn. They also collected tribute from as far away as present-day Bahrain and Iraq. The Al Bu Sa'id conquered the Dhofar region, which is part of present-day Oman but was not historically part of the Oman region (Peterson 2001). Although Ahmad bin Sa'id Al Bu Sa'id succeeded in uniting Oman under an Ibadi imamate, his family's *religious* authority did not last long. His son, Saiyid Sa'id bin Sultan Al Bu Sa'id (r. 1806–1856), was elected to the Imamate after him, but no other family member won the official approval of the religious establishment. The Al Bu Sa'id called themselves *Sultans*, a secular title having none of the religious associations of Imam. They further distanced themselves from Ibadi traditions by moving their capital from Rustaq, a traditional Ibadi centre in the interior, to the trading centre of Muscat. The result was that the traditional conflictual relationships between the coast and the interior – the land and the sea – were reconstituted. Starting in the eighteenth century, groups from the interior gradually began to settle on the coastal new centres.

9.3 Trade Places and International Communities

Within these new coastal centres, international trade witnessed the gradual emergence of the town of Muscat. During the nineteenth century, the picturesque Bay of Muscat was – and still is today – a semicircle, enclosed by the mountains and with cliffs dropping to the sea on which fortifications were built to keep a lookout for enemies. The hinterland of Muscat is so mountainous that, in the nineteenth century, it could only be reached on camel or donkey back; just outside the town, the coast was mainly desert, hilly and desolate. Water resources have always been scarce in Oman and, in 1800, the price of the famous sweet, clean water of Muscat was extremely high (Ward 1987: 4). A varied and vivacious world animated Muscat: merchants from all over travelled there, Arabs, Indians, Hebrews, Turks, Armenians, Africans, Persians… The dwellings were *barasti*, huts with roves of palm leaves and mud houses. The *suq* (old market) of Matrah, near Muscat, spread over a large area, almost entirely built up with dwellings and narrow and winding alleyways. Here, every kind of merchandise could be found, silk and linen, spices, dates, coffee brought across the desert by caravans, pearls, green and black grapes, bananas, figs, butter, fowl, goats and cattle, and even delicious mangos imported mainly by sea. The rich Omani merchants wore long, wide robes of extraordinarily clean white cotton, with wide sleeves and waists bound by belts from which emerged their beautiful silver knives, the *khanjar*, and swords. The most imposing were the Baluch warriors, naked to the waist and armed with a knife and a double-handed sword, with fierce glares and of threatening presence (Nicolini 2008: 327–344). In 1825 Saiyid Sa'id bin Sultan Al Bu Sa'id's income amounted to 522,000 Maria Theresa thalers (Broome 1972: 221–253; Semple 2005), of which 120,000 came from Zanzibar. The maritime city of Muscat, thanks to its strategic position at the entrance to the Gulf, was always held to be the best port of the entire Arabian Peninsula. The highest peak in the mountain ranges was mount Jabal Akhdar (2,743 m), where snow falls during the winter months, and even grapes were grown on its slopes, from which the Portuguese, during their presence there, made a wine called *muscatel*.

From the earliest times, the port had always been a lively and bustling place. Its position, almost hidden among the rocks, made it an ideal harbour for merchants, sailors, adventurers and pirates who found fruit and drinking water there. During the nineteenth century it was densely populated, a true crossroads for trade between East Africa, the eastern shores of the Gulf and Western India. The Marani and Djallali forts, built by the Portuguese in 1527, defended it. Towards the end of the eighteenth century, the English merchant and explorer Abraham Parsons (d. 1785) described Muscat as a quite cosmopolitan city, where the tolerance of the political leaders permitted flourishing trade and multi-religious, multi-ethnic coexistence (Ward 1987: 8). Numerous caravans arrived daily from the interior to unload ostrich feathers, animal horns, sheep and leather, honey and beeswax and to bear away knives, games, spices, rice, sugar, coffee and tobacco. The English explorer noted also that trade between Muscat and Mocha (al-Muqah) was extremely intense; the Omani city sent 20,000 bales of coffee to Basra, every year, destined for Constantinople. Trade towards the interior, in contrast, was mainly in Persian carpets and silk, along with pearls. He further commented that drinking water was taken on board ships by barges drawn by oxen because the land was too uneven for barrels to be rolled over it. Many merchants were semi-naked and attempted to cool themselves by the use of ingenuous fans since, as Parsons admitted, "Muscat is the hottest place on earth" (Ward 1987: 9). Lastly, he also remarked on how many of the inhabitants were ill or in need of treatment.

In the nineteenth century Muscat was mainly known as a fearsome den of pirates, and the British presence in the Omani port was permanent precisely from this century on. The assignment of a Resident there was, however, abolished as early as 1809 due to the deleterious impact of the Muscat climate on the English. The Omani port therefore came under the jurisdiction of Bushire, today in Iran (Onley 2007).

Among the many Indian merchants trading in Muscat and the Gulf there were the *Bhatta*, originally from Rajasthan (from *Bhatti*, *Subhatta*, Hindu warriors of the Vaishnavit caste). Another group of Bhatta were the Kutch, again Hindus who in the seventeenth century enjoyed great prestige in Muscat and whom the Arabs exempted from taxation. Together with these groups of merchants, there were also the Khoja, who were Isma'ilis. Mainly Muslims (*Bohra* and *Khoja*) were employed in foreign and seagoing trade, while Jains and Hindus (*Banya* and *Bhatta*) dominated the banking and finance fields. These merchants were vividly described by European explorers of the nineteenth century, who took note of their complexion, fairer than that of the Arabs, their fine features, long moustaches but no beards and a Chinese pigtail at the base of a shaved head. Stress was also laid on the elegance and sumptuousness of their attire: silk tunics with long, ruffled sleeves, a clear sign that they were not involved in any form of manual labour.

The multiple roles of these merchants were among the essential and deciding factors in development also on the East African island of Zanzibar during the nineteenth century, where they were extremely active. They were called *banyan* (*vaniya*, in Gujurati *vaniyo*, man of the merchant caste, from the Sanskrit *vanij*, merchant, later Anglicized as *banyan*, a term used to indicate Hindu as opposed to Muslim merchants) (Allen 1978: 128; Bhacker 1992: 209; Lodhi 2000: 68–71; Sheriff 2010: 183–189). There were, moreover, "money tasters", who tested and tasted the good quality of the coins, and *sarruf* moneychangers (from whence we have the English term *shroff*), called *mushrikun* by the Arabs, "pagans" but included in the Islamic institution of *aman* (protection) (Blanchy 2005). In their accounts and in the communiqués of the East India Company representatives, the British used the term *banyan* to designate both the Hindu castes and the Indian Isma'ili communities, this mix-up being quite frequent.

Since the end of the eighteenth century, the Al Bu Sa'id fostered the mercantile expansion towards the oceanic coasts of Africa; a cultural synthesis thereby developed across the Indian Ocean, represented by continuous migratory flows in which the land factor strongly influenced the sea factor. During the nineteenth century, Muscat's dominions consisted of the island of Bahrain, the coast of Makran, which today belongs to Pakistan (Nicolini 2009: 239–267), some areas along the Persian coast such as Chah Bahar, the island of Socotra (Yemen), the islands of Kuria Muria (a group of five islands in the Arabian Sea, southern Oman), the islands of Zanzibar and Pemba and adjacent ports of the East African coast from Cape Guardafui (also named Ras Asir, in Somalia) to Cabo Delgado (a promontory that gives today a Mozambican province its name). And it was in this very period that the presence of many economic opportunities on the East African littorals was a potent factor increasingly drawing the Omani Arabs to East Africa.

9.4 The Sultan's "Myth"

Saiyid Sa'id bin Sultan Al Bu Sa'id vitalised an important mercantile empire in the Indian Ocean. The main factors in the rise of a mighty maritime trade network were the expansion of the spice trade, especially by the cultivation of cloves in Zanzibar and the Pemba islands (*Unguja*), the slave trade, ivory exportation and their implications in relation to the European powers of the nineteenth century. The creation of a new niche of agricultural exploitation in Zanzibar itself and in Pemba was destined to transform both islands into new centres of global mercantile interests (Croucher 2007: 302–325).

Saiyid Sa'id bin Sultan Al Bu Sa'id spoke Arabic, Hindi, Persian and Swahili; he saw the island of Zanzibar for the first time in 1802, when he was only 11 years old – and remained bewitched (Maurizi 1984; Lorimer 1915: 440–469; Ruete 1929: 417–432; Farsi 1986; Badger 1986: 407). He was the major exponent of the revaluation of the spice trade as a means to create a new power elite by significantly expanding the cultivation of cloves in Zanzibar. This highlights one of the first major steps towards the importance of spice. At the end of the eighteenth century the introduction of cloves (*Eugenya Caryophyllata*, from the *Mirtacee* family, called *kavafuu* in Swahili) to this tropical island opened Al Bu Sa'id's eyes to new economic-commercial potential. At that time, the Sultan of the island, Saiyid Sa'id bin Sultan Al Bu Sa'id, had three wives, an infinite number of concubines and at least 120 children. His wives were Azza bin Seif bin Imam Ahmad, who lived in the palace at Mntoni on Zanzibar; the niece of the Shah of Persia, Fath 'Ali Shah Qajar, whom the Sultan had married in 1827 on the condition that she could spend long periods at her father's court in Teheran, from whence she no longer returned following a ferocious argument in 1832 during which Saiyid Sa'id bin Sultan Al Bu Sa'id was even called a "Sunni dog"; the third was Shahruzad bin Irish Mirza bin Muhammad, great granddaughter of Shah Muhammad of Persia, whom Saiyid Sa'id bin Sultan Al Bu Sa'id married in 1837. She arrived in Zanzibar with a valuable dowry, a following of 150 men and numerous horses on which to go hunting. Sharuzad had Persian baths built at Kidichi and Kizimbani, the ruins of which still bear witness today to the artistic sensitivity of this, the Sultan of Zanzibar's last wife

(Farsi 1986: 11–22). The mother of Hilal bin Sa'id Al Bu Sa'idi, son of Saiyid Sa'id bin Sultan Al Bu Sa'id, was a concubine.[6]

On the sea, the Sultan, himself a great sailor, possessed a fleet including the *Liverpool*, a magnificent vessel built in Bombay in 1826, with 74 cannon and a crew of 150. In an attempt to soften the inflexible stance of the British toward the slave trade, he sent this ship as a gift to British King William IV who, however, limited himself to renaming the ship *Imam*. A further 18 ships were also at the Sultan's disposal.

The Sultan had demonstrated his respect for Great Britain as an international sea power on numerous occasions, including with the marvellous gifts he sent to all British representatives and by permitting ships of the Royal Navy and the Bombay Marine to perform the thankless task of enforcing the terms of the abolition treaties in the Indian Ocean. His life was certainly long: Saiyid Sa'id bin Sultan Al Bu Sa'id died on 19 October 1856, when he was 65 years old, in the Seychelles on a dhow[7] (Hourani 1995: 89; Agius 2008) that was taking him from Muscat to Zanzibar. This marked the end of an epoch, but not the end of the multiple cultural and political "films" or of the numerous mercantile routes vitalised by the Omani red flag across the Indian Ocean.

9.5 Conclusion

As more than one cultural and political "film" unfolded, the power balances among regional and international leaderships shifted during the nineteenth century. In this regard, we agree with Lorenz and Mattheis (in this volume) when they affirm that "the region is both a setting and an instrument for emerging actors that claim more influence in the international political economy". Consequently, external presences of the time, such as the European powers, altered the dynamics and continuous movements in the Omani and other mercantile communities throughout the Indian Ocean and inevitably influenced future substantial changes in these seaboard regions. Probably, regional leaderships, such as those of Oman and Zanzibar, were not so rich (Deutsch and Reinwald 2002: 61–73), and the Omani sultans did not generally benefit that much from the trade. Moreover, they did not control, in the modern European meaning, the whole of the East African coast from Cape Guardafui to Cabo Delgado. Proof is found in the revolts of the Omani group in East Africa against the newly established dynasty of the Al Bu Sa'id in Oman. In this regard, the presence of the Mazaria group (sing. Mazrui) in Mombasa and along the coasts and on some islands of East Africa may have been an important factor hindering Omani control of its East African possessions. During the eighteenth century, the Mazaria group of Mombasa, of Arab origin, was an ally of the Ya'ariba of Oman. At that time the East African

[6]Personal conversation with Dr. Rashid Al-Dhyabi, Zawawi Group, Sultanate of Oman, 2009.

[7]Daw is a Swahili name, not used by the Arabs but adopted by English writers in the form "dhow".

littorals were divided into numerous small states owing allegiance to Oman because Oman had expelled the Portuguese from them in 1698. With the Al Bu Sa'id's accession to power in Oman, the Mazaria (1735–1837) remained a virtually independent dynasty. In 1822 the Al Bu Sa'id sent an expedition that drove the Mazaria not only from Mombasa, but also from Pemba Island. In 1827 the Al Bu Sa'id asserted their authority: one effect was a great increase in the revenues remitted. There ensued a struggle between the Al Bu Sa'id and the Mazaria for Mombasa that ended only in 1837 when, by a ruse, the Al Bu Sa'id took some 30 of the Mazaria captive. All were deported and some were killed (Gray 1957; Brown 1972; Ritchie 1995; Powels 1996: 301–318). Thus, starting from 1842, the presence of Omani Arabs on the East African coasts led to numerous intersections between regional and international interests, with Britain often turning new realities into new political scenarios. In this context, our working hypothesis concerning the re-reading of the role of Omani dynasties in the realities of the Indian Ocean must take into consideration also the perception of strength. Here regional and international trade followed ancient distributions of forces and power along ancient routes across the land as well as on the sea. And it is precisely along these land and sea routes that we should search for new explanations of the past and present.

References

Agius, D. (2008). *Classic ships of Islam: From Mesopotamia to the Indian Ocean*. Leiden: Brill Academic Publishers.

Allen, C. H. Jr. (1978). *Sayyids, Shets and Sultans: Politics and trade in Musqat under the Al Bu Sa'id, 1785–1914*. PhD dissertation, University of Washington, Seattle

Badger, G. P. (1986). *History of the imams and seyyids of Oman*. London: Darf Publishers.

Bhacker, M. R. (1992). *Trade and empire in Muscat and Zanzibar. Roots of British domination*. London: Routledge.

Blanchy, S. (2005). *Karana et Banians. Les Communautés commerçantes d'origine indienne à Madagascar*. Paris: L'Harmattan.

Broome, M. (1972). The 1780 restrike talers of Maria Theresa. Doris Stockwell memorial papers, *Numismatic Chronicle,* VII series, XII, Manchester.

Brown, R. T. (1972). *William Fitzwilliam Owen: Hydrographer of the African coast, 1774–1857*, History – Dissertations and Theses, 75. http://surface.syr.edu/hst_etd/75

Croucher, S. K. (2007). Clove plantations on nineteenth-century Zanzibar. *Journal of Social Archaeology, 7*, 302–325.

Deutsch, J. G., & Reinwald, B. (2002). *Space on the move. Transformations of the Indian Ocean seascape in the nineteenth and twentieth century*. Berlin: Klaus Schwarz Verlag.

Farsi, S. A. S. (1986). *Seyyid Said Bin Sultan. The joint ruler of Oman and Zanzibar (1804–1856)*. New Delhi: Lancers Books.

Floor, W. (2006). *The Persian Gulf. A political and economic history of five port cities 1500–1730*. Washington, DC: Mage Publishers.

Gray, J. M. (1957). *The British in Mombasa 1824–1826. Being the history of captain Owen's protectorate*. London: Macmillan.

Hourani, G. F. (1995). *Arab seafaring* (Rev. edn. [1951]). Princeton: Princeton University Press.

Lodhi, A. (2000). *Oriental influences in Swahili. A study in language and culture contacts*. Göteborg: Acta Universitatis Gothoburgensis.

Lorimer, J. G. (1915). *Gazetteer of the Persian Gulf, Oman and Central Arabia.* Calcutta: Superintendent Government Printing.

Maurizi, V. (1984). *History of Seyd Said, Sultan of Muscat.* Cambridge: Cambridge University Press.

Nicolini, B. (2008). Slave trade in the Western Indian Ocean during the 19th century: the role of Baloch mercenaries. In C. Jahani, P. Titus, & A. Korn (Eds.), *The Baloch and others: Linguistic, historical and socio-political perspectives on pluralism in Balochistan* (pp. 327–344). Wiesbaden: Reichert.

Nicolini, B. (2009). The myth of the sultans in the Western Indian Ocean during the nineteenth century: a new hypothesis. *African and Asian Studies, 8*(3), 239–267.

Onley, J. (2007). *The Arabian frontier of the British Raj: Merchants, rulers, and the British in the nineteenth-century Gulf.* Oxford: Oxford University Press.

Pallaver, K. (2008). *Lungo le piste d'Africa. Commerci locali e strategie imperiali in Tanzania (secoli XIX-XX).* Milan: Carocci.

Peterson, J. E. (2001). Oman. Originally: Entry "Oman" (part article of "Arabia"). In *Encyclopedia Britannica* (1990). http://www.jepeterson.net/sitebuildercontent/sitebuilderfiles /Oman_Encyclopedia_Britannica.pdf

Powels, R. L. (1996). The Pate chronicles revisited: Nineteenth-century history and historiography. *History in Africa, 23*, 301–318.

Ritchie, J. M. (1995). *The history of the Mazrui dynasty of Mombasa.* Oxford: Oxford University Press.

Rockel, S. (2006). *Carriers of culture, labor on the road in nineteenth-century East Africa.* Portsmouth: Heinemann.

Ruete, R. S. (1929). *Said Bin Sultan (1791–1856). Ruler of Oman and Zanzibar. His place in the history of Arabia and East Africa.* London: William Ouseley limited.

Ruete, R. S. (1929). The Al Bu Said Dynasty in Arabia and East Africa. *Journal of the Royal Asiatic and Central Asian Society, 16*, 417–432.

Semple, C. (2005). *A silver legend: The story of the Maria Theresa Thaler.* Manchester: Barzan Studies in Arabian Culture.

Sheriff, A. (2009). The Persian Gulf and the Swahili coast: A history of acculturation over the longue durée. In L. G. Potter (Ed.), *The Persian Gulf in history* (pp. 173–189). New York: Palgrave Macmillan.

Sheriff, A. (2010). *Dhow cultures and the Indian Ocean.* New York: Columbia University Press.

Smith, G. R. (1999). *Entry: Ya'rubids. Encyclopaedia of Islam* (CD-ROM Edition). Leiden: Brill Academic Publishers.

Tibbetts, G. R. (1981). *Arab Navigation in the Indian Ocean before the coming of the Portuguese.* London: The Royal Asiatic Society of Great Britain and Ireland.

Ward, P. (1987). *Travels in Oman.* Cambridge: Cambridge University Press.

Chapter 10
Oman and the Indian Ocean Rim – Economic Integration Across Conventional Meta-Regions

Steffen Wippel

10.1 The Region and Regionalisation Redefined

Very often economists and politicians tend to analyse past trends of and future opportunities for regional economic integration in terms of predefined regional entities. So the appeal to integrate the Arab world – politically and economically – has come up repeatedly. This was not only based on a Pan-Arab ideology that developed in the twentieth century in the wake of colonialism and decolonisation, but was also propelled from the outside by international observers and institutions. They thereby referred to ideas of distinct Middle Eastern and North African regions that had been conceptualised by European chancelleries since the late nineteenth century mainly for geopolitical reasons (Krause 1993). But the vacillation between such notions as "the MENA region" and "the Arab world" already shows the problem of giving a clearly defined geographical shape to a part of the world that is often essentialised in cultural and other terms. Against this background, the region has long been considered one of the least integrated areas in the world, in terms of both institutions and economic flows.

Yet, the latest concepts across the disciplines emphasise a more open approach to processes of region building. For this, one can rely on a broader range of conceptual ideas, like the "New Regionalism Approach" developed by scholars such as Hettne and Söderbaum (2000) and Bøås et al. (2005), primarily anchored in political studies; the broader "spatial turn", i.e. a new interest in "space" in social sciences and humanities, often closely linked to ideas of social constructivism (e.g., Bachmann-Medick 2006: 284 ff.); and a "geography from below" (Ben Arrous 1996), which examines actors' "daily regionalisations" (Werlen 2000) that produce and reproduce regional macro-contexts emerging out of them.

S. Wippel (✉)
Zentrum Moderner Orient (ZMO), Kirchweg 33, 14129 Berlin, Germany
e-mail: steffen.wippel@t-online.de; steffen.wippel@zmo.de

S. Wippel (ed.), *Regionalizing Oman: Political, Economic and Social Dynamics*, United Nations University Series on Regionalism 6, DOI 10.1007/978-94-007-6821-5_10,

Accordingly, the notion of "region" becomes very fluid and designates an entity that is rarely already defined, rarely restricted to one spatial scale, and rarely continuous in space and time; rather, it encompasses a wide range of forms, from institutionalised geographical settings and territories of regulation and control to very temporary spaces where relations and flows concentrate, with shifting and porous borders at different and interfering levels. Whereas "regionalisation" permits designating the broader phenomenon of both intentional and unintended region-making, but especially those processes of increasing interweavement that are furthered "from below", "regionalism" refers in particular to the process of constructing regions "from above" and to political ideas and projects of regional integration (Lorenz and Mattheis, in this volume).

In line with such reconceptualisation of space and region, Lewis and Wigen (1997) showed the ideational force that pre-established "metageographies" have on the perception and the ordering of the world by political actors, the media and the broader public. The tendency to compartmentalise the world into contiguous regional containers, regarded separately and ignoring links between them, is also strong in established academic "area studies". To overcome this situation, since 2000 the *Zentrum Moderner Orient* (ZMO) in Berlin, for example, has carried out a series of projects investigating relations between the Arab world, Sub-Saharan Africa and the Indian subcontinent and at the same time exploring overlapping – old and new – regional spaces such as the Trans-Saharan and Indian Ocean worlds (Freitag and von Oppen 2010; Bromber, in this volume). Newer projects consider the Gulf area, of which Oman is also a part, as an entangled region, linked to all three of the aforementioned conventional world regions.

Studies in regional integration, too, recognised the development of a kind of "open regionalism" (e.g., Soesastro 1998). This means not only openness to simultaneous processes of enhanced globalisation, but also allows for individual country membership in several regional institutions and, hence, the development of overlapping institutionalised areas. Others point to differentiated integration and the "fuzzy" borders of such regions (Christiansen et al. 2000).

In politics, academia and the media, Oman is also regularly regarded as being situated in the MENA region and/or the Arab world. In the following, a different perspective will see it as part of the Indian Ocean world to which Oman was always linked.[1] However, before considering its position(ing) in this region, it seems appropriate to briefly explain what can be understood by the term "Indian Ocean".

From a historical perspective, we do not have a continuous and homogenous Indian Ocean region. On the one hand, several largely overlapping Indian Ocean worlds

[1]The article is a result of the research project "Between the Arab World and the Indian Ocean: Oman's Regional Economic Orientations" (2008–2011) at the Institute for Oriental Studies at the University of Leipzig, funded by the *Deutsche Forschungsgemeinschaft* under the reference numbers GE 749/8-1 and 8-2. Additional aspects, mainly in relation to the Port of Salalah, have been developed in a second project, "Tanger – Salalah: Globalising 'Regional Cities'" (since 2008) at the *Zentrum Moderner Orient* (ZMO), Berlin, financed by the Federal Ministry for Education and Research (reference number 30/8845).

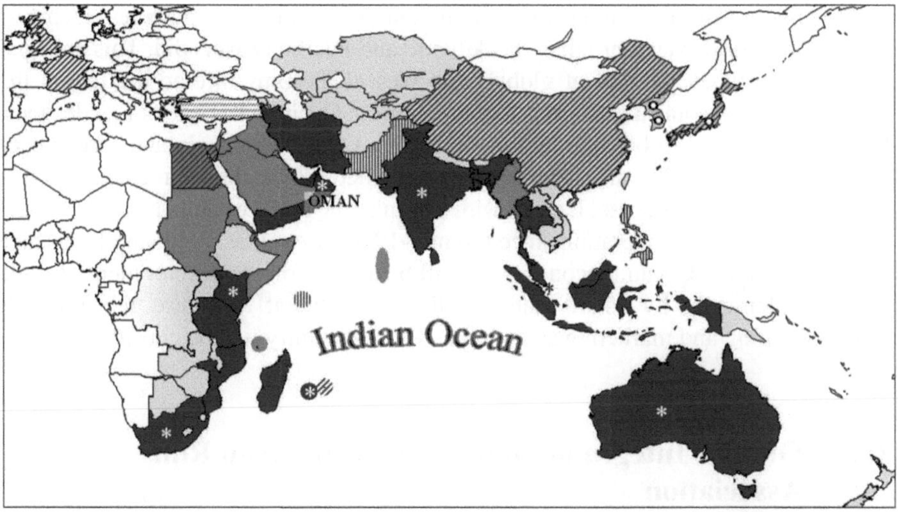

- Indian Ocean Rim Association for Regional Cooperation (IOR-ARC) member states – founding members are marked with an asterisk (*)
- IOR-ARC dialogue partners
- Other countries with direct access to the Indian Ocean or bordering the North-Western adjacent seas (Red Sea, Gulf)
- Wider hinterland: states bordering the Chinese Sea; African, South and Central Asian land-locked countries; other parts of Oceania
- Membership refused (Pakistan), adjourned (Qatar), accepted in principle (Philippines) or withdrawn (Seychelles)
- Partner status under study (Turkey)
- Other East Asian countries

Maps are not authoritative on international boundaries and do not endorse any political view. Sudan has meanwhile split into the Republics of Sudan and South Sudan (which has now become part of the wider hinterland).

Fig. 10.1 Definitions of the Indian Ocean region

existed, depending on actor-, place- and time-specific perspectives as exemplified by the notion of "seascape" developed at the ZMO (Bromber, in this volume). On the other hand, the Indian Ocean region need not be confined to its islands and immediate coastlines.[2] Authors very often integrated adjacent seas such as the Persian Gulf, the Red Sea or even the South China Sea and a large hinterland that encompasses inner-continental areas from the African Great Lakes and the Eastern Congo Basin up to Central Asia, which also showed strong commercial and social links to the sea. Most historians thereby also included China in this large world region. Today we can subsume several landlocked countries oriented towards Indian Ocean ports and trade lanes and should not totally ignore East Asia, from where major sea routes lead to the Indian Ocean rim states (Fig. 10.1).

---

[2]For understandings of the Indian Ocean world(s) and its sub-systems from various perspectives, see, e.g. Chaudhuri (1990), Wriggins (1992), McPherson (1993); for a critical assessment, see INORI (2005).

Despite its historical dimensions, the Indian Ocean attracted much less attention in the post-World War II era than the Atlantic and Pacific Oceans did. This changed considerably when the end of global East-West dichotomy offered the region the opportunity to become a new arena for cooperation. Over the last one or two decades, Oman also worked to become part of the Indian Ocean area again and forged economic links with it. This article takes a more detailed look at three dimensions of this regional integration process: It starts with Oman's role in the establishment of formal regional economic cooperation since the mid-1990s as well as its bilateral presence around the Indian Ocean. Second, there will be a focus on the development of trade links, supplemented by a short glance at direct investment. And third, the country's self-positioning and marketing as an Indian Ocean country will be considered.

10.2 Oman's Integration into the Indian Ocean Rim Association

Even compared with other countries around it, Oman was very for a long time reluctant to become a member of regional institutions. Even a slight relinquishment of sovereignty and harmonisation of policies seems to have been regarded as highly incompatible with its difficult nation-building process. Yet, in 1981, Oman was a founding member of the *Gulf Cooperation Council* (GCC), mainly pursuing security interests. Steps towards a customs union (2003) and a common market (2008) were not taken until recent years. As Oman's early opt-out from the planned currency union showed, it is still very hesitant about deeper economic integration. Oman also participated only late in pan-Arab trade cooperation when it became a member of the *Greater Arab Free Trade Area*, which has been gradually implemented since 1998. In between, it participated in launching the third regional association, in which it is a member now, with a focus on the Indian Ocean region.

Political consciousness of the Indian Ocean as a unifying factor did not start to develop again among the adjacent nations until the 1950s. Security concerns led the states of the region to propose in the 1970s and 1980s the establishment of a nuclear-free zone. In the 1990s, the strengthening of economic reforms and the establishment of the WTO pushed economic motives into the foreground. After a series of preliminary consultations, delegates of several states including Oman met in 1995 to discuss the *Indian Ocean Rim Initiative* (Fig. 10.1).[3] In parallel, a "second-track" dialogue was initiated among representatives from business and academic networks from 23 countries. In 1997, the first ministerial meeting of the then 14 participant states adopted the charter of the *Indian Ocean Rim Association for Regional Cooperation* (IOR-ARC). It is tripartite in nature and includes

[3] Kelegama (2000), Tiwari (2004), Bouchard (2000), Reddy (2000), Porter (1997) and Shand and Kalijaran (1997) give details on the launch, organisation and activities of current Indian Ocean cooperation and on the motives of its members.

representatives from government, business and academia who jointly develop the association's policies and work programs. At their second meeting in 1999, ministers established a permanent secretariat in Mauritius and admitted five new members. By 2001, five non-regional "dialogue partners", with specific stakes in the area, have been accepted.[4] Observer status has been granted to the *Indian Ocean Tourism Organisation*, and in 2010 extended to the *Indian Ocean Research Group*. Current membership therefore is limited to 18 out of 25 sovereign states with direct access to the ocean.

According to its fundamental principles, the association's main task is to facilitate and promote economic cooperation. It runs its affairs with an evolutionary approach and on a voluntary basis. Prevailing neoliberalism had put the ideal of "open regionalism" on the agenda. This meant that states would rely on market-driven integration in line with the Asian-Pacific model. Trade liberalisation was to be applied to members and non-members simultaneously on a "most favoured nation" basis. Other areas of cooperation were defined as trade and investment facilitation through the sharing of information and the harmonisation of standards and economic and technical cooperation in specific sectors. Intraregional trade between Indian Ocean states in the 1990s was only 20 percent to a quarter of the region's overall trade, but 65 percent of intraregional trade was among IOR-ARC members. McGuire's study (2003) revealed that, over the 1990s, trade barriers have been significantly lowered, concomitantly with a noteworthy expansion in trade. Oman had the third-lowest tariffs; yet, it still employed quite a number of non-tariff measures. With the GCC customs union in place, the Sultanate has now to stick to its common external tariff of mostly 5 percent.

According to local opinion, Oman has been one of the "most enthusiastic" members.[5] From 2000 to early 2003, the Sultanate held the presidency of the IOR-ARC. The extraordinary Council of Ministers' meeting in 2000 in Muscat adopted a trade and investment plan of action, and the 3rd ministerial meeting in 2001, in Muscat again, established a *High Level Task Force* to study the future direction of the association. Its report was presented to the Senior Officials' reunion in Oman in 2002. However, in its first decade, the IOR-ARC produced few tangible results.[6]

Among the main problems of the association is the great difference in the sizes of the member states' populations, economies and trade, as well as in the level of economic, social and technological development. Some observers noted a general

---

[4] Turkey's application is pending; Pakistan's accession was repeatedly opposed by India; the Seychelles withdrew from the IOR-ARC for financial reasons. Qatar's application was denied, but the sheikhdom was offered dialogue partner status, which it refused in turn. In 2009, the members accepted the Philippines' application to join, but are waiting for the Philippines to confirm its application.

[5] Additional information on Oman's role in the IOR-ARC has been gathered in interviews with observers and actors in Oman. For the sake of confidentiality, no interview partners are cited individually. Numerous newspaper articles and press releases with details have been consulted during the research, but are also not explicitly mentioned.

[6] For results as well as Oman's engagement, see also Vines and Oruitemeka (2008), Gopalan and Rajan (2009).

lack of economic compatibility and poor infrastructural links. The consensus-based approach needs time, too. The superposition with other regional organisations poses a problem. Unilateral trade liberalisation is politically extremely difficult to realise, and sectoral projects have been of limited interest to many of the members. Finally, the core group of initiators already has quite diverging strategic interests in participating in the IOR-ARC. Whereas India showed a preference for a more gradual approach to including new members and for a more rapid program of common trade liberalisation, Australia and Singapore were among the most fervent defenders of open regionalism and, together with South Africa, defended a more "inclusive" approach with a maximum of members. Oman itself felt in growing need to expand its economic space and wanted to profit from its strategic location in the middle of the Indian Ocean. It favoured a more rapid reduction of trade barriers among the partners. For the Sultanate, the IOR-ARC mainly serves to open opportunities for its business community, less to establish protective measures. Behind it is the strategic goal of strengthening the private sector in the country.

The association was only reenergized from the later 2000s on.[7] The institutional capacity of the IOR-ARC began to grow. In the meantime, a Preferential Trade Agreement (PTA) has been deemed useful to enhance economic cooperation among member countries (see also Business Information Services … 2004). In 2007, Oman organised an expert meeting on this type of cooperation, but negotiations showed slow progress. Up to mid-2011, only its feasibility was under study, and Oman, Sri Lanka, Iran and Yemen completed a draft framework to allow for a final decision by the member states. Not all members are sure about its usefulness in times of generalised WTO membership and free trade agreements. For Oman, a PTA would require permission from other GCC countries. This seems quite unlikely in light of the decision to tolerate free trade with the US as a one-time exception from customs union rules. In addition, during the 2010 summit, the establishment of a Clearing Payment Union came up again. Other Omani activities in the field of trade include a seminar on "Service Trade and Dispute Settlement under WTO", organised by the *Oman Chamber of Commerce and Industry* (OCCI)[8] in early 2011, that is to be regarded in the light of plans to establish a regional arbitration centre for commercial affairs (Iran Chamber … 2009).

At any rate, the focus on establishing tangible projects is widely welcome. Already in the 1996/97 work program, Oman was made responsible, together with South Africa, for a project on the development of seaports and maritime transport. Recent projects have been pushed forward mainly by Oman, Iran and India. Since

[7]This paper was finalised in early November 2011, shortly before the 11th ministerial meeting at Bengaluru, intended to advance Indian Ocean cooperation. In preparation for it, Indian delegations had visited all member countries, first among them Oman.

[8]Oman is one out of only four members represented by chambers of commerce in the business group, whereas the others send ministerial delegates.

the late 2000s, for example, these three countries (plus Yemen) supported the establishment of the association's Special Fund that aims to allow for implementing priority projects. Besides the financial contribution of USD 200,000 by the three main supporters together, China announced it would contribute an additional USD 100,000. Currently, they are launching three other "flagship" projects (see also IOR-ARC Secretariat 2010): The Iranian government has established the *Regional Centre of Sciences and Technology Transfer*. The *Fisheries Support Unit* that has recently been set up in Oman is based on an agreement between the Omani Ministry of Fisheries and the IOR-ARC to help member states manage fish stocks and combat illegal fishing. In 2011, the ministry organised a training workshop on fishery biology and stock assessment. The envisaged *Maritime Transport Council* is now to be established in Muscat, too, by the OCCI and the national Ministry of Transport and was to start work in 2011 (Iran Chamber ... 2009). In the light of current problems, Oman supported the establishment of a regional anti-piracy centre in neighbouring Yemen.

In addition, the OCCI is preparing a study on the development of tourism in the Indian Ocean region that is co-financed by the Omani Ministry of Tourism, the Regional Fund and Iran (Iran Chamber ... 2009). In 2010, Oman hosted the second of hitherto three Construction Business Seminars. Furthermore, the Indian Ocean region offers alternative study opportunities, increasingly also used by Omani students, as the UK and other Western countries become less attractive. Here, the joint *University Mobility in the Indian Ocean Rim* (UMIOR) program proposes scholarships for postgraduate studies. In 2002, Oman had organised the second UMIOR General Conference and offered 25 out of 450 exchange places provided by five countries (Mohamedbhai 2008: 292–293; Anon. 2003: 7).

10.3 Further Institutional Links with the Indian Ocean Region

On the bilateral level, Oman had established only a limited number of economically relevant agreements until the early 1980s, nearly exclusively with Western industrial countries and with India, from where it had been administered under the British protectorate; further agreements with Arab Mediterranean countries were then added. But only since the early 1990s did the Sultanate start to considerably expand its contractual network, especially to conclude numerous accords with Indian Ocean countries, mainly those with coastlines on the Gulf and the Red Sea, and in various parts of Asia (Wippel 2010: 12–17; Fig. 10.2). They include general trade and numerous sectoral agreements; in particular, the double taxation and investment treaties negotiated since then can be regarded as essential preconditions for enhancing economic contacts.

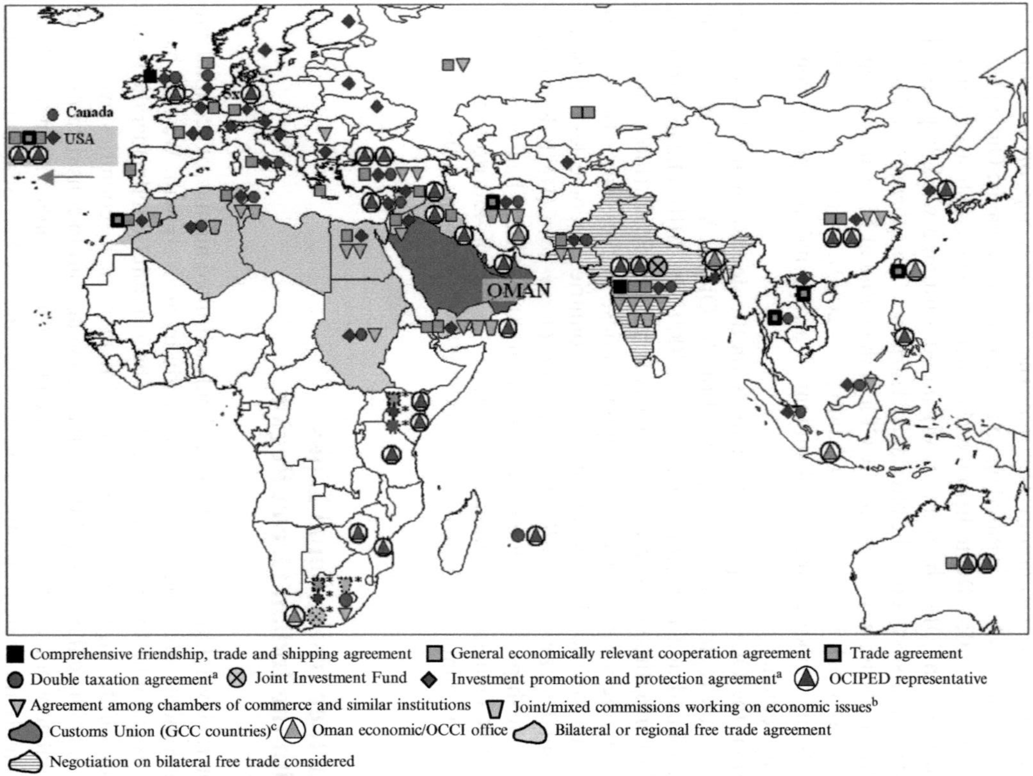

The map gives the situation in 2008 with partial updates. More recent sources are not completely consistent, mainly on some supplementary "trade agreements".

*Agreement in negotiation. a Only one agreement per country given. b No purely political or technical commissions. National and international sources.

c No further details given (except for representations).

Fig. 10.2 Oman's bilateral economic agreements

Table 10.1 Economic agreements of Oman

	With regions	With states
Direct agreements	Membership in regional agreements: Gulf Cooperation Council (GCC) 1981 Greater Arab Free Trade Area (GAFTA) 1997/2005 **Indian Ocean Rim Association for Regional Cooperation (IOR-ARC)** 1995/97	Free trade agreement with USA 2006/09 Negotiations on bilateral free trade occasionally considered with **India, Pakistan** Double taxation and investment treaties Other economically relevant agreements
Indirect agreements (via the GCC)	Cooperation agreement EU 1989 Cooperation declaration EFTA 2000 Framework agreement Mercosur 2005 Free trade agreement with European Free Trade Association (EFTA) 2009 Free trade negotiations with European Union (EU) **Association of Southeast Asian Nations (ASEAN)** Mercosur	Framework agreements with **China, India** 2004 Free trade agreements with Syria, Lebanon 2005, **Singapore** 2009 Negotiations on free trade with **Egypt, Jordan**, *Turkey*, **Azerbaijan, Pakistan, India, Thailand, China**, *Japan, South Korea*, **Australia**, *New Zealand*

Bold: Indian Ocean associations and countries; in italics: IOR-ARC partners or countries in the wider Indian Ocean area. National and international sources

In contrast, besides the Arab and Gulf regional accords, Oman has only one bilateral free trade agreement (FTA), with the US, signed in 2006. Zorob (in this volume) shows the inconsistencies that arose with the Gulf customs union. Instead of bilateral contracts, FTAs are basically being negotiated on the GCC regional level – either with other economic blocs or with individual countries. As Table 10.1 shows, most of these efforts are directed towards economies that can be considered part of the wider Indian Ocean realm. However, when negotiations with the GCC lasted too long, the idea of bilateral FTAs between Oman and Pakistan or India came up for a short moment.

Moreover, Oman began to establish more representations abroad. A few economic offices and OCCI delegations as well as a number of representatives of *The Omani Centre for Investment Promotion and Export Development* (Ociped) have a special focus on Indian Ocean countries, including in Africa. Diplomatic missions likewise centre on the region (besides other MENA and industrial countries) and fulfil important economic tasks.

10.4 Oman's Economic Exchange with Indian Ocean Countries

In the following, the study of import and export trade shares gives a first idea of the importance of Indian Ocean economies for Oman. As the definition of the region is not easy and depends on respective perspectives and circumstances, the analysis of trade data has to examine different geographical variants.[9]

10.4.1 Imports

Following the IMF trade statistics up to 2005, on the import side, the seven core IOR-ARC countries have provided more or less continuously 7–9 percent of Oman's imports since the early 1970s. Among them, India had a share of 3–4 percent in the country's total imports. In contrast, dependence on imports from all current 18 IOR-ARC member countries increased from 26 percent in the 1970s to about 36 percent since the 1990s. The difference and the increase are mainly due to the UAE's share, which grew from 15 percent to about a quarter. Non-members among the immediate rim states are not very significant; only if we include the Red Sea and the Gulf does the region's share rise again, to about 30 percent in the 1970s and 1980s and to 41–43 percent over the 15 years that followed. The landlocked hinterlands and the states littoral to the South China Sea contributed three further points to the supply side. Further east, Japan and Korea together added another 15–20 percent. Data for the years 2005–2010 accentuate tendencies (see also Table 10.2). The IOR-ARC countries together now provide almost 40 percent of the Sultanate's imports. Also increasing were the shares of the Indian Ocean region including the Gulf and the Red Sea (ca. 45–48 percent), as well as the hinterlands and South China Sea (ca. 50–53 percent). China more than doubled its share to 5 percent, whereas Japan's portion reduced perceptibly.

Thus, in the first decade after the year 2000 the Indian Ocean region as it is currently institutionalised supplied more than a third, and in a very wide definition well above two-thirds of the Sultanate's imports. However, deliveries mainly come from a limited range of countries, namely the UAE, India, Saudi Arabia and the more distant Japan, Korea and China.[10] Among the Indian Ocean sub-regions, GCC countries contribute the most to Oman's imports: their portion increased from 17 percent in the 1970s to roughly 30 percent in the 2000s. In the last three decades, East Asian countries followed suit (ca. 20 percent to a quarter more recently), if we stick to the very wide understanding of the whole region. South East Asian nations including Oceania (7–9 percent) as well as South Asian countries (4 percent; after 2005: ca. 7 percent) rank much lower, whereas African countries oriented towards the Indian Ocean are nearly insignificant (Fig. 10.3).

[9] Trade figures for 1980–2005 are based on IMF (2007); national data are extracted from MoNE (2008, 2010). Electronic IMF data have not been accessible for later than 2005. Additional data from ITC (2011) for 2001–2009 are not always consistent with IMF figures. DG Trade (2011) reports trade with Oman's Top 50 partners (with the EU regarded as a single partner) in 2010.

[10] Among Oman's top suppliers we also find the IOR-ARC's dialogue partner, the UK, whose share continuously decreased from 16 to 3 percent since the early 1980s, the US (6–7 percent) and Germany (5 percent).

Table 10.2 Omani Imports and Exports (2005–2009)

All imports		All exports		Non-oil & re-exports	
Rank country/region	Share (percent)	Rank country/region	Share (percent)	Rank country/region	Share (percent)
1. UAE	26.0	1. China	25.6	1. UAE	43.0
2. *Japan*	15.7	2. *Japan*	10.8	2. India	7.4
3. (United States)	5.9	3. Thailand	9.5	3. Iran	5.7
4. India	5.4	4. *South Korea*	9.3	4. Saudi Arabia	5.6
5. (Germany)	4.9	5. UAE	9.2	5. China	3.3
6. China	3.9	6. Taiwan	3.6	6. Qatar	3.0
7. *South Korea*	3.7	7. Iran	1.9	7. Singapore	2.4
8. Saudi Arabia	2.9	8. Singapore	1.7	8. (United States)	1.8
9. (United Kingdom)	2.8	9. Malaysia	1.6	9. Iraq	1.7
10. (Italy)	2.2	10. India	1.3	10. Yemen	1.6
11. Thailand	2.1	11. (United States)	1.2	11. Pakistan	1.6
12. Australia	1.9	12. Saudi Arabia	1.2	12. (United Kingdom)	1.6
IOR-ARC 7	8.8	IOR-ARC 7	3.9	IOR-ARC 7	10.9
IOR-ARC 18	39.9	IOR-ARC 18	26.1	IOR-ARC 18	63.1
IOR	41.1	IOR	26.7	IOR	65.9
IOR+Red Sea, Gulf	46.0	IOR+Red Sea. Gulf	29.8	IOR+Red Sea. Gulf	79.6
IOR+wider hinterland	50.8	IOR+wider hinterland	59.6	IOR+wider hinterland	86.7
IOR+East Asia	70.2	IOR+East Asia	79.7	IOR+East Asia	88.6
GCC	30.7	GCC	11.5	GCC	53.0
African IOR	1.1	African IOR	0.9	African IOR	3.8
South Asia	6.5	South Asia	2.4	South Asia	9.4
South East Asia/ Oceania	7.6	South East Asia/ Oceania	13.1	South East Asia/ Oceania	4.6
East Asia	23.8	East Asia	49.5	East Asia	7.3

Countries in italics: Far East; in parentheses: extra-regional. Regional definitions: IOR-ARC 7: founding members; IOR-ARC 18: all current members; IOR (Indian Ocean Rim): all littoral states; IOR+Red Sea, Gulf: plus states bordering the Red Sea and the Gulf; IOR+wider hinterland: plus land-locked hinterland and littoral states to the South China Sea; IOR+East Asia: plus Koreas and Japan; African IOR: includes littoral states, including the Red Sea, and land-locked hinterland; South Asia: South Asian Association for Regional Cooperation; South East Asia: Association of Southeast Asian Nations (ASEAN).
Sources: MoNE (2008, 2010), International Trade Centre (2011). The author's own calculations.

10.4.2 Exports

Oman's exports are much more difficult to evaluate as they mainly consist of hydrocarbons and concentrate on a few countries in East and South East Asia.[11] According to data for *all* goods, in the 1970s Oman directed 16 percent of its exports to the seven IOR-ARC core countries, a share that fell back to 4–5 percent in the subsequent decades (but was again 14 percent in 2010). Decreasing, under great fluctuation, from

[11] From 2007 to 2009, 71 percent of all oil went to East Asia, at least 16 percent to South East Asia (MoNE 2010: Table 8–4).

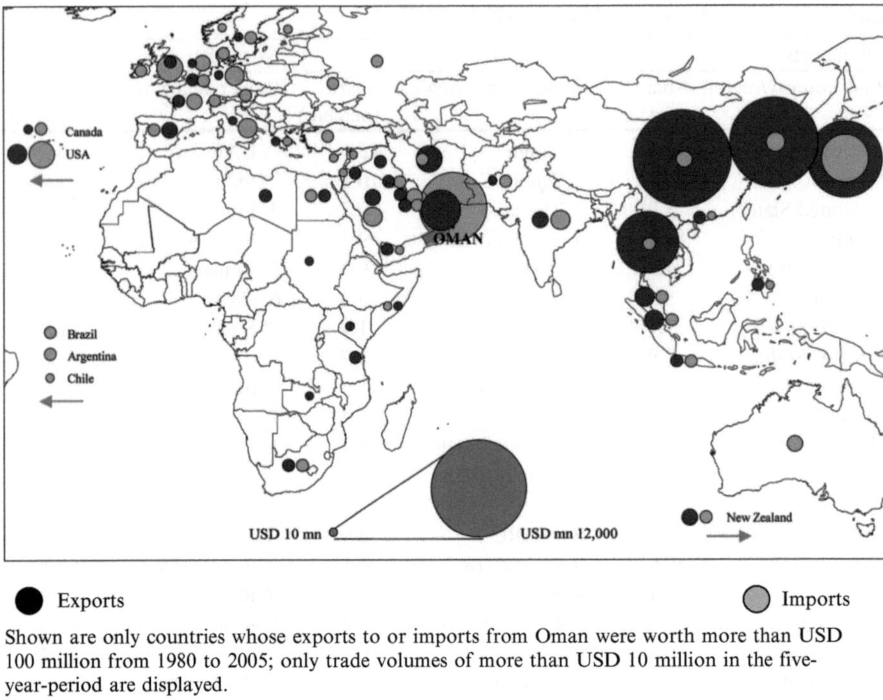

Fig. 10.3 Distribution of Omani exports and imports (2001–2005) (Source: IMF (2007). The author's own calculations)

19 to 2 percent, Singapore remained the main customer until the mid-2000s, seconded by India whose share by contrast grew from 1 to 11 percent in the 2000s. Among later association members, the UAE, in particular, increased its share from 0 percent in the early 1980s to approximately 10 percent,[12] and Thailand achieves about 11 percent since the 1990s. So about a third of all Omani exports has gone to the IOR-ARC of 18 since the early 1980s, irrespective of considerable fluctuations. Non-member rim and hinterland states add little to these shares, except China whose importance as a customer rose from 0 to 28 percent in the last decade[13] and made the Indian Ocean in its wider definition increase up to nearly 70 percent in 2010. Other East Asian countries always provided another 20–35 percentage points, with Japan increasingly supplemented by South Korea. Thus, on average 80–95 percent of Omani exports went to areas South and East of the Arabian Peninsula.

Hence, among the sub-regions, East Asia comes first, purchasing more than a quarter of all exports in the 1970s and more than one half since the 1990s. ASEAN plus Oceanian countries has fluctuated between 5 and 25 percent since the early 1980s, while the GCC countries were at around 14 percent (with a pronounced

[12] The UAE's share of 46 percent in the second half of the 1980s seems to be biased for statistical reasons.

[13] In addition, Taiwan's share, only evident from ITC data, was nearly 4 percent (2005–2009).

decrease). The eastern parts of Africa and South Asia attracted about 1–2 percent of all exported goods each (but the latter 13 percent in 2010). In general, exports are less widely spread than imports: at the top we have a strong concentration on a few major customers in the East whose demand is driven by booming economies. India and several Gulf neighbours are also among the top 12 destinations.[14]

The regional and national distribution changes considerably if we consider national data for *non-oil* and *re-exports* only, over the 2005–2009 period (Table 10.2).[15] Together they made up nearly a quarter of all exports during the second half of the last decade, compared with 6 percent in 1990. They concentrate more on nearby countries. The initiators of the IOR-ARC receive 11 percent, mainly India (7 percent), whereas the share of all current members bounces to 63 percent, due to the UAE's 43 percent stake, followed by nearby Iran (6 percent). The share increases to 80 percent if we add all littoral states, the Red Sea and the Gulf (including Saudi Arabia's 6 percent) and to 87 percent in the wider definition (with 5 percent for China plus Hong Kong). Other East Asian countries contribute only two further percentage points. Thus, the GCC states dominate by far (53 percent). Almost all 12 top destinations for Omani non-oil exports are situated around the Indian Ocean and its adjacent seas. Yet, as nearly half of these volumes consists of re-exports, there is a statistical distortion of trade flows that go via Dubai and other emirates, which however do not correspond to the final destination of the goods.

Summarised, Oman's exports display a greater orientation toward Indian Ocean countries than its imports do. Its whole Indian Ocean trade focuses on Gulf countries and South East Asia; East Asia is only indirectly linked to the region. For non-oil goods, South Asia also matters, whereas African countries garner only a very small percentage of Omani foreign trade. Yet, with regard to the outspokenly open and shallow regionalism of the IOR-ARC, elevated shares do not necessarily mean trade diversion in favour of a new economic bloc; on the contrary, strong links preceded the establishment of the association, mainly due to market forces. Accordingly, Ociped has defined African and Asian countries west and north of the Indian Ocean as its target markets for non-oil products and also concentrated its market studies on these countries (Ociped 2009b, http://www.ociped.com).

10.4.3 Trade Intensities

An analysis of regional trade orientation by shares ignores the size of partner countries; moreover, a regional sample's shares continuously increase the more countries it includes. Therefore, "relative trade intensities" that relate the respective parts in

---

[14] Among the non-Indian Ocean customers, only the US (1–3 percent) continuously ranked among the top 12 since the 1980s.

[15] Non-oil exports and re-exports consist mainly of machinery and transport equipment (42 percent), petroleum products (14 percent), chemicals (15 percent) and manufactured goods (13 percent). Cf. MoNE (2010: Table 4–11).

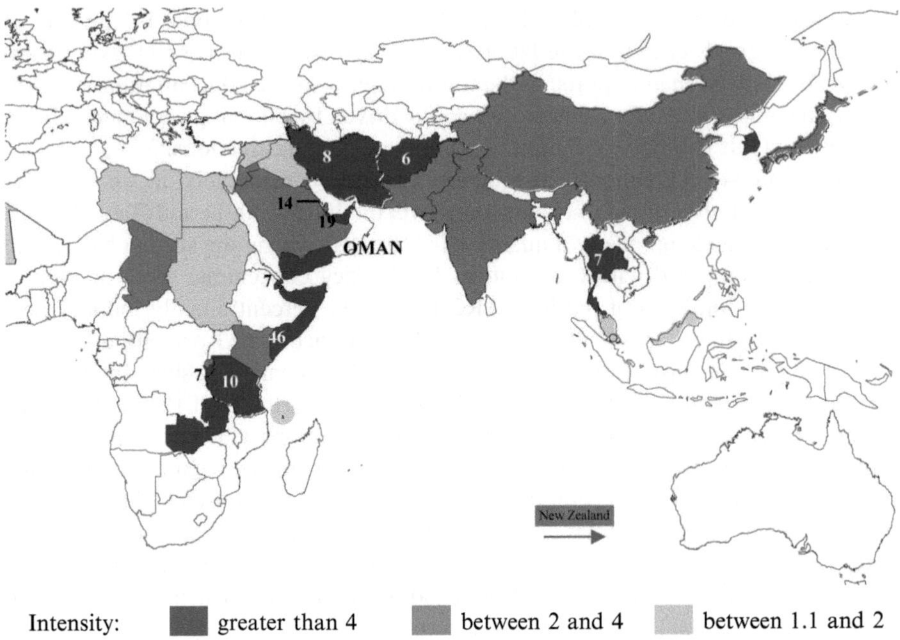

Fig. 10.4 Intensities of Omani International Trade (2001–2005). Figures are given for intensities greater than 6 (Sources: IMF (2007). The author's own calculations)

world trade of two partners give a complementary picture of regionalisation tendencies. The more the ratio exceeds the value of one, the more intense is trade, whereas for values between 0 and 1, trade is lower-volume than could be expected from the countries' importance in world trade.

The number of countries with which Oman trades intensely has continuously increased. The figures reveal that these countries are nearly exclusively located around the Indian Ocean (Fig. 10.4).[16] Trade intensities can reach very high values for some smaller (mostly African) countries. With 45–50, they have been very high in the case of Somalia in the 2000s, whereas for Tanzania they have been elevated more continuously since the mid-1980s (1980–2005: average of 16). For this 25-year period, the UAE displayed the top mean value (27). Trade with Yemen (14), Bahrain (10) and, since the 1990s, Thailand (fluctuating around 7) likewise

[16]For the sake of space and simplicity, only intensities for total trade are presented. Outside the wider region, elevated intensities of roughly 2 existed only with the Netherlands, Cyprus and Norway in parts of the 1970s and '1980s respectively.

Table 10.3 Relative intensities of Oman's regional trade

Partner regions	1981–1985	1986–1990	1991–1995	1996–2000	2001–2005	*1980–2005*	2005–2009
IOR-ARC 7	4.1	1.9	1.5	1.2	1.3	1.7	1.1
IOR-ARC 18	3.0	6.9	3.6	4.0	3.8	4.0	3.2
IOR	3.0	6.8	3.5	4.0	3.8	3.9	3.2
IOR+Red Sea, Gulf	1.9	6.0	3.1	3.6	3.4	3.4	2.7
IOR+wider hinterland	1.5	4.1	2.3	2.8	2.5	2.5	2.1
IOR+East Asia	2.4	2.8	2.9	3.0	2.8	2.8	2.2
GCC	3.0	23.0	9.7	11.1	8.5	9.1	7.1
East Africa	5.3	6.9	9.0	10.6	4.2	6.8	1.1
South Asia	1.1	3.3	1.9	2.1	2.0	2.0	2.2
South East Asia	3.4	0.9	1.5	2.2	2.2	2.1	1.7
East Asia	3.1	0.8	2.9	2.7	2.5	2.5	2.0

Sources: IMF (2007); International Trade Centre (2011). The author's own calculations
East Africa: East African Community. For further regional definitions see Table 10.2

showed elevated intensities.[17] Based on values between 2 and 7, goods exchange in the last three decades has also been quite intense with a wide range of African and Asian countries, from Zambia to Singapore, sometimes with pronounced variations over time. In the Far East, intensities of trade with Japan slightly decreased, whereas they grew with Korea (since the late 1980s) and China (since the early 1990s).

In a regional perspective (Table 10.3), the share of the IOR-ARC founding members in Oman's foreign trade was nearly double their share in world trade until 2005, whereas in the following years virtually no regionalisation took place. However, if we include the members that joined later, the regional trade intensity rises to about 3–4. With broader definitions of the Indian Ocean area, trade is slightly more diluted in the wider region. Here, after the second half of the 1980s, there were only moderate variations over time. On the sub-regional scale, trade with GCC members is extremely intense, especially since the mid-1980s (1980–2005: average of 9). After 1980, trade was also very intense with East African countries (nearly 7), but eased off in the last 5 years. To the east, exchange with East Asia was usually slightly more intense than with South and South East Asia. Consequently, trade intensities show a stronger orientation towards the Indian Ocean region in its narrower understanding with a central focus on its northwestern parts. In particular, they integrate nearby East African and South Asian countries in Oman's trade region, in contrast to shares.

[17] Figures for 2005–2009, e.g., decreased for the UAE (to 18), Bahrain (6), Yemen (5) and Tanzania (below 2) and were 6 for Thailand, but increased further for Djibouti (from 7 to 44).

10.5 Firm Cooperation Between Oman and Indian Ocean Countries

Considering further economic flows that link Oman to Indian Ocean partners, I will bypass such aspects as work migration (see Pradhan, in this volume) and tourism, but briefly want to point out foreign direct investment (FDI).

The value of FDI in Oman more than doubled between 2005 and 2009 (from OMR 2.2 to 5.1 bn).[18] Annual inflow peaked in 2007 (OMR 1.3 bn) and fell to less than half by 2009 due to the worldwide economic crisis. The bulk of annual flows and stocks came from the UK and US (Table 10.4). The third-largest investor was the UAE (15 percent of flows 2006–2009 and of stocks 2009). India, other Arab Gulf countries and Mauritius followed. Whereas most Asian and Arab countries disinvested considerably in 2009, Bahrain and Mauritius succeeded in raising their shares considerably. IOR-ARC members were responsible for 21 percent of inflows and stocks in the same periods, whereas all Indian Ocean rim countries plus the wider hinterland contributed 34 percent to both. Main investors came from the GCC (ca. 25 percent), with other Asian countries being far less important (ca. 5 percent). If we exclude investment in the Omani oil and gas sectors again, which contributed 57 percent to current FDI (2006–2009) and 53 percent to its stock (2009), the shares of Indian Ocean countries more than double.

Oman's stock of its own productive investment abroad increased steadily from almost 400 mn in 2006 to more than OMR 730 mn in 2009. Over two-thirds were invested in the Indian Ocean rim including its wider hinterland; IOR-ARC members alone accumulated more than a quarter.[19] The main countries of investment were Pakistan, the UAE and Bahrain. Recent FDI outflow was mainly directed to Pakistan (31 percent), followed by the UAE, Saudi Arabia and Egypt, whereas Western countries were of minor importance.

However, figures on foreign direct investment are even less accurate than trade data and ignore a wide range of forms of firm cooperation. With the *Oman India Fertiliser Company*, a USD 1 bn project inaugurated in 2006, Oman attracted the largest Indian investment abroad. The list provided by the Embassy of India (2011a) comprises 32 major Indian-owned enterprises in Oman. In total, more than 100 other large Indian companies are said to have a foothold in Oman, besides more than 1,500 joint ventures, and around 30 Omani firms are said to operate in India (Singh 2011). Indian companies (plan to) engage in a wide range of secondary and tertiary sectors. Vice versa, Oman has invested more than USD 200 mn in the Indian oil sector, in manufacturing and software industries (Embassy of India 2011b). Banks have branches and subsidiaries on both sides, mainly serving the Indian expatriate community. Further opportunities for collaboration have been recently identified in the fields of agriculture,

[18] The Omani Riyal (OMR) is pegged to the dollar at OMR 1 = USD 2.6. The calculations that follow are based on MoNE (2011).

[19] Regional shares might be underestimated, as 26 percent of FDI is located in "other" countries.

Table 10.4 Oman – direct investment

Foreign direct investment in Oman by country of origin					Omani direct investment by country of destination		
	All FDI		Non-oil FDI			All FDI	
Relative share	Flows 2006–2009 (percent)	Stock 2009 (percent)[a]	Flows 2006–2009 (percent)	Stock 2009 (percent)[a]	Relative share	Flows 2006–2009 (percent)	Stock 2009 (percent)[a]
UK	33.2	33.4	5.0	7.2	UAE	14.3	23.1
USA	25.3	19.6	3.0	2.7	Pakistan	31.0	14.3
UAE	15.2	14.7	32.9	29.4	Bahrain	4.5	8.2
India	2.2	3.7	4.8	7.6	Saudi Arabia	11.8	5.4
Qatar	3.1	3.4	7.2	7.2	Egypt	11.3	5.2
Kuwait	3.2	3.3	7.5	7.0	Kazakhstan	7.9	4.8
Bahrain	2.7	2.1	6.4	4.6	UK	6.0	3.6
Mauritius	3.0	2.1	7.0	4.4	India	0.2	2.7
Netherlands[b]	1.5	1.7	3.6	3.6	Korea	–0.3	2.5
GCC	25.6	24.6	56.1	50.5	GCC	30.5	36.7
IOR-ARC 18	21.0	21.0	46.7	42.7	IOR-ARC 18	14.5	25.8
IOR+wider hinterland	34.1	34.2	74.1	68.8	IOR+wider hinterland	89.4	67.6
IOR+East Asia	35.1	35.2	69.6	71.0	IOR+East Asia	89.1	70.0
Asia (w/o MENA)	4.6	6.4	0.4	11.6	Asia (w/o MENA)	47.2	28.1
Europe and Americas	36.9	40.6	67.4	78.3	Europe and Americas	94.0	96.4

Source: MoNE (2011). The author's own calculations
Countries: Major and wider Indian Ocean partners only. Regions: include only specified countries
[a]Provisional
[b]Followed by Jordan, Saudi Arabia, Korea, Iran, Pakistan

education and healthcare, and a USD 100 mn *India-Oman Investment Fund* has been initiated.[20] Other important cooperation partners include GCC countries, mainly Dubai, Thailand, Malaysia, Australia and Korea. Yet, this needs further investigation. On a more individual scale, business connections with East Africa have also revived (Verne and Müller-Mahn, in this volume).

10.6 Oman's Self-positioning in the Indian Ocean Region

Economic relations are accompanied by debates inside Oman about its regional orientation and belonging. Internally, the debate serves self-identification as part of the nation-building process after the takeover by the current Sultan, who tried hard

[20]There are plans to expand the fund to up to USD 1.5 bn. A similar USD 500 mn South Africa-Oman fund is currently in the pipeline.

to integrate the diverse regional, tribal, ethnic and linguistic groups within the country. Externally, however, it is to be primarily understood as a strategic endeavour to position the country on the economic world map and to brand it as a site of production, a trade hub and a tourist destination.

In their international political and economic activities, Omani institutions regularly refer to the country's glorious past as a seafaring nation and maritime empire with longstanding links to other parts of the Indian Ocean, from East Africa to South Asia and as far as China. The Sultanate's national narrative emphasises its openness to the outside world and its centuries-old transnational connections, which are exemplified by the cosmopolitan "Zanzibar-Omanis", the established Indian community in the country and the country's prominent location in the Indian Ocean between East and West, giving access to several sub-regional markets.

In 1996, in the process of founding the IOR-ARC, Sultan Qaboos postulated, "The Indian Ocean has always been the main gateway for Omanis, who explored its shores and travelled beyond as they established long-term ties" (cited by Kéchichian 2008: 127). In his speech on the occasion of the 26th National Day, he praised the "glorious seafaring traditions, in which all sons of Oman take pride", and continued:

> the Omani dhows sailed forth over the seas and oceans like white clouds, carrying a message of blessing to all mankind. Those dhows returned from their voyages laden with the produce of many lands in a mutually beneficial exchange. This sea borne intercourse resulted in Oman becoming one of the world's greatest commercial centres over the centuries (MoFA 1996).

One of the early highly symbolic and mediatised events during the effort to consolidate the Sultan's power was to rebuild a traditional vessel named after Sohar, the presumable hometown of Sinbad, and to send it along a traditional sea route to Canton, China in 1980, the same route that is supposed to have been used by the legendary sailor (Anon. 2005; Fig. 10.5). In 1990, the Sultan placed his own yacht at the disposal of the UNESCO for a "Maritime Route Expedition" from Venice to Osaka to explore the cultural cross-fertilizations generated by the historic Silk Road (UNESCO 1990). 30 years after the "Sinbad Voyage", the departure ceremonies for another reconstructed boat from the ninth century, the "Jewel of Muscat", took place in the port of Mutrah. After several stops in India, Sri Lanka and Malaysia, it arrived in Singapore after half a year, where it was exhibited as a gift from Oman. This voyage was regarded as an important sign of developing intraregional tourism as well as trade.

Traditional boats are displayed everywhere in the country. So the Sohar ship found its definite place at a roundabout in the outskirts of Muscat near the prestigious Al Bustan hotel. Other roundabouts show ship monuments or signs (Fig. 10.6). Pictorial representations of shipping activities are also to be found on centrally placed clock towers; museums' maritime departments display a broad range of traditional dhow types. Among the few publications on Oman that can be purchased in local bookshops are a reasonable number of coffee table books on traditional

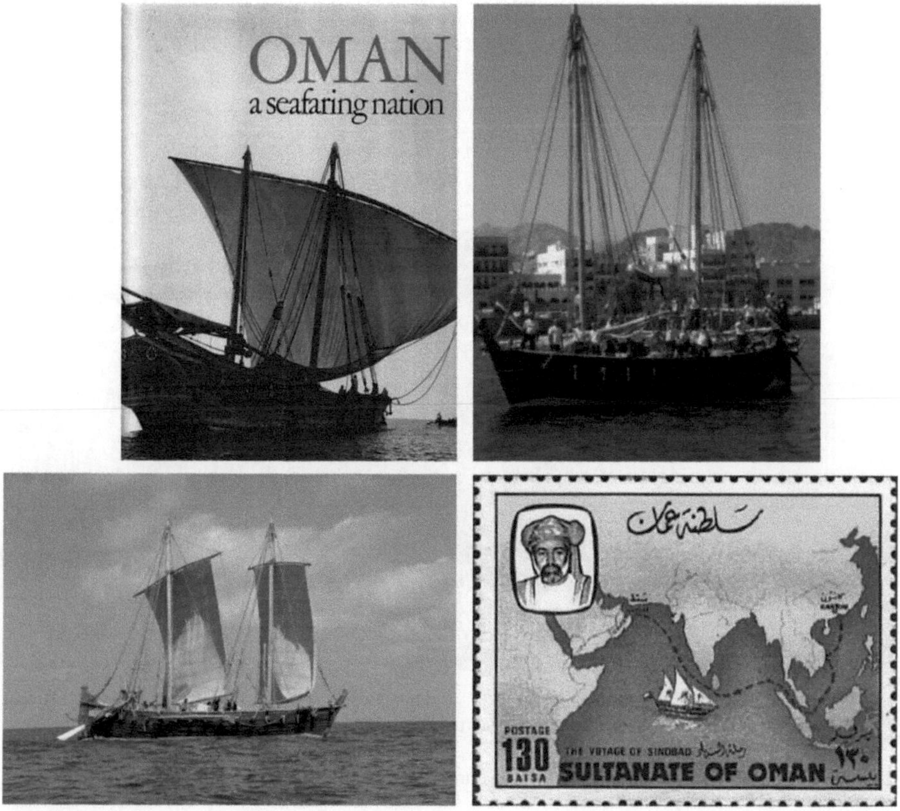

Fig. 10.5 A Seafaring Nation – From the "Sohar" (1980) to the "Jewel of Muscat" (2010) (Sources: http://www.maritimebooks.com.au/pix/55219.jpg, Photo by Steffen Wippel 2010, http://www.jewelofmuscat.tv/image/tid/31, http://www.danstopicals.com/oman219.jpg)

shipping. Enterprises – port operators and shipping agencies, but also car traders, insurance companies and firm holdings – use ships as symbols in their corporate design. The young national carrier Oman Air recently renamed its first-class and promotion campaigns after Oman's most famous ancestor, Sinbad.

At the same time, Oman's historic and strategic location on the Indian Ocean is repeatedly emphasised. The official Oman yearbook, which targets mainly the international public and is translated into several languages, emphasises twice that the Sultanate is "dominating the oldest and most important sea trade route in the world between the Gulf and the Indian Ocean" (Ministry of Information 2008: 12) and that, in the past, it has already been "a prosperous Indian Ocean commercial and maritime centre" (ibid.: 30). The recent public-private "Brand Oman" campaign underlines the sea as one of four central characteristics of the country: Its logo (Fig. 10.7) represents "the sultanate's historic leadership in trade and pioneering

New Industrial Estate Roundabout, Salalah / The "Sohar", Al Bustan Roundabout, Muscat
Al Wizarat Roundabout, Al Khuwair, Muscat / Al Mina' Roundabout, Mutrah

Fig. 10.6 Shipping monuments in Oman (Source: Photos by Steffen Wippel 2009, 2010)

Fig. 10.7 "Brand Oman" Logo (Source: http://www.brandoman.om)

role in exploration"; looking from right to left, it shows "the dhow (purple), the turtle and rich marine environment (marine green)" (Brand Oman 2011).

The travails of traditional seafaring also serve to convince contemporary countrymen of efforts needed to promote the country and foreigners of the national experience. In his aforementioned speech, Qaboos said:

> We wish to remind the new generation of the high purpose of their forefathers who braved the storms of the violent seas in order to provide us with a wholesome standard of living. The Omani youth who look forward to glorious horizons are called upon today to take their ancestors as an example of diligence, hard work, patience, persistence and sustained effort.

> They are also called upon to believe, as they believed, that productive work – no matter how small it is – is a key element in the structure of the nation (MoFA 1996).

He then concluded:

> We are here today to link our shining present with our historic past, within this new framework which embraces countries with historical commercial ties, and mutual economic interests and goals (ibid.).

Similarly, Ociped postulates: "With modern manufacturing plants, a fierce devotion to quality, entrepreneurial flair and centuries of seafaring export experience, the Sultanate's business community is an intrinsic part of Brand Oman" (Ociped 2009a: 18). The new IT park, which seeks to attract international investors, states: "for this nation of ancient seafarers, the concept of international trade is far from new. Indeed, since as far back as the first century AD, Oman has been an international trading hub" (Knowledge Oasis Muscat n.d.).

With the container port of Salalah, which was established in the southern governorate of Dhofar in 1998 and has grown to become one of the major transhipment hubs worldwide, the Omani government sought to re-establish the country's historic role as an *entrepôt* for trade (Wippel 2011). The port operator named its brochure for the port inauguration "Rewriting the History of an Important Ancient Trade Route" and underlined, "A key feature of this facility is its central location in the Indian Ocean …" (Salalah Port Services … 1998). The port advertises itself as a "Gateway to the Indian Ocean Rim Countries" (Salalah Port Services Co. n.d.), and its homepage states: "Situated right at the major East-West shipping lanes, Salalah enjoys an attractive strategic location in the heart of the Indian Ocean Rim …" "Set against the tranquil backdrop of passing time the vessels that brought about prosperity and growth is [sic!] but an instance in Omani seafaring tradition that goes back to over 4,000 years. … Salalah not only provides convenient access to the Middle East but is also a suitable channel for the Sub-continent, Red Sea, Upper Gulf and the East African markets with over 1.6 billion consumers" (http://www.salalahport.com). The same is true for the adjacent, newly established Salalah Free Zone. Its homepage also vaunts the favourable location on the world's main sea trade route as "The key to unfettered access to over 1.6 billion consumers in the Middle East, East Africa and the Indian Ocean Rim …" (SFZ n.d.). Correspondingly, both institutions visualise this geoeconomic positioning, integrating in their publicity materials maps showing their strategic location in the region.

Similarly, tourism marketing, which is by far the most advanced field of "selling" Oman, refers to the Sinbad legend, the country's maritime past and its position at intercontinental crossroads, reflected in cultural, linguistic, architectonic and culinary diversity and blending. Yet, according to Omani interlocutors, responsiveness in the business community to the GCC is still greater than for the IOR-ARC. Though they say that the media generally cover events well, they underline the need to further improve awareness of belonging to the Indian Ocean region and of the opportunities offered by it.

10.7 Conclusion: In Search of Economic Diversification and Regional Belonging

This study showed that Oman has and is developing strong economic links with Indian Ocean countries and actively places itself in the area. The main motives behind this are the desire to diversify the still very hydrocarbon-dependent national economy and to prepare it for the post-oil era, as is set down in the national "Vision 2020" postulated 15 years ago. This includes the development of export-oriented industries, the establishment of international free zones and development into a global transport hub, mainly by constructing and expanding ports.

To this end, Oman orientates itself towards the Indian Ocean, which is surrounded by some major emerging economies offering promising markets. With other countries, the Sultanate tries to build on historical links that help to create a certain degree of "proximity", even if the goods exchanged, the means of transport and the main actors have changed considerably. At the same time, this is part of broader reciprocal "Looking East" (from the Gulf) and "Looking West" strategies (from China or India) and of a recent engagement of Gulf countries in Africa (mainly to secure food supplies). Additionally, attempts to position Oman as an economically attractive place and to brand the hitherto relatively unknown country have been strengthened. All this means that Oman is trying to make use of its geographical location and to produce and communicate a favourable geoeconomic position.

At any rate, with its focus on Oman's current economic relations with the Indian Ocean area, the objective of the present paper is not to construct another exclusive world region. It is *but one* possible perspective to take or "story" to tell. It neither wants to deny Oman's identity as an "Arab" country nor to detach it from the MENA region. Finally, it is to be hoped that this chapter has made it clear that the Indian Ocean is not a homogenous and continuous entity, as Bromber already showed in the conceptual part of this volume. Instead, it divides into several sub-regions and has different, often quite vague shapes in accordance with different temporal, institutional, material and discursive perspectives. It turns out that the Gulf constitutes a central point of reference, simultaneously part of the Indian Ocean world and the Middle East, linking Asia, Europe and Africa. Instead of monolithic blocs and unique regional belonging, we should be aware of multiple, overlapping regional identities and orientations. Obviously this also extends to political, social and cultural spheres.

References

Anon. (2003). Second UMIOR general conference. *Thai Higher Education Review, 1*(3), 7.

Anon. (2005). *Oman, a seafaring nation* (3rd ed.). Muscat: Ministry of National Heritage and Culture.

Bachmann-Medick, D. (2006). *Cultural turns: Neuorientierungen in den Kulturwissenschaften*. Reinbek bei Hamburg: Rowohlt.

Ben Arrous, M. (1996). *Beyond territoriality: A geography of Africa from below*. Dakar: Codesria.

Bøås, M., Marchand, M. H., & Shaw, T. M. (Eds.). (2005). *The political economy of regions and regionalisms*. Houndmills/Basingstoke/New York: Palgrave Macmillan.

Bouchard, C. (2000). *L'espace indianocéanique: Un système géopolitique en recomposition.* Ph.D. thesis, Faculté des études supérieures & Faculté des Lettres, Département de géographie, Université Laval, Quebec.

Brand Oman. (2011). *The story behind the brand mark.* http://www.brandoman.om/en/brand_oman/story/. Accessed 17 Nov 2011.

Business Information Services for the Indian Ocean Rim Countries. (2004, August 23). *Report of the working group on trade and investment. Colombo, Democratic Socialist Republic of Sri Lanka.* http://www.iornet.com/newiornet/iorarc/wgti/wgti2004.htm. Accessed 21 Feb 2006.

Chaudhuri, K. N. (1990). *Asia before Europe: Economy and civilisation of the Indian Ocean from the rise of Islam to 1750.* Cambridge/New York: Cambridge University Press.

Christiansen, T., Petito, F., & Tonra, B. (2000). Fuzzy politics around fuzzy borders: The European Union's 'near abroad'. *Cooperation and Conflict, 35*(4), 389–415.

DG Trade (European Commission). (2011, June 8). *Oman: EU bilateral trade and trade with the World.* http://trade.ec.europa.eu/doclib/docs/2006/september/tradoc_113430.pdf. Accessed 12 Sept 2011.

Embassy of India. (2011a). *Major Indian companies represented in Oman.* http://www.indemb-oman.org/major_indian_companies.asp. Accessed 16 Sept 2011.

Embassy of India. (2011b). *India-Oman economic relations.* http://www.indemb-oman.org/economic_relations.asp. Accessed 16 Sept 2011.

Freitag, U., & von Oppen, A. (2010). Introduction: 'Translocality': An approach to connection and transfer in area studies. In U. Freitag & A. von Oppen (Eds.), *Translocality: The study of globalising processes from a Southern perspective* (pp. 1–21). Leiden/Boston: Brill.

Gopalan, S., & Rajan, R. S. (2009). *Indian Ocean Rim Association for Regional Cooperation (IOR-ARC).* Arlington: Mimeo. http://66.147.244.232/~lifeats1/ramkishenrajan/pdfs/publications/other_policy_briefs_and_opeds/2009/IOR.pdf. Accessed 15 Nov 2010.

Hettne, B., & Söderbaum, F. (2000). Theorising the rise of regionness. *New Political Economy, 5*(3), 457–473.

IMF – International Monetary Fund, Statistics Department. (2007). *Direction of trade statistics* (1980–2005). CD-ROM. Washington, DC.

INORI – Indian Ocean Research Initiative. (2005). Neuere Literatur zum Indischen Ozean – eine kritische Würdigung. In C. Marx (Ed.), *Periplus 2005: Jahrbuch für außereuropäische Geschichte, 15* (pp. 141–172). Münster/Hamburg/London: LIT.

IOR-ARC Secretariat. (2010). *Indian Ocean Rim Association for Regional Cooperation (IOR-ARC): Documents for the Twelfth Meeting of the Committee of Senior Officials (CSO).* Sana'a, Republic of Yemen, Tuesday August 3rd, Wednesday August 4th. http://www.madagascar-diplomatie.net/article.php?article_id=648. Accessed 22 July 2011.

Iran Chamber of Commerce, Industries and Mines. (2009, June 30). *15th Business Forum of Indian Ocean Rim Association for Regional Cooperation (IOR-ARC) to be held in Yemen.* Tehran. http://en.iccim.ir/index.php?option=com_content&view=article&id=1410:-15th-business-forum-of-indian-ocean-rim-association-for-regional-cooperation-ior-arc-to-be-held-in-yemen&catid=42:asian-pacific. Accessed 9 Mar 2011.

ITC – International Trade Centre, Market Analysis and Research. (2011). *Trade Map: Trade statistics for international business development.* http://www.trademap.org. Accessed 12 Sept 2011.

Kéchichian, J. A. (2008). A vision of Oman: State of the Sultanate speeches by Qaboos Bin Said, 1970–2006. *Middle East Policy, 15*(3), 112–133.

Kelegama, S. (2000). Open regionalism in the Indian Ocean: How relevant is the APEC model for IOR-ARC? *Journal of the Asia Pacific Economy, 5*(3), 255–274.

Knowledge Oasis Muscat. (n.d.). *A technology park.* Muscat.

Krause, R. F. (1993). Orient, Naher und Mittlerer Osten: Die Begriffe im Wandel der Zeit. *Geographische Rundschau, 45*(1), 4–9.

Lewis, M. W., & Wigen, K. E. (1997). *The myth of continents: A critique of metageography*. Berkeley/Los Angeles/London: University of California Press.

McGuire, G. (2003). *Barriers to trade in Indian Ocean rim countries*. Canberra: Commonwealth of Australia. http://www.dfat.gov.au/trade/iorarc/research_reports/trade_barriers_iorarc.pdf. Accessed 25 July 2005.

McPherson, K. (1993). *The Indian Ocean: A history of people and the sea*. Delhi/New York: Oxford University Press.

Ministry of Information, Sultanate of Oman. (2008). *Oman 2008–2009*. Muscat: Ministry of Information.

MoFA – Ministry of Foreign Affairs, Sultanate of Oman. (1996). *Speech of his Majesty Sultan Qaboos bin Said on the occasion of the 26th National Day*. http://www.mofa.gov.om/mofanew/hmspeech.asp?title=55. Accessed 11 Sept 2011.

Mohamedbhai, G. (2008). Mauritius. In D. Teferra & J. Knight (Eds.), *Higher education in Africa: The international dimension* (pp. 262–302). Chestnut Hill/Accra: Boston College Center for International Higher Education & Association of African Universities.

MoNE – Ministry of National Economy, Sultanate of Oman. (2008). *Statistical yearbook 2008* (Issue 36). Muscat. http://www.moneoman.gov.om/book/syb_2008/fscommand/english/index.htm. Accessed 4 Mar 2009.

MoNE – Ministry of National Economy, Sultanate of Oman. (2010). *The statistical year book 2010* (Issue 38). Muscat. http://www.moneoman.gov.om/book/SYB2010/index.htm. Accessed 22 Mar 2011.

MoNE – Ministry of National Economy, Directorate General of Economic Statistics, Sultanate of Oman. (2011). *Foreign investment 2005–2009* (5th issue). Muscat. http://www.mone.gov.om/PublicationAttachment/FOREIGN%20INVESTMENT11.pdf. Accessed 6 Aug 2011.

Ociped – The Omani Centre for Investment Promotion and Export Development. (2009a). *Solid value: Goods from the Sultanate of Oman*. Muscat: Ociped.

Ociped – The Omani Centre for Investment Promotion and Export Development. (2009b). *Market studies*. A collection of document files on USB-Stick, presented by Ociped [Muscat].

Porter, I. W. (1997). The Indian Ocean rim. *African Security Review*, *6*(6). http://www.iss.co.za/pubs/ASR/6No6/Porter.html. Accessed 2 Mar 2009.

Reddy, J. M. (2000). Overview. In J. M. Reddy (Ed.), *Trade and investment: Issues in the Indian Ocean rim* (pp. 1–20). New Delhi: Sterling Publishers Private Ltd.

Salalah Port Services Co. (n.d.). *The Port of Salalah – Your Gateway to the Indian Ocean rim countries*. Muscat/Salalah.

Salalah Port Services Company SAOG. (1998). *Rewriting the history of an important ancient trade route*. Muscat/Salalah.

SFZ – Salalah Free Zone. (n.d.). *Investor guide: One free zone. Many amazing advantages*. Muscat/Salalah.

Shand, R., & Kalijaran, K. P. (1997). Yamazawa's open economic association: An Indian Ocean grouping for economic cooperation. *The Developing Economies, 35*(1), 3–27.

Singh, M. (2011, August). Take off stage. *Oman Economic Review*. hhttp://www.oeronline.com/php/2011/Aug/interview.php. Accessed 16 Sep 2011.

Soesastro, H. (1998). "Offener Regionalismus" im asiatisch-pazifischen Raum. In H. W. Maull (Ed.), *Regionalismus in Asien Pazifik* (pp. 7–58). Bonn: DGAP.

Tiwari, S. K. (2004). *Indian Ocean Rim-Association for Regional Cooperation (IOR-ARC): Problems and prospects*. Delhi: Abhijeet Publications.

UNESCO – United Nations Educational, Scientific and Cultural Organization. (1990, October 30). *Address by Mr Federico Mayor, Director-General of the United Nations Educational, Scientific and Cultural Organization (Unesco) at the ceremony to launch the Maritime Route Expedition of the Unesco integral study of the silk roads: Roads of dialogue*. DG/90/39. Venice. http://unesdoc.unesco.org/images/0008/000880/088051eo.pdf. Accessed 17 Mar 2010.

Vines, A., & Oruitemeka, B. (2008). *India's engagement with the African Indian Ocean rim states*. London: Chatham House, Africa Programme Paper 1/08. http://www.chathamhouse.org.uk/files/11293_india_africa0408.pdf. Accessed 4 Mar 2009.

Werlen, B. (2000). Alltägliche Regionalisierungen unter räumlich-zeitlich entankerten Lebensbedingungen. *Informationen zur Raumentwicklung, 9*(10), 611–621.

Wippel, S. (2010). *Between the Arab world and the Indian Ocean: Dimensions of Oman's economic regionalisation*. Leipzig: Graduate Centre Humanities and Social Sciences of the Research Academy Leipzig.

Wippel, S. (2011, July 7). *Globalisation, regionalisation and economic change in Salalah (Oman)*. Paper, Gulf Research Meeting 2011, Workshop 5: Modernization and socio-economic changes in the Gulf Arabic cities. The Gulf Research Centre, University of Cambridge, Cambridge (in preparation).

Wriggins, H. W. (1992). The dynamics of regional politics: An orientation. In H. W. Wriggins & F. G. Gause III, et al. (Eds.), *Dynamics of regional politics: Four systems in the Indian Ocean rim* (pp. 1–21). New York/Oxford: Columbia University Press.

Internet Links

http://www.brandoman.om. Accessed 18 Mar 2010.
http://www.ociped.com. Accessed 12 Sept 2011.
http://www.salalahport.com. Accessed 3 Oct 2010.
http://www.maritimebooks.com.au/pix/55219.jpg. Accessed 20 Mar 2010.
http://www.jewelofmuscat.tv/image/tid/31. Accessed 20 Mar 2010.
http://www.danstopicals.com/oman219.jpg. Accessed 17 Nov 2011.

Chapter 11
Oman Caught Between the GCC Customs Union and Bilateral Free Trade with the US: Is It Worth Breaking the Rules?

Anja Zorob

11.1 Introduction

Oman has been a member of the Gulf Cooperation Council (GCC) since the latter's foundation in 1981. Although the creation of the GCC was primarily motivated by security concerns, stronger economic cooperation and integration among its members soon attracted the GCC leaders' attention. The GCC members early on aimed at establishing an economic bloc, to be achieved on a gradual basis. While succeeding in eliminating tariff barriers among each other in 1983, the decision to introduce a customs union (CU), had to wait almost another 20 years. Moreover, the GCC customs union, as well as all other initiatives aimed at deepening integration announced during the 2000s, still lack proper implementation.

Oman has always remained rather reluctant towards initiatives at deepening and widening the scope of economic integration among the GCC members, fearing in particular Saudi dominance. In 2006, however, Oman not only postponed its membership in the GCC Monetary Union, originally scheduled to be established by 2010. In addition, it signed a free trade agreement (FTA) with the United States of America. With this "deep" FTA going far beyond the removal of "border barriers" on merchandise trade, the Omani administration hopes to be able to significantly enhance exports and foreign direct investment as a means of achieving higher growth, employment and diversification of the Omani economy. According to theory, Oman and Bahrain who concluded a similar treaty with the United States, violated the rules of the GCC customs union, as the bilateral FTAs "break" the common external tariff (CET) agreed on with the other GCC members. Beyond potentially impeding implementation of the CU, the bilateral FTAs may, in the worst case,

A. Zorob (✉)
Institute of Development Research and Development Policy, Ruhr-Universität Bochum, Universitätsstr. 150, GB 1/161, 44801 Bochum, Germany
e-mail: anja.zorob@rub.de

S. Wippel (ed.), *Regionalizing Oman: Political, Economic and Social Dynamics*, United Nations University Series on Regionalism 6, DOI 10.1007/978-94-007-6821-5_11,

undermine the credibility of the GCC as a whole. Omani officials, however, don't miss any opportunity to stress that it is not the FTA that is hampering full implementation of the GCC customs union.

Against this background, the question arises how implementation of the bilateral FTA with the United States impacts the progress of GCC-internal integration. Moreover, what are the potential costs or risks the Omani economy will confront while trying to comply with a multiplicity of rules as part of different trade agreements? This chapter starts by reviewing developments inside the GCC and exploring Oman's economic relations with its Gulf neighbours. The subsequent part takes a look at the Oman-US FTA and discusses the Omani government's motives for concluding it. Then the costs and risks of "betraying" the customs union for GCC-internal economic integration and Omani companies and administration will be analysed in greater detail.

11.2 Developments Within the Gulf Cooperation Council and the Omani Perspective

11.2.1 Efforts at Deepening GCC Economic Integration

In 2011, the GCC celebrated its 30th anniversary. The establishment of the Council is generally viewed as a response of the six oil-rich Arab Gulf countries – Saudi Arabia, the United Arab Emirates (UAE), Kuwait, Qatar, Bahrain and Oman – to the Islamic Revolution in Iran in 1979 and the outbreak of the first Gulf War between Iran and Iraq. Accordingly, the motive behind its creation was first of all to gain security by helping to protect its members against their more highly populated and heavily armed neighbours Iran and Iraq (Koch 2010). Within the GCC, Saudi Arabia is not only the most populous and economically most powerful member country; it also maintains to this day a dominant position and usually forms the main driver behind measures to widen and deepen GCC-internal integration. Against this background, the other GCC countries, and in particular Oman and Bahrain as the least populous and least economically powerful countries of the Gulf region, traditionally take a back seat when it comes to deepening GCC integration, viewing it as an instrument employed by the Saudis to consolidate power and influence in the region (Holthaus 2010). However, Oman relies heavily on its neighbours in the Gulf with regard to non-oil trade, aid, investment and labour migration.

Although the creation of the GCC in 1981 was primarily motivated by security concerns, economic integration soon attracted GCC leaders' attention. Within a few weeks after its foundation, the members approved the Unified Economic Agreement (UEA). It aimed at establishing a common oil and energy policy, coordinating industrial policy and conducting common projects, among other things. In addition, it spelled out the target to establish an economic bloc, closely following Balassa's "stages of integration" (Balassa 1961; see also Lorenz and Mattheis, in this volume).

These stages define the process of integration as gradually developing from a free trade area to a customs union and common market to reach in the end a complete economic union. In recent years, those calling for deeper economic integration within the GCC increasingly held up the European Union as the "role model" to follow. While the GCC members relatively quickly managed to introduce a free trade area in 1983, other fields, such as coordinating oil policy among the GCC member countries, realized hardly any progress. The decision to establish a customs union had to wait almost another 20 years. Nevertheless, the GCC succeeded during the 1980s and 1990s in setting up some common organizations, such as the Gulf Investment Corporation, and launched some joint development projects. In addition, and benefiting from measures such as the abolition of visa requirements for GCC citizens when moving from one member country to another and the gradual easing of rights of establishment for Gulf companies, cooperation on the level of private business and civil society improved significantly, most importantly through professional associations (Legrenzi 2008).

The decision in 2001 to move to the next stage of economic integration was accompanied by a revision of the UEA. The new UEA agreement included harmonizing economic, fiscal and monetary policies among the GCC members as an additional target, set a specific timetable for the introduction of a CET and subsequent steps of integration and established mechanisms for implementation, monitoring and dispute settlement (GCC Secretariat 2009; Woertz 2008). According to this timetable, the GCC customs union should have been completed by 2005 at the latest. The GCC member countries managed to align their tariff regimes with a CET of 5 percent across more than 85 percent of all tariff lines with most of the rest to be exempted from duties full implementation of the customs union, however, still faced several obstacles. According to latest information, it shall be completed by 2015 (Anon. 2011a). The bumpy track record of the CU, however, did not prevent Gulf leaders from declaring that the GCC common market would come into force as scheduled with the beginning of 2008 (GCC Secretariat 2009; Woertz 2008). This means that the scope of integration is moving beyond the liberalization of merchandise trade to cover also free trade in services and free movement of capital and labour. Important steps in this direction and the achievement of a common "economic nationality" covering equal treatment and free movement, residence, work, investment, education, health and social services have been taken since the years prior to 2008. Yet, there are still many issues pertaining in particular to the liberalization of trade in services and government procurement, and the movement of migrant workers, that still need to be tackled more substantially (cf. also World Bank 2010b; Zarrouk 2011).

Beyond the common market, the UEA also included the target of establishing a monetary union and introducing a single currency by the year 2010. In 2002 a Monetary Union Committee was formed and tasked with carving out economic convergence criteria, which were approved by the Supreme Council at its meeting in December 2005. In addition, it was agreed that all members should adopt the US dollar as a common currency peg (GCC Secretariat 2009). However, in 2006 Oman decided to pull out of the monetary union plan. When asked for the reason behind this decision, Omani experts and officials emphasized the great differences in monetary and financial policies among GCC member countries.[1] In 2007, Kuwait decided to peg the Dinar to a currency basket instead of the US dollar. Finally, in 2009, the UAE opted out of the plan, too, reportedly because of disagreement with the Saudi brothers over the location of the future GCC central bank headquarters.

Finally, at the GCC summit in December 2011, the Saudi King raised the idea of transforming the GCC into a "Gulf Union". According to his words, the time was ripe to "move from a phase of cooperation to a phase of union within a single entity" (Anon. 2011b, 2012). Earlier, in May 2011, many were caught by surprise to learn that the Gulf leaders are considering requests by Jordan and Morocco to join the club just two weeks ahead of the GCC's 30th anniversary (Anon. 2011e, f). Both ideas seem to have been triggered by the events of the Arab Spring and the Arab Gulf countries' deteriorating relations with Iran.[2] Meanwhile, Oman is reported to be a strong opponent of the idea of admitting Morocco and Jordan as new members (Anon. 2011c, d). Moreover, in almost all GCC member countries many voices are critical of a Gulf Union and warn, among other things, that all obstacles impeding economic integration should be eliminated first or that such a step should not be taken as a response to specific events or threats, not to mention the deep political differences among GCC members. Regional observers emphasize that Oman in particular may find it problematic to accept the proposal, not only because of its distinct foreign policy in general and its relatively good relations with Iran specifically (Anon. 2012). Nevertheless, the Saudi proposal to transform the GCC into a single entity was formally adopted at the summit (Anon. 2011a).

11.2.2 GCC Negotiations on FTAs with External Partners

The first free trade agreement the GCC tried to negotiate jointly was the treaty with the EU. However, due to several "stumbling blocks", the latest of which revolved around the EU's insistence on a clause proscribing export duties, the GCC finally suspended negotiations in late 2008.[3] During the 2000s, the GCC members began to negotiate FTAs with a number of other external partners and in particular Asian countries (Table 11.1). This did not preclude negotiations on trade and cooperation agreements between individual GCC members and other countries on the bilateral level, as is best illustrated by the Oman-US and Bahrain-US FTAs.

[1] Interviews with Omani experts conducted in Muscat in early 2011.

[2] There have always been discussions about enlarging the GCC by adding new members since its establishment. However, only Yemen was approved in 2001 as a member or rather observer of some GCC-internal specialized councils. In 2006, the GCC leaders suggested a future full entry of Yemen into the GCC, albeit without presenting a formal plan of accession (World Bank 2010b: 19).

[3] The GCC and the EU are bound by a cooperation agreement concluded in 1989. For more details on the FTA negotiations which had begun as early as 1990, see Zorob (2009, 2010).

Table 11.1 The GCC's free trade agreements and negotiations with external partners

Partner	Start of negotiations	Status of negotiations
European Union	1990	Suspended in December 2008
China	2005	On-going
Turkey	2005	On-going
India	2006	On-going
Singapore	2006	FTA signed in December 2008 (pending ratification)
EFTA	2006	FTA signed in June 2009 (pending ratification)
MERCOSUR	2006	On-going
Japan	2006	On-going
Pakistan	2006	On-going
New Zealand	2007	FTA initialled in October 2010
Australia	2007	On-going
South Korea	2008	On-going

The author's compilation based on different national and regional sources

These bilateral FTAs soon sparked controversy among GCC members. Being aware of the potential trade deflection these treaties could generate, or in other words that the Saudi market could be flooded with highly competitive US products imported duty-free via Bahrain, the Saudi leadership reportedly "lambasted" their Bahraini brothers at a meeting in late 2004. Despite the potential harm these bilateral FTAs could do to future prospects of economic integration among the GCC members, regional leaders apparently preferred to keep their disagreement behind closed doors (Lawson 2011: 202). And indeed, beyond merely recording that Bahrain and Oman had each concluded a bilateral agreement with the US, the Gulf daily press kept more or less silent (Woertz 2006).

In the meantime, GCC leaders took steps to give the impression that they are sticking to former plans to implement the customs union and work hard at eliminating all obstacles impeding economic integration. At the summit in Abu Dhabi in 2005, they decided to adopt a "Common Trade Policy". As part of this new policy, all future free trade negotiations were to be conducted by the GCC members as a bloc, except in relation to the United States, with whom they are still allowed to negotiate on an individual basis (GCC Secretariat 2009). The GCC leaders may have sought to follow the example of the EU's supra-nationalized "Common Commercial Policy". However, for a genuine common trade policy, as the EU case shows, there must be an executive organ entrusted with full powers to conduct trade negotiations on the part of the member countries and to "speak with one voice". As of 2012 the GCC still lacked such a joint institution. Nevertheless, the GCC succeeded in concluding some FTAs with external partners, although both the GCC-Singapore and the GCC-EFTA FTAs, inked in 2008 and 2009 respectively, were still pending ratification as of early 2012. Another "deep" FTA was initialled in 2009 with New Zealand. Finally, all GCC member countries are members of the Greater Arab Free Trade Area (GAFTA) launched in 1997 under the auspices of the Arab League (Zorob 2008).

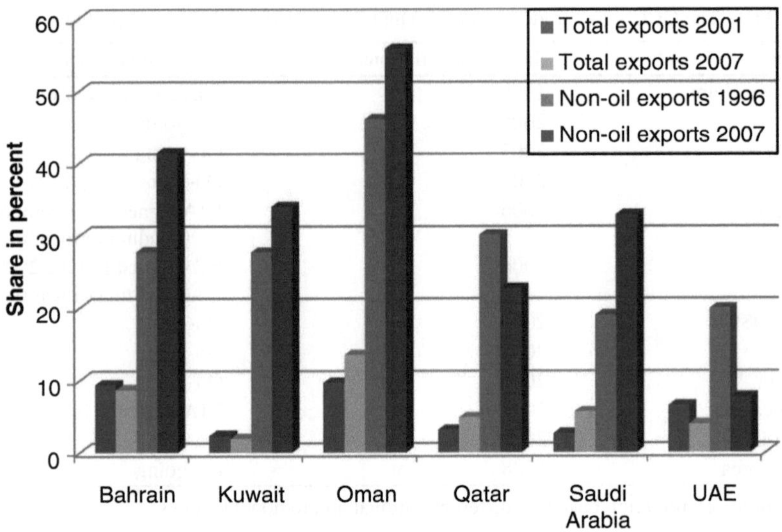

Fig. 11.1 Share of exports to other GCC Members in total and non-oil exports (The author's compilation based on Nechi (2011: Tables 2 and 5))

11.2.3 Oman and Its Neighbours in the Gulf: Trade, Aid and Investment

Merchandise trade among GCC members remains low-volume, despite the considerable growth it has witnessed since the beginning of the 1980s. In 2009 intra-GCC exports reached USD 31 billion or 6 percent of the GCC countries' total exports, whereas intra-GCC imports accounted for 6.2 percent of the total. This is far below the intraregional share of exports of more than 60 percent in case of the EU or 25 percent among ASEAN members (Zarrouk 2011: 4). The main reason behind low intraregional trade has often been attributed to weak trade complementarities among GCC members and the fact that the main customers of their oil and gas exports are outside the region. Oman's main trade partners are traditionally in East and South East Asia. In the first half of the 2000s, these markets absorbed around two-thirds of all Omani exports (Wippel 2010).

If oil is excluded, intraregional trade presents a significant share which amounted to some 17 percent of total non-oil exports of the GCC member countries in 2009 (Zarrouk 2011: 10). In the case of Oman this share is even higher. As illustrated in Fig. 11.1 Oman delivered some 13 percent of its total exports and more than half of its non-oil exports to the other GCC members. In addition, intraregional exports accounted for a substantial proportion of GDP, totalling 8.4 percent in 2007 (World Bank 2010b: 31). Around one-third of Omani imports came from other GCC countries, with the UAE being the largest Omani import partner in the world (Nechi 2011: 96; Wippel, in this volume; 2010).

Foreign direct investment (FDI) developed tremendously in Oman in recent years. Inflows amounted to an average of some USD 2.1 billion a year between 2005 and 2010 (UNCTAD 2011). Exact figures about the sources of FDI are, however, hard to find. Some references indicate that most FDI inflows to Oman came in the past from the UK and USA, in addition to the Gulf neighbours and, in recent years, also India. Most of them have been directed to the oil and gas sector, manufacturing and financial services and, more recently, tourism (ESCWA 2008: 10; U.S. & Foreign Commercial Service 2012).

Beyond trade and investment, Oman figures as a prominent tourism destination for Gulf citizens (ESCWA 2009: 32). In addition, Oman receives gas from Qatar, apparently at a preferential price, via the Dolphin Pipeline, as domestic gas reserves are limited and extraction is comparatively expensive (World Bank 2010b: 16). Finally, Oman was and still is one of the most important recipients of Arab aid. Although the volume of financial transfers decreased continuously after the 1980s, Oman always featured among the top ten recipients of Arab official development assistance from 1973 to 2008. Over this period it received some USD 4.4 billion in aid (World Bank 2010a: 12). More importantly, however, the GCC council pledged USD 10 billion each to Oman and Bahrain, just a few days after protests erupted in the port city and industrial hub of Sohar. Aid transfers were planned to be paid over the next 10 years "to upgrade their housing and infrastructure" or, in other words, to help both countries to quell the protests by speeding up public employment programs and other measures to enhance social security (Ali Khan 2011; Anon. 2011g; Bladd 2011).

11.3 The Oman-US Free Trade Agreement

11.3.1 Oman-US Relations and the Bush Administration's MEFTA Initiative

Oman and the United States are bound by strong relations that were put on a formal basis as early as in the 1830s, when the partners signed a treaty of friendship (Katzman 2012: 1). In the past, these relations concentrated primarily on a security or defence partnership. Convinced that Gulf security can't be reached without protection provided by the Western world, in 1980 Oman was the first country in the region to formally allow US troops to use its military facilities (Peterson 2004: 132). Nevertheless, US military presence in Omani facilities decreased substantially during the last decade, probably not least because a growing number of Omanis feel uncomfortable about it. Although the US ceased to provide Oman with development started to aid in the mid-1990s, in recent years it still offered Foreign Military Financing aimed at supporting, among other things, non-proliferation and combating terrorism (Katzman 2012: 10–11).

The FTA with Oman is one of the FTAs the United States signed with Middle Eastern countries in the framework of the MEFTA Initiative launched by the Bush

Table 11.2 Bilateral trade agreements between GCC members and the United States

Country	TIFAs	Status of FTA negotiations	Status of FTAs
Bahrain	2002	Concluded 05/2004	Signature 09/2004 In force since 2006
Kuwait	2004	–	–
Oman	2004	Concluded 10/2005	Signature 01/2006 In force since 2009
Qatar	2004	Preliminary negotiations stalled since 04/2006	–
Saudi Arabia	2003	–	–
UAE	2004	Stalled since 03/2007 Start of TIFA-plus 06/2007	–

The author's compilation based on Office of the United States Trade Representative (2012), and several media reports

Administration in 2003. This initiative was designed as a bottom-up approach by means of which "willing" Middle Eastern countries could become partners, provided that they fulfil a number of consecutive steps. Potential members should first join the World Trade Organization (WTO), take part in the Generalized System of Preferences (GSP) if applicable, and then conclude a Trade and Investment Framework Agreement (TIFA) with the United States. This should be followed by signing a Bilateral Investment Treaty (BIT) and finally a comprehensive FTA with the US. Finally, trade-capacity building programs, as part of a USD 1 billion financial and technical aid package, were conceived to help smoothing the implementation of the bilateral FTAs (Bolle 2006a). It was planned that the bilateral FTAs with Middle Eastern and North African countries would finally be merged into a single arrangement – the MEFTA – by 2013.

Almost in line with the MEFTA Initiative and its consecutive steps, Oman first became a member of WTO in 2000. Besides enjoying GSP, Oman signed a TIFA in July 2004, as shown in Table 11.2. In the course of the TIFA, a joint Council on Trade and Investment was established, which met for the first time in September 2004. Negotiations on the Oman-US FTA started in March 2005. They were concluded within an extremely short period only around half a year later. The agreement was signed in Washington in January 2006 (Bolle 2006b; MOCI 2006). At the time of its signature, it was the 5th FTA the United States had signed with a MENA country. The four other countries are Bahrain, Israel, Jordan and Morocco (Nelson et al. 2012). It took, however, three years until the treaty eventually went into force (for the alleged reasons behind the delay, see Oman Economic Review 2008).

11.3.2 The Broad Structure of the Oman-US FTA

The Oman-US FTA covers a wide range of topics and can therefore best be classified as a "deep" agreement which goes far beyond removing "border barriers" on merchandise trade. As the United States seem to present each partner with a "prototype" draft agreement at the outset of the FTA negotiations (Lawrence 2007: 22), the Oman-US FTA more or less resembles other agreements signed in the framework of the MEFTA initiative. Besides immediate free trade in industrial goods, the treaty provides for a substantial liberalization of trade in services, rights of establishment and strong rules for government procurement, the protection of intellectual property rights and streamlining and modernizing Omani customs procedures (Bolle 2006b; MOCI 2006).[4]

As regards merchandise trade, the partners provided each other immediate duty-free access for almost all industrial and consumer goods except textiles and apparel when the agreement went into force. Textiles and apparel were divided into three groups with respect to phasing out tariffs, ranging from immediate elimination to gradual reduction over 10 years. To enjoy duty-free access, goods must fulfil rules-of-origin criteria. With regard to textiles and apparel, these requirements cover, among others, the "yarn forward rule" and are therefore said to haven been primarily designed to protect the US market. Oman has been granted a Tariff Preference Level (TPL) that allows Omani companies to export an annual quantity of 50 million square meters of textile products duty-free to the US market which do not need to fully comply with the rules-of-origin requirements. However, the TPL is limited to a period of 10 years (MOCI 2006; Malkawi 2011). With respect to agricultural trade, Oman granted US products immediate duty-free access for "current" imports in 87 percent of all tariff lines, while the United States offered the same for all "current" Omani exports. Tariffs on remaining agricultural products will be phased out within 10 years after the agreement went into force.

As regards trade in services, including financial and telecom services, both parties provide each other with substantial market access that goes beyond the commitments Oman offered as part of its accession to the General Agreement on Trade in Services (GATS). However, Oman managed to include a negative list of services that will continue to restrict US service suppliers. With respect to investment, both parties grant each other national or most favoured nation treatment as regards the establishment, acquisition and operation of investments, except for sensitive sectors or branches included in a negative list attached to the agreement. US investors have to abide by Omanization rules that require up to 80 percent of those being employed by US companies to be Omani nationals. Provisions on government procurement require Oman to implement a system of fair, transparent and predictable procedures and to offer US suppliers the equivalent of national treatment when bidding on contracts with selected Omani government entities and state-owned enterprises. However, Oman retained the right to grant a preference margin to national small and medium-sized enterprises (MOCI 2006). Moreover, the Oman-US FTA includes several provisions on labour and environmental protection. These provisions do not oblige the parties to adhere to specific standards, but rather to commit to not weakening national protection as a way to promote trade and investment (Bolle 2006b: 8; Lawrence 2007: 27).

---

[4]The full text of the FTA including annexes is available at the Oman Ministry of Commerce & Industry and the Office of the United States Trade Representative website (2012).

11.3.3 *Motives Behind and Expected Effects of the Oman-US FTA*

In a rare critical statement on the bilateral FTAs in the Gulf media, Woertz (2006) asked how it could come that "Bahrain and Oman took this step with such ease; why Saudi Arabia did not oppose them more decisively; and finally what are the motives on the part of the US in deliberately driving a wedge between the GCC countries". He suggested that it might have been primarily political motives which were driving the behavior of all parties concerned.

As mentioned above, the Oman-US FTA is part of the MEFTA initiative launched by the Bush administration in 2003. This initiative was designed a year and a half after 9/11 to contribute to the new US strategy of combating international terrorism (Bolle 2006a). The logic behind was the Bush administration's firm belief that economic growth and democracy could be effectively promoted by free trade or, more precisely, by opening up the economies of the Middle East to US competition, anchoring reform and promoting diversification.[5] Along with the MEFTA Initiative, Woertz (2006) assumed the intention to isolate Saudi Arabia and containing the power of the GCC as a regional player as another motive behind the conclusion of bilateral FTAs which may have resounded "in some neoclassical circles" at least. Beyond political interests, another reason to opt for bilateral agreements instead of a regional agreement could simply be the complexity of trade negotiations. Following this logic it is hard to imagine that an arrangement as found in deep and comprehensive as the FTA with Oman could have been concluded with all MENA countries at once or even with a sub-group of them (for a similar argument, see Lawrence 2007). In addition, all FTAs necessarily need to be ratified "at home", i.e. in this case by the Omani parliament and the US Congress. Thus, and in particular if one recalls the United States' former disaffirmation of regional trade agreements, new FTAs in the framework of the MEFTA initiative had "to offer" benefits for the US economy beyond what could be achieved in the framework of the WTO.

Political and security motives may also have dominated Omani decision-making. As mentioned above, the Omani leadership is said to firmly believe that security in the Gulf region can only be achieved with the support of Western powers and among them, most importantly, the UK and United States.[6] In official statements, however, the expectations or rather hopes inspired by Oman's conclusion of the FTA with the United States coincide almost completely with the language used by the US administration and, likewise, what economic theory predicts. Potential positive effects of regional integration generally include increasing trade, efficiency and investment by enlarging market size as well as political benefits such as strengthening

---

[5]For a critical discussion of how free trade could help to fight terrorism, see Looney (2005).

[6]For detailed information on historical as well as recent relations between Oman and the UK, see Valeri (2009).

bargaining power. In this context, many economists maintain that an FTA with a strong industrialized country provides developing or emerging economies like Oman with better chances to benefit from static and dynamic effects of integration than a South-South agreement does. In addition, North-South FTAs offer partners gains from so-called non-traditional effects, such as securing and enhancing market access and/or locking-in reform and enhancing its credibility.[7] Accordingly, in Omani official statements and the majority of media coverage, the agreement with the United States was highlighted as a cornerstone of the country's strategy to liberalize the economy, diversify its productive base and prepare the Omani economy for the time after oil dries up. In other words, the bilateral FTA would provide an important instrument for generating growth and employment for a young and fast-growing population. Taking a similar line, the most recent CRS Report for Congress portrayed the FTA as some kind of a "gift" rewarding Oman for its strong support of US policy in the region: "It was partly in appreciation for this alliance that the United States entered into a free trade agreement (FTA) with Oman, which is also intended to help Oman diversify its economy to compensate for its relatively small reserves of crude oil" (Katzman 2012: Summary).

By liberalizing trade with the United States, it is hoped that access to the largest market in the world comprising more than 300 million consumers and a GDP worth USD 14 trillion will significantly improve. The GCC market, in contrast, appears to be rather small with a combined GDP of around USD 1 trillion and some 43 million consumers. Enhanced market access shall contribute to push non-oil exports and would also encourage US and other countries' companies to invest in Oman in order to produce and export goods to the vast US market, taking advantage of the duty-free preferential access" (MOCI 2006: 8). At the time of signature, a specific hope was attached to a potential revival of the "dying" Omani textile industry. Omani exports of apparel declined sharply in 2005 after quotas as part of the WTO agreement on textiles and clothing have been phased out (Bolle 2006b: 5). Moreover, the Omani government expected that opening up to US service suppliers will benefit Omani consumers and companies alike. In addition, granting US companies the same treatment as the Gulf neighbours will contribute to attracting US investment (MOCI 2006: 10). Finally, Oman could develop as a gateway of US goods to other GCC countries.

It should not be taken for granted, however, that the effects outlined above will in fact materialize. Usually, implementation of an FTA needs to be accompanied by a host of complementary measures to enable the tiny economy of Oman to benefit from such a far-reaching agreement. In addition, it will most probably come at a substantial cost. Beyond the "normal" adjustment costs, Oman might incur risks and opportunity costs by "obstructing" GCC internal economic integration.

[7] For a more detailed discussion of potential effects of integration and the debate about South-South vs. North-South RTAs, see Zorob (2008), Schiff and Winters (2003), and Kennes (2000).

11.4 Potential Costs and Risks of "Betraying" the GCC Customs Union

11.4.1 Impact of the Oman-US FTA on the Process of GCC-Internal Integration

As already mentioned, full implementation of the GCC customs union has been postponed several times in recent years. It is well-known that introducing a CET is a necessary but not sufficient condition for establishing a CU. It needs to be accompanied by the introduction of a common commercial policy and institutions capable of designing and implementing it. In addition, a system stipulating how duties are collected at the first point of entry and distributed among the CU members has to be set up and customs rules and procedures be harmonized. Finally, an effective CU that allows the eventual removal of customs inspection and verification of origin at internal borders requires a complete removal of non-tariff barriers in trade among members. Accordingly, the establishment of a CU is much more demanding than a FTA in terms of harmonisation and coordination efforts, as well as loss of national sovereignty over trade policy (Schiff and Winters 2003; Roy and Zarrouk 2002; Kennes 2000).

On the other hand, signing an FTA with an external partner while at the same time belonging to a CU means that the respective country hurts the common external tariff agreed on with the other partners of the CU. If customs inspection at GCC-internal borders was lifted, US goods imported via Oman or Bahrain would run the risk of being transhipped duty-free to other CU members, while these countries do not enjoy duty-free access to the US market. To avert such an outcome, verification of origin and inspection at GCC-internal borders would need to remain in place, generating administrative costs and hampering free trade among the GCC member countries. In addition, Oman would gain access to lower-priced imported inputs, enhancing the competitiveness of its own goods exported to the other GCC members. Moreover, Gulf neighbours might not be very delighted about forfeiting the preferential treatment over US suppliers they were assumed to have enjoyed previously on the Omani market in services trade and government procurement. As a consequence, other GCC members could think about retaliating in one way or another. In sum, opening up to US competition and adopting a whole range of US rules and regulations could seriously obstruct efforts at deepening integration and harmonizing rules within the GCC common market.

Omani officials often emphasized that at the time the FTA was negotiated the GCC customs union did not exist yet and thus they could not have "broken" the rules. They argued that the agreement with the United States presented a "window of opportunity" to lock in domestic reforms.[8] But even if the effects of the Oman-US

[8] Interviews with Omani experts conducted in Muscat in early 2011.

FTA contributed to preventing a full implementation of the GCC customs union, they may have formed only the tip of the iceberg. In fact, disagreement among the GCC members seems to go far beyond measures to prevent potential trade deflection. For many years, GCC private business has complained about the "daily agony at regional border points" and numerous restrictions of overland trade within the GCC. Pictures of kilometres-long queues of trucks standing in front of border check points were periodically shown in the Gulf media in recent years. In 2010, the Federation of GCC Chambers of Commerce and Industry (FGCCI) for the first time took part in a meeting of the GCC common market committee. In a report they presented at the meeting, FGCCI representatives mentioned a long list of obstacles that apparently go far beyond Gulf countries' national customs authorities asking to present rules of origin certificates for goods imported from other GCC members. The report pointed to additional fees requested to be paid at the border and facilities staying closed for longer times and being underequipped, prolonging cumbersome customs inspection procedures. Transport companies have been prevented from opening branches in other GCC member countries, and truck drivers have not been permitted to enter other GCC countries with empty trucks at night or have had to leave the country again within 12 h (Anon. 2010a, b). In addition, the UAE, for instance, will refuse to accept re-exports to its territory from other GCC member countries if a UAE agent holds exclusive agency rights (Zarrouk 2011; UAE Ministry of Foreign Trade 2010). The disagreement among the member countries on how to distribute customs revenues collected on goods imported from outside remained another sticky point while affairs were regulated by a temporary system (Anon. 2010b). As a result one may argue that the GCC members apparently lacked the will or were not prepared to introduce common rules and procedures that would enable the customs union to function effectively.

However, for Oman, the UAE is the sole window to the other GCC markets and many goods are imported to Oman via UAE ports.[9] Accordingly, the Oman-US FTA adds to existing problems traditionally. Although the countries agreed on a mechanism by which UAE customs authorities collect duties on imports of US products destined for Oman whereby customs receipts will be reimbursed later procedures like the latter will at least generate additional red tape. US sources, on the other hand, complained about cases in which Omani customs officials collected customs duties on US products when being transhipped to Oman via the UAE or when some non-American goods were in the same container (U.S. & Foreign Commercial Service 2012).

Yet, Omani experts, in line with all those upholding the credo of "open regionalism", dismissed any criticism or caveats. They rather argued that the bilateral FTA with the United States shall serve as a "building block" for deepening GCC-internal economic integration. By entering into an FTA with a "Northern" industrialized

[9]There are only four border checkpoints with UAE, and no checkpoint with Saudi Arabia, the largest GCC market. An overland route connecting Oman with Saudi Arabia has only just started to be built. Cf. Wippel (2010) and interviews in 2011.

partner, best practice rules and regulations as well as institutions could be imported, enabling the "Southern" or small "developing" economies to realize positive spill-over effects on intraregional integration. Such an objective could arguably best be reached if all GCC members, or even all MENA countries, concluded similar FTAs with the United States. Omani observers emphasized that this is exactly what the Omani government had in mind when concluding the agreement with the United States: that it should serve "as an important stepping stone towards an eventual Middle East Free Trade Agreement" (Oman Economic Review 2011).

Since the signature of the Oman-US FTA, however, no measures have apparently been taken to reach this end. In contrast, negotiations on an FTA with the UAE stalled in the early months of 2007 (Palmer 2006), and negotiations with Qatar never did really kick off. Although Egypt signed in 2004 an agreement with Israel and the United States to establish "Qualified Industrial Zones", FTA talks were put on hold in 2005 (Nelson et al. 2012: 18). Finally, the Trade Promotion Authority that allowed the Bush administration to enter into FTA negotiations under "fast track" procedures expired in mid-2007. In a speech delivered shortly before the G8, World Bank, IMF and others met in Deauville in May 2011, president Obama announced the launch of a new "Trade and Investment Partnership with the Middle East and North Africa". It was stated that this initiative would support MENA countries' integration with US and European markets by building on existing trade agreements and a future coordination of policies with the EU (The White House 2011). Yet, at the beginning of 2012, little seems to have been done to turn rhetoric into action. Moreover, a recent report casted doubts on both the feasibility of future FTAs with MENA countries and the effectiveness of increased trade and investment in supporting political transition (Nelson et al. 2012). Suggesting US commercial interests as a guiding principle for future trade policy towards the MENA region, the latter's markets were considered too small to be worth the price of negotiating trade and investment agreements. In other words, further FTAs with Gulf and other MENA countries seem to have been dropped from the US agenda.

This means, however, that one of the most important problems behind GCC economic integration – the duplication of Gulf countries' strategies to diversify their economies – may deepen even further in the future. If the bilateral FTAs with Oman and Bahrain remain the only ones or if differing rules keep them separated from other US trade agreements, a "hub-and-spokes" system must be expected to develop. In such a system, trade and investment risk being diverted from Oman and Bahrain to the United States as the "hub" of a larger network of FTAs, which now already stretches far beyond the MENA region.[10] Against this background, one could truly ask whether the bilateral FTA between Oman and the United States was really "worth breaking the rules"?

---

[10]For more details on potential costs and risks of a hub-and-spokes system applied to the case of the Euro-Mediterranean partnership, see Zorob (2008); on the difficulties of different rules-of-origin systems as part of MENA countries' agreements with the United States and the EU, see Lawrence (2007).

Finally, and beyond purely economic repercussions, the bilateral FTAs may have strengthened the Iranian government's belief in the GCC members' dwindling capability to join ranks: "Tehran has therefore adopted a more confrontational posture towards its southern neighbours" in recent years (Lawson 2011: 209–210). This apparent "credibility lack" of the GCC altogether – as an alliance for political, security, social and economic cooperation – may also have triggered the most recent proposal to establish a "Gulf Union". This Union, however, for the many reasons mentioned in this chapter, will most probably not see the light of day.

11.4.2 The Impact of Multiple Trade Agreements on Omani Business and Administration

The case of Oman trying to simultaneously integrate with different external partners and, accordingly, being obliged to comply with a multiplicity of rules as part of "overlapping" trade agreements presents an example of what is referred to in the literature as "spaghetti-bowl regionalism". The term was coined by Jagdish Bhagwati, accoring to whom FTAs are "inherently preferential and discriminatory" (Bhagwati 1995). The main problem or "systemic implications" of trade agreements include, most importantly, rules of origin. These are necessary features of all FTAs. However, both their formulation and implementation are characterized by a high degree of arbitrariness. In other words, rules of origin open the door for "protectionist capture" by domestic actors (Bhagwati et al. 1998). As a consequence, they contribute to setting up artificial production networks by discriminating against more efficient suppliers. At the same time, they create additional administrative burden. If different sets of rules of origin apply, producers have to know and differentiate among them when designing production processes, calculating of costs and fulfilling red tape to prove origin. In addition, the diversity of tariff reduction schedules and documents as part of FTAs with different partners causes delays as well as additional costs in customs procedures and requires experienced customs staff to determine which preferential schedule shall be applied to which assignment. Moreover, human capacities to negotiate trade agreements might soon be exhausted, in particular in small or developing countries (Bhagwati et al. 1998; Schiff and Winters 2003).

In this context a WTO report raised the issue that Omani ministerial capacities might have been overstretched already by negotiating the FTA with the United States (WTO 2008). Although Omani officials pointed out that, due to the customs union, rules-of-origin requirements have been lifted for trade among GCC members, other sourced maintained that they had still to be applied (World Bank 2010b). Yet, the GCC FTA rules of origin criteria, including the minimum of 40 percent local value added, seem in any case rather hard to fulfil for small economies with an underdeveloped production base. The same is true for the rules of origin covered by the Oman-US FTA. These do not only differ from the GCC-internal rules of origin. In addition, they were reported to be complex and restrictive as they have been primarily designed to protect the US market (see Section 11.3.2). Aside from product-specific rules, Omani exporters as of 2011 did still not enjoy the possibility to "cumulate origin" on a regional basis, i.e. to use inputs produced in other countries of the region that have concluded an FTA with the United States, despite a provision in the agreement to introduce such a system within six months after coming into force (Malkawi 2011). Beyond the GCC and the FTA with the United States, Oman is also a member of GAFTA and the Indian Ocean Rim Association for Regional Cooperation (IOR-ARC).[11] Moreover, the GCC already signed and is currently negotiating FTAs with other external partners. As it can't be expected that rules of origin and other regulations in all these agreements will be the same, difficulties in differentiation among the treaties' provisions, administrative burden and capacity bottlenecks on the part of Omani companies as well as public administration are doomed to grow even more.

Yet, the benefits of the Oman-US FTA were reported to have been rather limited up to the beginning of 2012, at least as regards the hoped-for expansion of Omani non-oil exports. Although exports to the US picked up during the last two years, non-oil exports concentrated on minerals, aluminium and petrochemicals; a significant expansion of textile exports, which had been announced as one of the most important beneficial effects, apparently did not materialize so far.

11.5 Conclusion

This chapter casted a glance on the progress of GCC economic integration in recent years. The analysis focussed on the GCC customs union which was announced in the early 2000s but still lacked proper implementation as of 2012. In addition, it introdced to the contents and expected effects of the Oman-US FTA. Bringing both things together the analysis put forward in this chapter concentrated on the question if or to what extent the bilateral FTA could be held responsible for the many delays and problems in implementation of the GCC customs union. As signing an FTA with an external partner while at the same time belonging to a CU means that the respective country is breaking the rules of the latter, it was claimed that the bilateral FTA concluded between Oman and the United States has contributed to seriously impeding implementation of the GCC customs union.

Although it is widely hoped for in Oman that the FTA with the United States will help to enhance exports and attract foreign investment as a means of achieving higher growth, employment and diversification of the Omani economy, its expected benefits should not be taken for granted. Moreover, the FTA might come at a substantial cost as a result of "betraying" GCC-internal integration, in particular if one takes into account that the Gulf neighbours as of 2012 still remain Oman's major

[11] The latter, however, is still in the process of preparing a preferential trade zone (Wippel, in this volume).

partners in trade, investment, financial aid and tourism. The bilateral FTAs with Oman and Bahrain surely can't be made responsible for all the numerous stumbling blocks impeding implementation of the GCC customs union. However, they seem at least to have contributed to hampering the progress of GCC-internal integration and will most probably do so even more in the future, thereby cementing a hub-and-spokes pattern of integration with the United States. Thus, Oman and the other GCC members risk confronting substantial opportunity costs in the years to come. Finally, Omani industry, business and public administration will be burdened with additional costs while trying to comply with a multiplicity of rules and regulations forming part of overlapping trade agreements Oman and the GCC as a bloc have signed and are about to conclude in the future. Although Oman always remained rather reluctant about initiatives aimed at deepening and widening the scope of economic integration among the GCC members during the last 30 years, the step to conclude and implement an FTA with the United States may eventually backfire.

References

Ali Khan, G. (2011, March 26). GCC aid could have significant positive impact on Oman, says S&P. *Muscat Daily*. http://www.muscatdaily.com/Archive/Stories-Files/GCC-aid-could-have-significant-positive-impact-on-Oman-says-S-P. Accessed 12 Mar 2012.

Anon. (2010a, September 22). GCC seeks to end common market hurdles. Private sector invited to attend joint meeting. *Emirates 24/7*. http://www.emirates247.com/business/economy-finance/gcc-seeks-to-end-common-market-hurdles-2010-09-22-1.293966. Accessed 22 Sept 2011.

Anon. (2010b, June 6). Tariff rift, delay block GCC customs union. Festering rift over distribution of tariff revenues blocks landmark customs union plan. *Emirates 24/7*. http://www.emirates247.com/eb247/companies-markets/logistics/tariff-rift-delays-block-gcc-customs-union-2010-06-06-1.251947. Accessed 22 Sept 2011.

Anon. (2011a, December 25). Gulf customs union begins January 2015, says Al Zayani. *Emirates 24/7*. http://www.emirates247.com/news/emirates/gulf-customs-union-begins-january-2015-says-al-zayani-2011-12-25-1.434434. Accessed 25 Feb 2012.

Anon. (2011b, December 20). GCC leaders stress the importance of unity. *Khaleej Times*. http://www.khaleejtimes.com/DisplayArticle09.asp?xfile=data/middleeast/2011/December/middleeast_December552.xml&section=middleeast. Accessed 25 Feb 2012.

Anon. (2011c, December 1). Oman and UAE insist on refusal to expand GCC. *Al-Quds al-Arabi*. Posted on MidEastWire, 2 Dec 2012. http://www.mideastwire.com/. Accessed 3 Dec 2011.

Anon. (2011d, December 1). UAE moves towards building a stronger union. *Khaleej Times*. http://www.khaleejtimes.com/darticlen.asp?xfile=data/theuae/2011/December/theuae_December21.xml&section=theuae. Accessed 25 Feb 2012.

Anon. (2011e, May 11). Jordan, Morocco to join GCC. *Khaleej Times*. http://www.khaleejtimes.com/DisplayArticle09.asp?xfile=data/middleeast/2011/May/middleeast_May233.xml&section=middleeast. Accessed 25 Feb 2012.

Anon. (2011f, May 11). Morocco and Jordan ask to join GCC. *The National*. http://www.thenational.ae/news/world/middle-east/morocco-and-jordan-ask-to-join-gcc. Accessed 25 Feb 2012.

Anon. (2011g, March 11). Duwal al-khaleej: 20 milyar dollar lil-Bahrain wa-'Oman. *Al-Iqtisadiyya al-electroniyya*. http://www.aleqt.com. Accessed 14 Mar 2012.

Anon. (2012, March 12). GCC union: Putting right step forward. *Gulf News*. http://gulfnews.com/news/region/general/gcc-union-putting-right-step-forward-1.992720. Accessed 15 Mar 2012.

Balassa, B. (1961). *The theory of economic integration*. London: George Allen & Unwin Ltd.

Bhagwati, J. (1995). *US trade policy: The infatuation with FTAs* (Columbia University discussion paper series, No. 726). New York: Columbia University Press.
Bhagwati, J., Greenaway, D., & Panagariya, A. (1998). Trading preferentially: Theory and policy. *The Economic Journal, 108*(449), 1128–1148.
Bladd, J. (2011, Mach 8). Gulf signs off $20bn aid deal for Oman, Bahrain. *Arabian Business*. http://www.arabianbusiness.com/gulf-signs-off-20bn-aid-deal-for-oman-bahrain-386099.html. Accessed 10 Mar 2012.
Bolle, M. J. (2006a). *Middle East free trade area: Progress Report*. Updated 26 June. CRS Report for Congress. No place: Congressional Research Service (CRS).
Bolle, M. J. (2006b). *U.S.-Oman free trade agreement*. Updated 10 October. CRS Report for Congress. No place: Congressional Research Service (CRS).
ESCWA – Economic and Social Commission for Western Asia. (2008). *Foreign direct investment report*. New York: United Nations.
ESCWA – Economic and Social Commission for Western Asia. (2009). *Annual review of developments in globalization and regional integration in the Arab countries 2009*. New York: United Nations.
GCC Secretariat – The Cooperation Council for the Arab States of the Gulf, Secretariat General. (2009). *The GCC process & achievement* (4th ed.). Riyadh: GCC Information Center.
Holthaus, L. (2010). *Regimelegitimität und regionale Kooperation im Golf-Kooperationsrat (Gulf Cooperation Council)*. Frankfurt am Main: Peter Lang.
Katzman, K. (2012). *Oman: Reform, Security, and U.S. Policy, 13 January* (CRS Report for Congress). No place: Congressional Research Service (CRS).
Kennes, W. (2000). *Small developing countries and global markets – Competing in the big league*. Basingstoke: Macmillan.
Koch, C. (2010). Der Golf-Kooperationsrat als regionale Sicherheitsorganisation. *KAS Auslandsinformationen, 26*(11), 24–39.
Lawrence, R. Z. (2007). Recent US free trade initiatives in the Middle East: Opportunities but No guarantees. In P. Cornelius & K. Schwab (Eds.), *The Arab World competitiveness report 2007* (pp. 21–30). Oxford: Oxford University Press.
Lawson, F. H. (2011). Geo-political complications of US free trade agreements with Gulf Arab countries. In M. Legrenzi & B. Momani (Eds.), *Shifting Geo-economic power of the Gulf: Oil, finance and institutions* (pp. 199–210). Aldershot/Burlington: Ashgate.
Legrenzi, M. (2008). Did the GCC make a difference? Institutional realities and (Un)intended consequences. In C. Harders & M. Legrenzi (Eds.), *Beyond regionalism? Regional cooperation, regionalism and regionalisation in the Middle East* (pp. 107–124). Aldershot/Burlington: Ashgate.
Looney, R. (2005). US Middle East economic policy: The use of free trade areas in the War on terrorism. *Mediterranean Quarterly, 16*(3), 102–117.
Malkawi, B. (2011). Rules of origin under US trade agreements with Arab countries: Are they helping and hindering free trade? *Journal of International Trade Law and Policy, 10*(1), 29–48.
MOCI – Ministry of Commerce & Industry, Sultanate of Oman. (2006). *Highlights of the free trade agreement (FTA) between the sultanate of Oman and the United States of America*. Muscat: MOCI.
Nechi, S. (2011). Determinants of trade flows among GCC countries: Potentials, limitations, and expectations. *World Review of Business Research, 1*(5), 91–109.
Nelson, R. M., Bolle, M. J., & Ilias, S. (2012, January 20). *U.S. trade and investment in the Middle East and North Africa: Overview and issues for Congress* (CRS Report for Congress). No place: Congressional Research Service (CRS).
Office of the United States Trade Representative. *Executive office of the President*. http://www.ustr.gov/trade-agreements/. Accessed 23 Jan 2012.
Oman Economic Review. (2008). *Oman-US FTA?* http://www.oeronline.com. Accessed 25 Oct 2011.
Oman Economic Review. (2011). *Oman-US FTA – Promising start*. http://www.oeronline.com/php/2011/jan/economy.php. Accessed 25 Oct 2011.

Oman Ministry of Commerce & Industry, & Office of the United States Trade Representative. *Oman-United States Free Trade Agreement*. http://www.omanusfta.com/documents.html. Accessed 24 Feb 2012.

Palmer, D. (2006, March 11). US, UAE postpone free trade talks amid ports row. *Reuters*. Posted on bilaterals.org 11 March 2006. http://www.bilaterals.org/spip.php?article4102&lang=en. Accessed 10 Feb 2012.

Peterson, J. E. (2004). Oman: Three and a half decades of change and development. *Middle East Policy, 11*(2), 125–137.

Roy, J., & Zarrouk, J. (2002). *Completing the GCC customs union*. Washington, DC: The World Bank.

Schiff, M., & Winters, L. A. (2003). *Regional integration and development*. Washington, DC: World Bank/Oxford University Press.

The White House. (2011). *Remarks by the President on the Middle East and North Africa*. http://www.whitehouse.gov/the-press-office/2011/05/19/remarks-president-middle-east-and-north-africa. Accessed 24 February 2012.

UAE Ministry of Foreign Trade. (2010). *Trade policy review – United Arab Emirates 2010. Update on the WTO TPR Report 2006*. Abu Dhabi: Ministry of Foreign Trade.

UNCTAD – United Nations Conference on Trade and Development . (2011). *World investment report 2011. Non-equity modes of international production and development*. New York: UNCTAD.

US Trade Information Center. (2012). *Helping U.S. companies export: U.S. free trade agreements*. http://export.gov/FTA/index.asp. Accessed 22 Jan 2012.

U.S. & Foreign Commercial Service and U.S. Department of State. (2012). *Doing business in Oman: 2012 country commercial guide for U.S. companies*. http://buyusainfo.net/docs/x_5348846.pdf. Accessed 15 Mar 2012.

Valeri, M. (2009). *Oman. Politics and society in the Qaboos state*. London: Hurst & Company.

Wippel, S. (2010). *Between the Arab world and the Indian Ocean: Dimensions of Oman's economic regionalisation* (Working Paper Series, No. 8). Leipzig: Graduate Centre Humanities and Social Sciences of the Research Academy Leipzig.

Woertz, E. (2006, October 6). FTAs ring alarm bells to Bahrain, Oman. *The Peninsula*. http://www.bilaterals.org/article-print.php3?id_article=6152. Accessed 24 Oct 2006.

Woertz, E. (2008, January). Common market more important than common currency. *The GRC Economic Research Bulletin*, No. 5, January.

World Bank. (2010a). *Arab development assistance: Four decades of cooperation*. Washington, DC: The World Bank.

World Bank. (2010b). *Economic integration in the GCC* (World Bank Middle East and North Africa region). Washington, DC: The World Bank.

WTO – World Trade Organization. (2008, August 5). *Trade policy review – Report by the Secretariat: Oman*. WT/TPR/S/201/Rev. 1. Geneva: WTO – World Trade Organization.

Zarrouk, J. (2011). *Muqarana bayna as-suq al-khaleejiyya al-mushtaraka was-suq al-urubiyya al-mushtaraka* (Arab Monetary Fund (AMF) economic studies). Abu Dhabi: AMF.

Zorob, A. (2008). Intraregional economic integration: The cases of GAFTA and MAFTA. In C. Harders & M. Legrenzi (Eds.), *Beyond regionalism? Regional cooperation, regionalism and regionalisation in the Middle East* (pp. 169–183). Aldershot/Burlington: Ashgate.

Zorob, A. (2009). EU-GCC-Freihandelsabkommen: Eine "unendliche Geschichte"? *INAMO – Informationsprojekt Naher und Mittlerer Osten, 15*(59), 63–64.

Zorob, A. (2010, July 7–10). *EU-GCC free trade negotiations: A never-ending story?* Paper presented at the Gulf Research Meeting 2010, organized by the Gulf Research Center Foundation in association with University of Cambridge, Cambridge.

Chapter 12
Musandam and Its Trade with Iran. Regional Linkages Across the Strait of Hormuz

Michael Benz

12.1 Introduction

The Omani exclave of Musandam is rarely known to researchers of modern social sciences. The last existing research is from the 1980s concerning social behaviour and mobility of the people of the hinterland (Zimmermann 1981). Still under the reign of Sultan Qaboos, the exclave is considered isolated and backward, although the government has launched several programs to develop the region since he came to power in 1970. On the one hand, this corresponds to general theoretical ideas about exclaves, which claim that they are of little importance for their mainlands (Melamid 1968; Robinson 1959). On the other hand there are some theories that do not seem to fit for Musandam at first glance, e.g. emphasising that exclaves "[…] do not exist in a vacuum. They exist in a world full of global players and powers with often contradictory interests" (Vinokurov 2007: 9). Yet, considering Musandam from this perspective also means to talk about exclaves and their transnational and regional connections. The terms "exclave" and "enclave" depend on the viewer's perspective. In this paper "exclave" refers to Oman's point of view on Musandam, excluded from the rest of the country's territory.

There is a serious national Omani interest in the small exclave, which constitutes a separate governorate, with its unique geographical position. Only because of Musandam, Oman has a short coastline with the Persian Gulf that made it directly eligible to become a member of the Gulf Cooperation Council.[1] The territorial possession makes it responsible for the two shipping lanes in the vital Strait of Hormuz, through which 20 percent of the world's total oil need is shipped. But also in a historic perspective, the region around the Strait of Hormuz has always

[1] For Oman in the GCC see Zorob, in this volume.

M. Benz, M.A. (✉)
Comeniusstr. 20, 04315 Leipzig, Germany
e-mail: michaelbenz2@gmx.de

S. Wippel (ed.), *Regionalizing Oman: Political, Economic and Social Dynamics*, United Nations University Series on Regionalism 6, DOI 10.1007/978-94-007-6821-5_12,

been of strategic importance for securing the waterways between the Persian Gulf and the Gulf of Oman.

The aim of my field research in March 2011 was to show the extensive regional linkages that connect the "isolated and backward" exclave with its neighbours, especially Iran and the UAE, and their meaning for the live of the people in Musandam. The main focus was the trade, which is often called smuggling, although we will see that this terminology is not precise. As it is often the case, this kind of trade is considered illegal on the one side, i.e. in Iran, while it is legal and partially taxed by the state on the other, the Omani side. My research on this phenomenon was based on the anthropological method of participant observation and narrative interviews. Local sources, such as telephone books, have been collected in Khasab, the governorate's capital, and I made surveys, e.g. of boats arriving in the local harbour.[2]

12.2 The Trade and Its History

Trade across the Strait of Hormuz is no new phenomenon. In ancient times the Kingdom of Hormuz controlled vast areas on both sides of the Persian Gulf from the island of the same name near the Northern coast. Since the colonial era, starting with the presence of the Portuguese, there have been serious conflicts about the trade routes in the Persian Gulf, e.g. to Basra and Bahrain. Later, the British recognized the Strait's strategic importance for trade in the whole region. This led, for instance, to the establishment of a telegraph station on Maqlab Island near Khasab in 1864, which connected Basra and Bombay (Lorimer 1915).

We get first detailed information about regional trade around the end of the nineteenth and the beginning of the twentieth century (Constable and Stiffe 1883; Lorimer 1915). Correspondence around 1925 shows commercial links between Khasab and trading partners in Bandar Abbas, India and Bahrain (Fig. 12.1).[3] Long-existing social linkages pushed the trade across the Strait of Hormuz. There have also been religious connections with the Iranian coast. In conversations with Zimmermann, he reported about strong social contacts and regular reciprocal visits of people of both coastal areas, e.g. for Friday prayers.

The trade in its modern form probably arose for the first time in the aftermath of the Islamic Revolution in Iran 1979. In the following years, sanctions against the new Iranian government, which were intended to harm the national economy, grew stronger. The years of the First Gulf War (1980–1988) are the turning point for the establishment of a complex and extensive trade between Musandam and the Iranian coast. Zimmermann reported that during his 9-month field research in 1979 the trade didn't exist in the form we know today.[4]

[2] If there is no reference given in the following text, all information, interviews, photographs and observations are from this field research.

[3] The letters are presented in the museum of Khasab.

[4] Author's conversation with Wolfgang Zimmermann in Leipzig, summer 2011.

Fig. 12.1 Letter from a Merchant of Bandar Abbas to the Governor of Bukha, Musandam 1925

As a consequence of the Islamic Revolution and the First Gulf War, there was a serious lack of goods of everyday life in Iran. Because Khasab is at the closest point on the opposite side of the Strait, small speedboats need only about 1 h to cross it. Later, the trade-route Dubai-Khasab-Bandar Abbas was even used to bring goods via Iran to Iraq (Anon. 1999). The construction of a paved road between Khasab and

Ras al-Khaimah, the northernmost emirate of the UAE, in the 1990s was another important step that contributed to the booming trade. Since that time, goods could be carried on trucks much faster and cheaper than before.

12.3 The Trade Today

Today, the trade with Iran is the main economic source of the exclave, and with stronger sanctions on Iran it even constitutes a fast growing economic basis. Traditional ways of income like goat herding and harvesting have a shrinking importance. Only fisheries and tourism are economic sectors, which are also of some importance today. Most of the fish captured at the coast is being exported to the markets of the UAE the same day.

As a general trend from 2006 to 2010, there was a 20 percent rise in the number of formal businesses in whole Musandam, from 137 to 164.[5] But these figures are for sure largely underestimated, as in March 2011 there were more than 120 shops in the trade area of Khasab and more than 212 in the whole city, which only traded goods with Iran.[6]

Today the trade is of such size and complexity, that it is unimaginable, that the Iranian government is not able to recognize and prevent it. But the trade across the Strait gives the Iranian government a good opportunity to circumvent the ongoing economic sanctions. In this way, there is a constant supply of the market with important goods from abroad and, at the same time, this assures that the sanctions do not hit the national economy too severely.

12.3.1 The Trade Sequence: Of Goats and Flat-Screens

The sequence of the trade seems to be the same since its establishment in the early 1980s. The Iranian speedboats (which were about 100–150 per day during my field research) arrive at sunrise in Khasab and carry goats and sheep or sometimes dried fruits with them. The goods are immediately sold in the harbour and transported to the UAE and Saudi Arabia. All transactions in Khasab are done in UAE Dirham (AED) or Iranian Rial (IRR). The Omani Rial seems not to be used at all and all transactions are done in cash only. There is no evidence that any kind of electronic form of money transaction is used. The Iranians get no visas by the Omani government, but are during daytime allowed to move in a certain area in Khasab, which comprises the harbour and the market districts, although the police does not seem to enforce that rule very strictly.

[5] According to firms registered in the respective issues of the official telephone book of Musandam Governorate.

[6] Based on own surveys in Khasab.

Fig. 12.2 Trading stores in Khasab

After selling their animals at the harbour, the Iranian traders go to the nearby commercial area, which is today called "Iranian souq" (Iranian market). There, more than 120 shops offer all kind of goods that are of interest for Iranian customers, such as LCD-televisions, motorbikes, cigarettes and refrigerators (Fig. 12.2). There the Iranian traders also find goods that are not sanctioned in Iran but taxed too much e.g. soft drinks or basic foodstuffs, such as flour. The goods are all transported on trucks to Khasab from the ports in the UAE, mainly Dubai. A list displayed in the trade area gives detailed information about transportation fees. According to that list, there is no "classic" customs in Khasab, but the government collects taxes for the transportation of the goods from the local warehouses to the harbour.

With the delivery note from the shops, the Iranians go to an office building in the middle of the trading area, where the Omani state organizes the delivery of the goods to the ships. After the distribution, the traders load the goods on their boats. At sundown almost all of the boats leave the harbour at the same time so that they can split into small groups and escape the Iranian coast guard if necessary (Fig. 12.3). From that point on, it becomes difficult to trace the commodity chains, because the trade is considered illegal in Iran. But signs on some of the goods and delivery notes give a hint, that they are not only destined for Iranian markets, but are also carried onward to Central Asia, e.g. to Turkmenistan and Uzbekistan.

12.3.2 Economic Importance

Theories about the economic importance of exclaves for their "mother state" usually suggest that the exclave is of little importance because of its small size and

Fig. 12.3 Loaded boat on the way back to Iran

geographic isolation (Robinson 1959; Melamid 1968). The latter characteristics are also true for Musandam. With a size of about 1,800 km^2 and approximately 30,000 inhabitants, the governorate represents less than 0.5 percent of Oman's surface and about 1 percent of its total population (Ministry of Information 2003).[7]

But looking at economic activities in Musandam, we recognize that while even small and geographically isolated, the exclave is of significant importance for the Omani state. But as there is no exact data, giving about export volumes can only be speculative. According to official statistics, total Omani exports to Iran have been worth USD 297 million in 2010 (European Commission 2012). Yet, for Khasab there are only rough estimates that rather resemble pure speculations about the volume of goods going across the strait, which range between USD 500,000 and 2.0 million per day. Even the lowest figures, which from my observations seem absolutely realistic, could have two implications. Either this means that Oman is exporting almost 62 percent of its supplies to Iran via Khasab. Or the "export" from (or rather the transit via) Khasab alone corresponds to about 62 percent of the deliveries to Iran from the rest of the country – which sounds much more probable. There is an average of more than 100 speedboats per day coming over from Iran with some of them crossing the strait more than once a day. This would mean that each boat has to carry goods worth minimum USD 5,000. This shows that exclaves don't have to be big in size or population to be of serious national interest.

[7]Because of its eccentric position Musandam is often excluded from considerations on Oman (cf., for example, the calculations by Mokhtar, in this volume).

For the exclave itself, the trade is the main source of income today. According to people interviewed, the shops are owned by Omanis, but partially run by expatriates (about 25 percent (Ministry of Information 2003) mostly Indian), whereas the people working in the transport sector are mainly of Omani nationality. In contrast, In another important economic field, fisheries, only 9.3 percent of the population has been employed in 2006 (Al Marshudi and Kotagama 2006). Data about other economic sectors in Musandam is not available. But e.g. the tourism sector consists of 17 tourist companies and about five hotels (construction of another two is in progress). Even though the tourist sector was fast growing between 2006 and 2010 (+142 percent in the number of tourism companies), there are not more than an estimated 500 people working directly in this sector, which would mean less than 2 percent of the population of Musandam.[8]

But it is not only the trade itself that is changing the city of Khasab. The trade functions as a regional job motor for several other businesses. There are numerous firms that are also linked to the trade, like restaurants and shops for boat spare parts etc. In some tourist programmes, the traders are even part of guided city tours.

12.3.3 Impact on Social Relations

The trade with Iran is not only influencing the economic situation in Khasab. Also social relations and everyday life are heavily impacted by the new forms of employment.

Traditionally, social relations in Musandam were based on three different levels of organization. The first one was a complex form of belonging to one of the main tribes in Musandam, Kumzari or Shehi. The second level of belonging depended on different kind of work (mainly fishing, date harvesting and goat herding) with, as the third level, seasonal changes of locality for different social groups (Zimmermann 1981). Each kind of work was combined with other kinds of work in a complex system. This regular geographical movement between different livelihood systems was an integral part of social identity in Musandam.

With more and more people working in business with Iran, this system is now going through a fundamental change. The social organization is not longer based on this three-tier system only. Many people today are leaving their traditional villages in the hinterland and moving to Khasab for better job opportunities. There, mobility is reduced to the area of Khasab and there is often only one form of employment. This process of littoralization has already been forecasted almost four decades ago by the PGA (1975).[9]

Also the UAE and Saudi Arabia are favourite destinations for Omanis to work. Three decades ago Zimmermann (1981) forecasted a fundamental change in social

---

[8] Based on own surveys in Khasab.

[9] For the process of littoralization in Oman in general, see Mokhtar, in this volume.

behaviour in Musandam if the system that he called "regional-mobility behaviour" ("Regional-Mobilitäts-Verhalten"; Zimmermann 1981: 201) changes. Because of the lack of reliable information on this issue, no definite conclusion can be made, what kind of consequences this change will have for the people in Musandam. However, only the social group of the fishermen seems to be less influenced, because their traditional way of work is still practiced today, although with different equipment and less seasonal mobility. For example many of the fishermen in the Khor Shamm area, north-west of Khasab, still remain in their traditional villages and refuse to move to Khasab.

12.3.4 Smuggling or Not? Discourses and Realities About Trade in Khasab

While talking about trade and other economic sectors, development economics likes to distinguish between formal and informal activities. Smuggling is then considered a part of the informal economy although a single definition of smuggling does not exist (Komlosy et al. 1997). On the Iranian side, the trade is to be classified as smuggling, because it is considered illegal and is officially prosecuted by the Iranian state. On the Omani side, the trade should be characterised as formal, because distribution is supported by the state and it levies taxes for the transportation of the goods exchanged. As there is nearly no research done, especially on the Iranian side, it is difficult to make more general statements, so predefining the Musandam trade phenomenon is not useful at the moment.

But if we look at the few articles about Musandam, most of them in newspapers, there is a different image about the trade across the strait. These articles always combine the trade activities in Khasab with the word "smuggling" (e.g. Anon. 2009; Pohl 2004). The lack of basic data about the phenomenon is giving rise to speculations, and even becomes part of political campaigns, e.g. in the case of the succession of Saqr ibn Muhammad al-Qasimi, Sheikh of Ras al-Khaimah, deceased in 2010 (Schult and Smoltczyck 2010).[10] Articles of interest for tourists systematically try to sound adventurous and mysterious; therefore smuggling is the word of choice for them. Almost all articles ignore, that it is the governments of Oman and the UAE that make the trade possible. It would be easy for the Omani government to close the harbour for traders, and because of the rough and inaccessible geography of Musandam, trade of such kind and size would hardly be possible anywhere else outside of Khasab.

[10]The designated successor was accused to support the smuggling of sanctioned goods to Iran, because these goods pass Ras al-Khaimah on their way to Khasab.

12.4 Exclave Status and National Sovereignty: The Mainland-Enclave-Surrounding State Triangle

As we have seen, there are various reasons behind the emergence of trade activities in Musandam in their nowadays form. But the main factor is the peninsula's special relation to its mainland and its status as an exclave. Since the reign of Sultan Said ibn Taymur (r. 1932–1970), the Omani state has lost substantial influence in the exclave. Compared to the close relations that existed, for instance, between Musandam and the Batinah coast around 1920, the linkages had shrunk extensively until the 1970s. The detailed PGA report (1975) shows that there were almost no economic relations with the mother state at that time any more. The very little regional trade existing in Musandam was almost completely organized with the UAE (or the "Trucial States" before 1971) and Iran, and consisted mainly of fish, pottery or lucerne.

Until today the main focus of economic orientation for the Musandam population is Iran and the UAE. There are several indicators, that the Omani government has only a formal presence. One hint is the general use of the Emirati dirham as the main currency throughout the exclave. The AED is used in Musandam since its establishment in 1971 (PGA 1975; Zimmermann 1981). Because up to 70 percent of the tourists visiting Musandam come from the neighbouring emirates and local import and export is mainly done with the UAE, the use of the AED has lots of advantages. Mainly, there are no costs for converting money, and, especially, because most transactions are done in cash, payment is much faster with one currency. Even at major tourist attractions, e.g. Khasab castle, the entry fees are officially listed in dirhams, as are the charges for expatriates' remittances at banks. So while Musandam shows some of the typical characteristics associated with exclaves, which differentiate them from their nations' mainland, it also benefits from its special position "between the chairs". This territorial intermediacy is one condition for the ongoing process of "trans-state regionalization" (Bach 2003). Only because of the possibility to exploit different rules, political systems and levels of development etc. the trade is lucrative.

From a theoretical perspective, Vinokurov's model of the "mainland-enclave-surrounding-state-triangle" (MES) (Vinokurov 2006) can help to understand Musandam's special position between Oman, Iran and the UAE (Fig. 12.4). It represents the interplay, in which an exclave has to balance its position. Vinokurov makes clear, that not all tensions in this tripolar field have to be of the same intensity.

For the mainland, the most important meaning of an exclave is the upholding of sovereignty on a detached part of its territory (Robinson 1959). Most important factors are the relative size and population of the exclave and its geographical distance from the mainland. Economically, an exclave means, first of all, costs for its mainland if no natural resources lie within it. The state incurs lots of expenses to keep territorial sovereignty. The use of foreign currencies (Robinson 1959) and illegal trade (Farran 1955) are also reducing state revenues because of missing taxes and customs.

In relation to the surrounding state, the existence of an exclave impacts the bilateral ties between it and the exclave's mainland nation. International security issues

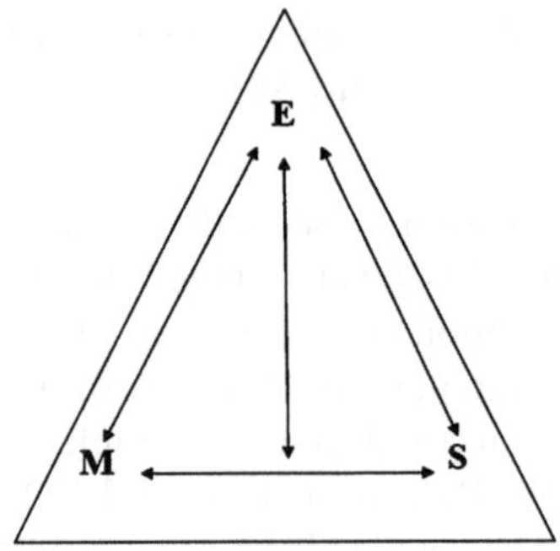

Fig. 12.4 Vinokurov's MES-Triangle (Design: Michael Benz)

therefore constitute the most important dimension (Farran 1955). In contrast to Farran's arguments, the surrounding state today is more affected by asymmetrical threats like terrorism and illicit trade, which have their origin in the in-laying area. The extra border within its own territory means greater expenses, too, in form of security measures, loss of territorial control etc. Economically, in contrast, the surrounding state often benefits from the exclave because of taxes and customs, as goods and services have to pass the surrounding states' borders.

For the exclave itself, its status means a series of specific advantages and disadvantages. The lack of sovereignty over its area for example impedes own decisions for improving development processes. Economically, because of its small size and population, an exclave is less capable of building own, self-sufficient economic structures. Because they often lack natural and human resources and adequate markets, economic activities traditionally focus on import. Vinokurov (2007: 10) states this as a "[…] considerable asymmetry between the structures of domestic consumption and domestic production." This means, that a prospering exclave has to be closely integrated into a network of global and regional linkages.

12.5 Conclusion

As we have seen, trade between Musandam and Iran is affected by many different factors, some of global, but many of regional character. The trade shows that regional linkages are likely to adapt to changing global conditions. A main factor is the geographical proximity between the Iranian coast and Khasab, traders make use of. It also shows that exclaves can be of serious economic and political importance, although they might be small in size or population.

Without historical connections and networks across the Strait of Hormuz, this kind of economic phenomenon would hardly exist. At the same time translocal[11] and trans-state relations across the Strait helped to develop a "new region" (Dietl,

[11] On the concept of transloacity, see Bromber and Verne and Müller-Mahn, in this volume.

in this volume) that is linking the actors in this triangle between Oman, Iran and the UAE closer together. Yet it was not a conscious "creation" as the term used by Dietl might suggest, because it was no organized top-down process that was leading to the emergence of this nowadays transnational region. It was a long-term bottom-up "regionalisation" process (Bach 2003) that was establishing the preconditions for today. The formal framework conditions were set later from the different governments.

The trade between Iran and Musandam still is an underexplored phenomenon. Giving a perspective on future developments is difficult. Among the various factors that will have an influence there is the planned establishment of a greater Free Trade Zone (FTZ) in Musandam. Already today Musandam acts in some ways like a FTZ with relative few bureaucratic restrictions. Yet this would formalize the almost tax- and customs-free status of the place, and thus potentially enlarge the regional operation range of this trade hub. The recent opening of a Lulu Hypermarket in Khasab can also be seen as a part of the ongoing process of regionalisation (Anon. 2012). The market is way too big for Khasab and gives rise to speculations as to also supply Iranian customers as well. Also a ferry service between Khasab and Bandar Abbas is being discussed (Anon. 2011a) and there are plans to create a transit corridor through Qatar, Iran, Turkmenistan and Uzbekistan (Anon. 2011b), which would make Khasab an essential part of this trade route. These policy-induced "top-down" development is [part of] what in contrast to "regionalisation" is called "regionalism" (Bach 2003).

A second factor are the ongoing sanctions against Iran. With growing punishment measures against the Iranian regime, the trade is probably going to increase in volume and revenues, as the huge Iranian markets are in a higher demand for goods. Also a possible military strike against Iran's nuclear facilities could – similar to the First Gulf War – give rise to trade across the strait. Simultaneously, higher international pressure (mainly by the US administration) on the Omani government to stop this flow of goods will harm this trade, as well as fewer sanctions against Iran, what will allow for alternative transport routes that are more formal and much cheaper.

Finally, the quality of bilateral relations between the different parties within the MES-Triangle will have an important role. Only when relations will be smooth, the trade is likely to be tolerated from all sides inside the MES-Triangle.

References

Al-Marshudi, A. S., & Kotagama, H. (2006). Socio-economic structure and performance of traditional fishermen in the sultanate of Oman. *Marine Resource Economics, 21*(2), 221–230.

Anon. (1999, April). Middle Eastern smugglers. A goat, a rug, special price? *The Economist*, 3.

Anon. (2009, November 2). US sanctions help Omani fishermen survive as smugglers. *The National*. http://www.thenational.ae/news/world/middle-east/us-sanctions-help-omani-fishermen-survive-as-smugglers. Accessed 18 Aug 2011.

Anon. (2011a, June 19). Khasab-Bandar Abbas ferry soon. *Oman Daily Observer*. http://omanobserver.om/node/55339. Accessed 18 Aug 2011.

Anon. (2011b, April 26). Sultanate, 4 states sign pact on transit corridor. *Oman Daily Observer*. http://omanobserver.om/node/48887. Accessed 18 Aug 2011.

Anon. (2012, January 15). Lulu Hypermarket inaugurated in Khasab. *Oman Daily Observer*. http://omanobserver.om/node/79378. Accessed 25 Mar 2012.

Bach, D. (2003). New regionalism as an alias: Regionalization through trans-state networks. In J. Andrew Grant & F. Söderbaum (Eds.), *The new regionalism in Africa* (pp. 21–30). Aldershot: Ashgate Publishing Limited.

Constable, C. G., & Stiffe, A. W. (1883). *The Persian Gulf Pilot, 1870-1932* (2nd ed.). Hydrographic Office, Admirality.

European Commission. (2012). *Oman*. http://trade.ec.europa.eu/doclib/docs/2006/september/tradoc_113430.pdf. Accessed 7 Apr 2012.

Farran, C. d.' O. (1955). International enclaves and the question of state servitudes. *The International and Comparative Law Quarterly, 4*(2), 294–307.

Komlosy, A., Parnreiter, C., et al. (1997). *Ungeregelt und Unterbezahlt. Der informelle Sektor in der Weltwirtschaft*. Frankfurt am Main: Brandes und Apsel.

Lorimer, J. G. (1915). *Gazetteer of the Persian Gulf. 'Oman and Central Arabia*. Calcutta: Superintendent Government Printing.

Melamid, A. (1968). Enclaves and exclaves. In D. L. Sillis (Ed.), *International encyclopedia of the social sciences* (Vol. 5, pp. 60–62). New York: Macmillan and The Free Press.

Ministry of Information. (2003). Counting of the population and housing 2003. http://www.omanet.om/english/regions/musandam3.asp. Accessed 18 Aug 2011.

PGA – Professional Group Australia. (1975). *Report. Development study. Musandam region. The Sultanate of Oman*.

Pohl, O. (2004, July 9). Khasab Journal; Sightseeing in Oman? You mustn't miss the smugglers. *The New York Times*. http://www.nytimes.com/2004/07/09/world/khasab-journal-sightseeing-in-oman-you-mustn-t-miss-the-smugglers.html. Accessed 18 Aug 2011.

Robinson, G. W. S. (1959). Exclaves. *Annals of the Association of American Geographers, 49*(3), 283–295.

Schult, C., & Smoltczyck, A. (2010, July 5). Ein Prinz zuviel. *Spiegel Online*. http://www.spiegel.de/spiegel/0,1518,704728,00.html. Accessed 21 Aug 2011.

Vinokurov, E. (2006). *Enclaves and exclaves of the world: Setting the framework for a theory of enclaves* (ZDES Working Paper). University of Bielefeld. http://depot.gdnet.org/newkb/submissions/1148717813_WP_Bielefeld_enclaves.doc. Accessed 14 Sept 2011.

Vinokurov, E. (2007). *Kaliningrad: Enclaves and economic integration* (Unpubl.) Special report. Munich personal RePEc archive. http://mpra.ub.uni-muenchen.de/20937/1/MPRA_paper_20937.pdf. Accessed 18 Aug 2011.

Zimmermann, W. (1981). *Tradition und integration mobiler Lebensformgruppen: Eine empirische Studie über Beduinen und Fischer in Musandam/Sultanat Oman*. Unpublished Ph.D. thesis, Georg-August-Universität Göttingen, Göttingen.

Chapter 13
Is Littoralization Reconfiguring the Omani Territory?

Belgacem Mokhtar

13.1 Introduction

The concept of territory is derived from the animal domain in the sense of appropriation, difference, control and defence. However, for humankind, a territory is not only lived in and controlled. It is especially conceived, represented and enforced by various codes, symbols and institutions. It resembles the notion of space of Lefebvre, who insisted on the abstract dimension of the space as conceived and imagined area (Lorenz and Mattheis, Chap. 3). Hereby, territory is the appropriated space "as it is suited with the feeling and pride of its appropriation. The term is very close to the term of nation or to homeland" (Belhedi 2002: 17). In the preindustrial phase, the territory of each human settlement is very close to the available natural resources, which enormously limits its extent and size. In such a case, small villages were often self-sufficient and communication and spatial interaction were merely occasional.

This statement implies three postulates: the first one is that a territory is determined by its unstable physical and human contents and by the social movement that develops within it. The second is that the dimensions, content and meanings of a territory constantly change. The third is that the precariousness of resources usually turns territorial attachment into an excessive feeling of territoriality, which ends in territorialism in its animal sense of ownership. Isolated settlements, a subdivided community, conflicts, and unsocial relations often characterize this stage of human civilization. At the spatial level, this situation led to auto-confinement of the spatial basic entities (very small units) and to fragmentation of the territory into a multitude of counties.

B. Mokhtar (✉)
Department of Geography, College of Arts and Social Sciences, Sultan Qaboos University, P.O. Box 164, PC 123 SQU Al-Khudh Muscat, Sultanate of Oman
e-mail: mokhtarbel@yahoo.fr; mokhtar@squ.edu.om

S. Wippel (ed.), *Regionalizing Oman: Political, Economic and Social Dynamics*, United Nations University Series on Regionalism 6, DOI 10.1007/978-94-007-6821-5_13,

In modern societies, the concept of territory “refers to the notion of the State, whose legitimacy consists partially in its capability to guarantee territorial integrity inside of the country (in relation to the population) as well as abroad (against other States)” (ibid.: 17). Hence the importance of the public role to transform the patchy counties “into a space structured and organized in networks” (Boukerzaza 2002: 33). Therefore, the concept of territory is associated with the socialization of space. It expresses the projection of specific human structures onto a specific area. This projection, essentially, includes the administrative division, the spatial management and governance, the multi-level operations of national, regional, local (urban and rural) and sectoral planning in view of a space’s unambiguous conception and representation.

However, these networks are more than material or physical. They also apprehend and enforce the feeling of identity with and belonging to a homeland, to the nation, by developing links throughout the country’s institutional space. This has great importance during any action between a region’s subdivisions, because it guarantees the national integrity in the regional context. This task becomes much more important if the region’s demographic or economic constituent weights are unequal.

Thus, the territory is the theatre of any material or social movement, any translocality in the sense of “spatial mobility”, and “as the sum of phenomena which result from a multitude of circulations and transfers” (Bromber, in this volume). It is the area that reflects the landscape configuration as shaped by translocality.

Littoralization is one of the diverse features of translocality. It designates the outcome of concrete movements of people and activities towards the coast with the accompanying or induced infrastructures, urban spread and harmful environmental impacts. At the time of globalization, littoralization appears as the unavoidable product of an outward-oriented economy. In fact, “globalization imperatively leads to a global frame defining functions and structures of geographic-spatial components” (Karray et al. 2002: 7). It predefines human activities’ axes and places and locates production plants and population concentrations. Fredotovic and Simunovic (2006: 1) noticed that “as a dynamic global process, littoralization is a part of the global trends because it encompasses demographic, geographic, economic phenomena as milestones of the changes, fast growth and relative decrease of the spatial dimension”.

However, the concept of littoralization does not make sense unless it creates spatial imbalance, regional disparities and environmental damages that can degrade the population’s living conditions.

13.2 The Omani Context

Historically, Oman has been known mainly as a sea-oriented country and maritime empire that dominated a large part of the Indian Ocean for more than a century. However, this was mostly in years of prosperity and internal peace. During periods of recession and austerity, the country had known many territorial tribulations between opposing regions, tribes and castes. Traditionally, the antagonism was multidimensional: it opposed the coasts to the interior, north to south, merchants to peasants (Al-Hanai 2002: 43–54) and the central government to local tribal chiefs. This later frequently manifested itself as religious conflict between the Imamate's and the Sultanate's standpoints about the nature of the political regime. At the regional level, the central Omani authority, whether it is in Muscat, Salalah or Zanzibar had to deal with constant external attempts to intervene, mainly in borderlands.

Thus, the historical Omani land appeared until 1970 as a vague space divided into several boundless counties. The lack of the slightest road infrastructure and the formless administrative organization had strengthened the territoriality of various tribes within their respective geographically and socially dislocated spaces. Practically, depending on circumstances and jointly for regions, this situation had placed human groups and the environment in a noticeable territorial dichotomy:

- Aggregation vs. Disaggregation
- Integration vs. Segregation
- Stability vs. Mobility
- Inclusion vs. Exclusion
- Equilibrium vs. Imbalance

In this arid area, "the lack of water resources, the poor soil, the harsh environment and the limited opportunities restricted population distribution and encouraged the tendency to concentrate on favourable sites on the coast or inland" (El-Arifi 1986: 224). However, since the site's resources were always limited, the optimal size rule constantly led to periodic migrations to new potentially liveable sites, redistributing people, reshaping spaces and reformulating socio-spatial relations. This confirms the meaning and output of translocality as "on the one hand, means spatial mobility as such and, on the other hand, physical, political, social and cultural spaces and localities that are shaped by it" (Bromber, in this volume).

However, after the "Renaissance" of Oman in 1970, the dominance of the export of hydrocarbons obviously shows the orientation of the country's economic activities towards the worldwide market. Thus, the first attempts to unify the country by modernizing activities and living conditions coincided with the emergence of the current trend of globalization, and the country had to face the challenge of reconverting this outward-oriented economy into an even-handed regional development able to uphold the socioeconomic conditions throughout all the Omani territory. This political will was expressed by successive five-year plans, a long-term economic vision (Oman Vision 2020) and the strategy of economic diversification focusing especially on agriculture, industry and tourism.

Paradoxically, the diversification of the economy seems to strengthen the connection to the world economy, strengthening the littoral regions. Indeed, these regions attract more and more people, activities and infrastructures, leading to an intense socio-spatial polarization. Fuelled by these trends, the historical spatial duality in Oman – between the interior as the main producer of national wealth and the coast as the central area of activity and growth – persists and involves more and more people and spaces. This current mobility seems to be reshaping the territory and hindering the political will to enforce the national identity and unity because of the inequality that it creates between the interior and the coast. In such a situation, people of the inland regions feel abandoned and frustrated.

13.3 Methodology

Since spatial configuration is a multiform product, the effect of littoralization on its patterns could be approached on both macro- and micro-scales. The macro-scale concerns the implications of the phenomenon on the national level and involves studying related major features, such as horizontal population movement and distribution, transport network characteristics, national and regional planning policy, infrastructure and the localization of activities, the urban hierarchical system etc. The micro-scale approach could deal with regional transformations resulting from littoralization, such as urban growth and patterns, the population's living conditions, environmental impacts, traffic problems, planning challenges and governance etc.

This research will focus on the national level, studying the horizontal population trends and concentrations by comparing data from the two available demographic censuses of 1993 and 2003 and the preliminary results of the 2010 General Census (Table 13.1 and Fig. 13.1). For this purpose, a Lorenz curve (Fig. 13.2) has been drawn to show the extent to which a population is equally or unequally distributed within its territory. A three-phase map (Fig. 13.3 and Box 13.1) is used here to illustrate how the mean centre of population, or centroid, has shifted during the last two decades. The mean centre, as the point on which a rigid weightless map would balance perfectly if the population members are represented as points of equal mass (Bellone and Cunningham 1993), demonstrates the direction a population is moving to as well as the attractive and repelling areas in the country.

Table 13.1 Population size and growth rates by region (1993–2003–2010)

	Population size in thousands and percentage of total						Annual growth rate (percent)	
Region	1993	percent	2003	percent	2010	percent	1993–2010	2003–2010
Muscat	549.2	27.2	632.1	27	734.7	27.3	1.70	2.14
Al-Batinah	565.0	28.0	564.4	28	761.1	28.3	1.75	2.19
Musandam	29.0	1.4	29.3	1	31.0	1.2	0.45	1.27
Al-Dhahira	181.2	9.0	207.0	9	147.6	8.2	1.14	0.87
Al-Dakhiliya	229.8	11.4	267.1	11	315.3	11.7	1.84	2.36
Al-Sharkiyah	258.3	12.8	313.8	13	348.1	13.0	1.76	1.52
Al-Wusta	17.0	0.8	22.9	1	32.7	1.2	3.70	5.00
Dhofar	189.0	9.4	216.0	9	249.4	9.3	1.60	2.00
Al-Buraimi					72.4			
Total	2018.5	100.0	2252.6	100	2694.0	100.0	1.70	2.00

Sources: MoNE (1993, 2004, 2010)

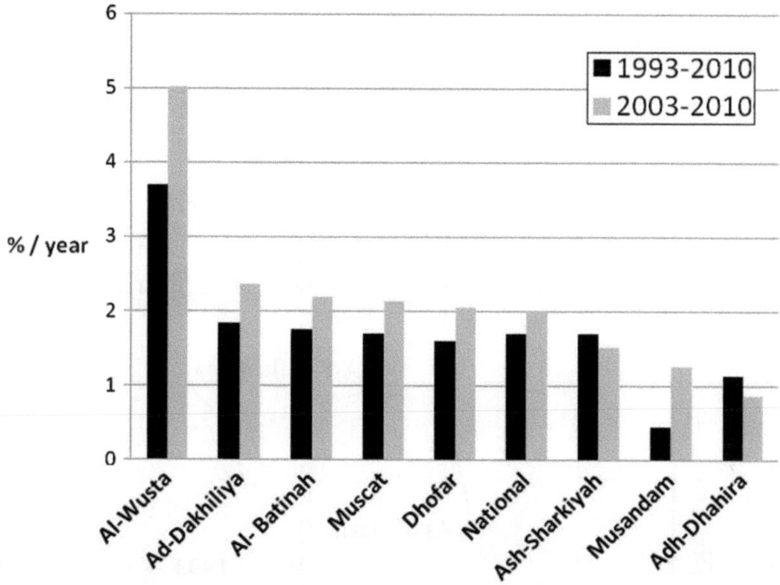

Fig. 13.1 Population growth by region in two periods (1993–2010 and 2003–2010) (Sources: MoNE 1993, 2004, 2010)

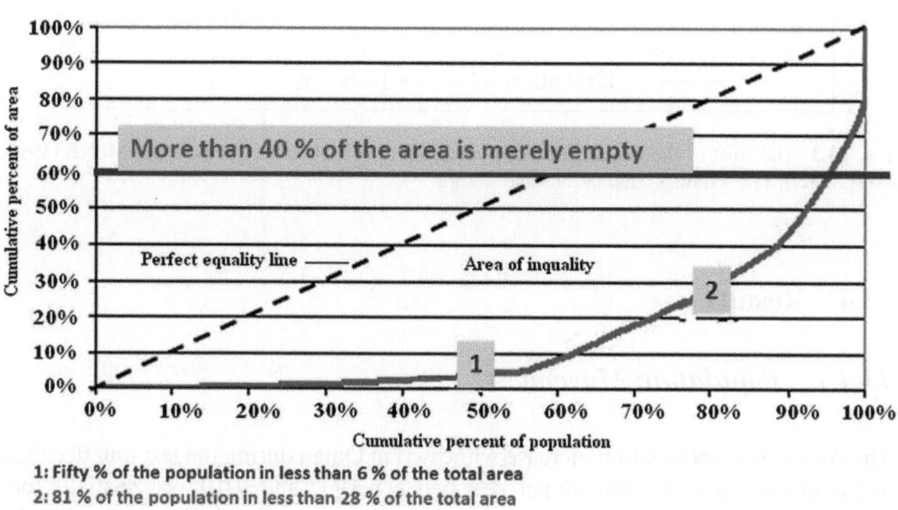

Fig. 13.2 Lorenz curve of Omani population distribution in 2008. *1*: 50 percent of the population in less than 6 percent of the total area; *2*: 81 percent of the population in less than 28 percent of the total area (Source: MoNE (2009). Own calculation)

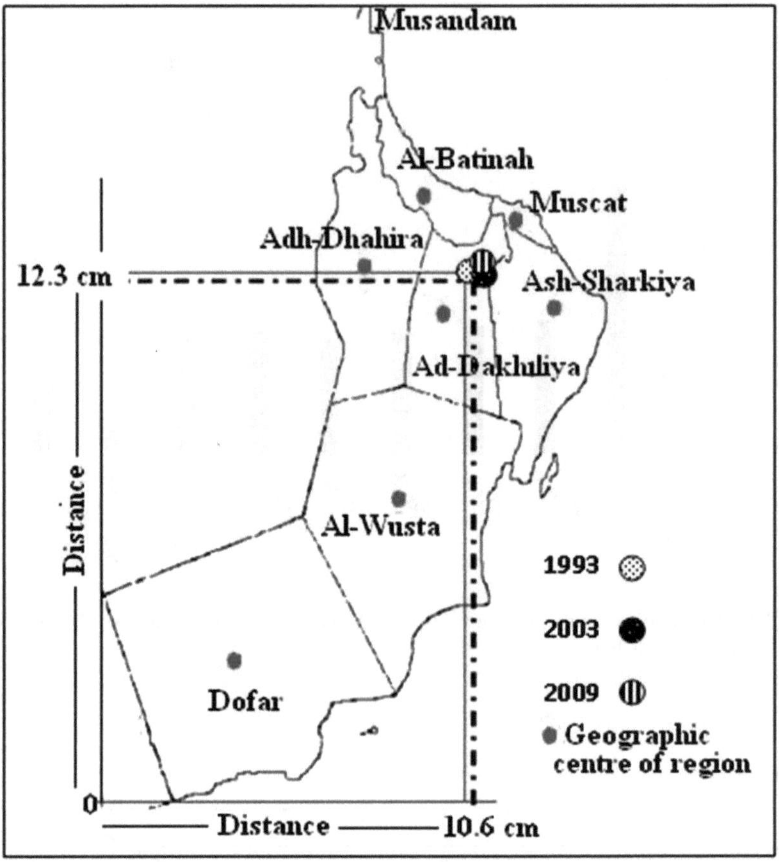

Fig. 13.3 The shift of the mean centre of population (1993–2003–2009) Sources: MoNE (1993, 2004, 2009). The author's calculations and design

13.4 Results

13.4.1 Population Movement

The conspicuous population increase witnessed in Oman during the last four decades, at the national rate of 2 percent per year between 1993 and 2010, was spatially lop-sided towards the coast. This phenomenon was most perceptible in the last decade: three main coastal regions, al-Wusta, al-Batinah and Muscat, registered higher annual growth rates than the 2 percent at the national level. In fact, between 2003 and 2010, the three regions registered annual rates of 5.00 percent, 2.19 percent and 2.14 percent respectively (Table 13.1). On the other hand, continental areas such as al-Sharkiyah and al-Dhahira experienced substantial decrease in population growth rates between

Box 13.1. The Mean Centre of Population

To find the mean centre of population, we used the regional administrative map of the Sultanate and drew two perpendicular axes (X and Y) that join at the southwest angle of the map. We determined the approximate geographical centre of each region except Musandam, which is too far removed, and calculated the position of each regional centre in relation to both perpendiculars. Then we built a table as follows:

Region	Population size (in 1993)	X (Distance from X = 0)	Y (Distance from Y = 0)	Pop size x X	Pop size x Y
Muscat	549,150	14.00	13.00	7,688	7,139
Dhofar	189,094	3.50	5.00	662	945
etc.	¦	¦	¦	¦	¦
Total	1,989,339[a]			24,548	21,052

[a]Musandam not included

We multiplied the population of each region by the distance separating it from X = 0 and from Y = 0. We divided the total population by the sum of the values obtained from the previous stage to find the distance of the mean centre from X and from Y in centimeters.

Example for 1993 (shown in Fig. 13.3):

Distance along the X axis: X = 24,548 / 1,989,339 = 12.33 cm

Distance along the Y axis: Y = 21,052 / 1,989,339 = 10.58 cm

This was separately calculated for each of the three periods 1993, 2003 and 2009

2003 and 2010. In the case of al-Sharkiyah and al-Dhahira, growth rates decreased respectively from 1.76 percent and 1.14 percent annually for the entire period 1993–2010 to 1.52 percent and 0.87 percent per year between 2003 and 2010 (Fig. 13.1).

13.4.2 Population Concentration

The population trend indicates that Muscat and al-Batinah regions the most heavily inhabited areas, grouping almost 56 percent of the whole population within 5.3 percent of the country's space. Furthermore, out of 60 wilayas (sub-governorates), 30 are coastal and contain more than 80 percent of the total population. Moreover, the five major coastal cities have about 1.27 million people, representing 62.7 percent of the whole population. The largest of these cities is the capital district, with almost 730,000 people (27.3 percent). The ten most populous agglomerations, among which nine are on the coast, comprise almost 63 percent of the population. The Lorenz curve of the distribution of Oman's inhabitants illustrates this fact.

The Lorenz curve measures how equally or unequally an economic or social phenomenon is distributed. The further the curve extends below or above the diagonal line of perfect distribution, the more unequal is the distribution of the phenomenon in space. The curve of Omani population distribution in 2008 (Fig. 13.2) lies far below the perfect equality line, and the magnitude of inequality appears to be too large, implying disproportionate spatial allocations and uses. Thus, some regions are relatively overcrowded while others are almost empty:

- 50 percent of residents are concentrated in less than 6 percent of the total national area.
- 81 percent of the population live in less than 28 percent of the total area.
- Almost 40 percent of the national area is uninhabited.

As Table 13.1 and Fig. 13.3 show, the trend of the mean towards the northeast centre of population, the concentrated regions are undoubtedly the coastal ones.

13.4.3 Shift of the Mean Centre of Population

The demographic boost in waterfront areas pushes the mean centre of population towards the northeast. Fig. 13.3, drawn from the author's calculation, shows the shift of this centre from the historical area of population concentration in al-Dakhiliya, near Nizwa, heading for the capital district in the Muscat governorate. Although the mean centre did not shift much in the years 1993, 2003 and 2009, the drift is noticeable over a short time, considering that this variable changes only very gradually over time. It might be clearer and nearer to the coast if a longer period were studied.

13.5 Conclusion

The current horizontal movement of population in Oman, the continuingly growing concentrations along the coast and the shift of the mean centre of population from the mountainous and isolated interior are of major significance. They symbolize a drift from an enclosed and tenable traditional world to an open and vulnerable new world. Indeed, the effects of recent transformations, added to the country's natural constraints, social dynamics and political concerns, are engendering great changes in the geographical space and the perception of national territory.

As population translocality – in the sense of movements and relations in space – has a major effect on the representation of territory and on identity formation in various stages of a country's history, as reflected in population distribution, activities and relationships, the new developments in Oman helped to overcome the traditional vulnerability of the inherited dislocated territory. Regional groups and tribes do not have a territorial basis anymore. They actually move in a bigger space, live from new activities and belong to a larger territory than the tribal ones. They identify themselves as a nation-state living in a national territory despite expressing their previous sentiment of territorialism through local customs, dialects and tribal showing off.

Neverthless, littoralization as a process stimulated the littoral zone to take an increasing role in the economy exacerbates the disparities in the continental regions: the Muscat governorate and al-Batinah region, although their area is only 5.3 percent of the national territory, monopolize currently 67 percent of large and medium-sized manufacturing units, 83 percent of the industrial labour force, 50 percent of the hotels, 90 percent of the 4- and 5-star hotels, 45 percent of all bank branches, 97.2 percent of the urban population and 54 percent of the housing units (Oman Chamber of Commerce and Industry 2009, calculation by the author).

The progressively growing regionalization along the Indian Ocean fringes reinforces this trend to littoralization. The ongoing development of littoral economic gates in the country naturally attracts more and more population and activities. This reminds one of the glorious ages when Oman was a maritime empire of prosperous transit hubs for goods and people in Asia and Africa. History is repeating itself, as decision makers in Oman now think, though in a new frame of regionalization. However, if economic aspects are widely privileged, the socio-political and environmental consequences begin to raise questions of the strategies capable of consolidating territorial integrity and national identity, on the one hand, and simultaneously, raising Omani responsibility to present and the future of the littoral zones, on the other.

References

Al-Hanai, A. (2002). Aspects des antagonismes sociaux en Oman: Marchands contre paysans (1861–1920). In M. Lavergne & B. Dumortier (Eds.), *L'Oman contemporain* (pp. 43–54). Paris: Karthala.

Belhedi, A. (2002). Du lieu....au territoire. In N. Karray et al. (Eds.), *Connaissance et pratiques des milieux et territoires* (pp. 13–30). Tunis: ENS.

Bellone, F., & Cunningham, R. (1993). *All roads lead to... Laxton, Digby and Longford.* Statistics Canada 1991 Census Short Articles Series. http://www.docstoc.com/docs/6124416/Center_of_population. Accessed 29 June 2011.

Boukerzaza, H. (2002). La limite et le lieu, références communes du milieu et du territoire. In N. Karray et al. (Eds.), *Connaissance et pratiques des milieux et territoires* (pp. 33–42). Tunis: ENS.

El-Arifi, S. (1986). The nature of urbanization in the gulf countries. *Geo-Journal, 13*(3), 223–235.

Fredotovic, M., & Simunovic, I. (2006, September 18–20). *New forms of littoralization in the Croatian coastal area: Retrospect – Prospect.* Paper for the meeting "Littoral 2006 Eurocoast: Coastal Innovations and Initiatives", Gdansk. http://bib.irb.hr/datoteka/279568.151-Fredotovic-Simunovic-New_Littoralization_in_Croatia.doc. Accessed 12 June 2011.

Karray, N., et al. (2002). Connaissance et pratiques des milieux et territoires. In *3eme colloque du Département de Géographie de la Faculté des Sciences Humaines et Sociales*, Tunis, 9–11 Mars 2000 (pp. 7–10). Tunis: ENS.

MoNE – Ministry of National Economy. (1993, 2004, 2008, 2009, 2010). *Statistical Year Book.* Muscat: MoNE, Information and documentation centre.

MoNE – Ministry of National Economy. (2004). *Selected data and indicators from (1993 & 2003) censuses.* Muscat: MoNE.

Oman Chamber of Commerce and Industry. (2009). *Industrial Directory 2009.* Muscat: OCCI.

Chapter 14
The Impact of Shopping Malls on Traditional Retail Stores in Muscat. Case Study of Al-Seeb Wilayat

Montasser I.M. Abdelghani

14.1 Introduction

Many of the cities in the Sultanate of Oman have witnessed a change in the function of retail trade and seen new components added to it, e.g. the emergence of giant hypermarkets. Since their appearance, at the beginning of the third millennium, shopping centres are a symbol of globalization and modernization. They have dramatically changed not only the Omani traditional retailing structure, but also consumption behaviour. The main objective of this paper is to analyze the relationship between transnational shopping centres and traditional retail trade. It focuses on the following questions: Are the products of small traditional retail shops able to compete with those of transnational shopping centres? What problems do small traditional retailers face as a result of the establishment of hypermarkets and shopping centres? What strategies do small retail commercial businesses use to deal with the competition of transnational shopping centres? Do the shopping centres lead to a restructuring and a new regionalizing of retail trade in Muscat?

14.2 Theoretical Background

Since their appearance in the structure of the city, shopping centres (shopping malls, hypermarkets) have attracted scientists' attentions (Wehrheim 2007). Numerous studies in the fields of urban studies, economic geography and economics shed light on this phenomenon. A wide range of studies has been conducted in the USA,

M.I.M. Abdelghani (✉)
Department of Geography, College of Arts and Social Sciences, Sultan Qaboos University, P.O. Box 42 Al-Khoud, Postal Code 123, Muscat, Sultanate of Oman

Department of Geography, Faculty of Arts, El-Minya University, El-Miya 61517, Egypt
e-mail: mabdelghani@hotmail.com; montaser@squ.edu.om

S. Wippel (ed.), *Regionalizing Oman: Political, Economic and Social Dynamics*, United Nations University Series on Regionalism 6, DOI 10.1007/978-94-007-6821-5_14,

Fig. 14.1 Shopping centres/malls and their various impacts (Designed by M. Abdelghani 2011)

the first country in which such centres were established. Since the 1980s, relatively new research has been conducted on European cities. After the establishment of several shopping centres in emerging and developing countries, researchers began to study this phenomenon there (Humphrey 2007).

The views and perspectives of these contributions are diverse (Hahn 2007). Some research sees the shopping centres as a new component in the physical structure of the city and links them and the city's development (Pump-Uhlmann 2007). Other research considers them a new type of architectural design or focuses on their economic impact, particularly their impact on traditional retailing in the cities and regions (Krüger and Walther 2007; Farhangmehr et al. 2001; Monheim 1998, 2003, 2006). Further research concentrates on it as places that create a new kind of social space, different from the social spaces of the traditional markets. Some highlight the relationship between these centres and changes in the consumption behaviour of the population (Sievers 2007; Mowen and Minor 1998). Past studies have established that shoppers view malls as a source of entertainment (Bloch et al. 1994). The scheme in Fig. 14.1 summarizes the various aspects of shopping centres and their impact on different sectors that can be considered (Fig. 14.1).

Although there are several studies in this research field in many countries and cities, the phenomena has not been researched adequately in the cities of the Arab world. This study aims to contribute to bridging the scientific gap on this topic.

14.3 Development of Retail Trading in Muscat

The structure of retail trade in Muscat is complex. An outline of the historical development of retail trading in Muscat will provide better understanding of its components and dynamics.

14.3.1 Before 1970

Before the 1970s, the small city of Muscat, situated along the coast, where the residence of the Sultan was at the time, had a lively and long-lived market (Suq Muscat) for retail trading (Scholz 1980: 256). More famous for trading was the Matrah area, which is located along the coast to the west of Muscat. The location of Matrah,

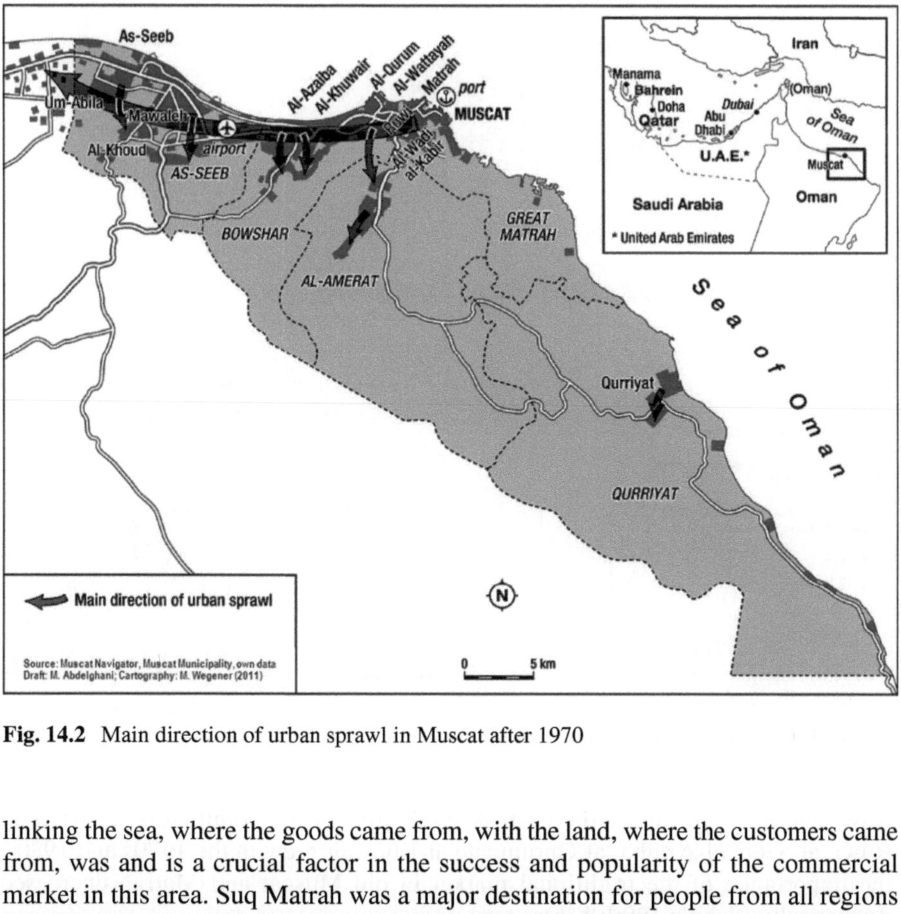

Fig. 14.2 Main direction of urban sprawl in Muscat after 1970

linking the sea, where the goods came from, with the land, where the customers came from, was and is a crucial factor in the success and popularity of the commercial market in this area. Suq Matrah was a major destination for people from all regions in the Sultanate of Oman; customers came there to shop from the inland areas such as Nizwa or from coastal areas such as the al-Batinah and Barka (Scholz 1990: 81). With the exception of Muscat as an administrative area and Matrah as the main commercial area, there were no other areas for retail trading in the vicinity of Muscat until the 1970s that could play the same role as a competing regional trade market.

14.3.2 1970–1995

With the beginning of the 'renaissance era' in Oman in the 1970s, and with the adoption of the concepts of planning, the government focused on the development of the capital, where there was an urgent need to develop the city and its urban functions so it could play the central role in politics, administration and the economy. The capital area expanded and grew, extending for a distance of more than 60 km (Scholz 1980: 265–267, 1990: 120) (see Fig. 14.2). The proposed business and commercial district, in a central place in the area of al-Azaiba, was completed through the growth of commercial areas in al-Seeb in the west and

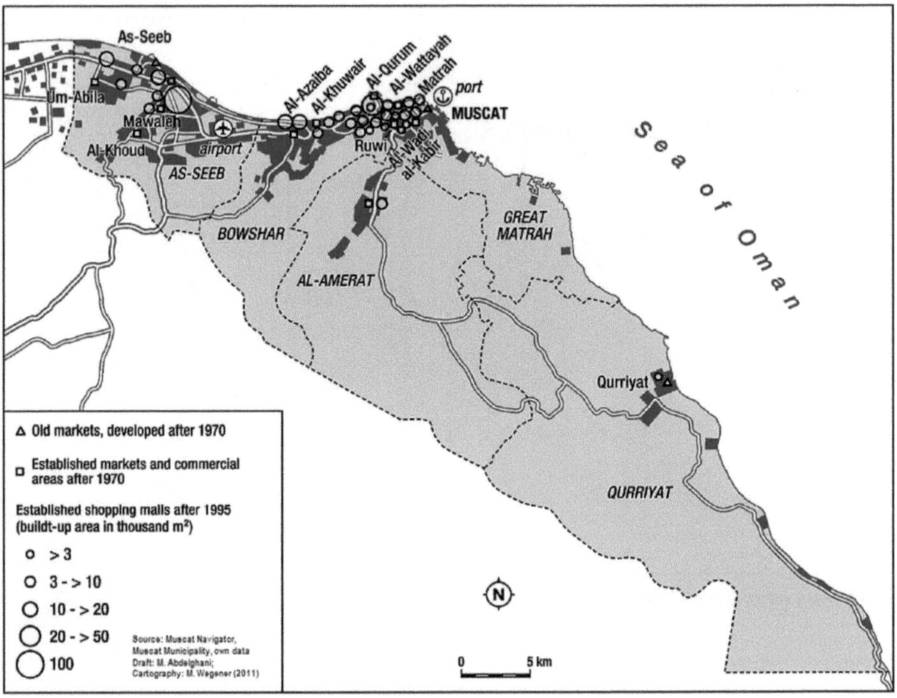

Fig. 14.3 General distribution of retail trade in Muscat

Ruwi and al-Wattayah in the east. Accordingly, as the commercial districts in Ruwi, al-Seeb, al-Azaiba, al-Qurum and al-Khuwair grew in the 1970s and 1980s, the importance of the traditional market in old Muscat and Matrah decreased dramatically (Scholz 1990: 126).

Nearly 40 years after the start of the implementation of development plans for the capital, areas of retail trade can be classified in two main categories: 1. The historical old markets, which were developed and modernized after 1970 (these include Suq Matrah, Suq al-Seeb and Suq Quriyat); 2. The markets newly established after 1970 as a result of the urban sprawl of greater Muscat (Ruwi business district, Suq al-Hamria, Suq al-Wadi al-Kabir, commercial areas of al-Wattayah, al-Qurum, al-Khuwair and al-Azaiba, al-Khoud and al-Hayl commercial streets, Mawaleh central market for vegetables and fruits, Um-Abila commercial area) (see Fig. 14.3).

14.3.3 Retail Trading Since 1995

Since 1995, retail trading in Muscat has experienced a stunning development and entered a new phase, represented by the emergence of shopping malls, which are displayed in Table 14.1. Shopping centres in Muscat can be classified into five

Table 14.1 Shopping centres/malls in Muscat 2011

Name of shopping centre	Location	Built area (square meter)	Parking surface (square meter)	Centre type
Sultan Centre (Tawfir)	Al-Mawalih	1,300	2,200	II
Khimji Mega Store	Ruwi	1,300	700	I
Al-Fair Supermarket	Al-Khoud	1,400	1,300	II
Mohsin Haider Darwish	Al-Seeb	1,500	650	II
Al-Khamees Plaza	Al-Qurum	1,800	1,600	I
Al-Sarooj Commercial Centre	Shatti al-Qurum	2,000	3,200	I
Al-Sarooj Plaza	Shatti al-Qurum	2,000	2,900	I
Mazoun Complex	Ruwi	2,100	400	I
Mohsin Haider Darwish	Ruwi	2,500	500	II
KMT Shopping Centre	Ruwi	2,700	1,200	II
Al-Masah Mall	Al-Qurum	2,750	2,000	I
Al-Seeb Mall	Al-Seeb	3,650	2,800	I
Lulu Hypermarket[a]	Al-Wadi al-Kabir	3,800	2,000	II
Mansoor Ali Centre	Ruwi	3,800	1,500	II
Sabco Centre	Al-Qurum	4,000	2,300	I
Sultan Centre[b]	Al-Qurum	4,100	2,500	II
Al-Wadi Commercial Centre	Al-Qurum	4,200	500	I
Jawharat al-Shatti	Shatti al-Qurum	4,600	5,000	I
Al-Maowli Complex	Al-Seeb	4,600	2,100	II
Al-Harthy Complex	Al-Qurum	5,400	3,000	I
Centre Point	Al-Khuwair	5,400	1,500	II
Oman Commercial Centre	Ruwi	5,500	1,200	I
City Plaza	Al-Khuwair	5,700	0	I
Al-Araimi Complex	Al-Qurum	6,000	6,000	I
Zakhir Mall	Al-Khuwair	6,000	6,800	I
Sultan Centre	Al-Amerat	6,350	5,500	II
Lulu Hypermarket	Darsait (Matrah)	8,000	9,500	II
Sultan Centre (al-Jomla)	Al-Khoud	8,000	10,000	II
Safeer Hypermarket	Al-Azaiba	8,000	4,500	II
Ramez[c]	Al-Seeb	8,500	5,200	II
Al-Qurum Complex (earlier name CCC)	Al-Qurum	9,500	3,000	I
Lulu Hypermarket	Al-Seeb	10,000	18,500	II
Lulu Hypermarket	Bowshar	10,250	25,000	II
Al-Bahja Centre	Al-Seeb	18,000	2,800 + 18,000 underground parking	I
Al-Qurum City Centre	Al-Qurum	36,000	20,000	I
Muscat City Centre	Al-Seeb	100,000	120,000 in 3 floors	I

Source: Own field survey and measurement of satellite images

[a]There are another six branches of the Lulu Hypermarket in Barka, Sohar, Khabora and Nizwa and two in Salalah

[b]There are another two branches of the Sultan Centre in Muscat (al-Azaiba and Quriyat) and another three branches in Rustaq, Samail and Nizwa

[c]There is another branch of Ramez in Salalah

categories, according to their size: the first category includes only one huge shopping centre, namely Muscat City Centre, located in al-Seeb, with a built-up area of 100,000 m^2. Second comes al-Qurum City Centre, a large shopping centre with 36,000 m^2. The third category includes centres with a built area from 10,000 to less than 20,000 m^2; this category comprises three centres, al-Bahja, Lulu hypermarket in al-Seeb and another Lulu in Bowshar. The fourth category, shopping centres between 3,000 to less than 10,000 m^2, includes 20 centres. The fifth category comprises centres from 2,000 m^2 to less than 3,000 m^2. In addition, there is a large chain of supermarkets less than 2,000 m^2 in size deployed in Muscat that were not taken into account in this study. In the table above, the five supermarkets mentioned with less than 2,000 m^2 are only examples of these supermarket chain and retail stores. There is no specific definition of shopping malls or hypermarkets in Omani law, for example, using the size as a standard or as a measure.

Generally, two types of shopping centres/malls can be distinguished. Type I comprises centres with a number of diverse shops (for food, clothes, electrical equipment, perfumes, pharmacies etc.). In addition, a number of restaurants, cafés and entertainment venues exist. Both international and local brands are represented here, including leading names in fashion, accessories, footwear and perfumes. Muscat City Centre, al-Qurum City Centre and al-Bahja are examples of these centres. Some centres of this type have neither restaurants nor cafés. Type II is characterised by shopping centres only for shopping. The centre is usually a single large shop or store and sells many items of food, clothing, electrical equipment etc. This type does not have a number of separate shops, and it is owned or managed as one unit by one company. Sultan Centre, Lulu and Ramez are examples of this type.

14.4 Factors Leading to the Establishment of Shopping Centres/Malls

A combination of factors led to the establishment of shopping centres in greater Muscat and in other Omani cities.

"Increase in Population": In 1972 the population of Oman was estimated at 600,000; in 1985 it rose to 1.4 million and became 3.17 million in 2009. In 1993, the population in Muscat was approximately 550,000 and increased in 2009 to 950,000 (Sultanate of Oman et al. 1972: 4; Sultanate of Oman 2002, 2010: Table 1–2). In addition to this number, it is estimated that there are at least 500,000 who travel to Muscat during the week for work or study and return home on weekends.

"Urbanization, changing consumption pattern": Parallel with the increase in the total population of Oman is the rise in the proportion of the urban population. According to the 1993 and 2003 censuses, the percentage of the urban population increased from 50 to 70 percent. In 2010, the urban population rose to 84 percent. A result of high urbanization is a change in consumption patterns. The population is consuming new types of goods adapted to their new urban life. Most of these goods have been imported from abroad, and reliance on local commodities and goods is clearly reduced.

"Development of incomes and purchasing power of consumers": Purchasing power is a decisive factor in the success of business. The more purchasing power, the greater the demand for goods and services; trade booms and there is an increased demand for investment in the commercial sector. To shed light on purchasing power in Oman, two indicators must be considered; first is per capita gross national income and second the average actual salaries in some job categories. In 1998 the per capita gross national income was about OMR 2,258, which increased in 2003 to 3,449 and reached OMR 7,790 in 2008 (Sultanate of Oman 2010: Table 1–14).[1] Regarding actual salaries, a driver in a government agency earns a monthly salary of OMR 300, a new graduate teacher working in primary school OMR 550, a civil engineer in the public sector about OMR 1,000 and an assistant professor at the university OMR 1,700. Remarkable is that the per capita gross national income and the actual salaries have clearly been rising over the last 30 years, leading to a strengthening of purchasing power in Oman.

"The development of a highway network": One of the important criteria for establishing a shopping centre/mall is easy access via paved roads for private cars, especially in the Gulf region, where the temperatures run very high, and important in the USA where people often have to travel long distances. By contrast, in South Asian countries and in China, shopping centres are being well connected to good public transportation networks, due to the lack of private cars there. In 1973, the total number of paved roads in Oman was 25 km. The length of the network of paved roads increased until it became about 23,233 km in 2008 (Scholz 1990: 144; Sultanate of Oman 2009: 244–245). The number of vehicles increased from 317,429 in 1996 to 560,302 in 2002. This enormous development of the paved road network and the increase in the number of private cars have greatly fuelled the retail boom, especially in Muscat, and have expanded the influential area of markets and shopping centres. It is now common for Omanis to travel long distances, more than 150 km, to do their weekly shopping or out of desire to buy a specific product from a specific market or mall. It is not rare for an Omani family to travel a distance of 300 km to purchase certain goods or to have a specific dress sewn for a woman.

"An increase in the number of expatriates and foreign tourism": In Gulf countries, the desire to consume global goods comes from the local population, whose consumption patterns are affected by urbanization and cultural globalization, on the one hand, and by immigrants with their culturally specific consumption behaviour and the increasing number of international tourists, on the other hand. Gulf societies are characterised by the multiplicity of nationalities living there. This is dictated by the conditions of the economic development and by population trends in these countries. These expatriates have specific purchasing desires for particular kinds of goods, in most cases strongly associated with their local consumption behaviour in their own home country. The immigrant communities, strongly affected by globalisation, increasingly consume global commodities. In 1985 there were about 314,000 expatriates living in Oman. In 2009 their number increased to 1.156 million.

---

[1] OMR (Rial Omani) 1 = 1,000 Baiza = EUR 1.79 (June 2011).

According to the data of the 2003 census, the number of expatriates in the Sultanate was 559,257; more than half of them were Indian (300,693; 154,453 of them living in Muscat). In second place are the Bengalis (83,038; 19,969 in Muscat), and then the Egyptians (23,711; 7,758 in Muscat), Sri Lankans (10,130; 6,605 are in Muscat), and Europeans (7,718; of them 6,437 in Muscat) (Census 2003, after Pfaffenbach 2011). In addition, in 2010, the number of tourists was estimated at 1.2 million (Anon. 2011).

"The state's desire to diversify the economic base, economic globalization and improvement in the investment environment": The Sultanate of Oman, like all Gulf Arab countries, is trying to diversify its economic base and to rid itself of its absolute dependence on oil. It tries to encourage investment in other economic sectors, such as tourism, real estate and trade. Improvements in the investment laws, advantages for investors, e.g. tax cuts, and attempts by the state to integrate into the global economy are factors leading to the increase of foreign investments in Oman. In 2005, their volume in all economic sectors was about OMR 1.7 billion. This value increased in 2009 to 3.46 billion. In the same period, foreign investment in the trade sector increased from 140.6 to OMR 248.2 million (Sultanate of Oman 2011: 24).

14.5 The Relative Importance of Traditional Markets and Shopping Malls

This paper will frequently use the terms traditional markets and retail trade, on the one hand, and big shopping centres/malls, on the other. Traditional retail trade means all types of grocery stores, minimarkets, stores selling only food and other stores selling goods like clothing, electronic appliances etc., which are distributed in traditional market areas such as al-Seeb and al-Khoud.[2] To answer the main question of this study, "To what degree have newly established shopping malls impacted retail trade in traditional markets?", the researcher and his team of male and female students from the Geography Department at the Sultan Qaboos University used two major approaches. The quantitative approach was based on a questionnaire that was answered by 96 visitors in Suq al-Seeb (73) and Suq al-Khoud (23) and by 269 visitors of shopping malls (81 in Lulu, 55 in al-Jomla, 52 in al-Bahja and 81 in Ramez).[3] The method used to collect data was a face-to-face interview based on a structured questionnaire with closed-ended questions. They were applied to visitors of markets and shopping malls during their visits to those places. In addition, I used the qualitative approach, in which 30 in-depth interviews were conducted, which gave the respondents a good opportunity to talk freely and to tell us their opinions

[2]The market of al-Seeb has been selected to study as an old market, further developed after 1970, and al-Khoud as a newly established market after 1970.

[3]We are still seeking the consent of Muscat City Centre, the largest shopping mall in the Sultanate, to survey its visitors with a questionnaire.

on many issues related to the study theme. The deeper interviews helped to get data that was not possible to obtain from the questionnaire. The results presented in this paper are part of the research project about retail trade in al-Seeb Wilayat; the project was funded by Sultan Qaboos University. The field study took about 1 year from 2009 to 2010.[4]

In an attempt to measure the relative importance of the traditional markets and shopping malls under study, respondents were asked about markets or shopping centres in which they prefer to purchase commodities like groceries, clothes, electrical appliances etc.[5]

14.5.1 *Groceries*

The interviewees were asked where they preferred to buy groceries. Taking into account the total of both samples together (shopping malls and traditional markets), we find that the Lulu hypermarket came in first, with nearly one-third of the respondents (32.3 percent; 34.4 percent of the sample of al-Seeb and al-Khoud, 31.5 percent of the sample of shopping malls). More than a quarter preferred Carrefour, 12 percent al-Jomla and 12.6 percent al-Seeb. The market of al-Khoud had a small percentage (3.8 percent). The importance of shopping malls in this sector is clearly higher than that of traditional markets.

14.5.2 *Purchase of Fish*

Due to its location on the Oman Gulf, its historical development as an old settlement for fishermen and the high percentage of workers in the fishing sector, al-Seeb is clearly especially important as a centre of marketing of fresh fish. More than half of the total samples preferred to buy fish from the market there, because it is characterized by high quality, guaranteed freshness and low price (Fig. 14.4). This proportion rises to more than 70 percent in the sample conducted in the market of al-Seeb and al-Khoud. Shopping malls do not have significant importance for this commodity, where 7.1 percent prefer to buy fish from Lulu and 5.2 percent from Carrefour. The importance of the market of al-Khoud is also low, with only 2.2 percent buying fish there, since there are very few fish shops located there.

[4]The writing was done at the University of Bayreuth, Department of Population and Social Geography, directed by Prof. Dr. Detlef Müller-Mahn, Germany, where I obtained a 3-month (June–August 2011) research scholarship from the German Academic Exchange Service (DAAD).
[5]The numbers of visitors and pedestrians at markets and shopping malls and the preferred time of shopping were also empirically researched. The results could not be included in this article for lack of space and will be published in another paper under preparation.

Fig. 14.4 Fresh fish market in al-Seeb (Picture: M. Abdelghani 2010)

14.5.3 Men's Clothing

One of the characteristics of Omani society is that people retain their traditional dress. Traditional markets offer great potential in sewing and selling Omani clothes for men and women. More than two-fifths of respondents prefer to buy or have men's clothes tailored at stores and workshops located in the market of al-Seeb. About one-fifth preferred other markets or places. Matrah was an important traditional market that was the first priority for them. For purchasing men's clothing, the four researched shopping malls together attracted only about one-fifth of the sample (Figs. 14.5 and 14.6).

14.5.4 Women's Clothes

The importance of shopping malls increases when we talk about the purchase of women's clothes. 27.4 percent of the respondents prefer to buy ready-made women's clothes from shops and stores located in shopping malls. The relative importance of Muscat City Centre rises here clearly; with about one-fifth of respondents it takes top priority. However, al-Seeb also remains in the first rank, with 30.4 percent buying ready-made women's clothes or having them sewn in shops and stores located there.

Fig. 14.5 Agglomeration of shops specialized in selling and sewing men's clothing in al-Seeb (Photo: M. Abdelghani 2010)

Fig. 14.6 Agglomeration of shops specialized in selling and sewing men's clothing in al-Seeb (Photo: M. Abdelghani 2010)

14.5.5 Electronic Appliances

The situation is different for electronic appliances. More than one-third of respondents prefer to purchase these items from Muscat City Centre. In addition to Carrefour, there is a branch of the world chain store E-MAX, one of the largest shops selling electronic appliances in the Sultanate of Oman. Lulu got a considerable proportion of about 14 percent. About one-fifth of respondents prefer to buy electronic appliances at al-Seeb; 12 percent purchase these items in other places. The market of Ruwi appears here as an important destination.

14.5.6 Women's Cosmetics

Shopping malls are also of great importance as centres for selling cosmetics for women. More than two-fifth of respondents prefer to buy these kinds of goods from shops located in shopping malls; they seek specific international brands in branches of global chains. Muscat City Centre, with its varied shops, is the most popular site; 29.6 percent prefer to purchase these items here. Lulu is the preferred destination for 6 percent. al-Seeb has a significant ratio, as about one-fifth of interviewers purchase those goods there. al-Khoud attracts about 6.9 percent of respondents.

14.5.7 Gold and Jewellery

Although there are some upscale shops selling gold and jewellery in Muscat City Centre, Lulu and al-Bahja, the traditional markets are always the favourite places of most Omanis for purchasing gold and jewellery. About two-fifths of respondents prefer to buy these items from the market of al-Seeb, whose gold shops and workshops are extensive, as is very clear from the land use in the area. Remarkable is the great importance of the market of Matrah, with more than a quarter of respondents buying gold only there, due to its long history and long experience in this sector. The trust enjoyed by the gold traders in traditional markets plays a major role in attracting customers to their shops. That confidence has not yet been established between consumers and the new gold shops in shopping malls, where only 2 percent of respondents purchase gold and jewellery.

In conclusion, Fig. 14.7 shows where the total sample of respondents said they purchased some goods.

The above explanation makes it clear that shopping malls affect customers' buying behaviour. These centres have become strong competitors for traditional markets, especially with some commodities such as groceries, women's cosmetics and electrical appliances. In addition to the brands offered by the international branches there, the

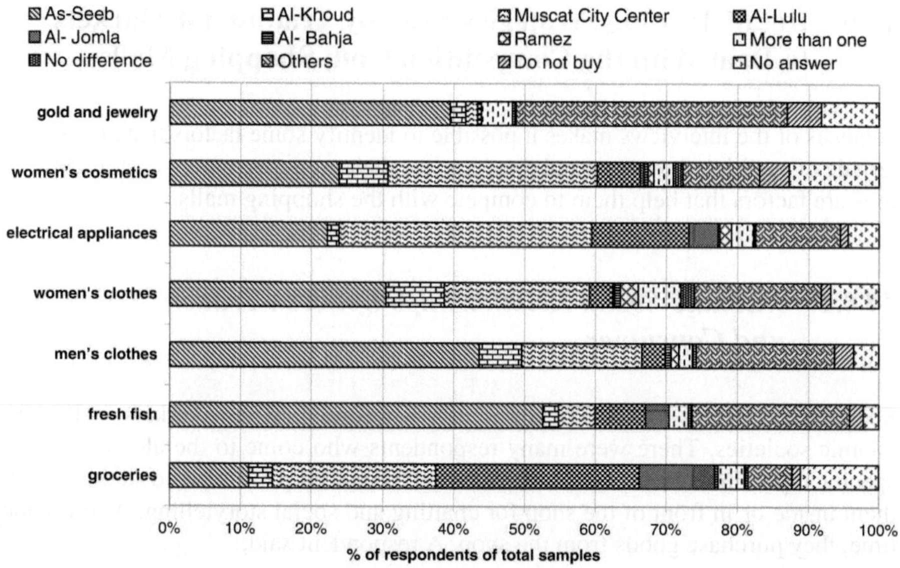

Fig. 14.7 Distribution of total sample among favoured markets/malls for the purchase of some goods (Draft & Cartography: M. Abdelghani)

centres are equipped with many comforts, such as air conditioning, parking facilities, children's play areas, prayer rooms, restaurants and coffee shops. For example, Table 14.1 shows that almost all malls have their own parking areas, free for customers. Sometimes the parking areas are larger than the mall itself.

The following quote from the case studies reflects people's preference to purchase from hypermarkets:

When Muscat City Centre and Carrefour were opened in 2000, it was a great event in Oman. If one were going to Carrefour, she or he would feel as if they were going to heaven. The people told their friends about their visit to Carrefour one week beforehand and continued the storytelling for another week after the visit (22-year-old male respondent, living in Wilayat Abri and in al-Khoud, Muscat).

Shopping malls have features that are not available in traditional markets. The malls have special offers and drawings. Traditional markets do not offer this. In the shopping malls there are signboards to guide the shopper. In the traditional markets these are not available. Malls have air conditioners that make us feel comfortable. There are no air conditioners when shopping in traditional markets. Especially in the summer, people prefer to shop at night to escape the intense heat during the day. In shopping malls, shopping carts are available for shopping and this is not available in traditional markets. There is an excellent feature of malls, in that there are security personnel, but in the markets there are no security people. In addition, shopping malls have an information centre, in case a child is lost (25-year-old female respondent).

"People are looking for convenience and saving time without having to resort to too many places to buy their requirements. Shopping malls provide all the supplies and goods that each individual needs (27-year-old male respondent).

14.6 Retail Trading Strategies Used by Traditional Markets to Deal With the Competition from Shopping Malls

Analysis of the interviews makes it possible to identify some factors that are characteristic of traditional markets and that increase their attractiveness to customers, and thus are factors that help them to compete with the shopping malls.

14.6.1 Intimate Social Relationships Between Trader and Consumer

Social relationships are one of the merits of economies and markets in Eastern Islamic societies. There were many respondents who come to the al-Seeb market specifically to meet their friends who are traders and shop owners and sit down with them inside or in front of the shop for chatting and social storytelling. At the same time, they purchase goods from the shop. A respondent said,

> I have come here every day for thirty years, and I come here after the Maghrib prayer. We are talking and telling, there is an affinity relationship between us and the owners of the shop, and every day when I go back home, I take the goods that we need at home.

For many individuals, traditional markets are not only a place for shopping, but more than that: a part of social life.

14.6.2 Instalment Sales

Whether in North African countries or in the Gulf Arab states, many buying and selling transactions are done on the basis of mutual trust between members of the community in the form of various social networks. Some respondents reported that they sometimes bought some goods in instalments, like electronic appliances or even groceries, with the assistance of a social relationship with traders. In an interview one of them told us, "The dealers know the circumstances of consumers, especially the Omani dealers." In most cases, official documents for the incurred debt or for the instalments paid (such as checks or receipts) are not required. Such transactions arise primarily as a result of the high trust between the parties. This type of trust is established between customers and traders in traditional markets, which gives greater scope to social life and revitalises conventions and traditions. Such advantages are not available in shopping malls. It is true that some stores like Carrefour could sell in instalments, but they make the following conditions:

- the buyer must have a fixed job in the official governmental or private sector;
- have a fixed monthly income;
- and submit a letter of guarantee from his or her employer;
- between 10 and 20 percent interest is charged;
- and many forms and signatures are required.

In contrast, customers making purchases from shops in al-Seeb and al-Khoud do not face such requirements and complications when they wish to make an instalment purchase. In a previous study by the author of squatter settlements in Egypt, he found that payment by instalments is one of the most important survival strategies of vulnerable groups (Abdelghani 2002; Abdelghani and Schrüfer 2005; Müller-Mahn and Abdelghani 2006). In Oman, despite the relatively high purchasing power of the population, this type of transaction exists, too.

14.6.3 Diversity of Goods and Products in Shops in Traditional Markets

The diverse companies supplying the shops in the traditional markets provide different goods to different shops, encouraging the customers to visit several shops. The shopping malls often have only one supplier for a product, so the goods are not varied to the same degree.

14.6.4 Haggling Over Price

Haggling over price is a widely reported feature of traditional markets in all Arabic countries. The seller knows that the first price he tells the buyer is not the final price of the commodity, just as the buyer is also confident that the first price he hears from the seller is not the final price. In most cases, a type of bargaining or haggling over the price between the buyer and seller arises and ends in an agreement on the final price, which satisfies both of them. Haggling over price is one of the features of the socioeconomic and cultural context when economic transactions are done. Such behaviours enhance social contact and networking among people, and often create new social relationships among them. This is in addition to the psychological and economic benefit enjoyed by the buyer when he knows that he got an item or service for a good price. To quote from an interview,

> You haggle over the price, he says to you the price is OMR 15, you do not give him OMR 15, you bargain, you offer him 12 or OMR 13. (Alcott) this (jacket) which surrounds the body and protects you from the cold, he reminds you its price OMR 15, you get it for OMR 13. I mean, you have a benefit of OMR 2. OMR 2 helps you to purchase goods satisfying other needs.

In contrast, the stores at shopping malls post fixed prices.

14.6.5 Al-Arsa Market (Auction)

There is in most traditional markets of Oman a selling in “al-Arsa”. This is a type of small auction, where the dealer calls aloud for the sale of a product. Customers compete with each other to get the product by increasing offers. This system is used to sell goods such as cattle, fish and dates.

14.6.6 Providing Traditional Goods

One of the important features of development in Oman is the effort to keep and support the local culture and national identity. This leads Omani people to keep consuming traditional goods. Every society is characterized by different kinds of traditional food. In Germany, for example, there are Bratwurst (sausages) and beer, in Egypt falafel and fava beans. Oman is well known for some traditional foods such as khubz al-tanour (oven bread), sambosa (a pastry filled with meat), orsia (mixture of wheat flour, water and chicken), Omani halwa (a sweet), dates and Omani coffee. The shops that sell the traditional Omani foods are concentrated in traditional markets, as in al-Seeb, where shops and small factories compete with each other to produce high-quality products. They have been practicing their activities for a long time and have a good reputation in this field. Many of these types of food commodities are sold only in traditional markets. Some shops in shopping malls offer some of these goods, but at high prices and in a lower quality, not coming close to the original products sold in traditional markets.

In addition to food, Omani culture features other traditional goods. One is traditional Omani clothing, which is worn by most Omani people. The men wear a dishdasha, an ankle-length robe. This costume is not complete without the headdress (masahar and kummah). The main components of the outfit for women are the black-collared abayas (cloaks) and hijabs (headscarves). The Omani depends largely on the tailors who sew their clothing in the many workshops in traditional markets, such as al-Seeb, Ruwi and al-Wadi al-Kabir. These workshops have considerable experience in this field. This experience allows them to provide an attractive, high-quality product at a price acceptable in the society. The heavily deployed workshops are one of the main factors attracting a lot of customers to traditional markets (photos 3 & 4).

Although China and some emerging countries in Asia have succeeded in making dishdasha, which are used in some other Gulf countries, as well as some other goods, such as the Islamic prayer mat and prayer beads, they have not succeeded so far in the design and manufacture of traditional Omani clothing. Therefore, a few shops in the shopping malls specialized in the sale of traditional Omani dress are in reality workshops that sew the traditional Omani dress. In the shopping malls there are some shops that sell ready-made women's abayas.

14.6.7 Fresh Fish, Live Birds and Animal Market

Al-Seeb market differs from other traditional markets, selling fresh fish, live poultry and animals. In the northern part of the al-Seeb market is a fresh fish market, where the fishermen offer freshly caught fish for sale, in a special area directly on the beach (Fig. 14.8). In 2004, the municipality of al-Seeb built a hall next to this place where fishermen can clean and cut up the fish. The visitors come to purchase the fish and let it be cleaned for the price of 200–300 Baiza per kilogram (Fig. 14.9).

Fig. 14.8 Fish auction in al-Seeb (al-Arsa), every day between 6 and 11 a.m. (Photo: M. Abdelghani 2010)

Fig. 14.9 Hall where fish is cleaned and cut up, built by the municipality of al-Seeb in 2004 (Photo: M. Abdelghani 2010)

Some shopping malls like Carrefour, al-Lulu and al-Jomla sell fresh fish. However, a number of respondents questioned the freshness of those fish.

At the front of the fish market is a good vegetable section. The wide variety of locally grown and imported products sells at relatively low prices, especially when

Fig. 14.10 Live birds such as pigeons and poultry are sold in al-Seeb (Photo: M. Abdelghani 2010)

a customer buys large quantities. At the entrance to the vegetable market is a row of meat shops selling fresh cuts of beef, mutton and camel. In the northern part of al-Seeb are also an open place and some shops that sell live birds, such as pigeons and poultry (Fig. 14.10). In a special place on the southern edge of the area is an open-air market for live animals such as sheep and goats. A large number of buyers move through this market in the early morning, particularly on Thursday and Friday. A large number of Omanis have a passion for consuming these fresh goods, and they come from far and wide. In malls, it is absolutely impossible to buy birds and live animals.

14.6.8 Selling of Animal Feed

There is a place on the southern edge of the al-Seeb market dedicated to selling animal feed, in the same area where live animals are sold. Some families raising livestock and birds in the yards of their homes, even in Muscat, always purchase their feed from al-Seeb (e.g. Zezza and Tasciotti 2010; Abdelghani 2002).

14.7 Regionalization of Retail Trade in Muscat

As previously mentioned, new commercial areas and shopping centres/malls in Muscat have been established since the 1970s. These areas and centres differ in composition and size from the old traditional markets and in the kinds of goods and commodities offered to customers. This main change has an enormous impact on the regionalization of retail trade and on the catchment areas of markets, not only in Muscat but throughout the Sultanate of Oman. Some of the results are:

- The importance of old markets has clearly decreased. For example, especially in regard to certain products like foodstuffs, Suq Matrah is no longer the main destination for customers in Muscat and from many regions of Oman. The newly established markets, such as the Suq Ruwi, have become more attractive.
- The emergence of the new markets after the 1970s was clearly associated with the urban sprawl and development of greater Muscat, whereas one of the objectives of urban planning from the outset was to provide commercial areas to serve the growing population. However, the boom of shopping centres/malls commenced rapidly after the population and urban growth. Two critical factors play a big role in the expansion of these malls. First, a population density associated with a high demand for goods, and second, the availability of areas and space that allows the construction of these enormous centres. We find, for example, small and medium-sized shopping centres located in the built-up area in Ruwi, where there is high population density, high structural (building) density and a severe lack of surfaces and space, while the large shopping centres/malls were constructed in the western parts of Muscat, particularly in al-Seeb Wilayat, where empty areas are more readily available.
- Shopping centres initially emerged in Muscat and in the last 3 years began to appear in some other cities such as Barka and Sohar. However, there are a lot of important settlements in Oman that have not yet seen the emergence of such centres, for example Nizwa, Bahla and Ibra. This forces the inhabitants of those settlements to go to Muscat to do their major shopping at malls like Carrefour and Lulu. Of course, the availability of private cars and the improved road network is a huge asset. The last weekend of each month, after workers are paid their salaries, shopping centres in Muscat are thronged with customers. They come to do their major shopping, or what one refers to in the Omani dialect as al-Azbah. This has led to a severe decline of the small stores and shops in many of the settlements. This is reported by many respondents during interviews. It can therefore be said that the shopping centres/malls have a negative impact on the small shops outside of the capital, Muscat.
- Yet, the traditional markets continue to have strong advantages in specific sectors and for specific commodities, and they strategically employ certain socio-economic practices to counter the competition of big malls and shopping centres. All these changes in the retail trade sector contribute to the formation of new shopping patterns and lead to a new local and regional distribution of shopping facilities.

All these findings lead us to believe that the emergence of shopping centres/malls in Muscat is one of the key factors that have led to the new regionalization of retail trade, not only in the capital area, but in the whole Sultanate of Oman. But it must be said that this point needs more detailed and comprehensive empirical research, which the author is currently conducting in the framework of the aforementioned research project.

14.8 Conclusion

The appearance of shopping malls in Oman is due to a number of factors: an increase in the population and high urbanization, improvement of the economic situation of the population, change in consumer behaviours, development of foreign investment opportunities, expansion of infrastructure (particularly transport and electricity), low prices of building areas until 2005 and low labour costs. Many of the studies conducted on the reality of retailing in European cities show that shopping malls have a major impact on traditional retail shops in the city centres. Many of these stores have closed because they were unable to compete with gigantic malls (Monheim 2003, 2006, 2007). The reality of retailing in Oman is different. Although the current study showed that shopping malls have impacted retail trade in the traditional markets, especially in regard to some particular kinds of goods, and have advantages in attracting large numbers of customers, the traditional markets continue to have their importance and attract customers purchasing local and traditional goods, such as clothing and traditional local foods. In addition, for Omanis the traditional markets are not only places to buy and sell, but also places of social interaction and places to renew the vitality of social networks. However, the question is: How long will the traditional markets in Muscat continue to resist the encroachment and invasion of huge global shopping malls?

Other results of this research have to do with the new regionalization of retail trade, not only in Muscat, but throughout the Sultanate of Oman. The concentration of retail trade areas and shopping malls with their new characteristics and attractiveness in Muscat, the availability of private vehicles and the improvement of the road network and the good accessibility of these new shopping destinations are all factors leading to a new map and to new distribution of retail trade in the country.

References

Abdelghani, M. (2002). *Handlungsstrategien verwundbarer Bevölkerungsgruppen zur Sicherung ihrer Existenz in den Hüttensiedlungen der Stadt El-Minya, Ägypten. Eine sozialgeographische Analyse mit kartographischer Auswertung*. Ph.D. thesis, University of Bayreuth, Bayreuth.

Abdelghani, M., & Schrüfer, G. (2005). Hüttenbewohner am Rand der Stadt: Die ägyptische Strukturanpassungspolitik. *Praxis Geographie, 35*(6), 30–33.

Anon. (2011, August 27). *Oman Daily Newspaper*. http://main.omandaily.om/node/65295

Bloch, P. H., Ridgway, N. M., & Dawson, S. A. (1994). The shopping mall as consumer habitat. *Journal of Retailing, 70*(1), 23–42.

Farhangmehr, M., Marques, S., & Joaquim, S. (2001). Hypermarkets versus traditional retail stores – Consumers' and retailers' perspectives in Braga: A case study. *Journal of Retailing and Consumer Services, 8*, 189–198.

Hahn, B. (2007). Shopping Center als Internationales Phänomen. In J. Wehrheim (Ed.), *Shopping Malls – Interdisziplinäre Betrachtungen eines neuen Raumtyps* (pp. 15–33). Wiesbaden: VS Verlag für Sozialwissenschaften.

Humphrey, J. (2007). The supermarket revolution in developing countries: Tidal Wave or Tough Competitive Struggle? *Journal of Economic Geography, 7*(4), 433–450.

Krüger, T., & Walther, M. (2007). Auswirkungen innerstädtischer Shopping Center. In J. Wehrheim (Ed.), *Shopping Malls – Interdisziplinäre Betrachtungen eines neuen Raumtyps* (pp. 191–208). Wiesbaden: VS Verlag für Sozialwissenschaften.
Monheim, R. (1998). Methodological aspects of surveying the volume, structure, activities and perceptions of city centre visitors. *GeoJournal, 45*, 273–287.
Monheim, R. (2003). Auswirkungen eines integrierten Einkaufszentrums auf die Innenstadt – das Beispiel des Rotmain-Centers in Bayreuth. In Bayerisches Staatsministerium für Landesentwicklung und Umweltfragen (Ed.), *Stadt-Umland-Management. Partnerschaft statt Konkurrenz. Zur Zukunft von Einzelhandel und Flächennutzung. Dokumentation der 2. Rosenheimer Stadt-Umland-Gespräche* (pp. 33–60). München.
Monheim, R. (2006). Das Rotmain-Center in Bayreuth: Chancen und Risiken eines innenstadt-integrierten Einkaufszentrums. In W. Brune, R. Junker, & H. Pump-Uhlmann (Eds.), *Angriff auf die City. Kritische Texte zur Konzeption, Planung und Wirkung von integrierten und nicht integrierten Shopping-Centern in zentralen Lagen* (pp. 225–253). Düsseldorf: Droste Verlag GmbH.
Monheim, R. (2007). Der Einzelhandel in der Bayreuther Innenstadt unter dem Einfluss eines integrierten Shopping Centers. In J. Maier (Ed.), *Wirtschaftsgeographie von Bayreuth* (pp. 107–131). Bayreuth: Arbeitsmaterialien zur Raumordnung und Raumplanung 255.
Mowen, J., & Minor, M. M. (1998). *Consumer behavior* (5th ed.). Upper Saddle River: Prentice Hall.
Müller-Mahn, D., & Abdelghani, M. (2006). Urbanisierung in Ägypten. *Geographische Rundschau, 58*(11), 12–20.
Pfaffenbach, C. (2011). *A City of Diasporas – Everyday practices and networks of expatriate communities in Muscat/Oman.* Paper presented in Gulf Research Meeting 2011, Cambridge.
Pump-Uhlmann, H. (2007). Shopping Center und Stadtentwicklung: unter Ausschluss der Öffentlichkeit? In J. Wehrheim (Ed.), *Shopping Malls – Interdisziplinäre Betrachtungen eines neuen Raumtyps* (pp. 175–189). Wiesbaden: VS Verlag für Sozialwissenschaften.
Scholz, F. (1980). *Sultanate of Oman. Geographical introduction.* Stuttgart: Klett (in Arabic).
Scholz, F. (1990). *Muscat, Sultanat Oman. Geographische Skizze einer einmaligen arabischen Stadt.* Berlin: Das Arabische Buch.
Sievers, K. (2007). Center-Science-Kunden- und Verhaltensforschung, als Grundlage der Planung und Betreibung von Shopping-Centern. In J. Wehrheim (Ed.), *Shopping Malls – Interdisziplinäre Betrachtungen eines neuen Raumtyps* (pp. 225–240). Wiesbaden: VS Verlag für Sozialwissenschaften.
Sultanate of Oman, General Development Organisation, National Statistical Department. (1972). *Statistical year book.* First Issue.
Sultanate of Oman. Ministry of National Economy. (2002). *Statistical year book.* Issue 30.
Sultanate of Oman. Ministry of National Economy. (2009). *Statistical year book.* Issue 37.
Sultanate of Oman. Ministry of National Economy. (2010). *Statistical year book.* Issue 38.
Sultanate of Oman. Ministry of National Economy. (2011). *Foreign investment 2005–2009.*
Wehrheim, J. (2007). *Shopping Malls – Interdisziplinäre Betrachtungen eines neuen Raumtypes.* Wiesbaden: VS Verlag für Sozialwissenschaften.
Zezza, A., & Tasciotti, L. (2010). Urban agriculture, poverty, and food security: Empirical evidence from a sample of developing countries. *Food Policy, 35*(4), 265–273.

Part IV
State and Society in Regional and Global Perspectives

Chapter 15
Private Documents as a Source for Regional History: The Archive of the ᶜAbrīyīn of Al-Ḥamrāʾ

Michaela Hoffmann-Ruf

15.1 Introduction

The year 2010 was highlighted by the ample festivities on the occasion of the 40th anniversary of Sultan Qābūs ibn Saʿīd's ascension to the throne. His coming to power in 1970 marked a turning point in the history of Oman. In the following decades, the country underwent a modernization of amazing breadth and speed. Building a modern infrastructure combined with modern employment facilities has changed people's life in a fundamental way. While there are countless advantages resulting from this development, it also has some less favourable facets. There is, for instance, the abandonment of the traditional settlement quarters in favour of modern houses, resulting in the almost complete decay of the old settlement cores with their mud-brick or stone constructions and their characteristic spatial and architectural features. Since the traditional architecture is closely linked to the socio-historical identity of the Omani society and is thus an important part of the cultural heritage, this threatens to bring about a considerable cultural loss. To counteract this development, an interdisciplinary research project was created in 1999 to document in detail the traditional architecture, economy and general way of life in the oasis towns of Oman (Gaube and Gangler 2011; Häser 2000).

15.2 The Discovery

Al-Ḥamrāʾ is an oasis town in the interior of Oman. The town's layout and inner structure, especially the densely built houses, is typical of the traditional Omani settlements (Fig. 15.1). During the architectural survey of the old city of al-Ḥamrāʾ, conducted in the

M. Hoffmann-Ruf (✉)
IOA, Abt. für Islamwissenschaft, Rheinische Friedrich-Wilhelms-Universität Bonn, Regina-Pacis-Weg 7, 53113 Bonn, Germany
e-mail: michaela.hoffmann-ruf@uni-tuebingen.de

S. Wippel (ed.), *Regionalizing Oman: Political, Economic and Social Dynamics*, United Nations University Series on Regionalism 6, DOI 10.1007/978-94-007-6821-5_15,

spring of 2000 in the framework of the aforementioned research project, a remarkable discovery was made. While measuring buildings, drawing plans and collecting information about individual houses and their inhabitants, a huge cache of documents was found in one of the storage rooms on the ground floor in one of the traditional houses in the centre of the city. These documents were kept in huge earthenware jars, similar to the jars traditionally used to store food (Richardson and Dorr 2003: 498–501).

With the permission of the owner, we were able to examine this remarkable find more closely. Most documents were folded very tightly and kept in bundles. To photograph and further analyse the documents, they first had to be unfolded. As is often the case, the paper was rather brittle, and it was inevitable that some fell apart (Fig. 15.2). After the photography of the documents was completed, the main features of every document were noted. The length, date (if present), kind of document (contract, private or business letter etc.) and the names of the people involved were recorded. It turned out that the find contained about 2,900 documents covering a time span of about 170 years from the second half of the eighteenth century to the middle of the twentieth century, more than 95 % of which were letters. Among the oldest documents is a letter from Imam Aḥmad ibn Saʿīd al-Būsaʿīdī, the founder of the current ruling family of Oman, dated June 1773.[1]

This first discovery was followed in the spring of 2002 by a second one that was at least as numerous as the first. While the second find still awaits closer investigation, this essay presents some results of the analysis of the documents of the first one.

The history of al-Ḥamrāʾ is inseparably connected to that of the ʿAbrīyīn. The city was founded by members of this tribe, originating from al-ʿArāqī in the region

Fig. 15.1 Al-Ḥamrāʾ

[1](B14-30: 24/25) 25.03.1187/16.06.1773, Aḥmad ibn Saʿīd ibn Aḥmad [al-Būsaʿīdī] to Rāshid ibn Masʿūd ibn Rāshid ibn Sālim al-ʿAbrī.

Fig. 15.2 Documents

al-Ẓāhira, around the middle of the seventeenth century and has been their tribal capital up to the present. Bayt al-Ṣafā', the house where the discovery was made, is one of the oldest houses of the settlement. According to the inscription on one of the wooden doors, the house was built in the year 1101 AH/1690 AD (Ott 2011: 155). To this day it is owned by a lineage of the local elite. Through many generations, the leader of the local community, the sheikh, came from this lineage (ʿAbrī 1959: 49–61). The fact that the find of Bayt al-Ṣafā' mainly consists of letters addressed to the actual sheikh of this lineage indicates that it is some kind of archive of the ʿAbrīyīn sheikhs of al-Ḥamrā'.

15.3 Theoretical Considerations

Most sources on the history of Oman focus on political history and present the political events from a macro-historical point of view. This holds true for the famous works of al-Sālimī (1961) and Ibn Ruzayq (1977) and even more so for European works (for example, Lorimer 1908–1915; Miles 1966; Saldanha 1986). However, they tell little about the everyday life of people and their daily social and political concerns.

Presently, research on the political, social or economic situation of a group or a region always brings the possibility of going beyond, or more correctly, *below* the macro-historical level by doing fieldwork, that is, asking people directly or watching them in the course of their everyday activities. With regard to the past, crossing this barrier between the macro- and the micro-historical level is more difficult and depends on the availability of a very special kind of written source material, such as travel accounts, testaments, biographies, diaries and account books. With regard to Oman, this type of material is rather scarce, the only exception being European travel accounts.

In this context, the special value of the ʿAbrīyīn-archive of al-Ḥamrāʾ is evident. The features that distinguish these documents from other existing sources and make them unique are their quantity and closeness and secondly their private nature. The letters from al-Ḥamrāʾ tell of the everyday political, economic and social life of a rural Omani community and reflect the interactions of this community's members on a local and regional level. Thus, they give us an insight into a reality that other sources fail to deliver.

The private character of the documents and their limited range make them an ideal material for a micro-historical approach. They allow us to gain a new perspective by reducing the scale of investigation, giving us a different view of previous knowledge. They allow a fascinating look below the macro level (Levi 1991; Ulbricht 1994). They throw new light on traditional interpretations and convictions, which qualitatively broadens the scope of existing macro-historical accounts and forms an important addition to the existing written material. As far as we know, no other archives similar to the one of al-Ḥamrāʾ have heretofore been discovered in Oman – a fact that only increases the significance of this discovery.

15.4 Choice of Focus: The Communication Network of Sheikh Muḥsin ibn Zahrān Al-ʿAbrī

Numerous ethnological studies have shown that in the Arab world a sheikh[2] was once a central person in the political, social and economic spheres of his community (cf. Dresch 1984; Fernea 1970; Gerholm 1977; Peters 1990). His position, although rather complex, was in general quite stable. Once elected, a man usually remained in his position until his death. But there are also examples in which the position of a sheikh was challenged, resulting in the loss of his influence and the loyalty of the people (Lienhardt 1975).

In the written sources on Oman, a sheikh is mostly portrayed as a leader in warfare. His most prominent features are his courage and fighting skills. Very little further information can be found on the other aspects of this position or the required personal abilities. As the archive of al-Ḥamrāʾ mostly consists of letters to the respective tribal sheikh, starting with Rāshid ibn Masʿūd ibn Rāshid al-ʿAbrī (d. 1191/1877) (ʿAbrī 1959: 50), the idea suggested itself to centre the analysis on the role of the sheikh as reflected in his correspondence, as well as on the function of the letters with regard to this position.

In our archive, about 1,300 letters were addressed directly or indirectly to Muḥsin ibn Zahrān al-ʿAbrī, who was the sheikh of al-Ḥamrāʾ from 1242 AH/1826-27 AD until his death in the year 1290 AH/1873 AD, almost a half-century later (about his life and rule, see ʿAbrī 1959: 61–98). On account of the huge number of letters linked to this person, it was clear that he was going to be the focus of my investigation

[2] Sheikh is capitalised when used as a title; otherwise it means a tribal leader in general.

(for the entire results, see Hoffmann-Ruf 2008). The central questions that were dealt with were the following:

- What do these letters say about the role of a sheikh in nineteenth-century Oman? What kind of tasks and expectations was he confronted with and how did he deal with them? Which other requirements, in addition to being courageous, did he have to fulfil in order to be successful?
- The large number of the letters – in addition to the fact that they were preserved and not destroyed – suggests that they served a certain purpose. So what was the function of the vast correspondence Muḥsin ibn Zahrān maintained? Did it help him in fulfilling the duties associated with his role?
- Another question is more general. Quite often in Arabic and European works (for example, Ross 1873; Miles 1881; al-Sālimī 1961, II: 175, 253–256) on the history of Oman, the terms "tribal dichotomy" and "tribal affiliation" are used when describing and explaining the social groupings and their behaviour. They convey the notion that the decisions and actions of people are to a great degree if not always determined by their affiliation with a certain tribal grouping, expressed by the same tribal *nisbah*. My intention was to find out whether the information drawn from the letters corresponds to this image, that is, whether the micro-historical and the macro-historical depictions were concordant or contradictory.

As it turned out these were not the only questions that were to be answered by analysing the letters.

15.5 Method

Muḥsin ibn Zahrān maintained correspondence with people and groups bearing various tribal *nisbahs* and living in various places in different regions. Thus, the first step was to choose a range of different letters/documents that promised to give a differentiated picture of the social, political and economic networks of Sheikh Muḥsin ibn Zahrān. The categorization of letters is mainly based on the tribal *nisbah* of the persons involved but also takes into consideration the respective place of residence.

The analysis involved a two-step process. First, the number of letters in conjunction with the period of time over which the contact existed was investigated, in order to gain a general overview of the correspondence and especially its frequency. Secondly, the content of the letters was analysed. What were the main topics dealt with and what were the reasons to establish and to maintain the contact? What can be said about the kind of relationship between the correspondents?

To answer these questions, 12 different groups of correspondence were examined. Letters were grouped with respect to the *nisbah* of the sender or the addressee.[3]

[3] Usually it is the *nisbah* of the sender that determines the classification. But sometimes the *nisbah* of the addressee is the relevant one. This is the case when the original addressee forwarded the letter to the ʿAbrīyīn of al-Ḥamrāʾ.

Then, a sub-classification was applied for those cases in which groups/people had the same *nisbah* but a different place of residence. To gain a better understanding of the situation, these documents were correlated, as far as possible, with other written sources, such as the works of Ibn Ruzayq (1977), al-Sālimī (1961), Lorimer (1908–1915) and the material in the British records (India Office Records/London: IOR/15/1, IOR 15/6; Public Records/Kew: F.O. 54).

Before now presenting some of the results of the study, I have to draw attention to the central handicap caused by the nature of this material. What this archive consists of are only the letters addressed to Sheikh Muḥsin ibn Zahrān, but not his answers. Apart from the cases in which the senders acknowledge the receipt of a letter or complain about not having received an answer, one simply does not know whether an answer had been sent or not. And even more precarious are conclusions about the content of such answers. Nevertheless, these letters did provide me with enough material to obtain a good picture of Muḥsin ibn Zahrān as the sheikh of al-Ḥamrā᾽ and the function of his vast correspondence.

15.6 Results

The analysis of the chosen letters showed first of all that there are clear differences between the correspondences in terms of their frequency and their content, as was to be expected. But regardless of the intensity of the contact and the content of the letters, the tone is always very polite and obliging.

The exchange of letters was often quite intense and lasted over several years or even decades. In some cases the letters revealed that the contact between Muḥsin ibn Zahrān and another person was later continued by the respective sons or nephews, for example in the case of the Banū Dhuhl of al-ʿAwābī or the Āl Yaʿrub. The correspondence with members of these two tribes contains well over a 100 letters each and lasted 62 and 85 years respectively. In contrast to that, there were also contacts of a temporarily limited nature, like the one with the Āl Ramāḥ that lasted only a few months, judging by the 11 letters found in the archive. Sometimes there were also alterations in frequency that seem to be due to political changes. The following diagram clearly shows the differences in the number of letters over the time span they cover (Fig. 15.3).

Considering the spatial aspects of the correspondence the letters from al-Ḥamrā᾽ provides interesting insights on two different levels.

First of all, there is the actual geographic range of the contacts. Muḥsin ibn Zahrān maintained a far-reaching and closely knit network of correspondences with people in the immediate neighbourhood of al-Ḥamrā᾽ and other regions (for example, al-Bāṭina, al-Ẓāhira) of what is known as Oman today. But the information contained in the letters is not restricted to that area, that is, they concern not only issues in Oman, but also in such far-flung places as today's Saudi Arabia and East Africa. Thus, there are two letters that report the capture of Dirʿīah, the first Saudi Arabian capital, by Egyptian troops under the command of Khālid ibn Suʿūd

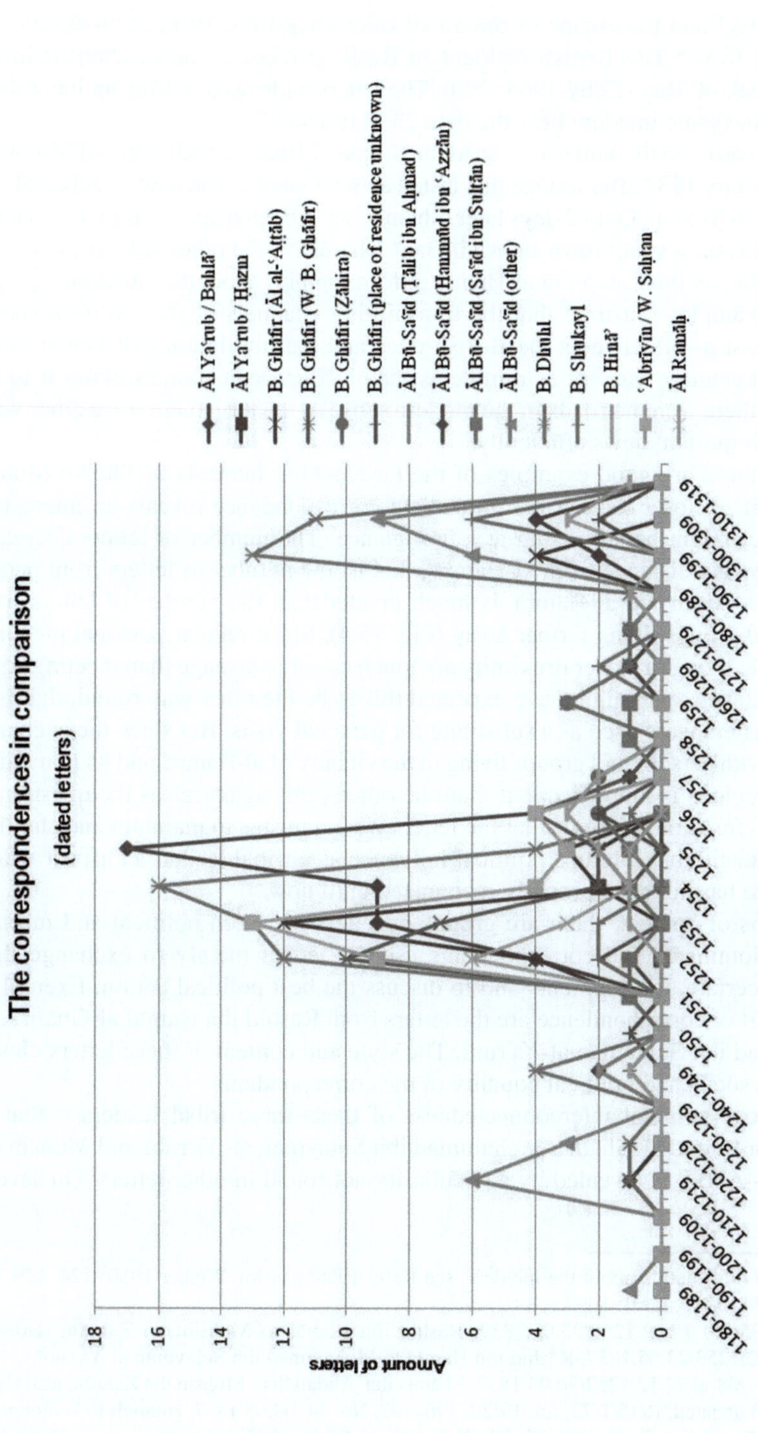

Fig. 15.3 The correspondences in comparison

in April 1837 and the escape of the Saudi ruler Fayṣal ibn Turkī to al-Buraymī in late April 1837.[4] The British resident in Bushehr received news about it in the second week of May (Kelly 1968: 290). The letters addressed to Muḥsin ibn Zahrān reporting the same incident bear the date 23 May 1837.[5]

A little earlier in the same year, Saʿīd ibn Sulṭān al-Būsaʿīdī had captured Mombasa on 12 February 1837 after a siege that lasted about 7 weeks. The news reached Oman on 28 March by ship. Only 2 days later, Shāmis ibn ʿAbdallāh al-Dhuhlī wrote a letter from al-ʿAwābī, a small town in Wādī Banī Khārūṣ on the other side of the mountains, to Muḥsin ibn Zahrān in al-Ḥamrāʾ informing him about the situation.[6]

Both examples illustrate that the transmitting channels of the ʿAbrīyīn sheikh were at least as effective as the British ones and that the interior of Oman in the nineteenth century was not as remote as mainly European sources claim it to be. Although there were no roads in the modern sense of the term there were other ways to spread important news efficiently.

While these are good examples of the far-reaching interests of Sheikh Muḥsin ibn Zahrān, a closer look at his immediate correspondence reveals an interesting pattern that might be surprising at a first glance. The number of letters decreases with increasing distance from al-Ḥamrāʾ, that is, the number of letters from people living in proximity to al-Ḥamrāʾ is much greater than the number of letters from people and groups living farther away (Fig. 15.4). Since regular personal meetings with people living in closer proximity are much easier to arrange than meetings over a great distance, one might have expected this to be the other way round, that is to say, that letters were used as a substitute for personal visits. But since the exchange of letters with persons and groups living in the vicinity of al-Ḥamrāʾ and its immediate adjacent regions is more frequent than the others, this again raises the question of the letters' function. It seems that the letters were a means to maintain and stabilize Sheikh Muḥsin ibn Zahrān's political influence as a tribal leader, an aspect whose importance has not been properly recognized until now.

In terms of content, there are groups of letters in which political and military subjects dominate. The correspondents use the letters mainly to exchange their views on certain developments and to discuss the best political action. Exemplary for this sort of correspondence are the letters from Rāshid ibn Ḥamīd al-Ghāfirī and Muḥammad ibn Sulaymān al-Yaʿrubī. The style and content of these letters clearly reflect the social and political equality of the correspondents.

The close political interconnectedness of these three tribal leaders – that is, Rāshid ibn Ḥamīd al-Ghāfirī, Muḥammad ibn Sulaymān al- Yaʿrubī and Muḥsin ibn Zahrān al-ʿAbrī – is revealed by a peculiarity not found in other letters. On several

[4]For further information about the incident, see Kelly 1968: passim, Winder 1950: 124–129, and Lorimer 1908–1915, I, 1B: 1097.

[5](B08-18: 35/36) 17.02.1253/23.05.1837, Rāshid ibn Ḥamīd to Muḥsin ibn Zahrān; (B08-18: 32/32) 17.02.1253/23.05.1837, Rāshid ibn Ḥamīd to Muḥammad ibn Sulaymān al-Yaʿrubī.

[6](B02-02: 07/08-a) 22.12.1252/30.03.1837, Shāmis ibn ʿAbdallāh to Muḥsin ibn Zahrān; also (B02-02: 07/08-b) undated; R/15/1/72, fol. 19/20, 196–197, No. 44, 08.05.1837, Hennell to Willoughby; R/15/1/75 (Translation Book), fol. 29, 20. Dhū al-Ḥijjah/28.03.1837, (sd.) Thuweyni to Hennell.

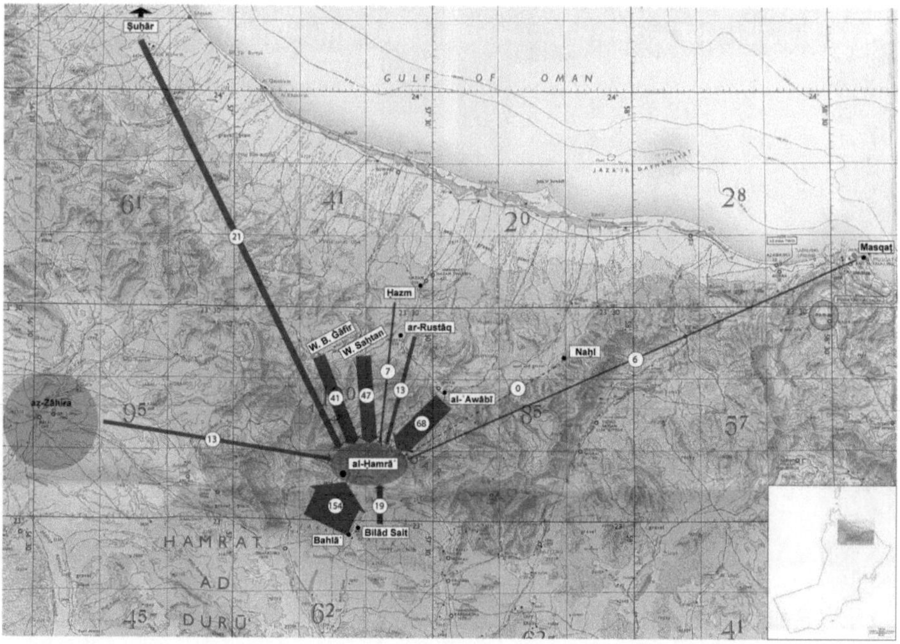

Fig. 15.4 Origin of letters (Source: Tactical Pilotage Chart, Series TPC, Sheet J-7B, Muscat and Oman, Saudi Arabia, Trucial States, Scale 1:500,000, Ministry of Defence, United Kingdom 1970)

occasions, Rāshid ibn Ḥamīd al-Ghāfirī wrote a letter to Muḥammad ibn Sulaymān al-Yaʿrubī who – after adding a statement on the reverse of the paper – forwarded this to Muḥsin ibn Zahrān in al-Ḥamrāʾ (Fig. 15.5).[7] In German, the term "postwendend" is used for this kind of correspondence, in English one might say "by return of post," which expresses (as in German) the idea that the letter was replied to quickly, but in German, the term originally referred to the fact that the paper was turned over ("gewendet") and used as a space in which to write a reply.

In letters from the Banū Dhuhl from al-ʿAwābī or from ʿAbrīyīn from Wādī Saḥtan, the main topics are requests for instructions and mediation, partly also for economic or military support. These letters reveal a clear social and political hierarchy with Sheikh Muḥsin ibn Zahrān as the dominant figure. A subject that is mentioned in all kinds of correspondence regardless of the parties' differences in political and social standing is commercial enterprises. There are also a considerable number of letters that merely announce the imminent arrival of a messenger conveying a verbally transmitted message. This indicates that there were sensitive topics that the writers preferred not to commit to writing.

[7](B02-03: 22) undated, Rāshid ibn Ḥamīd to Muḥammad ibn Sulaymān; (B02-03: 23) 04.03.1253/08.06.1837, Muḥammad ibn Sulaymān al-Yaʿrubī to Muḥsin ibn Zahrān; (B02-03: 20) 12.03.1253/16.06.1837, Rāshid ibn Ḥamīd to Muḥammad ibn Sulaymān; (B02-03: 21) 12.03.1253/16.06.1837, Muḥammad ibn Sulaymān al-Yaʿrubī to Muḥsin ibn Zahrān.

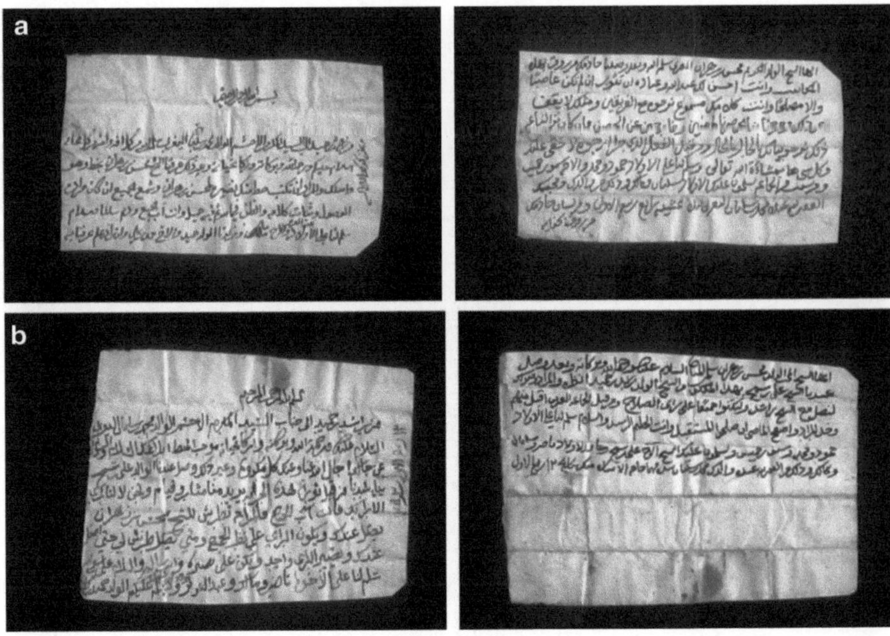

Fig. 15.5 Forwarded letter (**a**) (B02-03: 22) undated, Rāshid b. Ḥamīd to Muḥammad b. Sulaymān, (B02-03: 23) 04.03.1253/08.06.1837, Muḥammad b. Sulaymān al-Yaʿrubī to Muḥsin b. Zahrān. (**b**) (B02-03: 20) 12.03.1253/16.06.1837, Rāshid b. Ḥamīd to Muḥammad b. Sulaymān, (B02-03: 21) 12.03.1253/16.06.1837, Muḥammad b. Sulaymān al-Yaʿrubī to Muḥsin b. Zahrān

A second spatial aspect of the letters that is considerably reflected in their content is that of the tribal territory (*dār*). In the past in Oman, as in other tribal societies, a tribe's territory was never clearly defined in a modern sense, that is, with clearly drawn boundaries. Nevertheless, people were well aware of the boundaries of the territory they claimed to be theirs and of the sphere of control of the respective leader. In the course of time, the size and shape of a tribal *dār* would undergo changes: it might increase or decrease, and sometimes it also could vanish for good. These transformations depended mainly on political and economic developments and could result from militant as well as peaceful actions.

The growth of the tribal *dār* of the ʿAbrīyīn of al-Ḥamrāʾ since the foundation of the settlement in the seventeenth century was the result of both kinds of action, warlike and peaceful. For example, the Banū Dhuhl of al-ʿAwābī's submission to the ʿAbrīyīn sheikh's authority results from their wish to strengthen their position in the settlement against the Banū Kharūṣ (Wilkinson 1987: 114; Hoffmann-Ruf 2008: 230). But there are also examples of less peaceful agreements (Wilkinson 1987: 112–113).

The letters from al-Ḥamrāʾ provide a very good insight into the competing claims of the tribal leaders and the discussions about the range of their authority. These rival political and economic interests manifest themselves in discussions over the right to control the *bait al-māl* and the right to collect *zakāt* in a certain region, a frequent topic in the letters (Hoffmann-Ruf 2008: 207–208, 354–365). Reading the letters makes it evident that spatial structures such as the tribal *dār* were not fixed but fluctuating and that the successful achievement of one's objectives greatly depended on diplomatic and negotiation skills.

The letters show that Sheikh Muḥsin ibn Zahrān was confronted with many different tasks in his role as sheikh. He had to decide whether to participate in military actions and, if so, to lead his people, a role known from other sources (al- Sālimī 1961: passim; Ibn Ruzayq 1977: passim). Furthermore, he had to act as a judge in legal cases. But the aspect of his position as sheikh that appears most frequently in the letters is the request to act as a mediator in cases of conflict. Other sources do not mention this aspect at all, which makes it particularly interesting. Muḥsin ibn Zahrān's own community asked him to mediate in inner and outer communal conflicts. He also acted as mediator for people living elsewhere. This indicates that his authority and influence were not restricted to the immediate surroundings of al-Ḥamrā', but extended beyond them.

Besides clearly illustrating that Muḥsin ibn Zahrān had to respond to a variety of requests, the letters also show the difficulties connected with the role of sheikh. Especially in some legal cases or requests for mediation, when both parties addressed him for help and support, he must have been confronted with divergent, not to say contrary expectations. How did he handle them?

Even if it is obvious that Sheikh Muḥsin ibn Zahrān possessed great authority and influence that was not limited to al-Ḥamrā' and the ʿAbrīyīn, he did not pursue his interests and objectives merely by giving orders. In fact, a distinct command structure is hardly ever noticeable. Instead, Muḥsin ibn Zahrān relied on discussions and negotiations. Conflicts between groups or individuals were, as mentioned above, quite often the central topic of a letter. But in contrast to other written sources, it is not the fighting that prevails in the correspondence but the efforts to avoid open conflicts by peacefully solving the underlying problem.

In conclusion, the exchange of views and negotiations documented in these letters underlines that the important prerequisites to be a successful sheikh were the skills of persuasion and negotiation and the willingness to compromise. In my opinion, these personal communicative qualities were almost as important as courage and fighting skills. When taking into consideration that Muḥsin ibn Zahrān was a sheikh for nearly half a century, it can be assumed that he was quite successful in performing his duties as expected by his community.

The letters served different purposes. First of all, they were a means of transmitting news, personal views and instructions. In this respect, they can be considered an important addition to and, in some cases, even a substitute for personal meetings. The letters that announce the arrival of a messenger may have been a warrant of this individual's identity and reliability. A further purpose of the letters is to transmit various kinds of information. While acting as a judge and mediator, a sheikh needs to take into consideration every aspect of the relevant case. That is to say, he should know enough about the persons involved as well as about the wider circumstances of the case. It seems that the letters served the purpose of providing such information, enabling him to come to decisions that would find the consent and the support of the community. This is also an important but still underestimated factor in the role of a sheikh.

Finally, the letters clearly show that the often-mentioned notions of "tribal dichotomy" and interaction between people bearing the same tribal *nisbah* have to be revised. People sharing the same *nisbah* or belonging to the same tribal grouping do not necessarily have the same interests or pursue the same aims. Instead, their behaviour is, above all, determined by regional factors and changes in accordance with the political, social and economic situation. For example the right to collect *zakāt* in a certain village or valley is obviously only of interest to the people living there because the consent to pay *zakāt* to a certain person or this person's delegate means that they accept his authority. Other people with the same *nisbah* but living somewhere else are not immediately affected by this matter and accordingly do not participate in the discussions. Compared with other sources, the letters from al-Ḥamrāʾ provide a much more differentiated picture of the actual social and political behaviour of a person or a group.

15.7 Conclusion

Since this is the only archive of its kind and scope in Oman yet discovered and – most importantly – that has been made available for academic research, it is almost impossible to make a general statement on the importance of written communication in the Omani past. But the documents obviously played an important role in the life of the ʿAbrīyīn-sheikhs of al-Ḥamrāʾ. And there is no doubt that the letters addressed to Sheikh Muḥsin ibn Zahrān were more numerous than those addressed to his predecessors or his successors. This is of course partly due to the length of his rule, but it surely is also a result of his own intentions and actions (Fig. 15.6).

In accordance with the well-known proverb "Knowledge is power", Muḥsin ibn Zahrān seems to have consciously used his correspondences to obtain as much information as possible in order to fulfil his duties as community leader and, by doing this, also to consolidate his position. The letters were an important means of his communication; they were a complement or even stood in for personal meetings. Taking into consideration all these facts, the letters portray Sheikh Muḥsin ibn Zahrān as a man of great personal abilities and foresight who relied more on negotiations than on warfare.

Networks (social, economic and political) are not unchanging; they expand or contract according to the respective developments and changes in the framework. They do not necessarily correlate with modern political or administrative units. The spatial structures reflected in the letters are created by the people involved, by their perspectives and needs. Accordingly these structures show variations dependent on time, place and not at least on actor, a fact that the differences in quantity and durability of the correspondences clearly illustrate. What Katrin Bromber states in her introductory article (in this volume) about the "seascape" of the Indian Ocean also applies – to a large extent – to the regional level of the "land-scape" of al-Ḥamrāʾ, that is, that it formed a historical and symbolic space that was structured by people's ideas and actions.

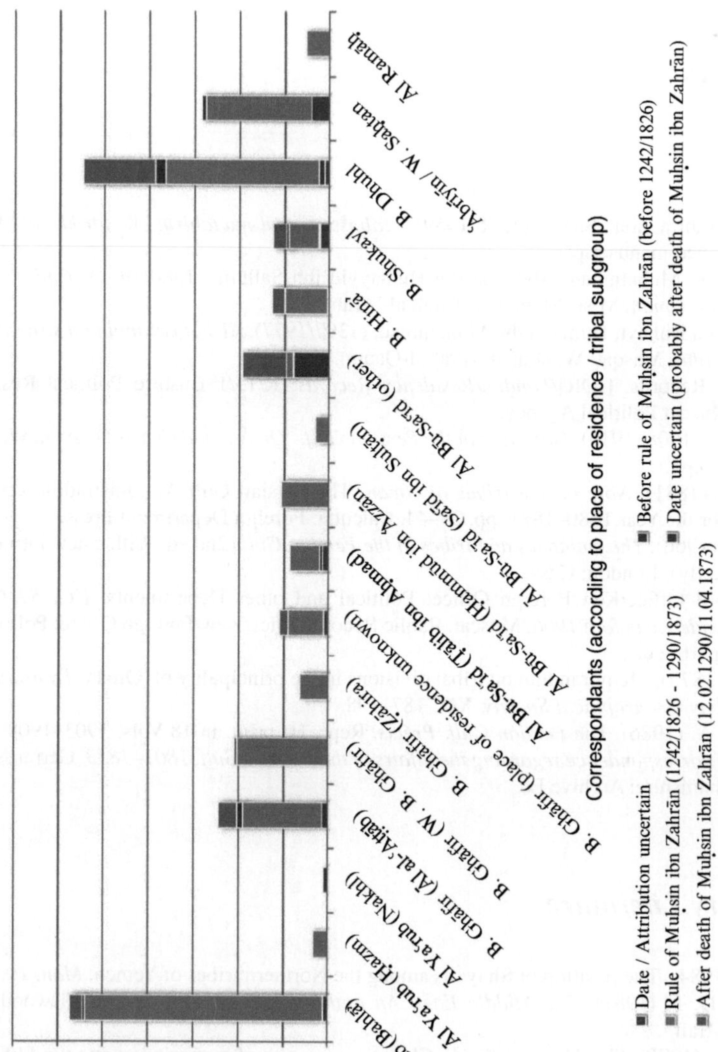

Fig. 15.6 Correspondants

In a more general sense, the letters from the ʿAbrīyīn archive of al-Ḥamrāʾ illustrate the importance of such material for the understanding of the Omani past. I therefore would like to express my wish that similar archives will be "unearthed" and studied in the future.

References

Sources

Al-ʿAbrī, Ibrāhīm ibn Saʿīd. (1378/1959). *Tabaṣṣurat al-muʿtabirīn fī tārīkh al-ʿAbrīyīn*. (Unpublished manuscript).

Al-Sālimī, Abū Muḥammad ʿAbdallāh ibn Ḥumayyid ibn Sallūm. (1380/1961). *Tuḥfat al-aʿyān bi-sīrat ahl ʿUmān*. Miṣr: Maṭābiʿ al-Kitāb al-ʿArabī.

Ibn Ruzayq ibn Buḥayt, Ḥumayd ibn Muḥammad. (1397/1977). *Al-Fatḥ al-mubīn fī sīrat al-sādah Āl-Bū-Saʿīdīn*. Masqaṭ: Wizārat at-Turāṯ al-Qaumī.

India Office Records. [IOR]/*London/Residency Records*: R/15/1 Bushire Political Residency; R/15/6 Muscat Political Agency.

Lorimer, J. G. (1908–1915). *Gazetteer of the Persian Gulf, 'OmÁn, and Central Arabia*. Westmead (et al.): Gregg.

Miles, S. B. (1881). *Note on the tribes of Oman*. The Persian Gulf Administration Report for Muscat for the Year 1880–1881, pp. 29–44. Calcutta: Foreign Department Press.

Miles, S. B. (1966). *The countries and tribes of the Persian Gulf* (2nd ed. With a new introduction by J.B. Kelly). London: Cass.

Public Record Office/Kew/Foreign Office: Political and other Departments. *F.O. 54 General Correspondence before 1906*. Muscat: Public Record Office/Kew/Foreign Office: Political and other Departments.

Ross, E. C. (1873). Memorandum on tribal divisions in the principality of ʿOmān. *Transactions of the Bombay Geographical Society, XIX*, 187–198.

Saldanha, J. A. (1986). *The Persian Gulf. Précis*. Repr. 1st print. in 18 Vols. 1903–1908. Vol. 2: *Précis of correspondence regarding the affairs of the Persian Gulf, 1801–1853*. Gerrards Cross, Buckinghamshire: Archive Ed.

Secondary Literature

Dresch, P. (1984). The position of Shaykhs among the Northern tribes of Yemen. *Man, 19*, 31–49.

Eickelman, D. F. (1981). *The Middle East: An anthropological approach*. Englewood Cliffs: Prentice-Hall.

Fernea, R. A. (1970). *Shaykh and Effendi. Changing patterns of authority among the El Shabana of Southern Iraq*. Cambridge: Harvard University Press.

Gaube, H., & Gangler, A. (2011). *Transformation processes in oasis settlements of Oman*. Muscat: Al-Roya.

Gerholm, T. (1977). *Market, mosque and mafraj: Social inequality in Yemeni town*. Stockholm: University Press.

Häser, J. (2000). Formation and transformation processes of oasis settlements in the Sultanate of Oman: Preliminary report on a new field project. *Proceedings of the Seminar for Arabian Studies, 30*, 115–118.

Hoffmann-Ruf, M. (2008). *Scheich Muḥsin bin Zahrān al-ʿAbrī. Tribale Macht im Oman des 19. Jahrhunderts*. Berlin: Schwarz.

Kelly, J. B. (1968). *Britain and the Persian Gulf 1795–1880*. Oxford: Clarendon.

Levi, G. (1991). On microhistory. In P. Burke (Ed.), *New perspectives on historical writing* (pp. 93–113). Oxford: Polity Press.

Lienhardt, P. (1975). The authority of shaykhs in the Gulf: An essay in nineteenth-century history. *Arabian Studies, 2*, 61–75.

Ott, C. (2011). Die Inschriften von al-Ḥamrāʾ. In H. Gaube & A. Gangler (Eds.), *Transformation processes in oasis settlements of Oman* (pp. 151–155). Muscat: Al-Roya.

Peters, E. L. (1990). The power of Sheikhs. In J. Goody & E. Marx (Eds.), *The Bedouin of Cyrenaica. Studies in personal and corporate power* (pp. 112–137). Cambridge: Cambridge University Press.

Richardson, N., & Dorr, M. (2003). *The craft heritage of Oman*. London: Motivate Publishers.

Ulbricht, O. (1994). Mikrogeschichte. Versuch einer Vorstellung. *Geschichte in Wissenschaft und Unterricht, 45*, 347–367.

Wilkinson, J. (1987). *The imamate tradition of Oman*. Cambridge: Cambridge University Press.

Winder, R. B. (1950). *A history of the Su'udi State from 1233/1818 until 1308/1891*. Princeton: University Dissertation.

Chapter 16
Domesticating Local Elites. Sheikhs, Walis and State-Building Under Sultan Qaboos

Marc Valeri

16.1 Introduction

Sultan Qaboos' overthrow of his father in July 1970 and his accession to the throne followed some 15 years of civil war. This instability had illustrated the social and political divisions of a territory officially known as the "Sultanate of Muscat and Oman" (Peterson 2007). Qaboos, who was not 30 yet and at the time unknown among the Omani population, inherited formal sovereignty over a political space without defined and recognised boundaries[1] and without a state apparatus. From this perspective, his room to manoeuvre with regard to the British was reduced to a minimum, and so was his legitimacy vis-à-vis the Omanis. He thus immediately faced the need to assert the legitimacy of his accession to the throne. The key element of the new regime's strategy of legitimization rests on the nation-building process implemented since 1970, which links the country's economic and social development to the modernizing state (as the administrator of the oil rent), on the one hand, and to the person of the new Sultan who embodies the state and has become the subject of a personality cult, on the other. By initiating a process of nation-building within the framework of a homogenizing central state that unified cultural and religious references, Qaboos has worked to legitimize his paternalistic authority. In pursuing this objective, the regime exploited the newly significant oil rent to implement previously unknown economic and social development through an extensive redistribution system.

[1] In 1970, two-thirds of the southern province of Dhofar was outside of the control of the Sultan and his British allies, following the uprising conducted by the Popular Front for the Liberation of the Occupied Arabian Gulf. In the North, the rulers did not ratify the final agreement on total delimitation of the Oman-UAE border until June 2002.

M. Valeri (✉)
Institute of Arab and Islamic Studies, University of Exeter,
Stocker Road, Exeter EX4 4ND, United Kingdom
e-mail: M.Valeri@exeter.ac.uk

S. Wippel (ed.), *Regionalizing Oman: Political, Economic and Social Dynamics*, United Nations University Series on Regionalism 6, DOI 10.1007/978-94-007-6821-5_16,

One of the regime's strategies was to undermine the legitimacy of the traditional *'asabiyyat* (tribes, ethno-linguistic groups and communities)[2] in which political references were formerly rooted and to replace them with a state apparatus that the Omanis were unlikely to turn against because they depended on it for their survival. Within a few years, the state was suddenly transformed into a concrete reality, becoming simultaneously the ground on which the competition for power and wealth takes place and, as the depository of oil rent, the object of all covetousness, the stake for which all actors contest – as an employer providing an inexhaustible pool of jobs open to the skilled and unskilled alike. This process made it easier to foster an Omani national identity, which reframed the references of identity by being centred on the person of Qaboos, who is identified in historiography with the state and, therefore, with contemporary Oman as a whole. To sum up, Sultan Qaboos has been able to set up the legitimacy of his authority by creating both an Omani state and an Omani nation.

In the 1990s, it was thus still generally accepted that the Omani tribes and clans were slowly disappearing under the blows of urbanisation and technological modernisation. Yet, while the omnipresent official discourse since the 1980s has constantly emphasized national unity feeling behind the ruler's authority, this process of substitution of identity allegiances, the local giving way to the national, was not to lead to the destruction of infra-national identities and structures of power. As Clifford Geertz explained in the 1960s,

> what the new States – or their leaders – must contrive to do as far as primordial attachments are concerned, is not, as they have so often tried to do, wish them out of existence by denying their reality, but instead domesticate them (Geertz 1963: 128).

For several decades, one of the guidelines of the Sultan's strategy of legitimisation has been "de-autonomising" local solidarities (ethno-linguistic tribes, groups etc.), i.e. neutralising their impact by subordinating them to the state and making them more and more dependent on a game that the regime controls. This has taken the form of a determined co-optation policy towards the most prominent tribes and noble families, as well as an integration of smaller local elites into the state apparatus.

This chapter focuses more particularly on one type of political personnel who are essential for understanding the political relationship between the centre and the periphery in Oman: the tribal elite and notables. While the most important sheikhly families have been offered economic opportunities and top positions in the state apparatus, the regime also hastened to attract local tribal elites into the system, by "bureaucratizing" them as an official intermediary between individuals and the public administration. Far from erasing the traditional local elite from the socio-political map, the advent of a nation-state has articulated itself with them, to maintain the old social order while depriving them of any potential for political harm to the new regime.

---

[2]Ibn Khaldun's notion of *'asabiyya*, usually translated as "group feeling", is understood as populations linked by blood ties or behaviours acting as a group or defining themselves as such (see Ibn Khaldun 1980: chapter 2).

16.2 The Encapsulation of the Tribal Elite into the State

No national debate on the role of tribes in the modern nation-state building has been started in Oman. In the promotion of a national identity, the official historiography has constantly done its best to present the state or the Sultan himself as the Omani citizens' only interlocutor. The tribe was never recognised as an official political entity. The taboo on the question of local groups' role in the state remains strict, and when the official rhetoric refers to tribes, it unambiguously evokes the division of the nation and historical regression, characteristic of the pre-1970 period, through the presupposition that the individual cannot claim several collective allegiances at the same time because one necessarily excludes the other.

Nevertheless, despite this official discourse, the tribal issue has remained a major concern of the authorities since the 1970s. The regime has strongly worked to co-opt the most powerful tribes, and the leading clans and families of the Imamate were soon offered a general amnesty to rally them to the side of the new regime. One of the most obvious examples of this is the noble lineage of the Khalili family, heir to a prestigious lineage of Ibadi *imams* and powerful actors in the Imamate until the 1950s. The new regime co-opted the nephew of one of the last Imams of Oman, Sa'ud bin 'Ali al-Khalili, at an early date and made him one of the four members of the very first Cabinet appointed on 15 August 1970 after Qaboos' accession to the throne. Sa'ud bin 'Ali also owns the Al Taher business group, which he founded in 1973; it is active in contracting (sole distributor of Caterpillar products in Oman), food and drink (Sprite, Coke, Zain, Al Sarooj supermarkets), industrial fisheries and the distribution of Shell products. In 2004 Al Taher was awarded Oman's fourth licence to sell petroleum products through his new business, Tammuz Oman Petroleum, and in May 2011, the Central Bank of Oman approved Sa'ud al-Khalili's application to establish the first Islamic bank in Oman (Bank Nizwa) (James 2011).

The course followed by his brother, Hilal bin 'Ali, is even more curious. Wali under Sultan Sa'id bin Taimur since 1943, he was thought likely to succeed his uncle as Imam, but tribal balance was not favourable to him. He took the Imam's side in the conflict that arose in Jabal Akhdar in the 1950s between the Ibadi Imamate, controlling the whole interior of the country, and Sultan Sa'id, backed by Britain, and was named the Imamate's Ambassador in Riyadh in 1954. Benefiting from the 1970 amnesty, he was immediately appointed Sultan Qaboos' Ambassador to Saudi Arabia. His son, Salim, currently a member of the appointed State Council, was formerly Chairman of the Omani Chamber of Commerce and Industry (OCCI) and then Minister of Agriculture from 2001 to March 2011. His grandson, Qais, chairs the OCCI's Oil and Gas Committee and the family business group, Al Khalili and Sons. One of Hilal bin 'Ali's nephews, 'Abd al-Malik bin 'Abd Allah – who had previously held successively the positions of executive chairman of the Royal Court Pension Fund, chairman of the first Omani banking group, Bank Muscat, and Minister for Tourism (2011–2012) – was appointed Minister of Justice in March 2012.

Another illustration of this "deal" with the authorities is given by the descendants of 'Abd Allah al-Salimi, one of the principal instigators of the Ibadi Imamate's renaissance at the beginning of the twentieth century. While his son Muhammad bin 'Abd Allah held a leading role within the Imamate's political authorities in exile, his grandson, 'Abd Allah bin Muhammad, has been Oman's Minister for Religious Affairs since 1997. Several of his relatives occupy crucial positions within the ministry. The minister's cousin, 'Abd Allah bin Salim, has occupied the post of Chairman of the Muscat Securities Market since 2002. Lastly, a member of the same tribe, Major-General Sa'id bin Nasir al-Salimi, is Commander of the Royal Army of Oman.

Similarly, the new state also hastened to integrate the small notability into the bureaucratic hierarchy. The Diwan of the Royal Court has regularly granted local sheikhs gifts in cash and in kind (cars, houses, etc.) so as to ensure their loyalty to the regime. Subsidies could reach OMR 30,000 per year.[3] Moreover, the *sheikh rashid*[4] is paid as a state employee and acts as an intermediary between individuals and the public administration. He officiates in a geographical district (*hara* or *hilla*), and not according to tribal or family criteria.[5] He carries out many daily acts aiming at facilitating relations between individuals and the state apparatus, such as certifying a person's lineage in order to deliver a passport and the solution of smaller disputes. The *sheikh rashid* has to give regular accounts of his acts to the wali, the highest representative of the Ministry of Interior (and of the state in general) in each *wilaya*.[6] When a *sheikh* dies, the choice of his successor is decided within the framework of the Ministry, in the presence of the notables of the district and with their approval.

This bureaucratisation of tribal sheikhs is also well illustrated by the human resources management of walis and other local representatives of the state. Before 1970, the sultan was represented locally by a wali, who was usually born either into the royal family or one of the most influential tribes and who was assisted by a *qadi* (judge) responsible for the resolution of conflicts. This pair of officials constituted in most cases the entire local state apparatus. One of the rules was to appoint a wali in a town far from his native region, so that he could be assumed to be impartial towards the local tribes. This rule would live on under Qaboos: the vast majority of walis are appointed outside the broader region they come from.[7]

Interestingly, no wali or governor (*muhafedh*) belongs to the Al Sa'id royal family, but all are either descended from a sheikhly lineage or collateral branches of the al-Busa'idi tribe. To this day, the regime has mostly resorted to groups historically allied to the Sultan of Oman (even during Sultan Sa'id bin Taimur's reign) and that have been seen historically as neutral in tribal issues and conflicts. This has led to

[3] Personal interview, 12 August 2004. OMR 1 = EUR 1.99 (6 May 2013).
[4] The tribe is organised in branches or sections (*far* or *fakhdh*), each one led by a *sheikh rashid*.
[5] Obviously, in the rural zones, the *hara* usually coincides with a clan's own settlement area, which strengthens the individuals' perception of a state in continuity with the pre-1970 period.
[6] There are 61 wilayas.
[7] In 2013, the only exception to this rule is Dhofar, where all but one walis (except the governor of the province and his deputy) are native from Dhofar governorate but from a different wilaya.

the perpetuation of the bureaucratic role played by some tribal lineages that have been working for the Sultan Sa'id and Sultan Qaboos for decades. Among them are collateral branches of the al-Busa'idi tribe, whose members served on a large scale under the twentieth-century sultans, especially as governors. Among the current governors and walis belonging to these collateral al-Busa'idi branches is the current governor of Muscat, *sayyid* Sa'ud bin Hilal al-Busa'idi, whose brother Sultan was himself governor of Muscat between 1983 and 1991, but also the current vice-governor of Muscat, *sayyid* Sa'id bin Ibrahim al-Busa'idi (whose brother Sa'ud was Minister of Interior until March 2011), the governor of Musandam, as well as seven walis in the country, including those of Seeb and Qurayat.[8]

Another bank of loyal wali office holders is the noble clans of the al-Ma'amari tribe. Their influence in the decision-making process had never faded until March 2011, when General 'Ali bin Majid al-Ma'amari, Minister of the Royal Office since 1989 and head of the office of the Sultan's Armed Forces Chief of Staff, and Lieutenant-General Malik bin Sulaiman, Inspector General of Police and Customs, with ministerial rank, were removed from their position. 'Ali bin Majid's brother-in-law, Muhammad bin Marhun al-Ma'amari, who was Ambassador to the UAE until 2007, has been Minister of State and Governor of Dhofar since then. Yahia bin Hamud al-Ma'amari, the current Governor of North Sharqiya, was wali of Nizwa in the 2000s and later governor of the highly sensitive Buraimi governorate (2006–2011), while four of his brothers are or were walis in the 2000s (one is the current vice-wali of Nizwa).

A similar move to encapsulate infra-national allegiances into state-building was the redistricting of the country in 1991. While initially composed of two governorates (*muhafadha*) and nine regions (*mintaqa*) – reminiscent of the pre-1970 political divisions – the national territory was re-divided into five regions – Batina, Sharqiyya, Dakhliyya, Dhahira and al-Wusta – and three governorates: Dhofar, Muscat, Musandam.[9] This administrative reform can be compared to France's 1790 redistricting, when the new Constituent Assembly replaced the administrative division of the territory inherited from the monarchy (with provinces of the Ancien Régime based on the Middle Age suzerainties and fiefdoms) by new *'départements'* the names of which refer to geographical criteria only. In Oman, the 1991 administrative re-organisation of the country into new geographical entities led to the appearance of new regional solidarities, because of the restructuring of the country's territory around regional capitals (such as Nizwa, Sur, and Sohar) that were destined to become conveyor belts between Muscat and their hinterland. This was a consequence of the location there of local branches of the administration and ministries and of new educational structures (universities, training centres for teachers and nurses, etc.). Rural-urban drift at the regional level, unknown until this time, brought about a dilution of former local identities in a wider regional community. In the eyes of the

[8] The title of *sayyid* is reserved in Oman to the royal family members.

[9] A new governorate (Buraimi) was created in 2006. These regions and governorates were themselves divided into wilayas.

new generations, the tribe or the village is now less important in identifying who is a member of another group than the regional centre in which the latter studied or trained. New regional identities have emerged all over the country (such as *dakhli*, from the interior; *sharqi*, from the east, etc.).

16.3 Recognition of the Tribal References by the State

This encapsulation process, which is a key element of the strategy of legitimisation Qaboos' regime, was not supposed to lead to – and has not marked – the extinction of tribal sheikhs and references though. Far from being destroyed, the tribal hierarchy has been rather recognised by the state apparatus and reshaped in order to adapt the state priorities. The regime's political strategy has been to domesticate the tribal elite, thus absorbing the benefits of their legitimacy while bringing them under his control.

The Omani authorities decided in 1980 to establish *shuyukh qabila* (sheikhs of tribe) for the Baharina and Lawatiyya[10] communities of the capital in order to act as intermediaries between the members of the community and the administration. While this process was not unanimously approved, the government wished, just after the Iranian revolution, to preserve Oman from any external religious influence, and to emphasise the anchoring of Oman's Shi'a into the nation by "tribalising" one of the non-Ibadi groups.

Another illustration of the way the former order's references have been encapsulated into the modern state is the official decision, in 1981, to give every citizen a patronymic referring to the tribe of his birth. This decision focused on the groups that cannot claim Arab tribal descent, like client groups of the noble tribes, and the Lawatiyya, the Baharina and Omanis of Baluchi descent. It was decided to give these last three groups the patronymics "al-Lawati", "al-Bahrani" and "al-Balushi". Many Lawatiyya still refuse to use this patronymic, so as not to be compared to a "nomadic tribe" (Eickelman 1990: 120) and not to reinforce stigmatisation to which they are still subjected by some Omanis of the interior.[11]

The existence of tribes within the state and the social status of their sheikhs have also been practically recognised by the Directorate of Tribal Affairs of the Ministry of Interior, which lays down an exhaustive list of tribes and their respective sheikhs. This determines the individuals officially allowed to hold the title of sheikh. In 1979 a "General Directory of Wilayas and Tribes of Oman" detailing the tribal composition of all villages, classified by wilaya, was printed but not put on sale. Last but not least, since 1970 the Ministry of Interior has required the signature of a sheikh to

[10] The Baharina and the Lawatiyya are two Twelver Shi'i groups present on the northern coast of Oman. While the Baharina are related to various Arab Shi'a communities of Bahrain and Southern Iraq, the Lawatiyya appear to have settled in Oman in several migration waves from Sindh (currently Pakistan) between 1780 and 1850.

[11] For more details, see Valeri (2010).

attest to an individual's affiliation with or membership in a tribe. The Ministry of Interior has thus made a takeover of the symbolic system of traditional local leaders to consolidate its own local anchoring.

Another very efficient tool used by Sultan Qaboos to consolidate his power has been the Council of Oman, composed of two chambers: the Majlis al-Shura (Consultative Council), elected since 2003 by universal suffrage, and the Majlis al-Dawla (State Council), appointed by royal decree. The Council of Oman has been depicted to the international community as an illustration of political liberalization for the last 15 years, but it is also obviously very useful in the internal agenda of the country, as a complementary way to domesticate the local elite and dispossess them of their social power. Dale Eickelman's sociological study of the members of the first State Consultative Council (1981–1983) members shed light on what he called "shaykhocracy" (Eickelman 1984: 59), given that 15 of the 18 members native to the interior belonged to tribal sheikhs' lineage.

Nowadays, it would be misleading to reduce the Majlis al-Shura elections to a political retribalisation only. Nevertheless the government has constantly worked to depoliticise the elections and reduce them to local and personal issues. Article 10 of the 1 March 2003 law dealing with the organisation of elections states that any citizen has the right to stand, provided, among other conditions, that he is a native Omani (*bi-l-asl*) and is a "son of the wilaya" (*min abna' al-wilaya*) in which he is a candidate or owns a residence there. In the 2003 and 2007 elections it was forbidden to discuss any general topic (like the role of the religion in present society or that of the assembly in the division of powers) or to present public promises or campaign together with a candidate from another wilaya. These limitations prevented the elaboration of political strategies. Candidates therefore stood in their own names only. If public gatherings were allowed in 2011 for the first time, campaigning remained very restricted and took place mostly in the *majlis* of the tribal sheikhs, but also through door-to-door and personal networks.

Voters residing in the capital were strongly encouraged to vote in their native wilayas through indirect measures, like the organisation of the voting on a working day and the granting of an additional holiday without loss of pay the next day on presentation of a stamped voter's card. Moreover, the organisation of voting on a local basis has tended in this direction. Similarly revealing was the absence of any members of the royal family, noble lineages of the al-Busa'idi tribe or leading historical merchant families among the candidates.[12] This was due both to reluctance to involve the royal name in a "vulgar" electoral game with popular voting and to the regime's unwillingness to face the implications of symbolic overinvestment in such candidatures: voters and observers would be tempted to interpret the results as a referendum on the authorities' general policies, and that would be inconceivable for Sultan Qaboos. These elections do not, in any case, question the legitimacy of the ruler, but that of all the local political elite.

[12] A notable exception is the winning candidacy in Sur in 2011 of Sa'ad Bahwan, the chairman of the OTE Group of Companies and youngest son of one of the leading Omani businessmen.

Thus it is not very surprising that the criteria of choice most commonly used by electors have related to primordial solidarities, especially in rural areas where choice mainly follows lines of tribal belonging. This tendency was reinforced by the format in which the candidates' names were given: first name, father's first name, grandfather's first name, great grandfather's first name, tribe's name. The candidate's name itself conveys his programme and defines by itself the social and political symbol the candidate embodies. Clientelism (*al-mahsubiyya*) and personal relations (*al-ma'arif al-shakhsiyya*) but also the sheikh's support for a certain candidate, were thus the most important determinants of choice in 2003 and 2007.

As a result of this absorption of tribal rhetoric and notabilities by the state, no social recognition remains except that granted by the state, which has appropriated the symbolic spaces that local authorities controlled before 1970, not by destroying them but rather by depriving them of any autonomous symbolic meaning. The social dubbing of the state has thus become crucial to all local elites. An example of this dilemma is the State Council, whose members are appointed by royal decree 1 week after the elections to the Majlis al-Shura. This gives the government the opportunity to establish closer links with key figures at very little cost. Moreover, it offers a second chance for groups whose members have not been elected in the Majlis al-Shura polls. In 'Ibri in 2003, for instance, the major tribe, the Ya'aqubi, was divided among several candidates. The failure to reach an agreement to group all the tribe's forces around a single name led to the defeat of all al-Ya'aqubi candidates. Fortunately for the tribe, the Sultan appointed Sultan al-Ya'aqubi to the State Council to compensate for this. The same situation arose in Mutrah, where the candidature of two Lawatiyya notables split the community's vote, the result being that there were no Lawati as Majlis al-Shura members. After the Sultan appointed two Lawatiyya to the State Council in the following days, the Lawatiyya remembered the lesson, organising "primary" elections within the community four years later to present only one candidate.

Thus, the State Council formalises the integration of local elites into the state apparatus. For instance, the Imamate's historical influential families are strongly represented, in particular by the presence of the last Imam of Oman's son, al-Khattab bin Ghalib al-Hina'i,[13] and, since 2003, of Zahra al-Nabhani, daughter of one of the Imamate's most powerful personalities. The Council therefore contributes to the central power's legitimisation through a redistribution of both material and symbolic powers. The de-politicisation process reaches its climax here, with the co-optation of traditional elites. By integrating them into the State Council and then officially recognizing their status, these elites will finally use their own social legitimacy, which has been independent of that of the nation-state built around the Sultan, in his favour. This political process is also the means of establishing a clear distinction between the royal family and the other citizens (including local elites). The latter group has been ordered to bring its social or traditional prestige into play. If a local

[13] He was appointed to the State Council in 2011, "replacing" his father's brother's son, 'Ali bin Talib al-Hina'i, who had been appointed for two terms (2003–2011).

notable or sheikh wins a seat in the Majlis al-Shura, his prestige is theoretically strengthened – but to the benefit of the central state, as this notability becomes an intermediary between state and society. If he is defeated, his fate lies in the hands of the Sultan, whose paternal benevolence can grant him a seat in the State Council, which will allow him to keep a bit of "social visibility". Thus his dependence upon royal goodwill is total. The social prestige of the tribal sheikhs consists merely of the one the state consents to confer to them, a phenomenon a growing part of the population has become aware of, as shown by the profound lack of interest in the 2007 Majlis al-Shura elections.

In one of his seminal papers on the persistence of monarchy in the Arabian Peninsula, Gregory Gause (2000: 174–175) explained,

> the successful monarchies are those which tamed tribalism [...]. All the monarchies of the [Arabian] Peninsula favoured the survival of tribalism as a personal marker of identity. They brought financial support and a recognized social position to tribal sheikhs. But they also achieved with success what their predecessors failed: to deny the tribes any autonomous political and military role in their societies.

As for Oman, one of the guidelines of the Sultan's strategy of legitimisation since his accession to the throne has been to re-adapt the Oman's social and political legacy to modern-day requirements and re-create it from a mould that makes sense to the modern consciousness. This has taken the form of the incorporation of the most powerful social groups (prominent tribal leaders, Ibadi religious *'ulama* etc.) into the political system in order to undermine their capacity to challenge his rule. The sovereign has hastened to turn infra-national legitimacies (tribes, ethno-linguistic groups etc.) to his own profit by integrating them into the new political order and using them to consolidate his authority. This has been particularly true when dealing with Cabinet positions. John Peterson (2004: 10) noted the prevalence in post-1970 cabinets of personalities from the very populated areas of Dhahira and West Batina; originating from tribes who had established ties with Riyadh in the 1950s, they were said to receive preferential treatment aimed at diverting them from the enticements of the late Sheikh Zayed since the 1970s. This extreme caution in composing Cabinets and balancing the regional and tribal origins of its members was illustrated once again in March 2011, when the Sultan restructured the Council of Ministers, a few days after the death of a protester shot by the security forces in Sohar: three of the newly appointed ministers were native to the Batina region, thus raising the total contingent of Cabinet members from Batina to six (out of a total of 29 ministers).

While the taboo on the question of local groups' role in the state remains strict, and with tribal issues in particular being unambiguously associated with the division of the nation, the modern state has come to terms with the *'asabiyyat* so as to absorb them. Far from eradicating tribal sheikhs, the regime has worked to absorb them and to co-opt them into the system. It has thereby sought to "de-autonomise" the traditional solidarity groups from the state, rendering them fully dependent on a political game that the regime controls and whose rules the regime establishes. In this way, the ruler has been freed from the constraints imposed by notables and traditional authorities and has stopped the latter from freeing themselves from the state's influence. He alone cannot be categorised as the representative of any particular interest: Sultan Qaboos is the only one who can claim to embody the whole political community.

Until recently, this policy has had very efficient political consequences for the regime's stability. It has avoided any socio-political polarisation on other criteria than that of local allegiances (tribal or ethno-linguistic bonds): by tacitly recognising the role of traditional infra-national legitimacies in the state architecture and channelling claims according to this identification, the ruler has prevented the emergence of "transversal" identifications, such as social class, religious allegiance or ideology, which have broader capacities to gather support. Any attempt to question the rules of the game incurs without fail the anger of the regime. Moreover, taking recourse to "reassuring" political and social references that are given the appearance of tradition has been part of a determination to fill the ideological gap between social infra-national structures and the state, and thus to facilitate individuals' acceptance of the new official order. Finally, this policy, which has made the sheikhs entirely dependent on the state's goodwill, has slowly deprived them of their potential for political harm, as there is no more social legitimacy and prestige besides that granted by the state. From this perspective, the regime has structurally contributed to eroding the sheikhs' credibility in the population's eyes – a grim finding for the authorities in February and March 2011, when the Ministry of Interior tried to involve tribal sheikhs and notables to appease the trouble in Sohar and Salalah. The protesters bluntly turned down the tribal leaders' mediation,[14] clearly illustrating the actual level of prestige and authority enjoyed by the tribal leaders in Oman after more than 40 years of Qaboos' rule.

The 2011 "Oman Spring" has shown how the long-practiced technique of "buying-off" tribal references with the aim of preventing any social claim or the emergence of alternative discourses has reached its limits. The 1991 redistricting of the territory, which intended to transcend infra-national solidarities (tribes, ethno-linguistic groups) with the creation of new regions organised around a central urban pole, produced long-term effects exceeding all expectations. In concentrating the frustrations of a whole region, with protests targeting symbols of the central state (particularly walis' offices and local branches of the Ministry of Manpower), in 2011 regional capitals like Sohar, Sur and Salalah epitomised the regime's inabilities to fulfil proclaimed promises of local development. From this perspective, the administrative re-organisation of the territory in October 2011 that dismantled the Batina and Sharqiyya regions, dividing them into two, transformed all regions into governorates. As all governors (except those of Muscat and Dhofar) will exercise their prerogatives under the strict supervision of the Minister of the Interior, this new reform illustrates an illusory attempt to re-assert the grip of the central state on turbulent peripheries.

[14] Personal interview, Muscat, 12 October 2011. See also *'Uman*, 11 April 2011 and *Muscat Daily*, 6 April 2011.

References

Eickelman, D. F. (1984). Kings and people: Oman's state consultative council. *Middle East Journal, 31*(1), 51–71.

Eickelman, D. F. (1990). Identité nationale et discours religieux en Oman. In G. Kepel & Y. Richard (Eds.), *Intellectuels et militants de l'Islam contemporain* (pp. 103–128). Paris: Le Seuil.

Gause, G. (2000). The persistence of monarchy in the Arabian Peninsula: A comparative analysis. In J. Kostiner (Ed.), *Middle East monarchies. The challenge of modernity* (pp. 167–186). Boulder/London: Lynne Rienner.

Geertz, C. (1963). The integrative revolution. Primordial sentiments and civil politics in the new states. In C. Geertz (Ed.), *Old societies and new states. The quest for modernity in Asia and Africa* (pp. 105–157). London: Free Press of Glencoe.

Ibn Khaldun. (1980). *The Muqaddimah: An introduction to history* (F. Rosenthal, Trans.). Princeton: Princeton University Press.

James, A. E. (2011, May 30). *Windows open for Islamic Banking Units. Times of Oman.* http://www.timesofoman.com/archivesdetails.asp?detail=45589.

Peterson, J. E. (2004). *The emergence of post-traditional Oman* (Durham Middle East Papers, Sir William Luce Publication Series, Sir William Luce Fellowship Paper, 5, 22 pp.). http://www.jepeterson.net/sitebuildercontent/sitebuilderfiles/Emergence_of_Post-Traditional_Oman.pdf.

Peterson, J. E. (2007). *Oman's insurgencies: The sultanate's struggle for supremacy*. London: Saqi.

Valeri, M. (2010). High visibility, low profile: The Shi'a in Oman under Sultan Qaboos. *International Journal of Middle East Studies, 42*(4), 251–268.

Chapter 17
Musandam: Creating a New Region Across the Water

Gulshan Dietl

17.1 Introduction

Oman is an island between the sand seas of Arabia to the west and the waters of the Gulf of Oman and the Arabian Sea to the east.

Oman lies in two distinct regions – the Arab Gulf States to its west and the Iranian landmass across the water to its east. This paper proposes to locate the country in both its neighbourhoods with a special reference to the Musandam peninsula.

The Musandam Peninsula is separated from the rest of Oman by a strip of territory belonging to the United Arab Emirates. It is this tip on the Gulf coast that has given Oman the status of a Gulf state and a berth on the Gulf Cooperation Council. Musandam juts into the Strait of Hormuz, which links the Persian Gulf with the Gulf of Oman. This location secures Oman a joint control, with Iran, of the Strait. The "Musandam phenomenon", as a result, explains Omani foreign policy behaviour to a very large extent. More specifically, it makes Oman's relations with Iran well worth scrutinizing.

17.2 Omani Foreign Policy: An Overview

Oman is the oldest Arab state. Between the seventeenth and the nineteenth century, Omanis built an empire from the Persian Gulf to the East African coast and Zanzibar. Geographically, the country borders Yemen in the southwest, Saudi Arabia in the west, the United Arab Emirates in the northwest (not taking Musandam into consideration), the Gulf of Oman in the north and the Arabian Sea in the east

G. Dietl, Ph.D. (✉)
Institute for Defence Studies and Analyses, 1, Development Enclave,
Rao Tula Ram Marg, New Delhi 110010, India
e-mail: dietl@hotmail.com; gdietl@mail.jnu.ac.in

S. Wippel (ed.), *Regionalizing Oman: Political, Economic and Social Dynamics*, United Nations University Series on Regionalism 6, DOI 10.1007/978-94-007-6821-5_17,

and south. Its total coastline is 1,200 miles. It has a small population of roughly 3.5 million. Like the rest of its neighbours, its economy is largely dependent on oil, though its production is much less than theirs. Like Bahrain, it is not a member of the Organization of Petroleum Exporting Countries. In fact, Oman is striving to reduce the importance of the oil sector within its overall economic performance (Al-Fil 2009). Tourism, trade, and banking sectors are promoted in pursuit of diversification. Agriculture and fishing are other main sectors of the economy.

Oman's central external linkage has been with the United States. The Treaty of Friendship and Navigation was signed between the two as early as 1833. It was the first treaty the US concluded with an Arab country. The Treaty of Amity, Economic Relations, and Consular Rights (1958) and the Free Trade Agreement (2006) are major landmarks in the economic sphere. There has been a close defence relationship between the two in terms of basing rights, weapons purchases and joint military exercises.

The relationship with the US is the foremost major determinant of the Omani foreign policy in general. It guides Omani behaviour on a wide range of issues. As a result, its views on and relations with Israel have always been at variance from the rest of the Arab world. When the Arab states broke off diplomatic relations with Egypt in 1979 in retaliation for its peace treaty with Israel, Oman – and Morocco – did not. In April 1996, the Israeli Prime Minister Shimon Peres, leading a high-level delegation, paid an official visit to Oman and Qatar. From then on, Oman and Israel exchanged trade offices till Oman closed them in October 2000 in the wake of the public demonstration against Israel at the start of the Second Intifada. Oman hosted the plenary meeting of the Water Working Group of the peace process, the first Gulf state to do so.

A second major determinant of Omani foreign policy is the domestic situation. At times, this factor has influenced and undermined the pro-US positions, but not beyond repair and not for long. The Omani population is believed to be divided equally between the Ibadis and the Sunnis. The Wahhabi version of Sunni Islam is seen to be making inroads in Oman. Omani Ibadis and Saudi Wahhabis have launched bitter theological tirades against each other. In 2008, for instance, the Omani religious establishment ordered the people not to follow the pronouncements of the Saudi religious authority on what day to celebrate Eid at the end of the fasting month of Ramadan. Police reportedly clashed with the Sunnis in Salalah over the dispute (Reuters 2009). The incident showed that Saudi religious influence can affect Omani social cohesion. The Shia minority is negligible, in comparison. The threat of Iran-inspired Shia radicalism, therefore, is limited. Omani regional policies, especially towards Saudi Arabia and Iran, are guided by sectarian considerations at times.

17.3 Oman and the GCC

Oman had been an ardent champion of the GCC. After the Iran-Iraq war broke out, Oman hosted in Muscat the final preparatory meeting prior to the GCC's formal founding session in May 1981 in Abu Dhabi. Over the years, however, it has followed distinctly oppositionist policies within the grouping, most of the time accompanied by Qatar. The two together constitute a counterbalance to the Saudi-led four.

At the GCC Kuwait summit in November 1984, the idea of a Gulf Deterrent Force was floated after the failed coup in Bahrain in 1982. The Saudis suggested that it must have a permanent land base, in Hafr al-Batin in the northeast of Saudi Arabia, near the Kuwaiti-Iraqi-Jordanian borders. Oman immediately expressed reservations on two grounds: 1. It could not afford the financial burden, because the discrepancies between the salaries and benefits provided to the forces serving inside and outside would be great. 2. In terms of its own security, it could not afford a whole unit of its armed forces to be stationed permanently in a faraway base outside its own territory. Eventually, so that Oman would not appear to be the odd man out, a compromise was reached: Oman agreed to send a token force to be stationed in Hafr al-Batin as a sign of good will towards Gulf solidarity (El-Rayyes 1987: 200–201). During the Iran-Iraq war, Oman was the only GCC member-state that maintained its ambassadors in both Baghdad and Tehran. The Omani navy, based on Masirah Island, did not intercept Iranian speedboats on their mission to explode under the oil carriers during the tanker war phase of the war. At the end of the war, Oman proposed Marshall Plan-like reconstruction assistance to Iran and Iraq both.

On the eve of the Iraqi invasion of Kuwait in 1990, Oman reportedly urged Kuwait to relieve Saddam Hussein's financial difficulties (Seale 2005). Its role during the war was mainly as a base and a staging post for the US and British air forces. Oman contributed a battalion to the ground war to liberate Kuwait, but its air force did not participate in attacks on Iraq. After the war, it was the only country that did not claim compensation for its citizens, even though several Omani residents in Kuwait suffered losses. It also advocated a 100,000-strong GCC army to avoid external military presence in the region. By the mid-1990s, Oman's stance toward the prolongation of economic sanctions against Iraq appeared ambivalent: Oman and Qatar were, notably, absent from talks held in March 1995 between US Secretary of State Warren Christopher and other members of the GCC on the continued maintenance of sanctions against Iraq. In November 1997, Oman expressed its opposition to possible military action to force Iraq to submit to inspections of its weapons capabilities by the UN Special Commission. In early 1998, as the crisis over United Nations Special Commission (UNSCOM) inspections deepened, Oman again urged the pursuit of a diplomatic solution. The Minister of State for Foreign Affairs expressed Oman's opinion that, should the UN Secretary-General's mission to Baghdad prove successful in facilitating the completion of UNSCOM's operations, the UN should then remove the economic sanctions against Iraq.

In the aftermath of the war against Iraq in 2003, Oman declined to send troops to stabilize the country. The Omani Minister in charge of foreign affairs, Yousuf bin Alawi Abdullah, replying to the request from the Iraqi government to send troops, said that the 15,000-strong international troops positioned in Iraq under US leadership were sufficient for the purpose and that Omani armed forces would not work outside the scope of the GCC security cooperation (Anon. 2004).

On the issues of internal integration, Oman has been a very selective participant, at times an advocate, at times reluctant, at times a dissenter. Oman asked to be exempted from the Economic Agreement signed in June 1981 that set the intra-GCC customs duty at 4 %. In January 2007, it decided to stay out of the GCC Monetary Union. It did not want to live up to the condition that public debt should not exceed 60 % of GDP. Also, the Omani riyal is the least expensive currency within the GCC, which is good for the tourism industry and exports (Ali 2007).[1] As the GCC has stuttered along on its path of a Monetary Union, it has not given up hope that Oman – and also the United Arab Emirates – will change their mind and come on board. The GCC Secretary General Abdulrahman Al Attiyah has sounded optimistic about the prospect, though nothing on the ground has changed (interview with Akhbar Al Khaleej, reproduced in Anon. 2010e).

Oman advocates a GCC-wide gas grid. Omani demand for gas has risen sharply in the recent years in view of heavy government spending on infrastructure and industrialization. Currently, Oman and the UAE together import gas from Qatar via a pipeline network developed by Dolphin Energy. It covers 18 % of total Omani demand for gas. Since Qatar has put a moratorium on further expansion of its huge North Field gas fields, Oman is looking for other supply sources.[2] At the Gas Arabia Summit 2009, the Oman Gas CEO Yousuf Al Ojaili made a strong case for a GCC-wide gas grid: the GCC countries with combined gas reserves of about 1,500 trillion cubic feet had enough gas in the ground to fuel the region's future industrial development and economic growth. They also had sufficient funds to develop the region's gas resources and existing gas processing and transportation infrastructure, which merely needs expanding (The National 2010).

17.4 Oman and Iran

In the fourth and third millennium BC, Oman-Iran relations amounted to "a general cultural convergence that is common to the whole of south-east Iran and Oman and leads to the technological level and production modes being the same" (Bowen-Jones 1987: 127). At a very different level of interaction, there were the complicated commercial and tribal control relationships between the Iranian city-ports of Qais, Huzu and Hormuz and Omani merchant families. Ethnically, both sides of the Straits are still virtually indistinguishable (Bowen-Jones 1987). Since time immemorial, the Strait of Hormuz has never operated as a barrier to contact, but rather as a filter.

In modern times, Oman's ties with Iran owe a lot to Iran's military support for Sultan Qaboos in his fight against the insurgency in Dhofar from the early to

[1] Ali agrees with Oman's position in view of the facts that 1. the Euro has appreciated since its launch in 2002, undermining the competitiveness of the Eurozone economies and 2. as in the Eurozone, where only 13 countries of the EU's 27 adopted the Euro, the GCC Monetary Union could go ahead in the absence of one of its members.

[2] The North Field reserves are estimated to be nearly 900,000 square cubic feet.

mid-1970s. Qaboos' personal appreciation and Oman's state interests converge when it comes to these bilateral relations. The past few years have witnessed close defence cooperation as well as common positions on regional issues. Very often, Omani ties with Iran have come at the expense of its role within the GCC and its relations with Saudi Arabia.

The first overt act of joining hands in defiance of the Arab consensus came in January 2009, when Qatar broke the Arab ranks and organized a summit in Doha to support Hamas in its struggle against Israel. The Iranian president Mahmoud Ahmadinejad and the Omani minister in charge of foreign affairs, Alawi Abdullah, both attended, together with the Palestinian resistance group.[3] A few months later, Alawi Abdullah was in Tehran, where he stated, "Hassan Nasrallah enjoys a high position. Iran's and Oman's position with regard to regional and global issues coincide" (Reuters 2009). Oman and Iran, an ally and an adversary of the US respectively, stood on the same side of the divide on Hamas and Hizbollah, the most non-grata groups for the US and the GCC states. Together, the Omani stands on Hamas and Hizbollah put it on the Iranian side of the fence in the GCC-Iran divide.

A bilateral security agreement was already in the works around that time. An annual defence cooperation commission meeting was instituted that was to be held in Tehran and Muscat alternately. Alawi Abdullah was in Tehran again in July 2009, when he and the Iranian foreign minister Manouchehr Mottaki addressed a joint press conference to announce that a move towards formal agreement was afoot and would be "a symbol of our strategic cooperation in preserving stability and security in the region" (Anon. 2009d).

The most visible sign of the relationship came with the Omani Sultan's visit to Iran in August 2009. Qaboos took more than three decades after coming to power to pay his very first visit to Iran. The timing of the visit, however, conveyed a lot more than the long interval. The incumbent Iranian president Mahmoud Ahmadinejad was re-elected for a second term in May 2009. There were massive protests within Iran because the election results were disputed. Qaboos chose the presidential inauguration for a high-profile visit (AFP 2009). During the visit, he stated that the "Persian Gulf littoral states must consider the region's common interests and with stepped up cooperation prepare the ground for its lasting security." The Iranian Supreme Leader Ayatollah Ali Khamenei added: "The US and some meddlesome states by continuously injecting insecurity and suspicion have never allowed the sensitive Persian Gulf region to witness calm." The two countries signed seven Memoranda of Understanding on various issues including political, economic and cultural cooperation (Anon. 2009b, c). An agreement on security cooperation was one of them, which covered the exchange of information and combating infiltration, smuggling and other crimes (Anon. 2009a). In February 2010, the two signed a formal Defence Cooperation Pact (Xinhua 2009).[4]

---

[3] Saudi Arabia and Egypt had boycotted the Summit and Oman was under pressure to do the same.
[4] On the eve of the Pact, in December 2009, the armed forces of Oman and Iran held a joint rescue drill off the coast of the Gulf.

Around that time, Yemen was in the throes of a rebellion by the Shia Huthi tribes, of which Iran was perceived to be the supporter. Even as the Saudis were insisting on a hard line on the issue, Oman called on the Yemeni government to hold a dialogue with the Huthis in the situation (Anon. 2010d). In the regional context, the Omanis were clearly out of step with their Arab neighbours to the west and closer to the Iranian position.

In April 2010, Tehran organized a high-profile conference on "International Disarmament and Non-proliferation: World Security without Weapons of Mass Destruction". The theme of the conference was "Nuclear Energy for All, Nuclear Weapons for None." The unstated aim of the conference was to assert the Iranian right to nuclear technology. Alawi Abdullah attended the conference and stated at its end that "Iran pursues the disarmament of the nuclear-armed countries" and that the event "offered proof of the peaceful nature of Iran's nuclear programme" (Anon. 2010a).

Underpinning the common stands on critical issues are solid economic reasons. There has been a sharp increase in demand for oil and gas in Oman as government investment in infrastructure and industrial development is increasing. Oman receives 18 % of its gas imports from the Dolphin project of Qatar. Qatar has now put a moratorium on its gas exports and Oman must look for other sources. Oman and Iran have agreed to develop gas on Iran's Kish Island and to transport it to Oman via a 200-km pipeline under the Gulf waters (UPI 2010; Reuters 2008). Oman has agreed to bear the entire cost of USD 12 billion. A joint development of Hengam/Bukha gas field at the cost of USD 200 million and transporting it to Oman via a 100-km pipeline is also agreed.

For Iran, Oman is a friend across the Gulf water and an economic ally. As the sanctions regime tightens around Iran, any opening that offers itself must surely be welcomed. Oman is one such. Additionally, Oman offers a window to reach out to the wider world. For example, the LNG plant in Qalhat in Oman has a small capacity of just under ten million tonnes a year. There are plans to expand it, which could be a future transit route for Iranian gas. In January 2010, Iran opened a trade centre in Muscat (Anon. 2010c), from where 60 Iranian companies will operate. This will be the second Iranian trade centre after Shanghai. The two have already established a Joint Investment Company worth USD 50 million with a 50 % share each (Anon. 2010b).

17.5 Musandam

As stated in the beginning, the Musandam Peninsula is separated from the rest of Oman by a strip of territory belonging to the United Arab Emirates. This tip on the Gulf coast has given Oman the status of a Gulf state and secured it a berth in the Gulf Cooperation Council. Most importantly, Oman and Iran share joint control over the Strait of Hormuz, which links the Persian Gulf with the Gulf of Oman. Roughly 40 % of all seaborne trade in oil passes through Hormuz, which works out to an average of 17 million barrels a day. It is a vital chokepoint point, because 90 %

of Japan's, 70 % of the European Union's and 50 % of America's oil supplies pass through it (Seale 2005).

Musandam consists of the northernmost tip of the Hajjar Gharbi Mountains. The coastline of the peninsula is rugged. Two inlets cut deep into it through the cliffs, providing spectacular views. The area is frequently compared to the fjords in Norway. There is enormous potential to develop tourism in the area. Khasab has been at the centre of touristic activities on Musandam. There are upmarket resorts catering to visitors from the Gulf States and to expatriates in Oman itself. Scuba diving, snorkelling, boating, trekking, car trips through the mountains and boat cruises through the fjords are attractions on offer. The introduction of two multi-purpose passenger vehicle ferries from Muscat to Musandam is expected to increase movement between the two. With a capacity to carry 208 passengers and 56 cars, the ferries cover an approximately 420-km route in a little more than 5 h (Benoy 2008).

Roughly 30,000 people live in this small area measuring 1,800 km^2. As already mentioned, the trans-Gulf contacts between Oman and Iran go back all the way to the fourth and third millennium BC. Ethnic intermixing has resulted in an indistinguishable population. Kumzari is the lingua franca used on both shores across the Strait of Hormuz.[5]

Since the Islamic Revolution in Iran, trade from there to the Iranian coast has boomed (for details cf. Benz, in this volume). The trade is illegal in Iran, but legal in Oman. The local government collects taxes, coordinates goods to the speedboats, distributes pickup and delivery orders to anyone with a small truck and grants de facto visas to incoming Iranian traders as long as they do not stray far from the port or stay overnight. The weathered speedboats line up along three small piers in Musandam every morning, right next to large police boats that patrol the strait. The trip is short, but many captains say it can be perilous because they have to dodge massive oil tankers and avoid Iranian coast guard patrols (Slackman 2009).

Goods worth USD 250,000 to USD 500,000 are estimated to cross the Strait each day. The route, the goods and the volume have changed with changing circumstances. In 1997, a paved road from the Omani town of Khasab to the UAE was completed, which facilitated a wider scope and brought the UAE into the loop. In 2002, the Iranian government signed agreements with cigarettes companies for imports. Cigarette smuggling was decimated as a result. The total volume since then was reported to be one-fifth of the level of a few years back. It may increase again as the sanctions on Iran intensify (Pohl 2004).

A wide variety of commodities, including cigarettes, food, clothing, electronics, pharmaceuticals, air conditioners and motorbikes, leave Oman; and loads of livestock, fruit and dried fruit come from Iran. The incoming cargo from Iran reportedly includes illegal migrants from Iran, India, Pakistan and Bangladesh hoping to reach the UAE, failing which they stay in Oman itself.[6] There are also accusations of drugs coming in from Iran (Dunlop 2007). The trade is said to represent over half the total economy of the Peninsula.

[5] Albeit in a very limited area and by very few people.

[6] Interview with Omani ship owners.

References

Chapter 18
The Political Economy of Internationalization and Privatization of Higher Education in the Sultanate of Oman

Torsten Brandenburg

18.1 Introduction: Building a Domestic Knowledge Base in Oman

While higher education has remained one of the GCC's most state-controlled sectors, a paradigm shift has taken place since the mid 1990s. In succession, the field of post-secondary education has been economically liberalized, resulting in an emergence of private institutions offering international degrees in academic cooperation with foreign universities. The impetus for the liberalization and an endorsement of higher education came after the early 1990s economic crisis, which placed limits on the expansion of public higher education. The primary purpose of the privatization agenda was to satisfy the educational aspirations of the young population, to enhance the competitiveness of the national economy and finally to be prepared for the upcoming end of the oil era. Thus, in response to these socio-economic challenges, Oman, like other countries in the region, launched an ambitious campaign to further enlarge and modernize its higher education system. The government's goal is that, despite its demographic challenge, at least 50 % of the 18- to 24-year-old Omanis will continue to post-secondary education by the year 2020, up from less than 15 % in 1995.

T. Brandenburg (✉)
Institute of Geography, Johannes Gutenberg University Mainz,
Johann-Joachim-Becher-Weg 21, 55099 Mainz, Aachen, Germany
e-mail: to.brandenburg@gmail.com

S. Wippel (ed.), *Regionalizing Oman: Political, Economic and Social Dynamics*, United Nations University Series on Regionalism 6, DOI 10.1007/978-94-007-6821-5_18,

18.1.1 Higher Education as the Main Pillar of the Arab Knowledge Revolution

The formation of human capital in the GCC lags behind its current economic progress. In relation to the size of the national economy, the per capita income or the human development index, educational outputs in all GCC states are far behind other regions. There is still no correlation between knowledge, productivity and wealth in the GCC, as long as wealth is produced by oil exports and not innovation- and knowledge-driven. The Arab Human Development Report 2003 emphasizes that the knowledge gap between Arab countries and advanced knowledge societies is large and widening. If Arab countries are to catch up with dynamic knowledge societies, they will have "to pursue a course of exponential growth of knowledge". Adopting such a course is a challenge, as "it requires (…) the dissemination, production and utilization of knowledge (…), at rates faster than those which historically prevailed in today's knowledge economies" (UNDP 2003: 40).

Bridging the knowledge gap may be achieved by increasing the number of academic programs, creating private institutions, developing distance learning, and engaging in internationalization activities, such as importing educational programs provided by foreign institutions, developing partnerships with local institutions, and allowing foreign institutions to operate locally. As a consequence, one might assume that the GCC's current trend towards internationalization and privatization in higher education contributes to this catching-up process, as suggested by the World Bank and other multinational organizations. These new educational services promise the required exponential growth to reach the knowledge level of advanced economies, in qualitative and quantitative terms. While internationalization is used to bridge the quality gap by importing foreign programs, the privatization addresses primarily the fiscal pressure of the massification in higher education.

18.1.2 Educational Services Across National Borders: Internationalization of Higher Education

In most countries, especially those in transition, the demand for post-secondary education is increasing. This is related to a number of socio-economic reasons: changing demographics, a greater number of school graduates, the movement towards lifelong learning and the impact of the knowledge-based economy concept. While the demand for higher education is growing, the capacity of the traditional public sector institutions to satisfy this need is being challenged. Alternative ways to provide higher education are being developed, including growth in the private (often profit-oriented) higher education sector, greater emphasis on distance and virtual learning, but also new developments in cross-border education (Knight 2007: 21).

The most visible aspects of the globalization of higher education include (i) the growing numbers of students (*consumption abroad*), professors and researchers (*presence of natural persons*) participating in mobility schemes, (ii) the growing numbers of cross-border academic programs (*commercial presence*), such as franchises and offshore campuses, and (iii) new regional and national level policies supporting academic mobility and other internationalization initiatives (Knight 2007: 21; Knight and Altbach 2007: 291–292). International students have become big business, bringing revenues to host universities and countries through tuition payments and other expenditures (Altbach et al. 2009: 8). Knight (2007: 21) assumes that the number of students moving to study in foreign countries will continue to increase, but supposes that particularly the mobility of academic programs and providers moving across national borders to deliver courses to students in their home countries will gain in importance. Traditionally, flows of students and scholars were largely a brain exchange within the North, or at least from the developing countries to North America and Europe. Today, the flows of programs and providers moving back and forth across borders have increased along other lines (Altbach 2004: 19). Besides the shift towards program and provider mobility, there is also a substantial change in orientation from cooperation to competitive commerce, visible in the growth of a mobility of educational services for commercial purposes (Knight 2005: 4, 2007: 22–28).

Program mobility means the physical or virtual "movement of individual courses and programs across national borders through face to face, distance or a combination of these modes" (Knight 2006: 28). Teaching is done by a local institution, credits towards a qualification are awarded by the foreign provider, by the domestic partner or jointly. The impetus to form international linkages can be viewed from the perspectives of the foreign and the local institutions. Universities are keen to export their programs to generate additional revenues and to create a branding as a global institution. Receiving institutions often aim to establish international links as a means of acquiring courses at minimal cost. Franchising, joint degrees and validation arrangements are the most popular modes of cross-border program mobility. By contrast, a non-collaborative provision is defined as "the physical movement of an education provider across a national border to establish a presence in order to offer education programs and services to students and other clients" (Knight 2007: 29). The most important mode of provider mobility in recent years is the international branch campus.

18.2 Oman's Renaissance: Knowledge Production and Dissemination Under Sultan Qaboos

This chapter describes the formation of Oman's publicly funded higher education system until the mid-1990s. As in other Gulf States, higher education has been treated as a public commodity. Consequently, the state had a monopoly over the provision of post-secondary education. Private higher education supplementary to the established public system was not allowed. The driving force of the publicly funded system was to establish the pillars of a modern society, a theme typical of the reign of Sultan Qaboos during the first years of what is often called Oman's Renaissance. Within the period, more than 30 public higher education institutions (HEI) were established, offering cost-free education exclusively for Omani citizens.

18.2.1 Closing the Educational Gap to Oman's Neighbouring Countries

Oman's modern educational system has only a short history. It began in 1970 under the guidance of Sultan Qaboos bin Said. Since then, most efforts focused on expanding primary and secondary schooling to absorb the growing masses of young people, to reverse low literacy and schooling levels, and to reduce urban-rural inequalities. The consequence of this catching-up process during the first period of Qaboos' reign was that a disproportionately large part of the public budget was spent on promoting primary schooling rather than on post-secondary education (Metz 1994; Scholz 1998: 150). The efforts to strengthen basic education were very successful, but produced numbers of secondary school graduates (SSGs) that far outstrip the nation's higher education capacities (Coffman 1996: 16). The subsequent great demand for higher education was met mainly by universities in Arab states, primarily in the United Arab Emirates (UAE) and Egypt, but also in Western countries, with the United States and the United Kingdom leading the way (MoNE 2008). The cost of this outsourced education was borne by public scholarships and private sources.

The early 1980s marked a watershed from a traditional to a more modern Oman. Well provided with income from oil exports, Sultan Qaboos was now capable of providing (more) services to the domestic population. In the late 1970s, the first colleges offering vocational and technical programs were established. These institutions were run by the government and focused on the national priorities of healthcare and teacher training. The inauguration of Sultan Qaboos University (SQU) as a comprehensive state university in 1986 was a further milestone in the process for higher education. Besides SQU, seven Technical Colleges, six Colleges of Education, 14 Health Institutes and an Institute of Financial Sciences were established by 1995, providing post-secondary opportunities to all corners of the country.

With the formation of SQU, several policy decisions were made to encourage students to continue in higher education and, therefore, to stay in Oman. While quite appropriate for the period, several of these policies are the origin of issues that now shape and constrain government decision making today (Chapman et al. 2009: 204–207). Firstly, the regime determined that higher education should be free, as was the standard in the region. Due to the high oil price in the early 1980s, financial resources were not a problem, and Oman could afford to provide free higher education for the relatively small number of school graduates. Secondly, university graduates were assured of public sector employment upon graduating. This early precursor of the later implemented Omanization was oriented toward reducing dependence on expatriate workers.

In the mid-1990s, the projected decline in oil production and its implications for government spending became visible. The increased enrolment in public higher education was a major cost that the government could no longer bear at previous levels. In addition, the implicit employment guarantee for graduates was unsustainable. Several incentives of the past had grown into entitlements that, in turn, were becoming liabilities for the future. The size of the public sector workforce increased – but the growth was driven more by supply than by demand. In addition, while the number of secondary school graduates increased to more than 15,000 in 1991, only 20 % of these certificate holders were admitted to one of the public higher education institutions (MoHE 2009). These figures indicate that admission to higher education was selective and competitive. Accordingly, despite the formation of a diverse and expensive public system, there was still a large number of Omanis who had to study abroad. Several thousand Omani students attended universities abroad, primarily public universities in the UAE, which were free of charge for GCC nationals (MoHE 2009). This student mobility illustrates the shortage of local admission capacity. However, institutions in the UAE had a bad reputation, as they offered primarily courses in Social and Islamic Sciences. Graduates of foreign institutions were also not entitled to work in Oman's lucrative public sector. As a result, Oman's higher education policy excluded a large number of students who had no chance to earn university merits and, consequently, no real opportunity to obtain lucrative public employment. Women in particular were disadvantaged because, for cultural reasons, they often could not enrol abroad, and in addition, a gender quota complicated admission to SQU. This situation put pressure on the regime, because it could cause dissatisfaction amongst the overlooked youth.

Figure 18.1 recaps the distinctive features of Oman's state-funded higher education system until the mid-1990s: the development of a modern, Western-style higher education system was the aim of the education policy. Within Qaboos' Renaissance policy, higher education became a vital part of the country's overall socio-economic agenda. Oman thereby used its oil funds to close the gap to the neighbouring states, which began to establish their state universities much earlier. Regional competition, prestige and the legitimacy of the ruling regime affected the higher education policy. Guided by Western educational standards and policies and following regional patterns, post-secondary education was seen as a public duty. There was a general conviction that only the state should offer higher education as a strategic investment in Oman's future. Private investments complementary to the public system were not allowed. Thus, in the initial phase, the government did not use a policy of privatization to increase admission capacities or to diversify the system. This changed later. In terms of internationalization, a presence of natural persons and consumption abroad can be assessed, but not in terms of a commercial presence. Like all GCC states, Oman relied on the import of experienced lecturers due to the lack of a local faculty with the required experience and qualification. Lecturers were hired mainly from India, but also from other Arab countries. In regard to consumption abroad, the government promoted the mobility of students and issued scholarships to high achievers to study abroad, while a large number of Omanis was forced to study abroad due to the limited admission capacities in Oman. The design of Oman's higher education system was also affected by transnational educational

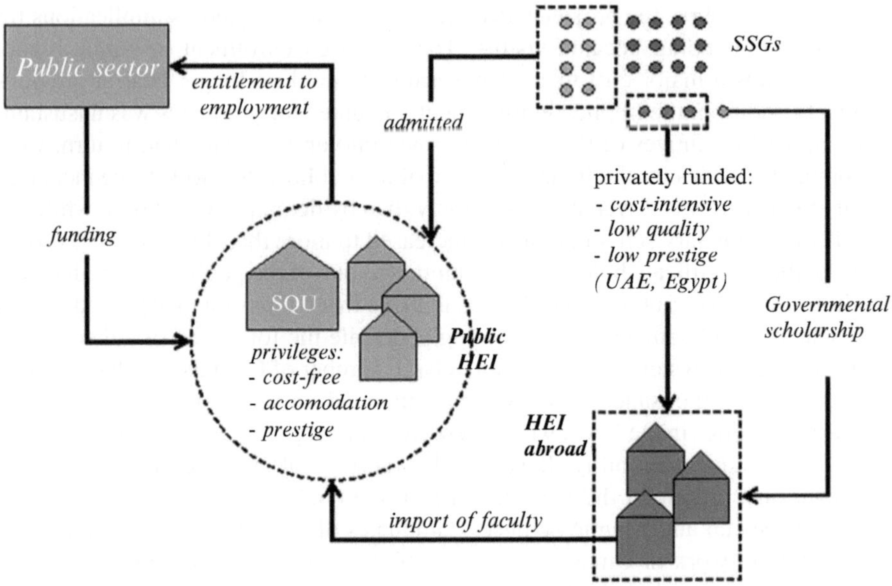

Fig. 18.1 Oman's higher education landscape until 1995 (Source: Brandenburg 2012)

concepts. As is the case in Qatar and Kuwait, SQU adopted Western academic and administrative concepts in order to become a "real" state university. All departments and degree programs bear the hallmarks of the Anglo-American university model.

The effects of the higher education policy till the mid-1990s are quite impressive. Within just 15 years, a diverse, publicly funded higher education system with more than 30 institutions was established. The admission capacities reached 3,000 university seats in 1995. All policies point to the creation of a broad range of higher education opportunities for Omani students. An important feature is that all institutions are limited to Omani nationals; the large number of expats was excluded from higher education. Despite efforts to increase admission capacities, the gross enrolment rate, as the major benchmark for policy-makers, declined in the early 1990s and oscillated around 15 %. The expansion could not keep pace with the demographic development! Faced with an estimated increase of SSGs, Oman's regime was forced to further expand and diversify its higher education system.

18.3 Oman's Shift to Privatization and Internationalization of Higher Education

To develop sufficient post-secondary educational opportunities, Sultan Qaboos issued a decree that legalized private higher education in 1995. The policy aims to support locally owned institutions that offer degree programs from international providers. Today, 27 private institutions offer more than 200 international degrees and cater to more than 33,000 students. It appears that a collaborative provision, such as franchise or validation agreements, became the predominant mode of transnational higher educational services. A distinctive feature of the liberalization policy is the subsidization of private, profit-oriented institutions, which are owned mainly by powerful members of Oman's society.

18.3.1 Promoting Higher Education to Set the Course for the Post-oil Era Since 1995

In the early 1990s, another fall in oil prices made Oman realize that its national economy, totally dependent on exporting oil, is economically unviable on the long run. In response to its socio-economic challenges, Oman's leadership adopted a liberal development agenda to modernize and diversify the national economy and to create much-needed jobs for the fast growing population. The long-term development strategy, Oman's Vision 2020, was the major testimony of intention to transform the economy into one "based on sustainable wealth-creating activities" (CFHEO 2005: 14). It also envisages greater participation rates in the workforce. The regime believes that university graduates in particular will have better opportunities to find employment in and outside the country (Al Barwani et al. 2009). As a consequence, higher education must respond to Oman's strategic plans in key sectors, because this is conducive to increasing the competitiveness of the national economy. Therewith, higher education became the central gateway to the realization of Oman's future aspirations. To achieve the transition to a knowledge-based economy, Oman aims to establish a mass higher education system characterized by a high participation rate (50–60 %). The vision of a knowledge-based economy also includes a commitment to strengthen the private sector as the key driver of economic growth. Statements from senior officials indicate that Oman's leadership is oriented toward a neoliberal development paradigm: "Till now, the government had a dominant role necessitated by the requirements of the previous stage. In the future, the role of the government should be limited to strategic guidance of an economy that depends on a dynamic private sector" (CFHEO 2005: 19). Thus the Vision 2020 emphasizes the state's commitment to shift from *publicness* (state-funded and -operated, cost-free) towards more *privateness* (privately owned and operated, cost-recovery) in higher education.

In line with the knowledge economy concept, a liberal human capital approach has become part of Oman's political agenda. In particular mass access to higher education has been regarded as a pivotal element of the transition from a rent seeking to a modern, market-driven economy, based on new foundations such as knowledge and innovation. Accordingly, the targeted value of higher education has changed over the past three decades: from an element within Oman's Renaissance to establish a modern state to a pivotal pillar of the Oman's ambition to become a globalized and competitive economy of the twenty-first century.

18.3.2 *Imperatives of Change: Satisfying the Increasing Demand for Higher Education*

By the year 2020, at least 50 % of the 18- to 24-year-old age group is to continue to post-secondary education (CFHEO 2005: 14). In meeting this target, the Sultanate faces huge challenges: firstly, the increasing number of SSGs demanding further access to tertiary education; secondly, limited admission capacities and high costs of public higher education; thirdly, declining oil revenues, which were previously used to finance post-secondary education; and finally, the need to raise the quality standards of the entire innovation system.

Demography: An analysis of Oman's age structure is helpful in assessing the impact of the demographic development on the demand for higher education. More than 35 % of Oman's population of 2.5 million is under the age of 15, and 63 % is under 25 (MoNE 2010). The growth in the number of secondary school graduates (SSG) between 1990 and 2020 illustrates the challenge to the higher education system. In 1995, the total number of SSGs reached 17,163 students; by the year 2000, the number had more than doubled, reaching 34,510 youngsters finishing school. In 2010, the number of SSGs peaked at almost 54,000 students (OMoI 2010; MoHE 2007). This means a tripling of SSGs within the period of just 15 years! To bring higher education to the masses, the government has to increase the annual admission capacity from about 3,000 in 1990 to almost 25,000 university seats in 2020.

Capacity Building: Only a few Gulf education officials will dispute that their higher education institutions have been characterized by a mediocre faculty, out-dated teaching methods and curricula, and poor materials and facilities (Coffman 2003: 18). Quality assessments have indicated unequivocally that school and university graduates from GCC states lag far behind graduates in East Asia and other developing nations (OECD 2008). As a consequence, enhancing the nation's human capital became an important rationale for reforming the higher education system. It is hoped that inputs and know-how transfers from well-established institutions abroad will foster Oman's innovation framework and that spill-over effects resulting from partnerships with foreign universities will promote research, development and academic excellence. The World Bank recommended this strategy because it has proven to be successful in a number of developing countries.

Rationalization: Since the early 1990s, the rate of increase in the cost of public higher education has accelerated because enrolments far exceed those ever imagined when SQU and the other institutions were founded. Oman does not have a large industrial or business sector outside of oil that can provide a meaningful tax base, and the country does not have a personal income tax. As a consequence, the government needed a strategy to limit costs while still encouraging system growth, requiring an expansion of the higher education system (Chapman et al. 2009: 202). This required a redefinition of the state-run economy, redistributing rents by providing jobs, free education, and healthcare for its citizens. The pressures of a globalized world undoubtedly had an impact on the domestic environment as neoliberal slogans of deregulation and liberalization found their way into governmental statements all over the region (Nonnemann 2008: 18–19). The Omani regime believed that liberalizing the economy, promoting greater financial openness to the rest of the world, and encouraging private investments would stimulate economic growth and address the demands of the young population. By legalizing private higher education, the government addressed three issues. Firstly, private institutions can charge tuition and recover at least a portion of the cost of education. Secondly, graduates of private institutions will not be entitled to public sector employment. However, they benefit from the Omanization policy. Finally, higher education is decoupled from the income from Oman's non-sustainable fossil resources (Chapman et al. 2009: 204).

Labour Market: Oman has to create 30,000 jobs per annum to reduce growing unemployment effectively (MoNE 2010). Concerns about the structure of the labour market, low productivity, and increasing unemployment, especially among the youth, affect education policy. In recent years the government has encouraged Omanis to work in the private sector and to take over jobs from expatriate workers. The objective is to achieve a greater participation rate in the workforce and to fight effectively against unemployment. As this requires a well-trained work force, a promotion of all types of education, from basic education to higher education, is essential to empower young Omanis to take up employment.

18.3.3 The Policy of Economic Liberalization of Higher Education in Oman

The privatization of higher education was enacted to meet the increasing demand for access to higher education that could no longer be met by the existing system (Al Lamki 2006: 59). Accordingly, the 1990s were a watershed for private investors, as they could enter lucrative markets that were previously reserved for public entities. In the years that followed, private 2-year colleges offering degrees at a diploma level started to mushroom in Oman. They later turned into 4-year colleges offering degree programs at under- and even postgraduate levels.

To encourage private investments in higher education, a generous set of public incentives was offered to those willing to operate private institutions. Subsidies include the provision of easy-term loans and the allocation of developed lands for the construction of educational institutes. Moreover, private institutions are exempted from most taxes for the first five years (Royal decrees 42/99 and 67/00). The subsidization policy was launched to attract private investments, but also to establish a formal cooperation between the government and the private sector. To reduce regional disparities, the government gave specific incentives for the formation of private universities: since 2001, they receive financial grants of up to OMR 17 million for the purpose of quality improvement related to teaching, learning and research. This includes instructional facilities and equipment. This is added to an initial capital grant of up to OMR three million (MoHE 2005). So far, seven consortia have made use of the royal fund to establish private universities in Sohar, Nizwa, Dhofar, Muscat, Ibra and al-Buraimi.

An important feature of Oman's privatization policy is that institutions are operated as profit-seeking enterprises. Private institutions have stockholders on record who invest in anticipation of a financial return. The government does not differentiate between for-profit and non-profit institutions, although it officially recommends that their main objective should not be profitmaking. This policy makes sense in Oman: a principal reason to establish a system of non-profit higher education institutions (as in the United States) is to encourage private philanthropy in support of higher education. Donors can receive tax breaks for their gifts. Because Oman does not have an individual income tax, there is no need for any tax advantages, and hence little reason to establish a special non-profit designation. Profit-orientation and public subsidization were needed to achieve the intended expansion of the higher education sector.

The time-variant analysis reveals that Oman's authorities have modified the privatization policy: in the first years, private higher education was offered only in addition to the existing public sector. Private colleges were only allowed to award degrees at the Diploma level. These 2-year colleges had a distinct vocational approach – more related to training than to academic education. Due to the pressure from the institutions, students, and economy, the profile and the scope of academic programs at private higher education were expanded. Today, all 27 private institutions in Oman award degrees up to the Bachelor's level; nine private institutions even have ministerial approval to award Master's degrees. The introduction of universities as a new type of private institution in 2001 was also a major application of the privatization policy. The adjustment was necessary due to the doubling of SSGs between 2000 and 2010 and the regional imbalances, as most private colleges operate in Muscat. Unlike private colleges, which enrol on average less than 1,000 students, private universities intend to contribute to a well-balanced development in all regions by enrolling up to 10,000 students. The government thereby used the income available after the oil price rally since 2003. In summary it can be said that Oman applied a liberalization policy to establish a private higher education system complementary to the existing public system. The policy was affected by the huge demand for educational services, the limited financial resources of the government (in the 1990s) and the liberal *Zeitgeist* of shifting responsibilities, duties and costs from public to private entities. Defining and distinguishing features of the application are the public support of private institutions, the status of private higher education as mass-absorbing, profit-oriented institutions and also the limitation on foreign ownership.

18.3.4 Internationalization of Higher Education: The Policy of Academic Affiliation

In conjunction with the privatization decree, the Omani government regulated an approach to promote the provision of transnational higher education services. To obtain the mandatory license, all private higher education institutions are legally bound to maintain an academic affiliation to a reputable international institution (MoHE 2005). In this way, the internationalization (in terms of a commercial presence) and the shift towards private higher education appeared simultaneously. This commitment is a defining feature of Oman's private higher education policy and is the root cause of the appearance of cross-border educational services.

The requirement to maintain academic cooperation with foreign institutions reveals that the government tries to control and guide the private sector initiatives. In line with the affiliation policy, Oman's government actively promotes the commercial presence of foreign providers in the country, but primarily in terms of collaborative arrangements: "Our higher education institutions need to build capacity so that they can manage their administrative and academic affairs efficiently and improve the quality of their curricula and programs" (interview with a senior official at the MoHE 2009). Although there are some formal requirements that must be included in an affiliation arrangement, there are no strict statutory provisions that define the mode or the scope of the cross-border services. Consequently, the intensity of academic cooperation, as well as the adapted models of cross-border services, varies from institution to institution (Brandenburg 2012). An important rule is that the association and the credentials of the academic partner must be officially recognized in the Sultanate. In addition, all offered degrees must be licensed by the MoHE prior to the first intake of students. The main objective of the affiliation system is a know-how transfer in line with a capacity-building strategy. Thus, the government's internationalization policy primarily addresses an import strategy rather than an export strategy as seen in other Gulf States, primarily in Dubai, where branch campuses try to attract large numbers of tuition-paying students (Meyer and Al Hamarneh 2008). As all private institutions in Oman must be owned by a majority of local shareholders, the government limits the provision of several types of non-collaborative arrangements, for example, an independently operated (and foreign-owned) branch campus. Both private and public higher education institutions use cross-border services to close the knowledge gap and to upgrade the quality standards of the post-secondary education system.

Thus, in terms of Knight's "Modes of Supply" (2007), there is a "commercial presence" of foreign providers (Mode 3) under Oman's specific regulation. In addition, an internationalization in the sense of (Mode 1) "cross-border supply" is taking place: distance-learning concepts noticeably emerged on Oman's higher education market. Moreover, the mobility of students, in the sense of (Mode 2) "consumption abroad", continued: the government still allocates a number of scholarships for high-achieving students to enrol in degree programs abroad that are not offered in Oman. In addition, the government encourages students to study abroad (self-paying) and recognizes foreign degrees from predetermined universities. In terms of the "presence of natural persons" (Mode 4), Oman's public and newly established private higher education institutions (still) rely on the import of lecturers from abroad. Indian lecturers form the vast majority of academic staff at private institutions. A supplement of faculty and management from the mother university is also often part of an affiliation agreement (Fig. 18.2).

The time-variant analysis shows that the government modified the affiliation policy in the past. In the first years after the privatization decree, the commercial presence of foreign providers and the provision of curricula and other services were limited to private higher education institutions. Since 2003, Oman's public higher

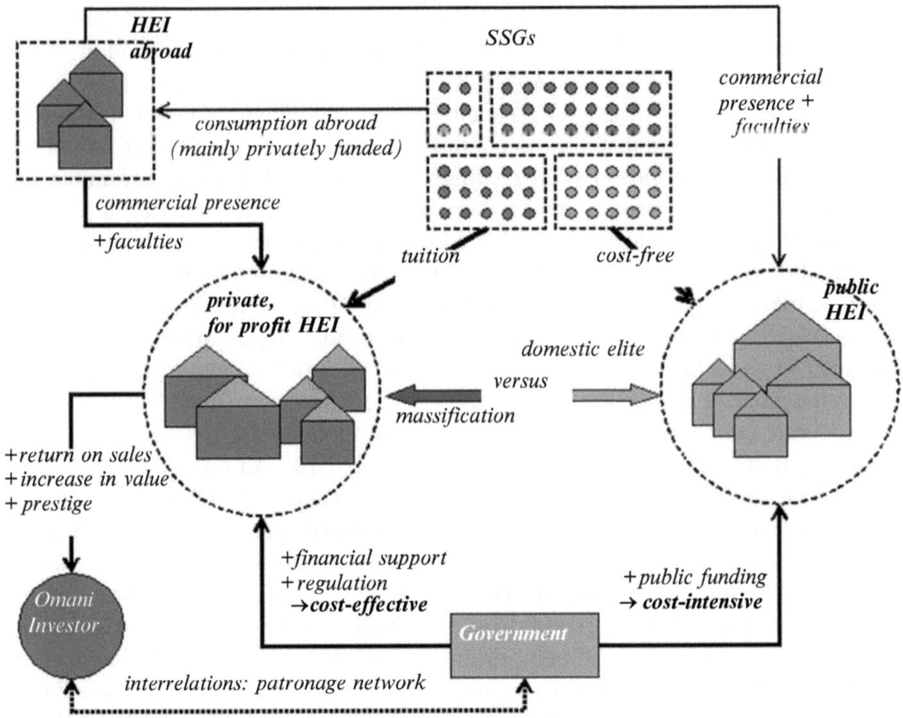

Fig. 18.2 Oman's higher education landscape since 1995 (Source: Brandenburg 2012)

education system also adopted several modes of cross-border services, such as validation agreements and international accreditations. Thus, private as well as public institutions increasingly rely on cross-border concepts. The government also eased some of the restrictions and allowed several private institutions to suspend the (costly) affiliation agreement. This concession shows that the affiliation policy aims primarily to bridge the educational gap in the initial phase by offering international programs. The defining feature of Oman's internationalization strategy is the focus on cross-border program mobility, while the mobility of foreign providers is limited. The internationalization agenda inhibits the formation of independently operating, foreign-owned branch campuses, as seen in other parts of the Arab world. All institutions are home-grown, foreign universities mainly provide academic services and assistance.

18.4 Conclusion: Oman's New Higher Education System, Public Versus Private Institutions

The policy to allow private higher education changed Oman's university landscape fundamentally. Oman's government used the privatization and internationalization of higher education to set a specific framework that focuses primarily on the expansion of admission capacities. The adjustment of the policy, particularly the subsidization of private, profit-oriented investments, is the main reason why the capacities developed rapidly. An important feature of Oman's liberalized higher education system is that the cost-intensive structures of the state-funded system have been sustained and that the government even increased the admission capacities of SQU and the other public colleges. Hence, both public and private institutions contributed to the growth of the post-secondary system. In terms of massification, the policy approach was successful, as it enabled more students to continue to higher education. The expansion even proceeded so fast that the strategic goal of an annual tertiary enrolment of 50 % was achieved already in 2010!

Figure 18.2 summarizes Oman's new higher education framework. With the formation of a tuition-based private higher education sector and the continuous development of the public education system, Qaboos' regime started a balancing act. Public higher education maintains its proven system of providing cost-free and well-recognized courses for highly achieving Omani students. The admission capacities of all publicly funded institutions, as well as the range of degree programs, were increased in the past decades. The annual intake of the public higher education sector amounts to 25 % of all SSGs and 55 % of all admitted students in 2010 (MoHE 2010). All students who are not admitted to the privileged public system have to bear the high costs of private higher education. Consequently, public institutions remain the institutions of first choice and can select the academically strongest students from a large group of applicants. Students who are refused admission have the option either to pay the high tuition for a private higher education, to study abroad, or to enter the labour market without higher education. Migrants, previously excluded from higher education in Oman, receive the opportunity to continue in private higher education. However, with less than ten per cent, the share of non-Omanis in the higher education system remains very low, as most children of expatriates still enrol at universities in their home countries.

In summary, therefore, the privatization of higher education caused segregation in Oman's higher education system. Public institutions, in particular SQU, keep their status as the national landmark institutions and address the domestic elite, whereas private, profit-oriented institutions primarily intend to absorb the mass of Oman's secondary school graduates. Investors in those private institutions take advantage of this situation and tap into a new, lucrative market. The private higher education market is a closed system that follows the hierarchal structures of Qaboos' regime. Long-established groups within the regime, such as merchant families, powerful tribes and members of the police and army, received the lucrative licenses to operate private institutions. The analysis of the political economy of private higher education shows that such investments guarantee high profit margins at low risk (Brandenburg 2012). In particular, the public subsidization and the low costs of operating the institutions constitute a solid business model. In fact, this segregation, public versus private, elite versus mass-absorbing, became a pivotal element of Oman's privatized higher education landscape since 1995.

The focus on home-grown higher education institutions rather than on international branch campuses is a characteristic that distinguishes Oman's higher education system from others in the region. While Qatar, Abu Dhabi and Dubai invested large sums of their petrodollars to attract Western top universities and to promote themselves as "globalized" educational hubs, Oman's higher education policy followed rather functional patterns: the main task was to satisfy domestic educational needs, not to export. However, local investors and governmental advisors emphasize that private institutions in Oman also intend to attract more foreign, tuition-paying students in the future (Brandenburg 2012). Due to its historical links to other Indian Ocean countries and its international degree programs, which are offered at a much cheaper rate than in Dubai or Qatar, the Sultanate might also become a regional hub for higher education services, especially for East African students. Thus in the coming years, Oman's higher education policy might shift more towards an export orientation to benefit from the country's location in the heart of the Indian Ocean Rim.

References

Al Barwani, T., Chapman, D., & Ameen, H. (2009). Strategic brain drain: Implications for higher education in Oman. *Higher Education Policy, 22*(4), 415–432.

Al Lamki, S. M. (2006). The development of private education in the Sultanate of Oman: Perceptions and analysis. *International Journal of Private Higher Education, 1*, 54–77.

Altbach, P. G. (2004). Higher education crosses borders. *Change, 36*, 18–25.

Altbach, P. G., Reisberg, L., & Rumbley, L. (2009). *Trends in global higher education: Tracking an academic revolution*. A report prepared for the UNESCO 2009 world conference on higher education, Paris. http://www.bc.edu/bc_org/avp/soe/cihe/publications/pub_pdf/UNESCO_TrendRpt.pdf. Accessed 12 June 2010.

Brandenburg, T. (2012). *Bridging the knowledge gap: Internationalization and privatization of higher education in the state of Qatar and the Sultanate of Oman*. Ph.D. thesis, Johannes Gutenberg-University, Mainz.

Chapman, D., Al Barwani, T., & Ameen, H. (2009). Expanding post-secondary access in Oman, and paying for it. In J. Knight (Ed.), *Financing access and equity in higher education* (pp. 201–218). Rotterdam: Sense Publishers.

Coffman, J. (1996). Current issues in higher education in the Arab world. *International Higher Education, 4*(Spring), 15–16.

Coffman, J. (2003). Higher education in the Gulf. Privatization and Americanization. *International Higher Education, 33*(Fall), 17–19.

Council for Higher Education Oman (CFHEO). (2005). *The strategy of higher education in Sultanate of Oman 2006–2020*. Unpublished dossier, Muscat.

Knight, J. (2005). New typologies for cross-border higher education. *International Higher Education, 38*(Winter), 3–5.

Knight, J. (2006). *Higher education crossing borders: A guide to the implications of the GATS for cross-border education*. Paris: Commonwealth of Learning/UNESCO. http://unesdoc. unesco. org/images/0014/001473/147363e.pdf. Accessed 9 Jan 2009.

Knight, J. (2007). Cross-border tertiary education: An introduction. In S. Vincent-Lancrin (Ed.), *Cross-border tertiary education. A way towards capacity building* (pp. 21–46). Paris: OECD.

Knight, J., & Altbach, P. G. (2007). The internationalization of higher education: Motivations and realities. *Journal of Studies in International Education, 11*(3–4), 290–305.

Metz, H. C. (Ed.). (1994). *Persian Gulf States: Country studies* (3rd ed.). Washington, DC: U.S. Government Printing Office. http://www.country-studies.com/persian-gulf-states. Accessed 26 July 2010.

Meyer, G., & Al Hamarneh, A. (2008, October 2–4). *Higher education in the Arab world – New strategies of expansion and models of international cooperation*. Paper presented at the 15th DAVO congress, University of Erfurt.

Ministry of Higher Education Oman (MoHE). (2005). Regulation and guidelines for establishing private universities, Colleges and Higher Education Institutes 2005. Unpublished dossier, Ruwi, Muscat.

Ministry of Higher Education Oman (MoHE). (2007). *Private higher education statistics*. Unpublished dossier, Ruwi, Muscat.

Ministry of Higher Education Oman (MoHE). (2009). *The general statistical book for higher education institutions in the Sultanate of Oman*. 6th Edition Academic year 2008–2009. Muscat. Ruwi. Unpublished dossier, Ruwi, Muscat.

Ministry of National Economy (MoNE). (2010). *Statistical yearbook 2010*. Retrieved February 17, 2011, from http://www.moneoman.gov.om

Ministry of Higher Education Oman (MoHE). (2010). The general statistical book for higher education institutions in the Sultanate of Oman. 7th edition academic year 2008–2009. Unpublished dossier, Ruwi, Muscat.

Ministry of National Economy Oman (MoNE). (2008). *Statistical yearbook 2008*. Muscat: Ruwi. http://www.moneoman.gov.om. Accessed 12 Apr 2010.

Nonneman, G. (2008). Political reform in the Gulf monarchies. From liberalisation to democratization? A comparative perspective. In A. Ehteshami & S. Wright (Eds.), *Reform in the middle east oil monarchies* (pp. 3–45). Reading: Ithaca Press.

OECD. (2008). *Tertiary education for the knowledge society. OECD thematic review of tertiary education* (Synthesis Report. Vols. 1–3). Paris. http://www.oecd.org/document/35/0,3343,en_2649_39263238_36021283_1_1_1_1,00.html. Accessed 9 Mar 2009.

Oman Ministry of Information (OMoI). (2010). *Oman 2009–2010*. http://www.omanet.om/english/oman2009-2010/main.asp. Accessed 13 Aug 2009.

Scholz, F. (Ed.). (1998). *Die Kleinen Golfstaaten*. Perthes Länderprofile. Gotha/Stuttgart: Klett-Perthes.

United Nations Development Program (UNDP). (2003). *Arab human development report 2003*. New York: Building a knowledge society.

[illegible]

Chapter 19
Bringing the Global and the Local Together Through English in Oman

Rahma Ibrahim Al-Mahrooqi and Victoria Tuzlukova

19.1 Introduction

Globalization is a pervasive phenomenon affecting the whole world, and Oman is no exception. While many insist that globalization wreaks havoc with the languages and cultures of some societies, others seem to be more optimistic about its effects. In large part globalization has been constructed by and retained through English. This chapter aims to examine ways in which English has assisted in modernizing Oman and its smooth entry into the global community. The chapter will also discuss the role of English in the local arena as a means for intercultural communication and the manifestation of Omani culture and its promotion around the world. The Omani culture is not only valuable to Oman, but is also important for the rest of the world. It is a part of the human heritage reflecting the impact of various historical, economic and social events that shaped and reshaped the world throughout history. Taking a look at how the two sides of the coin have been brought together will help us find middle ground where we can foster the unique identity of Oman while adapting to the accelerating changes in the globalized world. Examining how English, the vehicle that has enabled the spread of globalization (and vice versa), has functioned in Oman since 1970 will afford us an insight into how to forge strong connections between Omani culture and other cultures of the world.

R.I. Al-Mahrooqi (✉)
Department of English, Sultan Qaboos University, P.O. Box 42,
Postal Code 123 Al-Khoudh, Muscat, Oman
e-mail: mrahma@squ.edu.om

V. Tuzlukova
Professional Development and Research Unit, The Language Centre,
Sultan Qaboos University, P.O. Box 43, PC 123 Al-Khodh, Muscat, Sultanate of Oman
e-mail: victoria@squ.edu.om

S. Wippel (ed.), *Regionalizing Oman: Political, Economic and Social Dynamics*, United Nations University Series on Regionalism 6, DOI 10.1007/978-94-007-6821-5_19,

19.2 Globalization vs. Regionalization

"Globalization" is a word that started being used in the 1960s "as part of a wider debate about the social impact of new communication technologies" (Jackson 2004: 165) on diverse societies and cultural values. However, the concept itself is not new at all; it can be safely claimed that globalization commenced when people started travelling overland. Travel by sea and by air increased people's movement, and with the advent of modern communication technology, globalization commenced on a large scale. The Internet and cyberspace, being the fastest and most powerful tools of communication technology, have rapidly changed the world, making it possible to exchange vast amounts of information around the globe in almost no time at all. Communication technologies were first monopolized by certain powerful countries and corporations, and these entities sought economic advantages for themselves through the spread of their products and values to the rest of the world, a process that has led to both homogenization and/or hegemony, as many critiques would call it. Opinions of people who have pondered the effect of globalization have swung like a pendulum between opponents and proponents of globalization (O'Brian and Leichenko 2003).

The opponents believe that globalization leads to the spread of a capitalist mentality around the world, which in turn leads to the rule of competition and materialism. Other by-products of spreading capitalism – opponents argue – include the homogenization of the world and the standardization of global products, making big transnational corporations the main winners (Jackson 2004). They also hold that globalization causes lack of allegiance to people's countries, and so it could very well lead to the emigration of "brain power". Its homogenizing effect, it is predicted, will most probably lead to the erosion of local differences, loss of cultural identity and the spread of Western norms, values and languages, especially English, which has been the medium through which globalization was carried to the world (Jackson 2004; Short et al. 2001; O'Brian and Leichenko 2003).

The proponents argue that globalization spreads modernity, which involves the spread of technological advances around the world so everyone is a winner. They also contend that the spread of a capitalist market system can benefit all, as it increases economic efficiency and reduces prices of all types of commodities, which can lead to the betterment of life around the world. They claim that globalization has no real harmful effects on cultural identity, because this identity is deep-rooted in people and so cannot be affected in the short term by the acquisition of material goods. In fact – the proponents argue – globalization could actually foster a stronger sense of identity in the sense of creating a new identity for people coming from formerly non-cohesive societies. This was particularly true in Oman, which received many emigrants from different parts of Asia. These emigrants came to Oman for diverse reasons, such as political unrest in their countries of origin or in search of work and better opportunities. They settled in Oman and blended into the society, contributing to its development and welfare. In addition, globalization takes into consideration the "culture dimension" and adapts to local and cultural values and norms, and so it is continuously reshaped by them (Tomlinson 1999). This is consonant with Ronald Robertson's (1995) concept of glocalization, in which globalization is combined with local considerations.

Critically looking at the opinions of the opponents and the proponents, we realize that globalization does affect us in both negative and positive ways. Since it is a process that started a long time ago, its flow seems quite difficult to stop, and its effects cannot be undone (Rossiter 2001).

To minimize its effects, some analysts and critics suggested regionalization, "which refers to the growth of societal integration within a region and to the often undirected processes of social and economic interaction" (Guraziu 2008: 4). Therefore, regionalization builds and capitalizes on regional strengths as a component of globalization. In addition, it emphasizes cooperation and integration within a region with shared values and is characterized by geographic proximity. However, regionalization does not mean regional isolation, as it often leads to trans-regionalization – a process that is part of globalization. In the words of Hettne et al. (1999, cited in Guraziu 2008: 4) "the process of regionalization can only be understood within the context of globalization". Trans-regionalization is exemplified by the relationships a certain region has with another region. Arabian Gulf countries have formed the Gulf Cooperation Council, and European countries formed the European Union. These collective organizations may cooperate on various levels because there are issues of mutual concern to both entities. Hence, regionalization has become trans-regionalization.

On the other hand, Mittelman argues that "if globalization is understood to mean the compression of the time and space aspects of social relations, then regionalism is but one component of globalization. Properly understood, the dynamics of regionalism are a chapter of globalization." (Mittelman 1999, cited in Guraziu 2008: 5) Clearly, the issue of the relationship between regionalization and globalization is still controversial; nevertheless, they seem to be related.

19.3 Globalization and Culture

Having considered globalization thus far, we now turn to focus on culture, "the ontological foundation of a person's lived existence" (Heaven and Tubridy 2003: 152). According to Heaven and Tubridy, culture is "the ensemble of practices – linguistic, stylistic, religious etc. – that together form a way of being for a given community". To them, culture is "the language through which we learn to read the world. It is the daily practice of interpreting the meaning of our reality and ourselves" (ibid.). Our opinions, judgements and views of the world are influenced by our cultures, and unless we are confronted with another culture we continue to perceive the world through our own limited cultural lenses. Therefore, we might misinterpret the actions or words of people from other cultures. In the words of Heaven and Tubridy, "One's own cultural assumptions are so familiar that they seem obvious and natural, and the obviousness of our assumptions can frequently lead us to misinterpret the

7. It is the language of higher education.
8. It is the language of international safety.
9. It is the language of international law.
10. It is a "relay language" in interpretation and translation.
11. It is the language of technology transfer.
12. It is the language of Internet communication.

In addition to the above, English is the language of politics and diplomacy. It is the language of peacekeeping in the world, and it is the language used most in book publication.

Due to its dominance and presence in a multitude of domains, the English language has become the most-taught foreign and second language around the world. Teaching it effectively has entailed more than just teaching its vocabulary, structure and mechanics, because these isolated parts do not make up the whole. The whole is always greater than its parts: coherence, cohesion and the conveyance of meaning are essential parts of language. To convey meaning and communicate effectively, one has to know the conventions of the culture of the spoken language. The connection between language and culture seems to be quite obvious to many educators now; however, this was not always the case in language classrooms. In recent years, globalization has carried with it new methodologies that call for the integration of culture into the foreign language classroom. However, this has led to a dilemma about which culture into introduce and teach in the classroom: the foreign language culture or the native culture, or both, or the different cultures of the globalized world.

The current movement in foreign language education does not support a monocultural language classroom, which many view as a hindrance to effective understanding of the foreign language and to meaningful and positive communication between the native and foreign cultures. In Baker's words,

> Being positively acquainted with two languages and two cultures enables a person to have dual or multiple perspectives on society. Those who speak more than one language and own more than one culture are more sensitive and sympathetic, more likely to build bridges than barricades and boundaries… As an ideal, a person who is multicultural has more respect for other people and other cultures (Baker 2006: 375).

It follows that a person equipped with knowledge of various cultures is worldlier, less insular and less stereotypical in his or her views.

To foster positive communication in the world, it is important to educate students, especially foreign language students, about the validity of all cultural experiences, be it their own or those of the others. This can be accomplished by introducing a multicultural approach to curriculum that demonstrates that "rationality is not the monopoly of any one culture, and that understanding requires an interdependence of peoples" (ibid.: 383). English can be used to enhance and promote the identities of foreign language students through different programs. Since Oman is the focus of this chapter, two programs that are used to promote Omani culture through English will be discussed after addressing the presence of English in the Omani sociocultural context.

19.5 English in the Omani Sociocultural Context

As stated earlier, English has spread all over the world, and Oman is no exception. In its attempt to move Oman towards modernity, development and urbanization, the Omani government has realized – since the very first days of its "Renaissance" led by His Majesty Sultan Qaboos bin Said in 1970 – the importance of English in fostering Oman's advancement and its integration with the world. Therefore, English was initially included in the school curriculum starting in the fourth grade at first and then became part of school education from the first grade on. Al-Issa (2007: 199–200) holds that "Oman needs English, the only official foreign language in the country, as a fundamental tool for 'modernization', 'nationalization' and the acquisition of science and technology. The government and top Omani officials have supported the use of English in many domains such as the media and education." Nowadays, Omanis learn English for communicative and utilitarian purposes, and a "functional knowledge of English is important for travelling, pursuing higher education, finding a white-collar job, science and technology acquisition and cultural analysis and understanding" (ibid. 2007: 200). In addition, English is now essential for interacting and integrating with foreign tourists and expatriates in Oman (ibid.). English therefore coexists with Arabic almost everywhere in the country including road signage, business signage and the official documents of many government institutions. It is the medium of intercultural communication. It is also the language that cross-culturally represents Oman, offering its history, traditions, culture and natural beauty to potential tourists across the globe (Turner 2009).

The young Ministry of Tourism acknowledges the vital role that English can play in promoting Oman as a tourist destination and in the effective functioning of a multi-channel tourism communication network (Dann 1996). This network not only represents Oman cross-culturally as a tourist destination (Fodde and Denti 2005), but also assists in constructing and guiding the tourist's gaze (Urry 2002) both at the pre- and on-trip stages of the tourist experience (Capelli 2009). Tuzlukova and Al-Mahrooqi (2010) state that English has been an important tool in "featuring Oman as a tourist destination, converting marketing opportunities in tourism into sales, framing tourism as a customer-oriented industry, and enhancing tourism that is responsible and sustainable". They add, "In the tourism industry of Oman, English is an absolute necessity for effective special communication in the global tourism environment and for catering to international tourists. Therefore, English is not only the second language on almost all public signs, labels and writings, it is also the language of tourist brochures, guidebooks, web pages and websites that are aimed at promoting Oman in other parts of the world" (ibid.).

English is not only vital for the Omani tourism industry, it is also essential for communication and interaction among various interest groups in Oman. Since these groups are composed of people from different countries, not only are ideas about the areas of interest exchanged but also information about Oman and current events is circulated and discussed among members, which promotes an understanding of Oman among expatriate residents, who, in turn, often carry the message about Oman to their countries, hence spreading the word about Oman and its culture.

In addition, English is the only foreign language used in the media. There is an English Omani FM station, and the daily news is broadcast on TV in Arabic and English. There are four daily broadsheet English newspapers, which are the *Oman Observer*, the *Oman Tribune*, the *Times of Oman* and the *Muscat Daily*. Free weekly tabloid supplements or publications are also available, such as *The Week*, the *Y* and the *H!* There are monthly English publications such as *Al-Mar'a* [the Woman], a bilingual magazine directed towards women and focused on issues related to them. It has "often profiled important Omani and expatriate women personalities in Oman and tackled concerns and issues specifically impacting Omani women" (English Media in Oman 2011). The publication of a bilingual Omani women's magazine that portrays successful Omani women and addresses a range of women's issues in Oman plays a significant role in promoting the image of the country, among nationals and expatriates, as a place that believes in the equality of the sexes and provides equal opportunities in education, employment and other sectors for both men and women.

Oman Today, *Youth Observer* (a publication for school-age students, produced by the *Oman Observer* in cooperation with the Ministry of Education), *Living in the Gulf* and *Automan* are monthly English publications making reading in English available for the wider community in Oman. There are also three important publications focusing on business in Oman: *The Oman Economic Review*, *Business Today*, a bimonthly publication, and *The Business Directory of Oman*. The main feature of English publications in Oman is that they "are making available a varied range of voices reporting about the Sultanate as well as gradually raising issues that the general population was not either aware of or received erroneous information about from misinformed sources. It is also creating a platform where readers can dictate the content of the publications to a certain extent, pointing towards a certain issue or cause that they feel strongly about and urge the publications to highlight and further investigate" (English Media in Oman 2011).

Since English is the language of higher education, especially in science-based specializations, in Oman scientific publications in the form of journals are also produced in English, the most important of which are published by Sultan Qaboos University, such as SQU's *Medical Journal*, *Journal of Agricultural and Marine Sciences* and the *Science Journal*. *The Journal of Oman Studies*, published by the Ministry or Heritage and Culture, is very well known in Omani academic circles and abroad. These journals, among many others, showcase important scientific research done in the Omani context. In addition, the journals publish research by professionals in the field from the region and from around the world. Publishing such journals in English fosters communication between professionals in Oman and other professionals worldwide, providing an opportunity that raises the profile of Oman and Omani institutions in the international arena, thus promoting Oman globally.

19.6 English-Language Teaching in Oman: Its Role in Promoting Omani Culture

We are all born in a cultural milieu that instils in us certain beliefs, values and traditions that mark our identity and our perceptions of the world around us. The experiences a person has in one culture might be drastically different from the experiences another has in a second culture. And unless we are confronted with people whose values and beliefs or background are different from our own, we continue to see the world through our own cultural lenses (McGoldrick and Carter 1982). Cultures afford their members a shared identity and a cohesive framework that enables them to select, construct, interpret and assign meaning and value to the different elements and to the experiences they encounter.

Our experiences are grounded in our cultures and are stored in our mental records. Lucinda Clark paraphrases Applebee's description of these mental records when she writes:

> We function psychologically by building a systematic representation of experience. The system of representation is a mental record of our past experiences. Each new experience modifies the representation, which we have been constructing. The constructed representation guides us in interpreting experience (Clark 1997: 23–24).

Language is part of culture. It is the symbolic representation of experience. In Clark's words, "language is the personal interpretive symbol of experience" (Clark 1997: 23). The power of language to represent experience in symbols means that language is the carrier of culture and that the two are inseparable. Language is also the linguistic representation of thought. In his assertion that language contains three levels of organization – sound, form and meaning (where sound and form emphasize structure while meaning emphasizes the relationship between thought and language) – Michael Halliday (1975) seems to agree with the idea that language is the symbolic representation of thought. According to him, language is also organized as a system for making meaning, rather than a device for generating structures.

Language is not only a mechanism for conveying meaning, but also a signal of identification and a most eloquent symbol of group identity (Suleiman 1994, cited in Lin 1998). Louise Damen (1987) holds that culture is transmitted through language and that cultural patterns are actually reflected in the language of the group. The fact that language is the carrier of culture has many implications for learners of English as a foreign language. These learners come to the English classroom already literate in their mother tongue, which carries their native culture. Then, when these learners read in their mother tongue, they are familiar both with the language and its culture. This means comprehension difficulties are minimal in comparison to those they might face when reading a new language that reflects a culture foreign to them. Despite the difficulties foreign language learners may face when learning a foreign language due to cultural differences, it is important that they be exposed to the foreign language within its culture and in authentic situations. Authentic materials and tasks that are meaningful and purposeful have to be integrated in the curriculum. To acknowledge and validate the identities of learners, their own culture has to be reflected into the curriculum. This will empower them and give them a sense of pride in their own cultural traditions and will enable them to talk about their cultures to others. If given the opportunity to do so, learners can use the foreign language to exchange information about their own culture and heritage with students or individuals from other cultures inside and outside their country.

Hence, teaching a foreign language allows learners to find a new voice to express who and what they are as people of cultures that have similarities to and differences from all the other cultures around the world. Yen (2000: 25) asserts that foreign language instruction "is to help students both find and create voices in a new language". To the same effect, many educators argue that English is not the possession of native speakers alone but now belongs to the world. Yen states that "students should have the right to use the new language to introduce their own culture and maintain their own cultural heritage" (ibid.: 52). It is therefore crucial that teachers integrate students' culture into the foreign language classroom. And since literature embodies culture, it is the perfect avenue for bridging the differences between the native and the foreign cultures, or for nurturing the similarities between the two. Disciplined conversations and negotiation of meaning between the cultural situation of the text and the reader are essential in the foreign literature classroom (Corcoran 1991, cited in Jolly 2000: 5). In fostering communication between the two cultures, the social and psychological distance between the two will be minimized, allowing greater appreciation and more learning. When that is done, favourable attitudes and intrinsic and/or integrative motivation are bound to ensue (Matsui 2000; Thompson 1991).

Omani schools have realized the importance of opening dialogues between Omani students and English-speaking students in Oman and around the world. Fawzia Al-Seyabi (2010: 81–82) mentions two types of initiatives that promote students' cultural and intercultural awareness and foster their sense of pride in their national identity. The first of these initiatives is the Experiential Learning Program (henceforth ELP) offered at the Language Centre of Sultan Qaboos University. The ELP is a program that gives students specializing in English the opportunity to visit international schools in Muscat and to interact with staff and students in English. This is advantageous to the students, as they get the chance to practice their English and to listen to it in authentic settings, and it is advantageous to the international students and staff who are eager to learn about the culture that hosts them. In this program, students spend 1 day at school as teacher assistants in classes that teach subjects such as math, music, drama and information and computer technology (ICT) in English. In these classes, much cultural information is exchanged between these teacher assistants and students. In addition, the teacher assistants are required to prepare presentations on topics related to Omani culture, such as clothes, food, handicrafts and folktales. They also organize one very important event called the Omani Cultural Day, in which a repertoire of Omani cultural activities is planned and executed in the international school to allow its staff and students to get a dose of Omani culture.

The second example Al-Seyabi mentions is an initiative called "Connecting Classrooms" (Al-Seyabi 2010: 84). This is an international partnership program launched in 2006 and sponsored by the British Council in coordination with the

Ministry of Education in Oman. In this program, operating on the basis of Internet correspondence and parcel exchange (i.e. exchange of cultural goods, letters, folktales etc.), students from participating Omani schools work closely with British students in the UK on joint projects. The partnership lasts for 3 years, and participating schools from Oman and the UK engage their students in a variety of projects that take them outside the classroom and into an active process of learning about themselves and others as cultural beings. This has been a successful partnership program that has resulted in much collaboration and information exchange between students of both countries, Oman and Britain.

The two examples above are excellent initiatives that should be emulated by the various English-language institutions in Oman to foster cooperation and the exchange of information between Omani students and students around the globe.

19.7 Conclusion

English has been taken into the fabric of Omani social, economic and educational life. It has acquired a momentum and vitality of its own and has helped in promoting the local culture in many ways. In Oman, there is no heightened sense of fear that globalization and the spread of English use might endanger Omani cultural identity, and most students learn the language because it is a school subject and because it is needed in higher education. They learn it for instrumental and utilitarian purposes, such as getting better grades in school and securing good employment after graduation (Fahmy and Bilton 1992: 269–289). In fact, research has found that equipping Omani women with English fosters their sense of identity and affords them a feeling of freedom and confidence (Jabur 2008). Omani government and officials have supported the use of English in different domains due to the belief that English is an essential tool for the advancement of the country and its integration with the rest of the world. English is now used as a medium to promote Oman and its culture by fostering intercultural communication between Omanis and the rest of the world.

Because of English and many other economic, political and social factors, Oman is transcending locality and moving towards universality while maintaining its unique cultural identity, as a result of His Majesty Sultan Qaboos bin Said's wise and forward-looking vision for the country. Globalization has not thus far adversely affected the country, due to His Majesty's wise leadership. A process of glocalization has taken place in the country, and English has helped in the process of domesticating what is foreign to the local taste. The country is also taking part in a regionalization process. It is consolidating relationships with other Gulf countries that are dependent to a great extent on foreign labour, a fact that calls for the use of English since it is the language of international communication. However, this regionalization is just a step in the globalization process. English has helped in promoting the country worldwide. Tourism is a sector in which English is greatly needed. Other languages might also be needed in the future, but English is currently serving the purpose.

His Majesty Sultan Qaboos' vision and balanced policies and views regarding education, economy and politics are expected to lead to further accomplishment in the future.

References

Al-Issa, A. S. (2007). The implications of implementing a 'Flexible' syllabus for ESL policy in the Sultanate of Oman. *Regional Language Centre Journal, 38*(1), 199–215.
Al-Seyabi, F. (2010). Promoting Oman's cultural heritage through ELT. In R. Al-Mahrooqi & V. Tuzlukova (Eds.), *The Omani ELT symphony: Maintaining linguistic and socio-cultural equilibrium* (pp. 71–91). Muscat: Sultan Qaboos University Press.
Baker, C. (2006). *Foundations of bilingual education and bilingualism* (4th ed.). Portland: Multilingual Matters Ltd.
Billing, M. (1995). *Banal nationalism*. London: Sage.
Capelli, G. (2009). *Spatial representation in English and Italian guidebooks*. Paper presented at the 24th conference of the Italian Association for English Studies, challenges for the 21st century: Dilemmas, Ambiguities, Directions, Rome. http://www.gloriacappelli.it/blog/media/cappelli_abstractesp.pdf. Accessed 15 July 2010.
Clark, L. (1997). *Three students' sense of genre: A study of the oral language reconstruction of story and information books*. Ph.D. dissertation, University of Pittsburgh.
Damen, L. (1987). *Cultural learning: The fifth dimension in the language classroom*. Reading: Addison-Wesley.
Dann, G. (1996). *The language of tourism: A sociolinguistic perspective*. Wallingford: CABI Publishing.
English media in Oman. (2011). http://oumabdulaziz.jeeran.com/media.html. Accessed 27 Jan 2011.
Fahmy, J. J., & Bilton, L. (1992). The sociocultural dimension of TEFL education: The Omani file. *Journal of Multilingual and Multicultural Development, 13*(3), 269–289.
Fodde, L., & Denti, O. (2005). Cross-cultural representations in tourist discourse: The image of Sardinia in English tourist guides. In M. Bondi & N. Maxwell (Eds.), *Cross-cultural encounters – Linguistic perspective* (pp. 116–129). Rome: Officina Edizioni.
Gu, M. (2010). Identities constructed in difference: English language learners in China. *Journal of Pragmatics, 42*(1), 243–256.
Guraziu, R. (2008). *Is regionalism a stumbling block or a stepping stone in the process of globalization?* Unpublished MA Thesis in International Relations, Middlesex University.
Halliday, M. (1975). *Learning how to mean: Explorations in the development of language*. London: Edward Arnold.
Heaven, C., & Tubridy, M. (2003). *Global youth culture and youth identity*. In Oxfam International Youth Parliament (OIYP) Oxfam Community Aid Abroad. In Highly affected, rarely considered: IYP Youth Commission into globalization report (pp. 149–160). http://www.comminit.com/en/node/177170/306. Accessed 15 July 2010.
Jabur, Z. M. (2008). *A qualitative study of Omani Muslim women's perceived experiences as writers in English as a second language*. Ph.D. dissertation, Indiana University of Pennsylvania. http://dspace.lib.iup.edu:8080/dspace/bitstream/2069/130/Zainab+Jabur.pdf. Accessed 15 July 2010.
Jackson, P. (2004). Local consumption cultures in a globalizing world. *Royal Geographer Society, 29*, 165–178.
Jolly, C. N. (2000). *Reader response and the language minority students*. Unpublished Ph.D. dissertation, University of Calgary.
Lin, K. Y. (1998). *ESL students' comprehension and proficiency in Taiwan*. Ph.D. dissertation, University of South Dakota.

Matsui, Sh. (2000). *The relevance of native language in foreign language acquisition: The critical period hypothesis for foreign language pronunciation*. Ph.D. dissertation, The University of Texas.
McGoldrick, M., & Carter, B. (1982). Normal families: An ethnic perspective. In F. Walsh (Ed.), *Normal family processes* (pp. 167–195). New York: Guildford Press.
Norton, B., & Tang, C. (1997). The identity of the non-native ESL teacher on the power and status of non-native ESL teachers. *TESOL Quarterly, 31*(3), 577–580.
O'Brian, K., & Leichenko, R. (2003). Winners and losers in the context of global exchange. *Annals of the Association of American Geographers, 93*(1), 89–103.
Robertson, R. (1995). Glocalization: Time-space and homogeneity-heterogeneity. In M. Featherstone, S. Lash, & R. Robertson (Eds.), *Global modernities* (pp. 25–44). London: Sage.
Rossiter, A. (2001). *Globalization? What globalization? Linguapress EFL resource*. http://members.aol.com/linguapress/globaliz.htm. Accessed 15 Oct 2010.
Short, J., Boniche, A., et al. (2001). Cultural globalization, global English, and geography journals. *The Professional Geographer, 53*(1), 1–11.
Thompson, I. (1991). Foreign accents revisited: The English pronunciation of Russian immigrants. *Language Learning, 41*, 177–204.
Tomlinson, J. (1999). *Globalization and culture*. Chicago: University of Chicago Press.
Turner, L. (2009). Oman tourism: An international perspective on international tourist arrivals. *Omani Journal of Applied Sciences, 1*(1), 1–7. http://www.cas.edu.om/ojas/OJAS_OMAN%20Tourism%20An%20International%20Perspective.doc. Accessed 10 Aug 2010.
Tuzlukova, V., & Al-Mahrooqi, R. (2010). *The landscape of tourism in Oman within the context of the English language*. Paper presented at the 4th international conference on responsible tourism in destinations, Muscat.
Urry, J. (2002). *The tourist gaze. Leisure and travel in contemporary societies* (2nd ed.). London: Sage.
Yen, Y.-Y. (2000). *Identity issues in EFL and ESL textbooks: A socio-cultural perspective*. Ph.D. dissertation, Ohio State University.
Zaghoul, M. (2003). Globalization and EFL/ESL pedagogy in the Arab world. *Journal of Language and Learning, 1*(2), 106–146. http://www.jllonline.co.uk/journal/jllearn/1_2/zughoul.html. Accessed 15 July 2010.

Part V
Conclusion

Chapter 20
Concluding Remarks: Regionalizing Oman Beyond Conventional Metageographies

Steffen Wippel

20.1 Opening Up Spatial Containers to Complex Regional Contexts

The initial statement in this volume, that in politics, media and even academia the study of human agency and social relations is still often limited to the two spatio-scalar dimensions of the territorial nation-state and (quasi-)continental world-regions, is also true for the southeastern part of the peninsular landmass that stretches between the northwestern part of the Indian Ocean, the Persian Gulf, the Red Sea and the Syrian Desert. Political, social, economic and even cultural activities are mostly inscribed into the territorial boundaries of the state called the "Sultanate of Oman", which in turn is itself regularly subsumed as an allegedly self-evident part of the "Arab world" or the "Middle East (and North Africa)".

Even history is being realigned to the territory of the state, whose current form and name have only been consolidated since 1970. Yet, in the past, like other pre-modern states, for certain periods Oman constituted an empire with blurred, fluctuating frontiers, changing allegiances and loyalties, overlapping and graded areas of power, partly extending to distant lands across large waters (Fig. 20.1). Inheriting a relatively weak state and a neither clearly defined nor thoroughly controlled territory, modern Oman experienced a difficult national process of integrating previously quite autonomous regions, dispersed (and, to this day with Musandam, territorially non-contiguous) parts[1] and of various social and ethno-linguistic groups, including those that immigrated or remigrated over the last decades.

[1] The last Omani "overseas" possession, Gwadar, on the Makran coast of what is now Pakistan, was relinquished in 1958.

S. Wippel (✉)
Zentrum Moderner Orient (ZMO), Kirchweg 33, 14129 Berlin, Germany
e-mail: steffen.wippel@t-online.de; steffen.wippel@zmo.de

S. Wippel (ed.), *Regionalizing Oman: Political, Economic and Social Dynamics*, United Nations University Series on Regionalism 6, DOI 10.1007/978-94-007-6821-5_20,

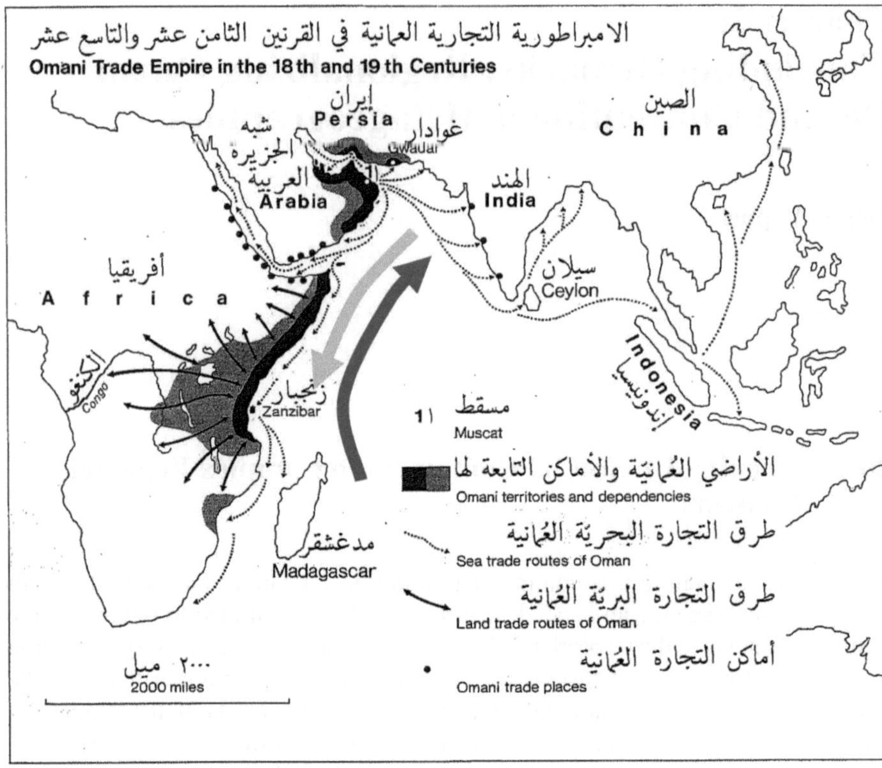

Fig. 20.1 The Omani Empire in the eighteenth and nineteenth centuries. *Black*: Territories and dependencies. *Grey*: Territories under strong Omani influence. ◀— Prevailing monsoon winds in winter —▶ Prevailing monsoon winds in summer. By courtesy of Fred Scholz, Berlin (Source: Scholz (1980: 102). Supplemented by the author)

Assertion of continuous territorial control was particularly difficult. In contrast to other non-Western parts of the world, the territorialisation of the Arab Peninsula was not completed during colonial times (Gabriel 1999). Only the discovery of oil and the contracting of exploration concessions increasingly called for the definition of borders since the 1930s. But agreements and demarcation were slow and produced a number of conflicts. The Buraimi border crisis that culminated in the 1950s (cf. also Kelly 1956; Steinbeck 1962, 1965; Al-Sayegh 2002), Saudi interference in other local conflicts and the Dhofar War from the mid-1960s to the mid-1970s, demonstrate that tensions between Oman and its immediate neighbours also included conflicts about territorial sovereignty and delimitation.[2] Besides, covert imaginations of a prolonged nation actually reaching into the "Trucial Oman" cut off by the British still seem to circulate (Al-Sayegh 2002; Valeri 2007: 348). Finally,

[2]For these conflicts, please consult the general literature on Oman mentioned in the introduction to this volume.

state borders were not entirely determined until the early 2000s.[3] Even more, the previously open border zones increasingly become more severally monitored and securitized, such as in the Buraimi area, where the UAE recently built a fence along the border. As a quite young state, it is comprehensible that Oman for a long time and to this day shows reluctance to abandon sovereignty (as in the case of the Gulf monetary union) and engages in "shallow" regional integration (such as in the Indian Ocean scheme).

Yet, this volume endeavours to show the diverse facets, the multiple dimensions and the continuous flux of the regionalisation processes of which Oman, its people and society are part. Several authors point to the political fiction of a united and homogenous state as well as highlighting endeavours to create such a national unity (e.g. Pradhan, Valeri, Chatty, Verne and Müller-Mahn, Al-Mahrooqi and Tuzlukova). They illustrate that it will not be sufficient to regard Oman from the sole perspective of either a national or regional container, which concentrates on processes, developments and interlacements within well-defined, closed and contiguous geographical entities. Instead, authors demonstrate multiple passages, relations and links to the "outside" world as well as Oman's belonging to, involvement in and orientation towards manifold regional contexts. However, regions and scales are often difficult to define, just as exact attribution of concrete places, activities and life conditions proves to be problematic. Whereas both regions and scales are repeatedly in motion, some regional settings are starting to sediment and to be institutionalized, even if geographical outlines, e.g. of regional organisations, also regularly shift or are disputed. At the same time, "fuzzy" shapes contrast with the difficult task of finding adequate categories and names to designate "regions" without fixing them permanently.

Contributing to this is not only the central state as a unitary actor, but also a large number of diverse individual and collective social agents within and outside the state and the country. They are part of and act in a large range of political, economic, social and cultural fields and are of various geographical and social origin. They often present themselves in multiple roles simultaneously or change fields of action over time. Regularly, several social fields and material, institutional and symbolic dimensions are closely interrelated, and institutionalised and informal activities complement and interpenetrate each other. Yet they do not necessarily shape congruent spaces, but often show spatial mismatch.

Contributions to this volume also show the importance of discourses and symbols in the building of regions. Historical aspects matter, too: evolutions of the past open out into contemporary development paths; and recourse to historical interconnections strategically ties, substantiates and legitimises current ones. Reference is thereby often made to the historical Omani land and sea empire from before modern

[3]Borders with Saudi Arabia were not agreed upon until 1990 and the border agreements with Yemen and the UAE were not signed until 1992 and 2002 respectively (demarcation with the UAE was finalized in 2008). Maritime boundaries were delimitated with Iran in 1974, with Pakistan in 2000, and with Yemen in 2003 (UN 2010).

territorial states were established. But when historical links are continued or revived, mostly it is now other, new actors, such as multinational companies, state or regional institutions and transnational migrants, who are involved in their re-emergence and consolidation.

Finally, region-making can be regarded from different conceptual angles, from different observers' and actors' viewpoints and with quite different foci and underlying questions. Contributions to this book take a wide range of approaches and open up a lot of new perspectives on regionalisation processes in and around Oman. Whereas some of the present papers concentrate on institutional forms of regionalisation, highly formalized flows and attempts at interstate regulation, many others focus on the translocal character of places, people and their activities, relations and networks, which are quite often informal and transgress territorial borders by trying to evade state control. Regionalisation takes place not only through harmonious cooperation, but also through diverse conflicts; at the same time flows, interconnections and spaces encompass delimitations, oppositions as well as power asymmetries.

In the next paragraphs, this concluding chapter will sum up the emerging multiplex social geographies from above and below, as demonstrated in the previous chapters, first with respect to different regional contexts and scales, then from the perspective of the diverse social actors and fields that participate in region-building.

20.2 A Multidirectional and Multiscalar Regionalisation Process

The processes of regionalisation studied in this volume point in different geographical directions and occur on multiple spatial scales. Very often, the previous chapters refer to the Gulf region, mainly the Arab part of it, and sometimes to the Arabian Peninsula. In the past, the Gulf already featured centres of interregional trade (Pradhan) and was part of Oman's maritime empire and network of trade routes (Dietl, Nicolini). In more recent times, the Gulf economies have been important partners and hubs for the Sultanate's external economic relations (Wippel) and a main destination for migrants, e.g. from India (Pradhan), Zanzibar (Verne and Müller-Mahn) and Oman (Benz). For the last 30 years, the Arab side of the Gulf has become more and more institutionalized in the Gulf Cooperation Council (GCC), which fuses economic and security dimensions and increasingly shows a "differentiated" type of integration (Zorob, Dietl, Wippel). For Brandenburg, the area constitutes a regional university landscape. Common matrimonial practices create similar health problems and foster exchange and cooperation on these issues (Beaudevin). But as already demonstrated for the Middle East and the Arab world (Wippel, in Chap. 1), the controversy about the "right" name for the "Persian" or "Arab" Gulf (Krause 2001) – or even its geographical extension (Zorob) – is subject to strategic considerations and reveals again the political sensitivity of allegedly value-free geographical designations.

Implicitly or explicitly, Oman is also regarded as a part of the Indian Ocean region (historically, see e.g. Nicolini). Wippel shows how institutional links, economic flows and strategic communication contribute to its constitution. According to Brandenburg, Oman should make use of its location in the heart of the Indian Ocean to become a regional hub for higher education. He especially points to its potential role for East Africa. This part of Africa in particular is mentioned as part of Oman's former transcontinental empire and trade connections, which extended along the coast and far into the hinterland (cf. also Nicolini, Dietl). Even diseases remind us of such historical links (Beaudevin). In this context, there is special interest in the relationship with Oman's former political and economic centre, Zanzibar, itself regarded as a commercial and cultural node in regional and global networks (Nicolini, Verne and Müller-Mahn). Verne and Müller-Mahn extensively investigate family, business and imaginary ties between remigrants to Oman and their former home, Zanzibar. "Zanzibar" stands not only for this island of relatively small size, but also for Oman's wider historical interests and presence in Eastern Africa. Asia, the other metageographical world region linked by the Indian Ocean, is mentioned mostly in economic contexts (e.g. Wippel) and itself divides into subregions. Among them, Central Asia was part of historical trade relations of the Gulf economies (Pradhan) as well as being included in the wider trans-Hormuz trade and future transport networks (Benz).

In contrast to these regions, the authors rarely bring up the subject of belonging to the "Arab" (or even "Muslim") world. Beaudevin points to common health problems and the role of "Arabness" in social status. Faculty has been imported from Arab countries, and Gulf universities are models for the other Arab countries. Egypt in particular was a traditional destination for studies abroad (Brandenburg) and a refuge for Zanzibaris after the revolution (Verne and Müller-Mahn).

Finally, from the Western world, colonial powers, such as the Portuguese and the British, arrived in the Indian Ocean and the Gulf areas in earlier centuries (Pradhan, Nicolini, Benz). Rather early, Indian traders already mediated exchange with Great Britain, the United States and Germany (Pradhan). Zanzibaris emigrated to Europe (Verne and Müller-Mahn), and in the health sector Europe is linked with Oman by training and expertise (Beaudevin). In particular the US and the UK are main destinations for studying abroad. In turn, the higher education system in the Gulf region is mostly modelled on the Anglo-American pattern (Brandenburg). Al-Mahrooqi and Tuzlukova point to the English-speaking world as a discontinuous and nearly globally-spanning linguistic macro-region.

As this volume focuses on "regional" processes and entanglement, bilateral relations are not in the centre of interest. Yet, they can also produce, initiate, counter or be part of regionalisation trends (for Oman's network of bilateral agreements cf. Wippel). Thus, several articles refer to formal interstate and informal transborder links and concomitant or competing region-building.

Besides Zanzibar, an "independent" political entity only until 1964, India is certainly among the most important references, due to the long history of interconnections, their multifacetedness and complexity. Pradhan actually sees Omani-Indian relations as (part of) a multiple regionalisation process. This not only concerns links between the two countries, specifically with areas along India's western coast, but also integration into far larger, plurilocal migration and sea trade networks. In the field of health, India is a source of medical practices and staff as well as, together with Pakistan, a destination for therapeutic journeys (Beaudevin); in the education sector, it is a major origin of faculty (Brandenburg).

Another important counterpart is Iran, and especially its coastal areas, too. Nicolini refers to historical links with Persia. For Dietl, historical ties, past military support and common interests count in making Iran a main political partner for Oman, whereas Benz concentrates on the intense trade and social links between Musandam and the opposite coast. With respect to regional organisations, Iran provided a main motivation to found the GCC (Zorob). In the IOR-ARC, Iran and India are among the most engaged members, together with Oman (Wippel).

Among the nearby countries, the United Arab Emirates (and particularly Abu Dhabi) also has a special role for Oman as an associate in the GCC, a direct neighbour, relations with which are sometimes ambivalent (Zorob), an important trade partner (Benz, Wippel, Zorob) and a main destination for students (Brandenburg) and migrants (Benz). The UAE is also part of the translocal desertscape of the Harasiis (Chatty), together with the southern edge of Saudi Arabia. The kingdom itself is a second economic partner among the Arab Gulf states (Benz, Wippel), but above all a neighbour rather feared for its interference in domestic affairs and attempts to dominate the GCC (Dietl, Zorob).

More distant, "interregional" relations exist with the United States. Zorob studies the common free trade area, with wider Middle East aspirations behind it, and its interferences with the Gulf project; Dietl regards the US as Oman's central (and disputed) political partner that ultimately will impact on other regional relations.

Several authors in this volume study mainly intranational processes and describe the multiple internal regional antagonisms and cleavages. As already mentioned in my conceptual chapter, this includes in particular spatially reflected binary oppositions – traditional and contemporary, observed and alleged – within Oman; at the same time, the close social and economic interaction, and even symbiosis, between these different spaces is demonstrated (cf. also Chatty, Beaudevin, Nicolini). In this context, Mokhtar investigates the economic and demographic strengthening of littoral areas. Abdelghani studies the regionalisation of retail trade, in particular in the capital area. In contrast, private universities contribute to reducing regional imbalances (Brandenburg). Valeri looks at the de-autonomising of infranational solidarities and legitimacies that have become subordinated to the central state; administrative territories, repeatedly reorganised (Fig. 20.2) and superseding tribal areas, themselves became arenas for regional identification and socio-political protest. At the same time, the power of the sheikhs became more territorialized, yet outside their areas of origin.

Finally, other authors look at transborder regions, such as Musandam (Benz) and the Jiddat il-Harasiis (Chatty), and their ambivalent relations with the contemporary territorial nation-state, including links with other parts of Oman. For Dietl, a geopolitical area emerges that centres on the Strait of Hormuz. In her historical study, Hoffmann-Ruf rewrites the regional micro-history of a rural community with

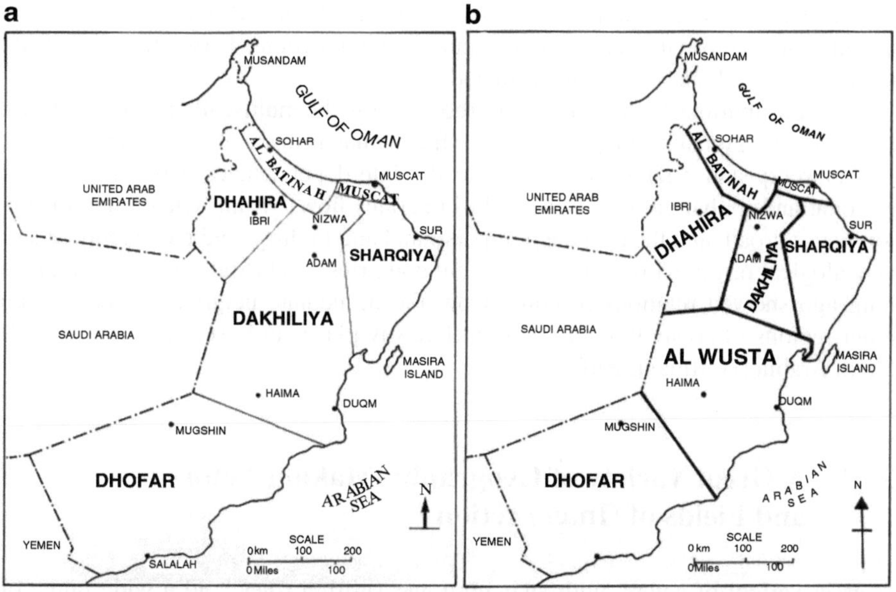

Fig. 20.2 Administrative division of Oman prior to and after 1991. **a**) Oman prior to 1991. **b**) Oman after 1991 (Notes: Al-Buraimi was created from parts of al-Dhahira in 2006. In 2011 al-Batinah and al-Sharqiya were divided in two Northern and Southern governorates each. By courtesy of Dawn Chatty, Oxford)

fluctuating translocal links. Additional authors have a strong focus on translocal and transnational connections in a wider context, too (Pradhan, Verne and Müller-Mahn, Beaudevin). Historically existing links and moves often became transnational when territorial borders were drawn and nation-states were established.

Regional belonging, however, is not unidimensional. Some authors emphasise actors' and places' location at the interface between several world regions, exemplifying Oman's multiple regional orientations. Nicolini thereby underlines Oman's historical situation at the crossroads between East Africa, the Gulf and Western India, with people pouring in from different directions and trade networks reaching far into the respective hinterlands. Similarly, Verne and Müller-Mahn point to the multidirectional links of Zanzibar; and for Pradhan, the Gulf economies are old trade hubs between the Fertile Crescent, the historic Silk Road and India. Geostrategically speaking, Dietl situates Oman today between the Arab Gulf states and the Iranian landmass. Institutionally, Oman is simultaneously embedded in the GCC, GAFTA and IOR-ARC (Wippel, Zorob), and Omani self-marketing emphasises the country's multi- and interregional location (Wippel). Brandenburg, finally, shows an entangled regionalisation process in higher education between the Western and the English-speaking world and the Gulf region.

Given Oman's special location and history, the interpenetration of sea and land is underlined as well. Thus, Nicolini insists on the reciprocal and common influence of land and maritime factors, whereas Verne and Müller-Mahn's seascape in fact reaches far into the coastal hinterlands of Africa and Oman. But also contemporary Oman shows a close interconnection – and often opposition – between the coast and the interior (Mokhtar, Abdelghani, Beaudevin).

The contributions to this volume moreover show the multiscalar and multidistant character of regionalisation processes in which Oman is involved. Thus, for example, Al-Mahrooqi and Tuzlukova investigate the interdependencies between national, regional and global culture. Beaudevin integrates flows within Oman, therapeutic journeys abroad, and the exchange of personnel and findings and reconstructions of genealogical origin with even more distant countries. And local tribal communities long ago showed relations reaching from the immediate neighbourhood through other regions of contemporary Oman to faraway places in East Africa and today's Saudi Arabia (Hoffmann-Ruf).

20.3 A Great Variety of Geography-Making Actors and Fields of (Inter)Action

A great variety of actors, with switching and shifting roles, and a wide range of fields of activities and interaction, of discourses and imaginaries and of types of flows contribute to the multilayered and multidirectional regionalisation processes investigated in this volume. Even actors having the same "national" background come from widely diverging social settings, act in different social fields and have diverse motives to do so. In this context, other geographical perspectives emerge in this section, e.g. on specific Omani "trade" or "migration regions" besides those in other social fields and from other local standpoints.

As already mentioned, "states", that represent governments and official authorities and are often equated with respective rulers, their policies, strategies and activities in a regional perspective are still an important object of study (e.g. for Dietl, Zorob, Wippel) as well as state intervention in other actors' everyday life (esp. Chatty, Valeri). However, in many chapters more differentiated groups and actors appear inside the "state" with eventually diverging interests and positions, such as the security apparatus (Nicolini, Verne and Müller-Mahn), the administrative and development bureaucracy (Valeri, Chatty) and ministries of health and education (Beaudevin, Brandenburg). Others investigate the changing influence and contacts of sheikhs as additional political leaders and their ambivalent relationship with central authorities (Hoffmann-Ruf, Nicolini, Valeri).

From a state perspective, political fields are at the forefront of regionalisation. Here, we often have to do with the making of geopolitics and geoeconomics. Security issues are of primary concern: whereas Nicolini addresses past wars and conflicts in the northwestern Indian Ocean, Verne and Müller-Mahn have to start with revolution in and expulsion from Zanzibar and Dietl basically concentrates on geostrategies around the Strait of Hormuz. Conflicts in the Gulf area also form the background for trade relations and motives for regional cooperation (Benz, Zorob). People from the Indian subcontinent have long been recruited into Omani military and police forces (Pradhan). Problems and attempts to achieve control over modern Oman's territory are considered by Valeri and Benz.

In the economic realm, over the last years Oman's cooperation and integration policies concentrated on the Gulf, the Arab world, the Indian Ocean rim and the US (Zorob, Wippel). The regional dimension of monetary policy is shown in the Sultanate's renouncing position towards GCC monetary integration (Zorob) and in effectively overlapping currency zones in Musandam (Benz). Infrastructure development – inland road networks (Abdelghani, Mokhtar), Indian Ocean ports (Wippel), planned ferry lines to Iran and transport corridors to Central Asia (Benz) – is an essential physical basis for regional movement and integration. Strategic positioning of Oman in the context of the Indian Ocean and major contemporary sea trade routes takes place in the marketing and branding of the country with the aim of legitimising and promoting trade, tourism and transport policies and projects (Wippel). Finally, regional profiles of domestic policies in areas such as health (Beaudevin) and education (Brandenburg) are related to the Gulf, the West and India, among other regions.

Also regularly participating in regionalisation processes are other economic actors such as seafarers, traders, businessmen, bankers, carriers, consumers and retail traders (Pradhan, Benz, Verne and Müller-Mahn, Nicolini, Benz, Abdelghani). In regard to trade in the past, Oman's position in the triangle of the Gulf, the Indian subcontinent and Eastern Africa is considered in particular (Nicolini, Pradhan). Contemporary trade extends, in varying degrees (also depending on commodities and measurement methods), to all regions adjacent to the wider Indian Ocean, but there are also considerable economic links with Western Europe and the USA (Zorob, Wippel). Transstate trade networks stretch from Musandam to both sides of the Persian Gulf and – to a degree not yet investigated – also towards Central Asia (Benz, Dietl), whereas translocal business ties are being re-established between Oman and Zanzibar (Verne and Müller-Mahn). Regional flows of money take place in direct investment, primarily between Oman and Western countries, Arab Gulf economies and India (Wippel), in Gulf aid (Zorob), in financial support for relatives in Zanzibar and in migrants' remittances, e.g. to India (Pradhan).

Social relations form quite different spaces. Family relations, involving multiform exchange, are the basis for a renewed Oman-Zanzibar relationship (Verne and Müller-Mahn). Nicolini mentions the marriages arranged to establish good relations between different countries' rulers in the past. Migrants play another important role in translocal processes linked with Oman. Besides Verne and Müller-Mahn's focus on the Zanzibar-Omanis, who are refugees and remigrants, others consider work migration in its regional dimensions, with people coming to Oman mainly from Asian and Arab countries: Pradhan, in particular, investigates Indian migrants of different ethno-religious, socio-professional and regional origin in the past (cf. also Nicolini) and present, whereas the Omani university and health systems offer employment opportunities for a wide range of expatriates (Brandenburg, Beaudevin). In modern times, Omani workers have also left for neighbouring Gulf countries (Benz). Illegal migrants from Iran and South Asia transit via Musandam to the UAE or, if blocked, stay in Oman (Dietl).

Other regular, often seasonal movements are engaged in by tribe members, for example, by the Harasiis moving nomadically between Oman and the UAE (Chatty) and in Musandam moving between the coast and the mountains as fishermen and peasants (Benz). Others investigate historical tribal areas in and beyond the contemporary al-Dakhiliya governorate (Hoffmann Ruf) and the disrobing of the political content of traditional tribal territories all over the Sultanate (Valeri). In parallel to that, these tribes, together with other ethno-linguistic groups, show changing roles and activities in the processes of nation-building, modernisation and globalisation. They are markers of ancestry, but also of health issues (Beaudevin). Pradhan and Verne and Müller-Mahn consider the Indian expat community's and the Zanzibaris' ambivalent links with contemporary Omani society in translocal and multi-ethnic places, such as Muscat or Oman in general, respectively.

Tourism – in particular from Western and Gulf countries – constitutes an important element in economic regionalisation processes (Zorob, Wippel), and tourism facilities are being built to help develop remote parts of Oman (Benz). Due to migration and tourism, consumption patterns in Oman are subject to multiple influences of cuisines of the East and the West, and regular shuttling for shopping takes place between the hinterland and Muscat (Abdelghani). The medical landscape emerging from the treatment of genetic diseases includes several flows of patients, staff and expertise: they go from the Omani countryside to the capital and to and from the Indian subcontinent, the Gulf and Europe, and they encompass imaginations of opposing national regions and ancestral links with Africa and Asia (Beaudevin).

The cultural field comprises moves for purposes of higher education: this includes students and faculty, consultants and investors, as well as ideas and role models, shifting mainly among Oman, the West, the Gulf and India, and potentially East Africa and other Indian Ocean countries (Brandenburg). Language and the media serve communication, information and the promotion of Omani culture, especially with expatriates and tourists within Oman and in the wider English-speaking community (Al-Mahrooqi and Tuzlukova). News exchange is also an essential basis on which social relations between Zanzibar-Omanis and their relatives in Eastern Africa are maintained (Verne and Müller-Mahn).

Finally, "external" actors and powers have an important role in regionalisation, too. Not of Omani descent, they can interfere from outside Oman as well as be directly present inside the country. Colonial powers, such as the Portuguese and the British, who arrived in different centuries in the Indian Ocean and the Gulf areas (Pradhan, Nicolini, Benz), and the US administration (Dietl, Zorob) have played important roles. International agencies, NGOs and experts (Chatty) and multi- and transnational companies, e.g. in retail and extractive sectors (Chatty, Abdelghani), intervene to different degrees and in different places. Even the transnational and partly elitist Zanzibar-Omani community displays traits of being outsiders (Verne and Müller-Mahn). Yet, a clear division between actors internal and external to a region becomes quite difficult, and even inappropriate, when we consider transnational and translocal entanglement and regional contexts with blurring and intersecting shapes, limits and scales.

20.4 A Need for Further Investigation from a Regional Perspective

The present volume shows the multiform, multidirectional and multiscalar regionalisation processes in, across and around contemporary Oman. Despite being quite extensive, this publication cannot be exhaustive. More insights already exist – sometimes implicitly rather than explicitly – in other publications, but in many more respects Oman and the Gulf area still need to be explored from a frankly regional perspective; micro-, transstate and translocal approaches are of special interest. For example, Omanis' shopping tour destinations include Dubai and thus display a transnational element; piracy recently arising off Oman's coasts is of transterritorial character, too; and maritime and overland infrastructure, now more urgently under construction or in the pipeline, will help to foster regional linkages. In contrast, previously intense cross-border relations in the twin-city of Al Ain–Buraimi have obviously been affected by the recently erected border fence. In other terms, Valeri (2007: 336 ff.) points to growing influences from and embedding in the Arab-Muslim world, whereas e.g. Mühlböck's (2010) study on the transnational links of clans and tribes between Dhofar and Yemeni al-Mahra and Hadramawt could not be integrated in this volume.

References

Al-Sayegh, F. (2002). The UAE and Oman: Opportunities and challenges in the twenty-first century. *Middle East Policy, 9*(3), 124–137.

Gabriel, E. (1999). Zur Grenzbildung in Arabien. *Geographische Rundschau, 51*(11), 593–599.

Kelly, J. B. (1956). The Buraimi Oasis Dispute. *International Affairs, 32*(3), 318–326.

Krause, R. F. (2001). Wem gehört der Golf? *Petermanns Geographische Mitteilungen, 145*(2), 14–17.

Mühlböck, M. F. (2010, March 26). *The history of tribes in Dhofar: Transnational links*. Paper presented at the international conference "Regionalizing Oman – Political, Economic and Social Dynamics", Department of Economics and Social Geography of the Middle East and North Africa, Institute of Oriental Studies, University of Leipzig.

Scholz, F. (1980). *Sultanate of Oman. Part 1: A geographical introduction to the country of Oman, its natural resources, its people, its settlements, its economy, and its modern development (reader)*. Stuttgart: Ernst Klett.

Steinbeck, E. G. (1962). Zur Frage der Grenzen in Südost-Arabien. The question of boundaries in South East Arabia. *Orient, 3*(1), 14–19.

Steinbeck, E. G. (1965). Zur Frage der Grenzen in Trucial Oman. *Orient, 6*(4/5), 134–137.

UN – United Nations, Office of Legal Affairs, Division for Ocean Affairs and the Law of the Sea. (2010). *Oman*. Updated 9 September. http://www.un.org/depts/los/LEGISLATIONANDTREATIES/STATEFILES/OMN.htm. Accessed 13 April 2012.

Valeri, M. (2007). *Le sultanat d'Oman: Une révolution en trompe-l'œil*. Paris: Karthala.

Author Bios

Montasser I.M. Abdelghani is an Assistant Professor of Social and Urban Geography at Sultan Qaboos University in the Sultanate of Oman. He was born in 1970 in the province of El-Minya, Egypt. From 1988 to 1992, he studied geography at the University of El-Minya. In 1996, he received a scholarship from the Egyptian government for postgraduate studies in Germany. He studied the German language in Frankfurt am Main and Mainz and obtained his doctoral degree in Social Geography in 2002 at the University of Bayreuth, in Bavaria. From 2003 to 2006, he taught Geography at a number of institutions in Egypt. In 2004, he worked as a Visiting Professor at the University of Bayreuth in Germany. Worldwide, he has participated in many international conferences and workshops and published several papers in Arabic, German and English. His research has focused on the issues of Arab cities, urbanization, retail trade, vulnerability, and international migration. He has been living and working in Oman since 2007.

Rahma Al-Mahrooqi is an Assistant Professor at Sultan Qaboos University, Oman. She has been working in the field of ELT for 17 years. She has a Ph.D. in English and Communications Education from the University of Pittsburgh, USA. Rahma Al-Mahrooqi has presented at many international ELT conferences and forums. Her research interests focus on teaching English as a foreign language, sociolinguistic issues, intercultural communication, literature and language teaching.

Claire Beaudevin is a social anthropologist; her main research field is the anthropology of health and her doctoral research (2010) has been dedicated to the study of the social representations and stakes of inherited blood disorders in the Sultanate of Oman. She teaches anthropology in Paris Descartes University, France, and is a postdoctoral researcher in the Cermes3 (Centre de Recherche Médecine, Sciences, Santé, Santé Mentale, Société – CNRS UMR 8211-Inserm U988, Paris, France), a multidisciplinary team of social scientists working on health-related issues. Her current research activities deal, on one hand, with users' experiences of direct-to-consumer genetic tests sold on the Internet and, on the other hand, the development of human genomics in the Gulf.

S. Wippel (ed.), *Regionalizing Oman: Political, Economic and Social Dynamics*, United Nations University Series on Regionalism 6, DOI 10.1007/978-94-007-6821-5,

Michael Benz completed a B.A. in Islamic Studies and Social Anthropology at the University of Freiburg im Breisgau. He finished his M.A. in Arabic Studies with a focus on Economics and Social Geography of the MENA Region at the University of Leipzig in October 2011. In October 2011 he presented the results of his M.A. thesis on Musandam at the 18th international DAVO congress. He is currently working for the Fraunhofer Institute in Leipzig and is preparing his Ph.D. thesis.

Torsten Brandenburg studied Geography and Political Sciences at the Universities of Passau and Mainz. His research at the Center for Research on the Arab World (CERAW) in Mainz focuses on economic and political developments in the member states of the Gulf Cooperation Council. His recently finished thesis "Bridging the Knowledge Gap: Internationalization and Privatization of Higher Education in the State of Qatar and the Sultanate of Oman" compares recent higher education policies in the GCC under the banner of globalization. Areas of interest also include labour market policies, the knowledge-based economy and migration regimes in the Gulf.

Katrin Bromber received her Ph.D. in African Linguistics from the University of Leipzig (Germany) and her habilitation degree from the University of Vienna (Austria). She specialized in Swahili Studies and currently works on sports in Ethiopia and the Gulf States. Since 2001, she has been affiliated to the *Zentrum Moderner Orient* (ZMO) in Berlin. Her books include *The Jurisdiction of the Sultan of Zanzibar and the Subjects of Foreign Nations* (2001), *Imperiale Propaganda. Die ostafrikanische Militärpresse im Zweiten Weltkrieg* (2009) *Sport Across Asia: Politics, Cultures and Identities* (2013; co-edited with Birgit Krawietz and Joseph Maguire) and *Globalisation and African Languages: Risks and Benefits* (2004; co-edited with Birgit Smieja).

Dawn Chatty is University Reader in Anthropology and Forced Migration and Deputy Director of the Refugee Studies Centre, Queen Elizabeth House, University of Oxford, UK. Her research interests include the coping strategies and resilience of refugee youth, nomadic pastoralism and conservation, gender and development, health, illness and culture. Her most recent books include: *Dispossession and Displacement in the Modern Middle East*, Cambridge University Press, 2010; *Dispossession and Forced Migration in the Middle East and North Africa* (eds. with Bill Finlayson), Oxford University Press, 2010; *Deterritorialized Youth: Sahrawi and Afghan Refugees at the Margins of the Middle East,* (ed.) Berghahn Books, 2010; *Nomadic Societies in the Middle East and North Africa: Facing the 21*st *Century*, Leiden, Brill, 2006; *Children of Palestine: Experiencing Forced Migration in the Middle East* (eds. with Gillian Lewando-Hundt), Berghahn Books, 2005; and *Conservation and Mobile Peoples: Displacement, Forced Settlement and Sustainable Development* (eds. with Marcus Colchester), Berghahn Press, 2002.

Gulshan Dietl is a Professor at the School of International Studies, Jawaharlal Nehru University, New Delhi. She has served as the Chairperson, Centre for West Asian and African Studies and Director, the Gulf Studies Programme at her University. Her areas of teaching, research and research guidance are domestic developments, foreign policies and security issues in the Gulf and West Asia. She has been a Fulbright

Scholar-in-Residence at the Mount Saint Mary College, Newburgh, New York (1993–1994), a Guest Research Fellow at the Copenhagen Peace Research Institute (1998–1999), a Visiting Professor at the University of Kashmir (2004), a Visiting Professor at the Fondation de la Maison des Sciences de l'Homme, Paris (2008) and a Visiting Professor at the University of Southern Denmark (2010).

Her publications include *The Dulles Era: America Enters West Asia* (Lancer International, New Delhi, 1985), *Through Two Wars and Beyond: A Study of the Gulf Cooperation Council* (Lancer Books, New Delhi, 1991), *Saudi Arabia: People, Politics and Policies* (National Book Trust, New Delhi, 2006), *Contemporary Saudi Arabia and the Emerging Indo-Saudi Relations* (Shipra Publications, New Delhi, 2007; Co-edited), and *Democracy and Democratization in the Gulf* (Shipra Publications, 2010; Edited). She has contributed book chapters and articles that have appeared in a wider range of Indian and international journals and papers series.

Michaela Hoffmann-Ruf studied Languages and Civilizations of the Islamic Middle East and Cultural Anthropology in Tübingen. From 2004 to 2007, she worked as a research assistant in the interdisciplinary project "Oasis Settlements of Oman" (University of Tübingen) and wrote her doctoral thesis on "Sheikh MuÎsin ibn ZahrÁn al-ÝAbrÐ. Tribal power in Oman in the 19th century." From 2007 to 2010, she was Lecturer at the Oriental Institute of the University of Tübingen. At present she is working on the edition of the German Orientalist Gildemeister's (1812–1890) letters to his family (a DFG-funded project) at the Rheinische Friedrich-Wilhelms-Universität Bonn. In parallel to her academic activities, since 1996 she has worked as a museum docent in the Department of Art and History of the Islamic Orient at the Linden-Museum Stuttgart (State Museum of Ethnology).

Ulrike Lorenz is Assistant Professor at the Chair of International Politics at the University of Potsdam. She was a Postdoctoral Fellow at the Freie Universität Berlin in the Kolleg-Forschergruppe "The Transformative Power of Europe" until early 2012 and holds a Ph.D. from the University of Leipzig with a Doctoral Fellowship at Stellenbosch University (South Africa). Having published and co-authored articles and book chapters on EU-Southern African trade relations and negotiations, she is currently researching energy and non-proliferation policies between the EU and Sub-Saharan Africa and lectures on the EU in international relations, the EU's external relations with the ACP countries and International Political Economy.

Frank Mattheis is a research fellow at the Global and European Studies Institute of the University of Leipzig in Germany. A global studies scholar by training, he is currently engaged in a research project on the changing nature of stateness in Africa. In addition, he has worked extensively in the fields of comparative regional integration and interregionalism. His regional focus has been on southern Africa and South America.

Belgacem Mokhtar is a Ph.D. in Economic Geography, (regional and urban planning) from the University François Rabelais, Tours, France. He taught Geography at a number of institutions of higher education in Tunisia (Colleges of Sfax and Sousse, 1989–1996) and in the Sultanate of Oman (Colleges of Sur and Rustaq, 1996–2003) and at Sultan Qaboos University (since 2003). Worldwide, he has participated in more than 20 international conferences and workshops and published 2 books and 15 scientific papers in Arabic, French and English. His research has focused on the recent socioeconomic changes in Oman as a GCC country and their impact on urbanization, settlement patterns and spatial reconfiguration. His last published paper (with Cybergeo) is about the role of real-estate values in the relocation of socio-economic categories in Muscat urban area, Oman.

Detlef Müller-Mahn is a Professor of Development Geography at the Department of Human Geography, Rheinische Friedrich-Wilhelms-Universität Bonn since April 2013 and former professor of Social Geography at the University of Bayreuth, Germany. In his research, he is interested in questions of development and social change in the Middle East and Eastern Africa. His current works include a study about water and urbanization in Khartoum, a number of projects about negotiations and practices of adaptation to climate change and social learning in Eastern Africa, and about the transformation of nomadic pastoralism in Ethiopia. The paper in this book presents findings of a study conducted as part of a collaborative research project (SFB 560) "Local agency in Africa in the context of global influences".

Beatrice Nicolini (Ph.D. in History of Africa, Siena University 1995) graduated in International Relations and Comparative Government, Harvard University, USA, and in Political Science, Catholic University of the Sacred Heart, Milan, Italy. She teaches History and Institutions of Africa in the Faculty of Political Science and in the Faculty of Letters and Philosophy, Catholic University of the Sacred Heart, Milan, Italy. She is a Member of the Ph.D. School in Politics and Institutions, Faculty of Political Science, Catholic University. She focused her research on the history of the Indian Ocean, combining fieldwork (South Central Asia, the Persian/Arab Gulf, Oman, India, Tanzania-Zanzibar, Mozambique) and archival research carried out in both Western and Afro-Asian countries. She attended numerous international conferences and workshops as the only invited Italian expert. Among her 98 publications (2004) is *Makran, Oman and Zanzibar: Three-Terminal Cultural Corridor in the Western Indian Ocean (1799–1856)*, Leiden: Brill Academic Publishers. (2006). Editor of *Studies in Magic, Witchcraft, War and Peace in Africa: 19th and 20th century*, New York: Mellen Press. (2009). The Myth of the Sultans in the Western Indian Ocean during the 19th century: A New Hypothesis. *African & Asian Studies*, 8 (3), 239–287. (2010). The Indian Ocean: A Cultural Bow. *Crissma Working Papers*, 19, 46–67; (2011) *The First Sultan of Zanzibar. Scrambling for Power and Trade in the Nineteenth Century Indian Ocean*. Princeton: M. Wiener.

Samir Pradhan is a senior consultant in macroeconomics research at a leading consultancy in Qatar. Prior to this, he was senior researcher for GCC economics and Gulf-Asia programmes at the Gulf Research Center, Dubai, UAE, the leading think tank of the Gulf region. He has extensive research and consultancy experience in GCC and emerging Asia. His research interests include the political economy of the Gulf, GCC-Asia interdependence, GCC-India relations, energy security and regional economic integration. Dr. Pradhan is a regular contributor to and commentator for major international and regional newspapers in the Gulf region. He has also several peer-reviewed publications to his credit, including two books. He holds an M.A. in Economics and a Ph.D. in West Asian Studies from the School of International Studies, Jawaharlal Nehru University, where he conducted research on emerging energy interdependence between the GCC and India from the perspective of international economic relations.

Fred Scholz is a retired University Professor of Geography at the Institute for Geographical Sciences and former Head of the Centre of Development Studies (ZELF) at the Free University of Berlin. He is also a Honorary Professor at the National University of Mongolia, Ulaan Baatar. Professor Scholz received his Ph.D. in 1967 from the Technical University (TU) Karlsruhe and passed his "habilitation" in 1973 at the University of Göttingen, both Germany. He became an extraordinary Professor at Göttingen University in 1975 and was a Full Professor in Berlin from 1980 to 2004. In 1982 he held a Visiting Professorship at the University of Kuwait, and in 2010 he obtained his honorary doctorate and professorship. His scientific specialization is in nomadism, development studies, globalization and fragmentation. In a regional perspective, his main interests are the Gulf States, in particular Oman, West and Central Asia, and North and West Africa.

Among his manifold publications are *Geographische Entwicklungsforschung. Methoden und Theorien.* Studienbücher der Geographie. Berlin, Stuttgart: Borntraeger 2004; *Nomadism & colonialism. A hundred years of Baluchistan: 1872–1972.* Oxford, New York: Oxford University Press 2002; *Die kleinen Golfstaaten.* 2nd, completely revised ed. Gotha, Stuttgart: Klett-Perthes 1999 (editor); *Muscat, Sultanat Oman. Geographische Skizze einer einmaligen arabischen Stadt.* 2 volumes. Berlin: Das Arabische Buch 1990.

Victoria Tuzlukova is currently working in the Language Centre at Sultan Qaboos University in Oman. She has been working in the field of English-language teaching for 27 years. Her research interests focus on sociolinguistics, intercultural communication, foreign language acquisition and the role of culture in foreign-language teaching and learning. She is the author and co-author of papers on professional discourse, language of professional communication, language teaching and education.

Marc Valeri is Lecturer in Political Economy and Director of the M.A. in Gulf Studies at the Institute of Arab and Islamic Studies (University of Exeter, UK). His main areas of interest are social, political and economic transformations and reform in the Arabian Peninsula. Moreover, he is developing researches on the issues of the stability and legitimacy of authoritarian regimes in the Middle East. He is the author of Oman. Politics and Society in the Qaboos-State (London/New York: Hurst/Columbia University Press, 2009).

Since November 2011, **Julia Verne** has worked in the Department of Human Geography at the University of Frankfurt, Germany. After having completed her B.A. in Geography and Development Studies (University of Bayreuth), she did her M.A. in Cultural Geography at Royal Holloway, University of London. From 2006 to 2010, she worked as a Research Assistant at the University of Bayreuth, Germany. During her studies and as part of her Ph.D. project on “Living translocality: Space, Culture and Economy in contemporary Swahili trading connections”, which she completed in 2010, she did extensive ethnographic research in East Africa, the Comoros, Dubai and Muscat, London and Jakarta.

So far, in her work she has mainly concentrated on everyday experiences and practices of mobility, translocality and trade, engaging with theoretical reflections on networks, rhizomes and relational space. Her publications include “Finding One’s Way through Places: A Contemporary Trade Journey of Young Zanzibari Traders”, in H.P. Hahn and G. Klute (eds.) *Cultures of Migration*, Muenster: LIT, 2007, pp. 61–88, “Mobile Phone Geographies” (*Cultural Geography Compass* 2010, 4/10, 1433–1447), and “A mobile phone: Mobility, materiality and everyday Swahili trading practices” (*cultural geographies* 2010, 17 (3), pp. 341–357). Julia Verne has spent the academic year 2010–2011 as a post-doc research scholar at the History Department of UCLA, where she embarked on a new research project engaging with relations between culture and space in constructions of the Indian Ocean.

Steffen Wippel is presently a Senior Researcher at the *Zentrum Moderner Orient* (ZMO), Berlin, with an on-going research project on port cities and urban development in Oman and Morocco. In parallel to that, he worked on the Sultanate’s regional economic orientations at the Department for the Economy and Social Geography of the Arab World at the Institute of Oriental Studies, Leipzig University, from 2008 to 2011. At the same time he is a Lecturer (*Privatdozent*) at the Department for Research on the Contemporary Middle East, Friedrich Alexander University Erlangen-Nuremberg, where he finished his habilitation thesis on processes of territorialisation and regionalisation in the larger Western Sahara area in 2008. Steffen Wippel studied Economics and Islamic Studies at the Universities of Freiburg i. Br. and Aix-en-Provence. He holds a Ph.D. from the Free University of Berlin, where he worked on Egypt’s Islamic economic institutions at the Department for Middle Eastern Economics. His main research interests are issues of economic and more recently urban development in North Africa and the Gulf region. Besides the workshop on “Regionalizing Oman”, he co-organised another international conference on “The Material and Symbolic Meaning of Architecture and Infrastructure in the Gulf Region” in 2010.

Among the monographs he has published are *Gott, Geld und Staat: Aufstieg und Niedergang der Islamischen Investmentgesellschaften in Ägypten im Spannungsfeld von Ökonomie, Politik und Religion*. Hamburg/Münster: LIT, 1994; *Islamische Wirtschafts- und Wohlfahrtseinrichtungen in Ägypten zwischen Markt und Moral*. Hamburg, Münster: LIT, 1997; and *Wirtschaft, Politik und Raum. Territoriale und regionale Prozesse in der westlichen Sahara*. Berlin: Hans Schiler (2012). Steffen Wippel is (co-)editor of several publications, a series of working papers and a book series on Middle Eastern economics.

Anja Zorob is a Senior Researcher and Assistant Dean, coordinating the Ph.D. Program in Development Studies at the Institute of Development Research and

Development Policy (IEE), Ruhr University Bochum, Germany. Her research record includes the policies, processes and outcomes of Middle Eastern and North African intra- and interregional economic integration (Euro-Mediterranean relations and intra-Arab integration), the political economy of reform in MENA countries (Syria and other Mashreq states) and issues of peace and conflict studies, among them Israeli-Palestinian relations. Her current research activities concentrate on the role of female entrepreneurs in the economies and societies of Arab countries, the political economy of international trade negotiations and the chances and risks of overlapping RTAs. In addition to research and teaching, Anja Zorob served in recent years as a consultant for German development organizations and the Federal Ministry for Economic Cooperation. Before joining the IEE, she was a Professor (*Juniorprofessor*) at the Center for Middle Eastern and North African Politics at the Freie Universität Berlin and did research at the IEE and at the Institute of Middle East Studies, German Institute of Global and Area Studies (GIGA) in Hamburg, Germany. She studied Economics, Islamic Sciences and Oriental Philology at the Universities of Freiburg, Damascus and Bochum and obtained her Ph.D. in Economics from the University of Erlangen.

Index

** Refer to instances more than 250. We have picked first instances page number from each chapter.

S. Wippel (ed.), *Regionalizing Oman: Political, Economic and Social Dynamics*, United Nations University Series on Regionalism 6, DOI 10.1007/978-94-007-6821-5,

L

M

T

Y

Z

MIX
Papier aus verantwortungsvollen Quellen
Paper from responsible sources
FSC® C105338

If you have any concerns about our products,
you can contact us on
ProductSafety@springernature.com

In case Publisher is established outside the EU,
the EU authorized representative is:
Springer Nature Customer Service Center GmbH
Europaplatz 3, 69115 Heidelberg, Germany

Printed by Libri Plureos GmbH
in Hamburg, Germany